Comparative Programming Languages

▶ SECOND EDITION ◀

INTERNATIONAL COMPUTER SCIENCE SERIES

Consulting Editor　　**A D McGettrick**　University of Strathclyde

SELECTED TITLES IN THE SERIES

Distributed Systems: Concepts and Design　*G Coulouris and J Dollimore*

Software Prototyping, Formal Methods and VDM　*S Hekmatpour and D Ince*

High-Level Languages and Their Compilers　*D Watson*

Interactive Computer Graphics: Functional, Procedural and Device-Level Methods
　P Burger and D Gillies

Real Time Systems and Their Programming Languages　*A Burns and A Wellings*

Fortran 77 Programming (2nd Edn)　*T M R Ellis*

Prolog Programming for Artificial Intelligence (2nd Edn)　*I Bratko*

Introduction to Expert Systems (2nd Edn)　*P Jackson*

Logic for Computer Science　*S Reeves and M Clarke*

Computer Architecture　*M De Blasi*

The Programming Process: an Introduction using VDM and Pascal　*J T Latham, V J Bush
　and D Cottam*

Analysis of Algorithms and Data Structures　*L Banachowski, A Kreczmar and W Rytter*

Handbook of Algorithms and Data Structures in Pascal and C (2nd Edn)　*G Gonnet and
　R Baeza-Yates*

Algorithms and Data Structures　*J H Kingston*

Principles of Expert Systems　*P Lucas and L van der Gaag*

Discrete Mathematics for Computer Scientists　*J K Truss*

Programming in Ada plus Language Reference Manual (3rd Edn)　*J G P Barnes*

Software Engineering (4th Edn)　*I Sommerville*

Distributed Database Systems　*D Bell and J Grimson*

Software Development with Z　*J B Wordsworth*

Program Verification　*N Francez*

Concurrent Programming　*A Burns and G L Davies*

Concurrent Systems: An Integrated Approach to Operating Systems, Database, and
　Distributed Systems　*J Bacon*

Comparative Programming Languages

▶ SECOND EDITION ◀

Leslie B. Wilson
Robert G. Clark

University of Stirling

ADDISON-WESLEY
PUBLISHING
COMPANY

Wokingham, England · Reading, Massachusetts · Menlo Park, California · New York
Don Mills, Ontario · Amsterdam · Bonn · Sydney · Singapore
Tokyo · Madrid · San Juan · Milan · Paris · Mexico City · Seoul · Taipei

The programs in this book have been included for their instructional value. They have been tested with care but are not guaranteed for any particular purpose. The publisher does not offer any warranties or representations, nor does it accept any liabilities with respect to the programs.

Many of the designations used by manufacturers and sellers to distinguish their products are claimed as trademarks. Addison-Wesley has made every attempt to supply trademark information about manufacturers and their products mentioned in this book. A list of the trademark designations and their owners appears on p. xii.

Cover designed by Chris Eley incorporating photograph
supplied by Tony Stone Photo Library and
printed by The Riverside Printing Co. (Reading) Ltd.
Typeset by VAP Publishing Services, Kidlington, Oxfordshire.
Printed in the United States of America.

First edition published 1988. Reprinted 1988.
Second edition printed 1993.

British Library Cataloguing in Publication Data
A catalogue record for this book is available from the British Library

Library of Congress Cataloging in Publication Data
Wilson, Leslie B.
    Comparative programming languages / Leslie B. Wilson, Robert G. Clark. — 2nd ed.
      p. cm. — (International computer science series)
    Includes index.
    ISBN 0-201-56885-3
    1. Programming languages (Electronic computers)   I. Clark, Robert G. (Robert George), 1944– . II. Title. III. Series.
QA76.7.W56   1993   92-36067
005.13—dc20   CIP

Preface to the second edition

Aims and objectives

In this book we consider the principal programming language concepts and show how they are dealt with in traditional imperative languages, such as Pascal, C and Ada, in functional languages such as ML, in logic languages like PROLOG, in purely object-oriented languages such as Smalltalk and Eiffel and in hybrid object-oriented languages such as C++.

The programming language scene has always been bedevilled by protagonists pushing their favourite language. This often leads to a reluctance to examine rival languages and to a 'love me, love my language' approach. The lack of a scientific approach to languages tends to emphasize the differences between them, even when these are quite minor. Our approach is to find common ground between languages and to identify the underlying principles. Although the approach of logic languages, functional languages and object-oriented languages is different from that of the traditional imperative languages, there are many areas of similarity, and seeing these helps us to understand the differences better.

This approach is important at the present time when there are major and important controversies as to which way we should be heading. To what extent is it worthwhile developing new versions of the old faithfuls as has happened with FORTRAN 90? Should we standardize instead on modern imperative languages like Ada? Are imperative languages themselves outdated, or will they be given a new lease of life by the incorporation of object-oriented features as happened with C++? Is the future likely to be dominated by functional languages, by logic languages or by object-oriented languages? What effect will new hardware designs have on programming languages? Are fourth-generation languages to end the rule of COBOL as the most widely used programming language? Although it is likely that many of these issues will not be resolved for many years, it is important that they are addressed.

The type of course taught in our department is, we think, fairly typical. It combines both theoretical and practical work and so there is a limit to the amount of material that can be covered. We feel that it is important to get the balance right. A purely theoretical approach usually leaves most computer science students unable to fit the theory with their practical experience, while an approach that merely piles one language on top of the other leaves the students ignorant of the common threads in language design.

Changes from the first edition

Initially we set out to write a relatively short book on comparative languages, but the first edition turned out slightly larger than we had hoped. In the second edition we hoped to offset additions by reductions but, while this has happened to a certain extent, there has been an inevitable increase in size.

Revisions have been made throughout the book to bring material up to date and as a result of feedback from students both at Stirling University and at New Mexico State University where one of us (LBW) was a Visiting Professor in 1989/90. There are two new chapters, as the book now contains:

- a much fuller account of object-oriented programming languages,
- an introduction to the formal definition of syntax.

Other changes include:

- an increase in the prominance of (ANSI) C and C++ throughout the book,
- the use of ML as the main example of a modern functional programming language,
- a fuller discussion of static, strong and dynamic typing,
- a revised discussion on exceptions with exception handling in PL/I being replaced by exception handling in Eiffel,
- an introduction to the use of lazy evaluation in the handling of infinite data structures,
- an update of occam to occam 2,
- more on denotational and axiomatic semantics,
- a significant increase in the number of exercises and solutions.

Intended audience

Although this book is intended primarily as a student text for a comparative language course, we hope that it will also be read by practising computer programmers. It is easy to be overwhelmed by the large number of available programming languages and we hope this book provides some guidance through the programming jungle. We have assumed a reading knowledge of Pascal together with proficiency in a structured imperative language such as Pascal, C or Ada. We have not assumed any prior knowledge of logic, functional or object-oriented languages.

Structure and contents

Many books on comparative programming languages have separate chapters on each of the main languages covered. We have not adopted this approach, but we have organized the book so that there are separate chapters on the main language concepts with examples and discussion of how they are dealt with in particular languages. The emphasis is on imperative languages and although a wide range of languages are covered, Pascal, Ada and C are used in a central role.

Chapter 1 Introduction: This shows how programming languages fit into the software development process and the effect this has had on language design.

Chapter 2 Historical survey: This provides a historical survey so that the development of present languages can be traced.

Chapter 3 Types, objects and declarations: This deals with variables, types and declarations. It is shown that many of the differences between languages can be explained in terms of the binding time of their attributes.

Chapter 4 Expressions and statements: This discusses expressions and statements with the emphasis on structured control statements.

Chapter 5 Subprograms: This looks at program structure and the importance of subprograms. Particular attention is paid to parameter-passing mechanisms.

Chapter 6 Data structures: This deals with arrays, records and dynamic data structures.

Chapter 7 Modules: This considers the problem of programming in the large and the need to decompose large problems into self-contained units with small strictly defined interfaces. This leads to a discussion of information hiding and abstract data types.

Chapter 8 Object-oriented programming languages: The concepts of inheritance and dynamic binding are introduced and explained through examples in Eiffel and C++.

Chapter 9 Functional languages: This introduces functional languages and describes both the traditional LISP approach, together with its modern dialect Scheme, and the approach taken in newer languages such as FP and ML.

Chapter 10 Logic programming: This deals with logic programming and is mainly concerned with the language PROLOG.

Chapter 11 Concurrency: This describes how concurrency is handled in Ada, Modula-2 and occam and how these languages deal with inter-process communication and synchronization.

Chapter 12 Syntax and semantics: This describes how the syntax of programming languages can be descibed formally in BNF and outlines two approaches, denotational and axiomatic semantics, for formally describing the semantics of programming language constructs.

Chapter 13 Input and output: This describes input and output, which always seem to be the Cinderella of language design.

Chapter 14 The future: This reviews the present situation and attempts to predict the direction in which language design is likely to go.

Appendix 1   Language summaries: This summarizes the features of the principal languages dealt with in the text.

Appendix 2   Language texts: This gives an annotated biography for a wide range of programming languages.

Chapters 1, 2, 3, 4, 5, 6 and 7 introduce the basic concepts and are best read in the given order, while Chapters 8, 9, 10, 11, 12 and 13 build on earlier material and, as they are largely self-contained, can be taken in any order. Each chapter contains a synopsis outlining the major topics to be covered, a concise end-of-chapter summary, exercises and an annotated bibliography. Solutions to selected exercises are given at the back of the book.

Finally we should make clear what this book is not. It is not a language reference manual or a text on language implementation. We make no attempt to teach any particular language, but the annotated bibliography at the end of the book gives suggestions for further reading in all the languages covered. It is also not a book on the principles of program construction, although throughout the book we view each language construct from the point of view of whether or not it helps or hinders the construction of readable and reliable programs.

Acknowledgements

We would like to thank our colleagues in the Computing Science Department at the University of Stirling, in particular Alan Hamilton, Simon Jones, Ana Moreira, Sam Nelson, Charles Rattray and Leslie Smith. They have acted as an ideal sounding board and their helpful criticisms of various chapter drafts have prevented us from straying too far into error.

In addition, we would like to thank Simon Plumtree of Addison-Wesley for his help and encouragement.

Leslie B. Wilson
Robert G. Clark
Stirling, December 1992

Contents

Preface   v

1 Introduction   1

1.1   The diversity of languages   2
1.2   The problem-solving process   2
1.3   Language design   4
1.4   The lexical elements   8
Summary   11
Bibliography   12

2 Historical survey   13

2.1   Early machines   14
2.2   FORTRAN   15
2.3   ALGOL   18
2.4   Business data processing languages   22
2.5   General or multipurpose languages   27
2.6   Interactive languages   30
2.7   Special-purpose languages   33
2.8   Programming languages in the 1970s and 1980s   38
Summary   46
Exercises   47
Bibliography   48

3 Types, objects and declarations   51

3.1   Names   52
3.2   Declarations and binding   53
3.3   Type definitions   59
3.4   Numeric data types   61
3.5   Logical types   65
3.6   Character types   66
3.7   Enumeration types   66
3.8   Pointers   68
Summary   72
Exercises   73
Bibliography   74

4   Expressions and statements   75

4.1   Expressions   76
4.2   Statements   79
4.3   Sequencing and control   82
4.4   Iterative statements   85
4.5   goto statement   91
4.6   Exception handling   91
Summary   95
Exercises   95
Bibliography   96

5   Subprograms   97

5.1   Stepwise refinement   98
5.2   Using subprograms   98
5.3   Program structure   102
5.4   Parameters   106
5.5   Functions   116
5.6   Storage management   119
5.7   Recursion   123
5.8   Forward references   125
5.9   Subprograms as parameters   127
Summary   129
Exercises   130
Bibliography   131

6   Data structures   133

6.1   Introduction   134
6.2   Arrays   135
6.3   Records   143
6.4   Dynamic data structures   148
6.5   Strings   152
6.6   Sets   156
6.7   Files   158
Summary   159
Exercises   159
Bibliography   161

7   Modules   163

7.1   Large programs   164
7.2   Information hiding   168
7.3   Abstract data types   172
7.4   Separate compilation   179
7.5   Generics   182
7.6   Object-oriented development   183
Summary   187
Exercises   188
Bibliography   189

8   Object-oriented programming languages   **191**

8.1   Object-oriented programming   192
8.2   Inheritance   193
8.3   Dynamic binding   196
8.4   Eiffel   198
8.5   Concluding remarks   206
Summary   207
Exercises   208
Bibliography   209

9   Functional languages   **211**

9.1   Von Neumann influence   212
9.2   LISP   218
9.3   LOGO   226
9.4   FP systems   229
9.5   ML   232
9.6   Concluding remarks   238
Summary   239
Exercises   240
Bibliography   241

10   Logic programming   **243**

10.1   The PROLOG approach   244
10.2   The basics of PROLOG   244
10.3   Data objects   250
10.4   Efficiency in PROLOG   252
10.5   A PROLOG example   253
10.6   The future of PROLOG   255
Summary   256
Exercises   257
Bibliography   258

11   Concurrency   **259**

11.1   Introduction   260
11.2   UNIX pipes   264
11.3   Monitors   265
11.4   The rendezvous   268
11.5   Real-time programming   276
Summary   279
Exercises   280
Bibliography   281

12   Syntax and semantics   **283**

12.1   Syntax   284
12.2   Semantics   290
Summary   294
Exercises   294
Bibliography   296

13   Input and output   **297**

13.1   Introduction   298
13.2   Input and output of text   299
13.3   Binary and direct access files   307
13.4   Concluding remarks   309
Summary   311
Exercises   311
Bibliography   312

14   The future   **313**

14.1   Imperative languages   314
14.2   Fourth-generation languages   316
14.3   Declarative languages   316
14.4   Object-oriented languages   317
14.5   Language design   318
14.6   Implementation considerations   320
14.7   Reasoning about programs   321
14.8   Efficiency versus ease of use   322
Summary   323
Bibliography   324

Appendix 1   Language summaries   **325**

Appendix 2   Language texts   **341**

Solutions to selected exercises   *349*

Index   *361*

Introduction

CONTENTS

1.1 **The diversity of languages**   2
1.2 **The problem-solving process**   2
1.3 **Language design**   4
1.4 **The lexical elements**   8

This chapter looks at the different stages involved in the development of software and concludes that the main purpose of a programming language is to help in the construction of *reliable* software. It also discusses how designers have tried to include expressive power, simplicity and orthogonality in their languages while noting that pragmatic matters such as implementation and error detection have a significant influence.

The basic building blocks used in the construction of a language are considered; that is, the character set, the rules for identifiers and special symbols, and how comments, blanks and layout are handled.

1.1 The diversity of languages

Although over a thousand different programming languages have been designed by various research groups, international committees and computer companies, most of these languages have never been used outside the group which designed them while others, once popular, have been replaced by newer languages. Nevertheless, a large number of languages remain in current use and newer languages continue to emerge. This situation can appear very confusing to students who have mastered one language, often Pascal, and perhaps have a reading knowledge of a couple of others. They might well ask: 'Does a lifetime of learning new languages await them?'

Fortunately, the situation is not as bleak as it appears because, although two languages may seem to be superficially very different, they often have many more similarities than differences. Individual languages are not usually built on separate principles; in fact, their differences are often due to quite minor variations in the same principle.

The aim of this book is to consider the principal programming language concepts and to show how they have been dealt with in various languages. We shall see that by studying these features and principles we can better understand why languages have been designed in the way they have. Furthermore, when faced with a new language, we can identify where the language differs from those we already know and where it provides the same facilities disguised in a different syntax.

1.2 The problem-solving process

A computer is a tool that solves problems by means of programs (or **software**) written in a programming language. The development of software is a multi-stage process and Figure 1.1 shows the different stages involved. First, it is necessary to determine what needs to be done. This is called **requirements analysis** and often necessitates extensive discussion with potential users – that is, the customers. The next step is to produce a document, the **specification**, that defines as accurately as possible the problem to be solved; in other words, it determines what the system is to do. Requirements analysis and specification are the most difficult stages of software development.

Having defined what the system is to achieve, the next step is to **design** a solution, which can then be implemented on a computer. It is only at this last stage (**implementation**) that a programming language is directly involved.

The aim of the fifth stage (**verification**) is to show that the implemented solution satisfies the original specification. Although there has been a lot of theoretical work on verification, or **program proving**, it is usually still necessary at this stage to run the program with carefully chosen test data. But the problem with program testing is that it can only show the *presence* of errors, it can never prove their absence.

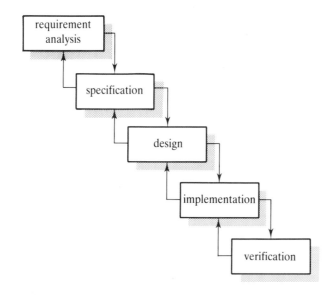

Figure 1.1
Software
development.

The final stage of software development, usually termed **maintenance**, covers two quite distinct activities:

(1) The correction of errors that were missed at an earlier stage but have been detected after the program has been in active service.

(2) Modification of the program to take account of additions or changes in the user's requirements.

It is important to realize that the software development process is iterative, not sequential. Therefore, knowledge gained at any one of the stages outlined can (and should) be used to give feedback to earlier stages.

Although a programming language is only explicitly involved in the implementation stage, it has traditionally influenced the other stages of the process. Designers are, for example, usually aware of the implementation language to be used and bias their designs to take account of the language's strong points.

In describing the software development process, the different stages of requirements analysis, specification, design and implementation were discussed, but the boundaries between the different stages are not always clear cut. For example, the need for a notation in which a specification or design can be written down has led to the development of both **specification** and **program design languages**. Such languages are at a higher level and give fewer details than implementation languages. Furthermore, as they are mathematical in form, they are amenable to proof techniques. As a specification or design contains all the information necessary to solve the problem, it is possible, at least in theory, to execute them directly instead of generating a program in an implementation language. Indeed, some specification and design languages have been developed so that this is possible. This approach is known as **rapid prototyping**, where rapid does not refer to the speed of execution, for such systems usually execute very slowly, but to the speed at which the prototype can be developed.

However, languages of this type are outside the scope of this book and so we only look at what are conventionally considered to be implementation languages, although some of the **functional languages** such as ML, described in Chapter 9, have been used for rapid prototyping and with **object-oriented languages**, described in Chapter 8, the distinction between design and implementation is often blurred.

The use of a systematic software development process has greatly influenced both language design and how languages are used. For example, Pascal was designed to support the ideas of **structured programming** while Ada and Modula-2, which were developed from Pascal, have additional features, such as modules, to enable them to be used effectively and safely in the construction of large systems. In most modern languages, type checking takes place at compile time, which is a considerable help in program testing. Also, the problems of program maintenance have led to the introduction of features that allow large systems to be broken down into self-contained modules. It is clear, therefore, that programming languages do not exist in a vacuum; rather, the design of modern languages is a direct response to the needs and problems of the software development process.

1.3 Language design

Most widely used programming languages are **imperative**; examples are FORTRAN, ALGOL, COBOL, C, Pascal, Ada and Modula-2. A program written in an imperative language achieves its effect by changing the value of variables by means of assignment statements. Other approaches to language design include **object-oriented languages** (such as Smalltalk and Eiffel), **functional languages** (such as pure LISP and ML) and **logic languages** (such as PROLOG). These alternative approaches are dealt with in Chapters 8, 9 and 10 respectively.

The primary purpose of a programming language is to support the construction of reliable software. However, a language should also be user friendly so that it is straightforward to design, write, test, run, document and modify programs written in that language. To understand how these objectives may be achieved, the issues of language design can be divided into several broad categories:

- expressive power,
- simplicity and orthogonality,
- implementation,
- error detection and correction,
- correctness and standards.

Expressive power

A programming language with high expressive power enables solutions to be expressed in terms of the problem being solved rather than in terms of the computer on which the solution is to be implemented. Hence, the programmer can concentrate on problem solving. Such a language should provide a convenient notation to describe both algorithms and data structures in addition to supporting the ideas of structured programming and modularization.

Another aspect of expressive power is the range of operations provided. If a language does not include a suitable range of operations, then the programmer generally has to provide these by function declarations, thereby distracting the programmer's attention to the lower level aspects of solving the problem. Often, languages may have high expressive power in some areas, but not in others; for example, Ada has a range of numerical operations that give it expressive power for numerical work, but it is less effective in data processing applications.

Also included under the heading of expressive power is **readability**; that is, the ease with which someone familiar with the language can read and understand programs written by other people. Readability is considerably enhanced by a well-designed comment facility, and good layout and naming conventions. In practice, it should be possible to write programs that can act, to an extent, as their own documentation, thereby making maintenance and extension of the program much easier.

Simplicity and orthogonality

Simplicity implies that a language allows programs to be expressed concisely in a manner that is easily written, understood and read. This objective is often underrated by computer scientists, but is a high priority for non-professional programmers. The success of BASIC and fourth-generation languages is an eloquent commentary on the importance users place on simplicity.

A simple language either avoids complexity or handles it well. Inherent in most simple languages is the avoidance of features that most human programmers find difficult. Simple languages should not allow alternative ways of implementing constructs nor should they produce surprising results from standard applications of their rules.

An orthogonal language is one in which any combination of the basic language constructs is allowed and so there are few, if any, restrictions or special cases. Examples of orthogonal languages are ALGOL 68 and Smalltalk which were both designed with the aim of keeping the number of basic concepts as small as possible. The idea was that the resulting language would be simple as it would only consist of combinations of features from this small set of basic concepts.

There can, however, be a clash between the ideas of orthogonality and simplicity. For example, Pascal, which is not orthogonal, is simpler to learn and use than ALGOL 68. Where a new special construct is introduced in Pascal, the same effect is achieved in ALGOL 68 by the combination of simpler existing constructs. As an example, Pascal separates the notion of the type of a parameter from whether it is a value or a variable parameter. (Details are given in Chapter 5.) ALGOL 68, on the other hand, combines both pieces of information within the parameter type. Although the ALGOL 68 approach is elegant and powerful, the more pragmatic approach (Wirth, 1975) taken in the design of Pascal has led to a more understandable language.

What is generally agreed is that the use of constructs should be **consistent**; that is, they should have a similar effect wherever they appear. This is an important design principle for any language although it is obviously of great importance in an orthogonal language which gets its expressive power from a large number of combinations of basic concepts. Whether simplicity or orthogonality is the goal, once the basic constructs are known, their combination should be predictable. This is sometimes called the **law of minimum surprise**.

Implementation

Execution of a program written in imperative languages such as Pascal, Ada and C normally takes place by translating (compiling) the source program into an equivalent machine code program. This machine code program is then executed. The ease with which a language can be translated and the efficiency of the resulting code can be major factors in a language's success. Large languages, for example, have an inherent disadvantage in this respect because the compiler will, almost inevitably, be large and indeed may be beyond the scope of small computers.

An alternative to compiling a source program is to use an **interpreter**. An interpreter can directly execute a source program, but what is more common is for a source program to be translated into some intermediate form which is then executed by the interpreter. Executing a program under the control of an interpreter is much slower than running the equivalent machine code program, but does give much more flexibility at run time. The added flexibility is important in languages whose main purpose is symbolic manipulation rather than numerical calculation. Examples of such languages are the string processing language SNOBOL4, the object-oriented language Smalltalk, the functional language LISP and the logic language PROLOG.

The use of an interpreter also supports an **interactive programming environment** in which programs may be developed incrementally. When developing a LISP program, for example, a programmer can interact directly with the LISP interpreter and type in the definition of functions followed by expressions which call these functions. The expressions are immediately executed and the results made available. This allows the early detection, and easy correction, of logical errors. Once the complete program has been developed, it can be compiled so that it will run faster.

Some language designers, notably Wirth, the designer of Pascal and Modula-2, have made many of their design decisions on the basis of the ease with which a feature can be compiled and executed efficiently. One of the many advantages of having a close working relationship between the language design and language implementation teams is that the designers can obtain early feedback on constructs that are causing trouble. Often, features that are difficult to translate are also difficult for human programmers to understand. ALGOL 68 is a prime example of a language that had a lack of success due to the fact that it was designed by a committee who largely ignored implementation considerations, as they felt that such considerations would restrict the ability to produce a powerful language. In contrast, the implementation of C, C++, Pascal and Modula-2 went hand in hand with their design and the Ada design team was dominated by language implementors.

However, it is necessary to achieve a proper balance between the introduction of powerful new features and their ease of implementation. For example, ISO Standard Pascal, has features, such as procedures being able to accept array parameters of differing lengths, that were omitted from the original version of the language on the grounds that they were too expensive to implement.

Error detection and correction

It is important that programs are correct and satisfy their original specification. However, demonstrating that this is indeed the case is no easy matter. As most programmers still rely on program testing as a means of showing that a program is error free, a good language should assist in this task. It is therefore sensible for language designers to include features that help in error detection and to omit features that are difficult to check.

Ideally, errors should be found at compile time when they are easier to pinpoint and correct. The later an error is detected in the software development process, the more difficult it is to find and correct without destroying the program structure.

As an example of the importance of language design on error detection, consider the FORTRAN method of type declarations where the initial letter of a variable name implicitly determines the type of the variable. Although this method is convenient and greatly reduces the number of declarations required, it is in fact inherently unsound since any misspelling of variable names is not detected at compile time and leads to run-time errors.

Conversely, explicit type declarations have the following advantages. Firstly, they provide extra information that enables more checking to be carried out at compile time and, secondly, they act as part of the program documentation.

Correctness and standards

The most exacting requirement of correctness is proving that a program satisfies its original specification. With the major exception of purely functional languages, which are amenable to mathematical reasoning, such proofs of correctness have not, as yet, had a major influence on language design. However, the basic ideas of structured programming do support the notion of proving the correctness of a program, as it is clearly easier to reason about a program with high-level control structures than about one with unrestricted **goto** statements.

To prove that a program is correct, or to reason about the meaning of a program, it is necessary to have a rigorous definition of the meaning of each language construct. (Methods for defining the syntax and semantics of a language are discussed in Chapter 12.) However, although it is not difficult to provide a precise definition of the syntax of a language, it is very difficult, if not impossible, to produce a full semantic definition, and as far as most programmers are concerned it is unreadable anyway.

It is therefore vital in the early stages of a language's development to have an informal description that is understandable by programmers. As in many aspects of computer science, there needs to be a compromise between exactness and informality.

A programming language should also have an official standard definition to which all implementors adhere. Unfortunately, this seldom happens as implementors often omit features that are difficult to implement and add features that they feel will improve the language. As a result, program portability suffers. The exception to this is Ada. An Ada compiler must be validated using a specially constructed suite of test programs before it can be called an Ada compiler. It is interesting that one of the aims of these tests is to rule out supersets as well as subsets of the language. This is an excellent idea and it is hoped that it will become the norm.

1.4   The lexical elements

The basic building blocks used in writing programs in a particular language are often known as the **lexical elements** and cover such items as the character set, the rules for identifiers and operators, the use of keywords or reserved words, how comments are written, and the manner in which blanks and layout are handled.

Character set

The character set can be thought of as containing the basic building blocks of a programming language – letters, digits and special characters such as arithmetic operators and punctuation symbols. Two approaches can be taken when deciding the character set to be used in a language. One is to choose all the characters deemed necessary. This is the approach taken with APL and ALGOL 60, but it has the drawback that either special input/output equipment has to be used or changes have to be made in the published language when it is used on a computer.

The other approach is to use only the characters commonly available with current input and output devices. Hence, the character set of early versions of

FORTRAN was restricted by the 64 characters available with punched cards, whereas Pascal initially was constrained by the character set available with the CDC 6000 series computer on which it was first implemented. In contrast, ALGOL 60 allows both upper and lower case letters in addition to many more special characters. In most modern languages such as Pascal, capital letters and their lower case counterparts are considered to be the same, and so they are suitable for use both on devices with large and small character sets.

Since the early 1970s, most input and output devices have supported internationally accepted character sets such as ASCII (American Standard Code for Information Interchange) and this has been reflected in the character sets of languages. The ASCII character set has 128 characters of which 95 are printable; the remaining characters are special control characters. The printable characters are the upper and lower case letters, digits, punctuation characters, arithmetic operators and three different sets of brackets (), [] and {}.

Composite symbols are used to extend the range of symbols available. Commonly used examples are the relational operators <= and >= and the assignment operator :=.

Identifiers and reserved words

The character set is the collection from which the symbols making up the vocabulary of a programming language are formed. Clearly, a language needs conventions for grouping characters into words so that names (usually known as **identifiers** in computing) can be given to entities such as variables, constants, etc. (Naming conventions are discussed in Chapter 3.)

Some of the words in a programming language are given a special meaning. Examples of this are DO and GOTO in FORTRAN and **begin**, **end** and **for** in Pascal. Two methods are used for including such words in a language. The method adopted by FORTRAN is to allow such words to have their special well-defined meaning in certain contexts. The words are then called **keywords**. This method was also adopted by the designers of PL/I since it limited the number of special words that the programmer had to remember – the scientific programmer using PL/I is unlikely to know all the business-oriented keywords, while the business programmer is unlikely to know all the scientific keywords. However, the drawback of this method is that the reader of a program written in a language with keywords has the task of deciding whether a keyword is being used for its *special* meaning or is an occurrence of an *ordinary* identifier. Furthermore, when an error occurs due to the inadvertent use of an unknown keyword, it is not always clear when a word has its special meaning, without consulting all the declarations.

The alternative method, used initially by COBOL and adopted by most modern languages, is to restrict the use of such words to their special meaning. The words are then called **reserved words**. The advantage of the reserved word method is best seen in languages like Pascal where the number of such words is quite small. In COBOL, however, the number of reserved words is much larger – over 300 – and so the programmer has the task of remembering a large number of words that must not be used for such things as variables. As well as reserved words, languages often have **predefined identifiers**. These are ordinary identifiers that have been given an initial definition by the system, but which may be redefined by the programmer. Examples, in Pascal, are the predefined type *integer* and the input and output procedures *read* and *write*.

In ALGOL 60 programs, reserved words are written in a different typeface, either underlined or bold face, depending on the situation. The drawback of this is that many input devices cannot cope with underlined words, so less attractive alternatives, such as writing reserved words in quotes, had to be used. In hand-written versions of programs in Pascal and Ada, for example, reserved words are often underlined so that they stand out while in books they are often printed in boldface. In the version presented to a compiler, however, they are typed in the same way as ordinary identifiers.

Comments

Almost all languages allow comments, thereby making the program more readily understood by the human reader. Such comments are, however, ignored by the compiler. In early languages such as FORTRAN, which has a fixed format of one statement per line, comments are terminated by the end of a line. In FORTRAN's case, the comment lines were started by a P in column 1. A similar method is used in other early languages such as COBOL and SNOBOL4.

ALGOL 60 uses a different method for comments: they begin with the reserved word **comment** and terminate with a semicolon. However, the problem with this method is that programmers often fail to terminate comments correctly. Often carried away by what they were saying in the comment, the fullstop was used instead of the semicolon. Consequently, the compiler, interpreting the program exactly, ignores the next declaration or statement. Errors caused in this way are difficult to find as the error message, if one is generated, is usually quite unrelated to the actual error.

Most later languages enclose comments in brackets. Pascal, for example, uses either (* and *) or { and } while C uses /* and */. But this approach still leaves the problem of terminating a comment unresolved. Some compilers alleviate this problem by giving a warning if a statement separator – that is, a semicolon – occurs within a comment. Ada, in contrast, commences a comment with two hyphens and ends it by the end of a line, so reverting to the methods of the earliest high-level languages.

Blanks and line termination

Programming languages vary considerably in the importance they attach to blanks (spaces). At one extreme, languages such as ALGOL 60 (and FORTRAN within columns 7 to 72 of a line) ignore blanks wherever they occur while, at the other extreme, SNOBOL4 uses blanks as separators and as the primitive operation of concatenating two strings. Most languages, however, use blanks as separators in a manner similar to that of natural language. Several blanks may also be used wherever one is allowed. Blanks in identifiers are normally forbidden, but to aid readability many languages, such as C and Ada, include the underscore character so identifiers like *current_account* and *centre_of_gravity* can be used. FORTRAN 90 does include a free format option in which blanks are significant and in which columns 1 to 6 have no special significance.

The significance of the end of a line also varies according to the language. Early versions of FORTRAN and COBOL, because they were card oriented, adopted the convention that the end of a line terminated a statement. If the statement could not be contained within one line, a continuation character was then used in the following line. Most recent high-level languages use the semicolon either to separate or to terminate statements. This method is often known as **free format** since it means that a new line can be started anywhere that a space may occur in a statement.

Summary

(1) Although there are many different programming languages in existence, these languages do, in fact, have more similarities than they have differences.

(2) The stages in software development are requirements analysis, specification, design, implementation, verification and maintenance. A programming language is not directly involved until the implementation stage.

(3) The evolution of a systematic software development process has greatly influenced language design.

(4) The primary purpose of a programming language is to support the construction of reliable software.

(5) A programming language should be simple, have high expressive power and language constructs that are consistent – that is, they should have a similar effect wherever they appear.

(6) It is important to have a proper balance between the introduction of powerful language features and their ease of implementation.

(7) Languages should support the detection of as many errors as possible at compile time.

(8) A language should have a single official definition to which all implementors adhere.

(9) The lexical elements of a language cover such items as the character set and the rules for identifiers and special symbols.

(10) FORTRAN and PL/I have keywords while most other languages such as Pascal have reserved words.

BIBLIOGRAPHY

The approach taken in this book to focus on language concepts and show how these concepts are realized in different programming languages is similar to that adopted by Horowitz (1983), Ghezzi (1987) and Meyer (1986). The book by Sethi (1988) also takes this approach but is more theoretical, as is the book by Watt (1990).

The alternative approach of having separate chapters on the main programming languages has been adopted by Tucker (1986), MacLennan (1987) and Friedman (1991). Pratt (1984), on the other hand, has combined both approaches: the language features are discussed in the first part of the book while the second part is devoted to individual languages. The result is comprehensive, although it leads to a very large text. Both Pratt and MacLennan also contain a large amount of material on language implementation.

Friedman, L. W. (1991), *Comparative Programming Languages*, Prentice-Hall.

Ghezzi, C. and Jazayeri, M. (1987), *Programming Language Concepts* (Second Edition), John Wiley.

Horowitz, E. (1983), *Fundamentals of Programming Languages*, Springer-Verlag.

MacLennan, B. J. (1987), *Principles of Programming Languages* (Second Edition), Holt, Rinehart and Winston.

Meyer, H. G. (1986), *Programming Languages*, Burgess Communications.

Pratt, T. W. (1984), *Programming Languages : Design and Implementation* (Second Edition), Prentice-Hall.

Sethi, R. (1988), *Programming Languages*, Addison-Wesley.

Tucker, A. B. (1986), *Programming Languages* (Second Edition), McGraw-Hill.

Watt, D. A. (1990), *Programming Language Concepts and Paradigms*, Prentice-Hall.

Wirth, N. (1975), 'On the Design of Programming Languages', *IFIP*, **74**, pp. 386–393, North-Holland.

Historical survey

2

CONTENTS

2.1 **Early machines**   14
2.2 **FORTRAN**   15
2.3 **ALGOL**   18
2.4 **Business data processing languages**   22
2.5 **General or multipurpose languages**   27
2.6 **Interactive languages**   30
2.7 **Special-purpose languages**   33
2.8 **Programming languages in the 1970s and 1980s**   38

There are two main reasons for studying the history of programming languages. Firstly, the languages available today are only explicable by examining how they grew up. One has to look at their development to understand why, for example, two of the major languages, FORTRAN and COBOL, are still in use over 30 years after their first appearance. There is in fact a huge inertia in the programming field, which means that once a language has been successful, it is very difficult to supersede it by a newer language. The large investment in established systems ensures the continuing use of old languages.

The second reason for looking at the history of programming languages is to pinpoint some of the errors made in the past and so try to avoid repeating them. A prime example where this was not the case was the rise of the microprocessor whose development paralleled that of the early computers in many respects. Unfortunately, many of the same mistakes were repeated because the software designers were unaware of the historical lessons.

This chapter starts its survey from the languages used with the early computers and traces their development as far as Ada, PROLOG, C++, ML and Smalltalk. While every attempt has been made to be historically accurate, the main purpose of this survey is to give the flavour of programming language development and to try to recapture the feelings of programmers at the time when each new language arrived on the scene.

2.1 Early machines

The birth of programming languages is a matter for some conjecture. Some people might consider that Ada, Countess of Lovelace, was the first programmer because she worked with Charles Babbage on the Analytical Engine. However, such academic speculations are best left to the historians. Likewise, the early work on the machines and languages of the late 1940s is of little interest in the development of programming languages.

The early languages, called **order codes** or **instruction codes**, were in fact very primitive, even in comparison with assemblers. They used numbers for operation codes as well as for storage locations and special registers which were called accumulators. Often, there were no mnemonics or floating point, and library routines, which were used for routine calculations and for input and output, were not called, but were inserted in the code. Also, loops, in which the instructions were changed, were far from the modern **for** loop in ease of operation although their purpose was the same.

An example of machine code instructions typical of the early machines (in this case, for the Ferranti Pegasus computer) is as follows:

```
1.3    521

3.0    1125
```

The first instruction (21) multiplies the number in location 1.3 by the number in accumulator 5. The result is a double-length number which is held in accumulators 6 and 7. The second instruction (12) transfers the contents of accumulator 1 to location 3.0, as modified by the number in accumulator 5.

Although order codes with mnemonics were used on machines such as the EDSAC I, programming at this level was soon seen to be a considerable drawback in the advance of computers. Machine codes were both hard to learn and difficult to use, which meant that early programs were full of errors and the 'patch' – that is, actually changing the executable code – was the standard method of correction. However, the middle and late 1950s saw a surge in the attempt to improve programming languages on both sides of the Atlantic.

First attempts to improve machine code

SHORTCODE for the UNIVAC, Speedcode for the IBM 701 and Matrix Interpretive schemes were all early attempts to improve machine code. An example of an early autocode program is as follows.

Autocode instruction	Comment
v10=TAPEB*	Read in n, then n numbers
n1=v10	Set n1 = n
n0=n1	
v0=0.0	Initialize v0
1)v0=v0+v(10+n0)	Form sum of the numbers

```
n0=n0-1
->1,n0≠0
v1=v0/n1                      Mean
n2=0                          Initialize counter n2
2)v2=v(10+n1)
->3,v1>=v2
n2=n2+1                       If number > mean add one to counter
3)n1=n1-1
->2,n1≠0
PRINTv1,1025
PRINTn2,2025                  Print answers
(->0)
```

Although this program was specifically written for the Ferranti Pegasus computer, it is fairly typical of autocodes. It has two types of variables, floating point variables v1, v2, v3 ... and integer variables n0, n1, n2 ... which were mainly used as indices, or what we would now call subscripts. The program itself reads in a list of numbers and finds the mean and the number of values that are greater than the mean.

Although autocodes were not high-level languages, they did have the beauty of being very simple and, therefore, easy to learn. They also avoided two of the problems inherent in early machines: fixed-point working and the transfer of information between the high-speed store and the backing store (usually a magnetic drum). However, as each instruction of an autocode program is interpreted, they were inefficient at run time and were also not very readable. Despite these drawbacks, autocodes were widely used.

2.2   FORTRAN

The birth of FORTRAN

The big breakthrough in the early years was 'The IBM Mathematical FORmula TRANslating system', known then and subsequently as FORTRAN. This was by no means an isolated development, but depended very much on the previous attempts to raise the level of programming languages. The manual for FORTRAN I was released in 1956, but it was 1958 before successful compilers were running programs correctly. After this, FORTRAN took off in a manner that probably surprised even its most ardent advocates.

One of the principal designers of FORTRAN, Backus, has made it clear that the motivating factor behind the language was not the beauty of programming in a mathematical notation but the economics of programming at that time (Wexelblat, 1981). Programming and debugging costs exceeded running costs and the situation was worsening with the advent of faster computers, which included hard-wired floating point. The only solution was to design a language for scientific computations that allowed the programmer to use mathematical notation. However, the designers of FORTRAN felt that this had to be done in a way that produced efficient object code, otherwise practising programmers would reject the language if they could produce a hand-coded version that ran much faster than the compiled FORTRAN program. Such worries have left their mark on FORTRAN and, as can be seen, considerations of run-time efficiency played a major role in its design, as did the IBM 704 machine and its punched card input.

Since FORTRAN was designed primarily for scientific calculations, string handling facilities were almost non-existent, and the only data structure was the array. Although the array was hedged about with limitations, it did represent a considerable step forward. Other FORTRAN features that were equally acceptable to its new devotees were:

- Comments.
- Assignment statements that allowed mathematical expressions of some complexity on the 'right-hand' side.
- The simplicity of writing loops with the DO statement.
- Subroutines and functions: the idea of the subroutine and function was not new, but FORTRAN did improve on them by employing a symbolic notation close to mathematics.
- Formats for input and output: input and output conversions were notoriously difficult on early computers, but FORTRAN formatting took a lot of the pain away.
- Machine independence: a FORTRAN program could be run on different machines.

Considering the state of ignorance about compiling in the late 1950s, the early FORTRAN compilers were remarkably good; but even so they were unable to achieve the aim of their designers, which was to produce code that was as efficient as hand-coded versions. Despite this, FORTRAN became enormously popular in a very short time, the main reasons for its success being the following:

- It made efficient use of programmers' time.
- It was easy to learn and opened the door to the computer for non-specialist programmers.
- It was supported by IBM, which soon became the most powerful firm in computing; in effect, FORTRAN and IBM rose together.
- When it was introduced, most applications and users were scientific, and FORTRAN had the right facilities for such users.
- It simplified several areas of computing in which programming was very tedious; notably, input and output.

A FORTRAN program

In Section 2.1, a simple autocode program was given for finding the mean of a list of numbers and the number of values that are greater than the mean. Here is the same problem solved in FORTRAN.

```
C    FORTRAN PROGRAM TO FIND MEAN OF N NUMBERS AND NUMBER OF
C    VALUES GREATER THAN THE MEAN
     DIMENSION A(99)
     REAL MEAN
     READ(1,5)N
5    FORMAT(I2)
     READ(1,10)(A(I),I=1,N)
10   FORMAT(6F10.5)
     SUM=0.0
     DO 15 I=1,N
15   SUM=SUM+A(I)
     MEAN=SUM/FLOAT(N)
     NUMBER=0
     DO 20 I=1,N
     IF (A(I).LE. MEAN) GOTO 20
     NUMBER=NUMBER+1
20   CONTINUE
     WRITE(2,25) MEAN,NUMBER
25   FORMAT(8H MEAN = ,F10.5,5X,20H NUMBER OVER MEAN = ,I5)
     STOP
     END
```

Notes

(1) The first two lines are comments.

(2) In the third line, the array has to be declared and its size given; in this case 99 elements with subscripts from 1 to 99. (The ALGOL 60 program in Section 2.3 shows the use of an array with variable bounds.)

(3) Most FORTRAN variables are declared implicitly by use. However, MEAN is declared explicitly as REAL because if it was declared implicitly, it would be an INTEGER variable, as its first letter is between I and N.

The development of FORTRAN

The success of FORTRAN was not without its problems, the principal one being that programmers were reluctant to use any other language. Thus, FORTRAN was used in circumstances for which it lacked the relevant language features – for example, for data processing applications and as an interactive language.

Another problem encountered was that there was no standard for FORTRAN and so slightly different versions were used in the compilers. Hence, a program that ran successfully on one FORTRAN compiler would more than likely fail when used with a different compiler. The clear need for a standard was underlined by the development of ALGOL 60 with its more precise definition. Eventually, the American National Standards Institute (ANSI) developed a standard for FORTRAN in 1966 while FORTRAN 77 emerged in 1978 and FORTRAN 90 in 1991.

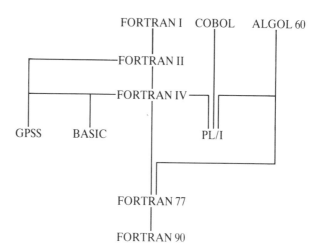

Figure 2.1
Development of
FORTRAN.

The new standard, FORTRAN 90, incorporates all the features expected in a modern language (allocation of space for arrays on block entry, records, modules, pointers, etc.). However, to protect the huge investment in existing FORTRAN programs, all legal FORTRAN 77 programs are also legal in FORTRAN 90. This means that the language is a mixture of old and new features.

Producing a new standard can also lead to the presence of multiple standards. For example, in the United States there are now two standards, FORTRAN 77 (known as FORTRAN) and FORTRAN 90. In the rest of the world, FORTRAN 90 has replaced FORTRAN 77 as the official standard FORTRAN.

Backus has pointed out (1978) that FORTRAN is very firmly based on traditional computer architecture, as indeed are most of the current high-level languages. While this promotes run-time efficiency, it considerably limits the programmer's thinking and inhibits the problem-solving process. The development of FORTRAN and associated languages is shown in Figure 2.1.

2.3 ALGOL

The period of the late 1950s was a very important one in the history of programming languages. Not only did it see the development of FORTRAN and COBOL but also a third major language – namely, ALGOL. No other language has had such a profound influence on programming language design and definition as that of ALGOL.

ALGOL emerged from a joint committee of European and American programming language experts that was set up with the aim of producing a common language (Wexelblat, 1981). Originally, this language was called IAL (International

Algebraic Language) but later it became known as ALGOL (ALGOrithmic Language). The objectives of the language were stated as follows:

- It should be as close as possible to standard mathematical notation and be readable without too much additional explanation.

- It should be possible to use it for the description of computing processes in publications.

- It should be mechanically translatable into machine code.

The committee's first product, usually known as ALGOL 58, was never implemented but the criticisms raised did help in the development of a subsequent version, ALGOL 60. The 'Report on the Algorithmic Language ALGOL 60' (Naur, 1960) was a major event in the history of programming languages and the 'Revised Report' (Naur, 1963), published three years later, was a classic. It may seem surprising to make such a song and dance about a language that was never in widespread use in the United States. However, its influence has been greater than that of FORTRAN and no other language has added so much to programming language theory.

The major concepts introduced by ALGOL 60 were:

- Language definition: BNF was used to define the syntax for the first time, a concept that led naturally to syntax-directed compilers. The semantics, however, proved more difficult and the definitions in English did lead to some ambiguity.

- ALGOL 60 was structured: it was the original block-structured language and variables in ALGOL 60 were only valid within the block in which they were declared.

- Arrays could have variable bounds at compile time, although the bounds had to be fixed when the block, in which the array was declared, was entered at run time so that suitable storage could be allocated.

- ALGOL 60 contained several structured control statements. The **if** statement and **for** statement were considerable advances on similar constructs in FORTRAN although the ALGOL 60 control statements were simplified in later ALGOL-like languages.

- ALGOL 60 was the first language to introduce recursion using recursive procedures. However, there was some argument as to whether the original committee realized the full import of their proposals in this area. Originally, recursion was decried as 'academic' and of little practical utility. But this view was partly caused by the difficulties the early ALGOL 60 compilers had in implementing the concept. However, there is no doubt now that the ability to use recursion is a very important programming skill and with improved compilers it is not inefficient.

As already indicated, ALGOL 60 was intended as a reference and publication language as well as a language for writing programs to run on computers. This led to its use by, among others, the Association for Computing Machinery (ACM) to communicate algorithms between users. But despite its powerful and improved facilities, ALGOL 60 was unable to supersede FORTRAN as the main scientific language. Several reasons have been advanced for this, but it was probably a combination of factors that kept FORTRAN well ahead, namely:

- Since ALGOL 60 compilers came out approximately three years after FORTRAN, the latter was strongly entrenched and programmers were reluctant to change. This was the first (but not last) instance of a new language being unable to supersede an established competitor.

- Since ALGOL 60 had more features, it was harder to learn.

- Although IBM initially supported ALGOL 60, they eventually decided that its customers were happy with FORTRAN and so did not wish to change. The great success of IBM in the 1960s helped to boost FORTRAN.

- FORTRAN compilers were simpler and produced more efficient code than ALGOL 60 compilers.

- ALGOL 60 had no official input/output (I/O). It was decided to leave this to the individual manufacturers so that they could tailor it to their computers. Although this seemed a reasonable decision, if a semi-official standard I/O had been agreed, then many manufacturers would have used it and a *de facto* standard ALGOL 60 would have been formulated.

An ALGOL 60 program

The following ALGOL 60 program solves the problem of finding the mean of a list of numbers and how many numbers are greater than the mean.

```
begin comment this program is the ALGOL 60 version of finding the mean and the
              number of those greater than the mean;
   integer n;
   read(n);
   begin real array a[1:n];
      integer i, number; real sum, mean;
      for i:= 1 step 1 until n do read (a[i]);
      sum:= 0.0;
      for i:= 1 step 1 until n do
         sum:= sum + a[i];
      mean:= sum/n;
      number:= 0;
      for i:= 1 step 1 until n do
         if a[i] > mean then number:= number + 1;
      write("MEAN =", mean, "NUMBER OVER MEAN =", number)
   end
end
```

Notes

(1) Unlike FORTRAN, the array declarations in ALGOL 60 could have variable bounds, as the array *a* has in this program. Variable bounded arrays can only be declared in an inner block and the value of the variable bound must be known before the block is entered at run time.

(2) There are no implicit declarations in ALGOL 60 – all variables must be declared.

The development of ALGOL-like languages

ALGOL has had a strong influence on many subsequent languages as is shown diagrammatically in Figure 2.2. The immediate successor to ALGOL 60 was ALGOL W (Wirth, 1966). In essence, this represented a tidying up of ALGOL 60 with a few new features. The most important changes and additions were:

- Records and references: they provided data structures other than arrays and allowed linked lists, trees and graphs.

- The **case** statement.

- Changes that separated the **for** and **while** statements and made the **for** statement more restricted and less prone to error.

- Procedure and function parameters could be called by value, result and value-result. The call-by-name method of parameter passing introduced by ALGOL 60 used the obvious mathematical approach of replacing a formal parameter by the corresponding actual parameter wherever it occurred. However, this method had been found to be inefficient and in some instances it led to unexpected results. Although it was still available in ALGOL W, it was discouraged.

- *Long real* and *complex* data types were introduced to enable double-length and complex arithmetic.

- The *bits* data type gave low-level processing ability.

- Assert statements were allowed and the assertions tested during a program run.

- Some string facilities were included, but they were still very primitive.

ALGOL W was indeed a worthy successor to ALGOL 60 and although not widely available, it was well liked by its users.

      The next ALGOL-like language was ALGOL 68, which was produced amid much controversy by the International Federation for Information Processing (IFIP) ALGOL working party in 1968. Its initial specification was so abstruse that there was some delay in its implementation and simple guides were produced before even partial acceptance of the language was achieved. Although ALGOL 68 had many virtues, these were rather lost in the controversy about its specification. Consequently, the large claims made for ALGOL 68 were never achieved. The idea of it being a universal language and ideally suited for data processing applications may have had some validity, but this made little impact on practising programmers.

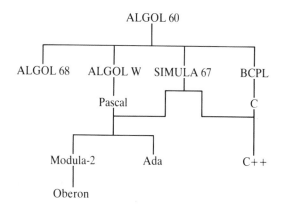

Figure 2.2
The main members
of the ALGOL
family.

The better points of ALGOL 68 were:

- An economy of constructs: the idea was to produce a core language with a small number of powerful constructs. (Note that PL/I, which is discussed in Section 2.5, went the other way by trying to be a comprehensive language.)
- Orthogonality: this was a major design goal of ALGOL 68. Having determined how a feature worked in one situation, it could be expected to behave in a similar way in any other situation; that is, there were no interactions between constructs when they were combined.

2.4 Business data processing languages

In the early stages of their development, computers were thought of as instruments for carrying out scientific calculations. However, it was soon realized that computers manipulated symbols and that these symbols did not necessarily have to be in the form of numbers. This realization led to some consideration of how the computer could be used to help solve the data processing problems inherent in large businesses. One of the major problems that existed in trying to develop a language for this purpose was the lack of a recognized notation – applications of this type were quite different from scientific calculations for which the language of mathematics had for years been the notational basis. One possible language that provided a basis on which to build a notation was the English language; however, on examination, it was found to have too many ambiguities and was unsuited in its natural form to the precision of a computer.

The first business programming language, started in about 1955, was FLOW-MATIC and this led on to the development of COBOL. FLOW-MATIC used English words for operations and data and the data designs were written independently of the manipulation routines. It was planned and implemented only on the UNIVAC 1.

COBOL

COBOL (COmmon Business Oriented Language) was yet another important language developed in the late 1950s. Its development was coordinated by a committee consisting mainly of representatives of computer manufacturers in the United States (US Department of Defense: 1960, 1961). Although the major influence on the design of COBOL was FLOW-MATIC, other earlier languages, notably Commercial Translator and AIMACO, also had some effect. COBOL was in fact a development from previous languages and ideas rather than a designed language. Its use has been widespread and for many years it was the single most-used programming language in the world. Undoubtedly, the policy of the US Department of Defense (DOD), which was strongly influenced by Grace Hopper, had a considerable effect on the success of COBOL. Apart from being one of the prime protagonists of the early meetings and committees when COBOL was introduced, the Department made it its policy to award contracts only where a COBOL compiler was available, and all computers purchased with Government funds had to have such a compiler. In fact, the DOD made COBOL a *de facto* standard long before it had an ANSI (1968) definition.

Since COBOL is essentially a data processing language, it differs significantly from FORTRAN and ALGOL, which emerged at about the same time. It places considerable emphasis on data and its input and output while keeping language features necessary for calculations very simple. As the language statements have an English-like syntax, COBOL is verbose. This was a deliberate design feature, its intention being that managers as well as programmers would find the final programs readable. The verbosity does cause some experienced programmers anguish and attempts were made, via systems like Rapidwrite (Humby, 1964), to allow a shorthand version of COBOL to be written by the professional programmer, from which the compiler could produce full COBOL.

While COBOL was never intended as an innovative language – indeed, it has had very little influence on subsequent languages – it did introduce the basic idea of distinguishing between the description of the data, the physical environment in which the computing was to be done and the actual processes performed on the data. Thus, the logical description of the data of the problem could be described independently of the physical characteristics of the media on which it was stored and manipulated; that is, the description is machine independent without being too inefficient. This separation is an important feature of COBOL and represented a major advance in its time.

A COBOL program is divided into four parts:

(1) The identification division, which provides commentary and program documentation.

(2) The environment division, which contains machine-dependent program specifications. Thus, it specifies the connections between the COBOL program and the external data files.

(3) The data division, which gives a logical description of the data.

(4) The procedure division, which contains the algorithms necessary to solve the problem.

Not all of the design features of COBOL have proved successful. For example, few programmers consider that the English-like form of the COBOL statement makes the overall program easily comprehensible. The difficulties of readability are even more noticeable when a complete COBOL program is examined and the lack of structure in the language becomes evident.

A COBOL program

Programming in COBOL, as in most business data processing, uses the concept of a file as the central data entity. Since the problem given previously is not really suitable for COBOL, as it is essentially scientific, the following COBOL program is a simple data processing application – it reads in one file, extends each record and writes out a new file.

```
        IDENTIFICATION DIVISION.


        PROGRAM-ID.  INOUT.
        *Comments are placed on a line which has an asterisk
        *in the first column. It is a very good idea to put
        *your NAME and the date of writing on your program.
        *You should also include a brief description of the
        *function of the program.
        *This program reads in one file, extends each record,
        *and writes out a new file.
        *
        ENVIRONMENT DIVISION.
        INPUT-OUTPUT SECTION.
        FILE-CONTROL.

                SELECT INP-FIL ASSIGN TO INFILE.
                SELECT OUT-FIL ASSIGN TO OUTFILE.

        DATA DIVISION.
        FILE SECTION.

        FD      INP-FIL
                LABEL RECORDS STANDARD
                DATA RECORD IS REC-IN.
        01      REC-IN.
                  05 ALPHA-IN PIC A(4).
                  05 SP-CH-IN PIC X(4).
                  05 NUM-IN   PIC 9(4).
        FD      OUT-FIL
                LABEL RECORDS STANDARD
                DATA RECORD IS REC-OUT.
        01      REC-OUT.
```

```
            05 ALPHA-OUT PIC A(4).
            05 SP-CH-OUT PIC X(4).
            05 NUM-OUT   PIC 9(4).
            05 EXTRAS     PIC X(16).

WORKING-STORAGE SECTION.

01          EOF PIC X VALUE IS 'N'.

PROCEDURE DIVISION.
AA.
            OPEN INPUT INP-FIL
            OPEN OUTPUT OUT-FIL

            PERFORM CC
            PERFORM BB THRU CC UNTIL EOF = 'Y'

            CLOSE INP-FIL, OUT-FIL
            DISPLAY "End of Run"

            STOP RUN.

BB.
            MOVE REC-IN TO REC-OUT
            MOVE 'EXTRA CHARACTERS' TO EXTRAS
            WRITE REC-OUT.

CC.
            READ INP-FIL
                    AT END MOVE 'Y' TO EOF.

            ************* END OF LISTING **************
```

Note

This shows how COBOL divides programs into the four standard parts:
IDENTIFICATION DIVISION, ENVIRONMENT DIVISION, DATA DIVISION
and PROCEDURE DIVISION.

The development of COBOL

The development of COBOL for use in business data processing paralleled that of
FORTRAN in the scientific community in many respects. However, the proliferation of different dialects of COBOL never happened to the extent that it did with
FORTRAN due to its tightly controlled development. The syntax of COBOL was
formalized very early in its development (1965). (The meta-language used was not
the BNF of ALGOL 60 but one more suited to COBOL's statements and structures.) The control of COBOL has been exercised through the Executive

Committee of CODASYL (COnference on DAta SYstems Languages), which was instrumental in its initial development. This control has led to an orderly mainte- nance and enhancement of the language, something that is not so necessary for a dynamic, new language but is necessary for a language that is intended for wide use in business data processing.

Although the tight control on COBOL has had some good effects – for ex- ample, making it effectively a universal language for data processing – it has had the drawback that the language has hardly changed in the first 25 years of its active life. Those changes (for example, the 1974 and 1985 standards) that have come about have been mainly to keep up with major equipment advances, but these have been relatively modest.

Fourth-generation languages

Programming languages are sometimes classified by their generation. Machine codes formed the first generation, autocodes and symbolic assemblers formed the second, while high-level languages such as FORTRAN, COBOL and Pascal are often referred to as being of the third generation. A feature that distinguishes third- generation languages from their predecessors is their independence from particular computer hardware. The aim of the fourth generation is to make languages much more problem oriented.

Fourth-generation languages (4GLs) are languages that were developed as a result of the dissatisfaction of business users with large conventional languages like COBOL. These users were often not professional programmers and wished to obtain quick results from data stored in the computer. The availability of terminals and, more recently, IBM PCs and their clones has had a major influence on the wide use of 4GLs. A business manager sitting at a desk with a PC wants quick results and is neither able nor prepared to embark on a large programming exercise to get them.

The problem in discussing 4GLs is their bewildering number and variety. Most are commercially produced for a particular computer or range of computers and the distinction between a language and a package is not always clear. The following tries to distinguish the main strands in this somewhat confused area.

Report Program Generator (RPG)

This was probably the first 4GL and was produced in the 1960s in response to customer requests for a simple language for the generation of reports. The requests were usually from users of small IBM computers who found the COBOL compiler too large and the assembler too difficult to use. RPG has a fixed coding structure with formats for input, switch specification (Booleans), calculation and processing, and output.

Application generators

These 4GLs generate solutions for routine applications. Typical operations include data entry, ideally with full checking, and updating of files or databases. Examples are FOCUS and RAMIS.

Query languages

These 4GLs are used with databases and allow the user to ask questions relating to several fields of the basic data records. More sophisticated languages in this category also allow the user to update the database. The most widely used language in this category is SQL.

Decision-support languages

The intention of the designers of 4GLs of this type was to help the user make informed and therefore better decisions. Such languages, for example ORACLE and INGRES, provide the user with facilities to build databases and to then perform statistical calculations, such as an analysis of trends on the data. Decision-support languages are usually business oriented and are typically used in the planning stage for analysing projected financial investment. They may include graphics facilities to enhance the display of material and vary from the simple, but effective, spread-sheets of LOTUS 1–2–3 to languages with sophisticated statistical and operations research features for decision making. Most of them also include windowing and data scrolling as important facilities.

In practice, 4GLs are not clearly divided into these four categories. While many 4GLs include report generators and graphics facilities as part of the language, others have such facilities provided as separate packages. Certainly, the ability of such languages to provide easy access to interactive graphics is an important factor for the business user on his or her PC.

4GLs are currently the most fluid area in programming language design, with new languages springing up and others withering away through lack of users. What is not being produced are well-designed and thought-out languages carefully tailored to the needs of the customer and which take into account current and future computer hardware.

2.5   General or multipurpose languages

In the late 1950s and early 1960s, language designers started working on the integration of the data processing ideas that had resulted in COBOL with the principles underlying scientific languages such as ALGOL and FORTRAN. The first multipurpose language was JOVIAL (Jules Own Version of the International

Algorithmic Language), which was developed at System Development Corporation (SDC). The major influence on its design was IAL (or ALGOL 58 as it is now more commonly known). The language is, therefore, much closer to the ideas of ALGOL than FORTRAN. As the language was developed to program a very large real-time system called SAGE, which had previously been written in machine code, the major objective in developing JOVIAL was to produce a language for programming large complex systems. In effect, JOVIAL combined the ability of doing numerical scientific computations with non-trivial data handling, manipulation and storage as well as adequate input/output facilities.

PL/I

In the early 1960s, two categories of programmer could be fairly clearly distinguished. On the one hand, there was the scientific programmer, usually using FORTRAN, whose needs were floating-point arithmetic, arrays, procedures and fast computation, usually via batch job processing. On the other hand, there was the commercial user who merely required decimal arithmetic, but who also required fast and asynchronous input/output, string handling facilities and efficient searching and sorting routines. However, there was also a growing band of special-purpose users who had diverse requirements, such as efficient real-time working, pattern matching facilities, variable length bit string arithmetic and list processing.

IBM was very much in the forefront of progress at this time and saw the opportunity in providing a computer system suitable for a wide range of users. The system that emerged was the IBM 360. Together with the new hardware, a new programming language was to be developed. It was originally called NPL, but that acronym was later dropped in favour of PL/I (Programming Language I) to avoid confusion with the National Physical Laboratory at Teddington, UK.

The new programming language was originally designed by a committee of IBM and their users who solicited views from a wide range of people as well as studying the major current languages FORTRAN, ALGOL, COBOL and JOVIAL. The guiding principles of the designers were as follows.

- Programmers' time is an important asset and should not be wasted.
- There is a unity in programming which the current division between scientific and commercial languages did not reflect.

The designers hoped, therefore, to produce a language that was comprehensive, easy to learn, teach and use, and capable of extension and subsetting. There were to be as few machine dependencies as possible while allowing the programmer to have full access to machine and operating system facilities without resorting to assembly language coding.

To accomplish all these design criteria, a large language was obviously going to be required. However, the designers felt that the programmers need not know all the features of the language to be able to use it efficiently. The result was the crucial and controversial idea at the heart of PL/I – namely, default. Every attribute of a variable, every option and every specification had a default interpretation; this was set to be the one most likely to be required by a programmer who does not know that alternatives exist. However, the implications of the default criterion were much wider than users had at first envisaged.

As the original version of PL/I (the NPL version) was too broad and incompletely specified, IBM took on the task of clarifying and refining the original specification. The version of PL/I that finally emerged combined many of the ideas of FORTRAN, ALGOL and COBOL. From FORTRAN came the parameter passing mechanisms, independently compiled subprograms, formatted input/output and COMMON blocks; from ALGOL, block structure and structured statements; from COBOL, record input/output, PICTURE type declarations and heterogeneous data structures. There were, however, ideas culled from elsewhere; namely, list processing concepts, control structures and methods for storage management. One new feature was exception handling by means of ON-conditions.

Before PL/I, language designers had either opted for run-time efficiency at the expense of flexibility (as was done, for example, in FORTRAN and COBOL) or else had allowed flexibility at the expense of run-time inefficiency (for example, SNOBOL and LISP). PL/I, in contrast, attempted to have both run-time efficiency and flexibility, but the penalty it paid was language complexity. It did by its existence highlight the problems in trying to design a general-purpose language that aims to satisfy all programmers. Nevertheless, it represents one extreme in design philosophy; that is, providing features for all applications within a fixed framework – what might be called a 'complete' language.

The alternative strategy to PL/I, probably best (although not ideally) represented by ALGOL 68, was to have a small core of basic language features that could be easily extended. The argument of core vs complete languages was much debated in the late 1960s and early 1970s but no worthwhile conclusions were reached.

A PL/I program

Here is a PL/I solution to the problem of finding the mean of a list of numbers and the number of values that are greater than the mean:

```
EXAMPLE : PROCEDURE OPTIONS (MAIN);
   /* This is the PL/I version of the mean and the number
      of values greater than the mean */
   GET LIST (N);
   IF N > 0 THEN BEGIN;
     DECLARE MEAN, A(N) DECIMAL FLOAT,
       SUM DEC FLOAT INITIAL(0), NUMBER FIXED INITIAL (0);
     GET LIST (A);
     DO I = 1 TO N;
       SUM = SUM + A(I);
     END;
     MEAN = SUM/N;
     DO I = 1 TO N;
```

```
            IF A(I) > MEAN THEN
                NUMBER = NUMBER + 1;
        END;
        PUT LIST ('MEAN=', MEAN,
                    'NUMBER GREATER THAN MEAN=', NUMBER);
    END EXAMPLE;
```

Notes

(1) PL/I allows both explicit and implicit declarations which can include initialization as in the case of SUM and NUMBER above.

(2) It allows operations with entire arrays like GET LIST (A).

(3) The final END can be used to terminate any inner blocks as well as the outermost block.

The future of general-purpose languages

PL/I suffered from considerable teething problems and, indeed, without the massive backing of IBM, it would probably have died an early death. IBM's support kept it alive but even they could not force users to accept it. At one stage, IBM tried to replace FORTRAN and COBOL by PL/I, making it the universal language. However, customer resistance was too strong and many people threatened to take their business elsewhere if IBM would not provide FORTRAN and COBOL compilers. Hence, IBM being a sound commercial organization, capitulated. So PL/I had to exist and justify itself in competition with FORTRAN and COBOL.

The size of PL/I produced large compilers and hence slow compile times, particularly with small machines where the overlaying of code for the compiler was necessary. The increase in core storage and the production of optimizing compilers did help to alleviate these problems but, even so, PL/I never replaced either FORTRAN or COBOL, never mind both. The search for a universal language did not stop with PL/I, although its lack of success considerably dented the hopes of designers.

2.6   Interactive languages

Early computers only ran one program at a time, but as computers developed and became more complex, operating systems were designed to use the available facilities – high-speed store, backing store, input/output devices – more efficiently. For example, the slowness of the input/output operations in comparison with the speed of the central processor led to **time sharing** with many remote stations sharing the time of the central computer. Eventually, the remote terminal became the normal tool of the programmer. Changes such as these started in the early 1960s and gradually gathered momentum until by the mid 1970s it was commonplace.

Although programming languages began to adapt to these changing circumstances, the provisions varied widely. Most language compilers were available to programmers at their terminals in more or less the same way as that for batch processing. Programmers put their programs into a file and then ran the appropriate language compiler using the file as the source program. Errors, if there were any, were output to the terminal and, if necessary, placed in a scratch file for reference. The programmer could then modify the original file and re-run the compiler. There were, however, some attempts to provide the programmer with better interactive facilities for on-line programming.

JOSS (Johnniac Open Shop System), developed in the early 1960s at the RAND Corporation, was probably the first interactive language. It demonstrated the value of on-line access to a computer and provided simple calculating facilities, a feature that was particularly useful to non-specialist engineers. QUIKTRAN, which emerged a little later, was the result of an attempt to adapt an existing language, FORTRAN, for use on a remote terminal: features of FORTRAN that were unsuitable for an interactive environment were omitted while a number of features that facilitated on-line debugging were added. QUIKTRAN was kept compatible with FORTRAN so that programs developed and debugged on a terminal could also use the regular FORTRAN compiler in batch mode.

For quite different reasons, two interactive languages, BASIC and APL, have made a considerable impact on programming.

BASIC

BASIC (Beginner's All-purpose Symbolic Instruction Code) was developed at Dartmouth College by Kemeny and Kurtz in the mid 1960s. Their intention was to produce a language that was very simple for students to learn and one that was easy to translate. The idea was that students could be merely casual users or go on from BASIC to more sophisticated and powerful languages, and that a casual programmer who has done nothing for six months can still remember how to program in BASIC (JOSS also claims this benefit). As someone described it, it is like learning to ride a bicycle or swim, once learned never forgotten. For many programmers, BASIC was like a return to the early autocodes: it could be learnt very quickly and programs written after one or two day's practice. However, it was not without its problems, particularly when larger more comprehensive work was required.

Like FORTRAN, a decade earlier, the success of BASIC surprised its inventors. However, this success was, no doubt, due mainly to the need for a simple high-level language for the new microcomputers of the mid 1970s, and BASIC was available, well known and certainly simple. It caught on in a big way.

In addition to the normal statements of a traditional programming language, BASIC has a few simple user commands which represent the interactive part of the language. The NEW command is used to create a BASIC program, which may be listed by the LIST command, edited by the DELETE command, executed by the RUN command and saved by the SAVE command. Any previously saved program can be retrieved for further use by the OLD command. BASIC is therefore not just a language, but incorporates sufficient operating system commands to make it complete in itself.

A BASIC program

The solution to the problem of finding the mean and the number of values greater than the mean is given here in BASIC for comparison:

```
10 REM THIS IS A BASIC PROGRAM FOR FINDING THE MEAN
20 DIM A(99)
30 INPUT N
40 FOR I = 1 TO N
50 INPUT A(I)
60 LET S = S + A(I)
70 NEXT I
80 LET M = S/N
90 LET K = 0
100 FOR I = 1 TO N
110 IF A(I) < M THEN 130
120 LET K = K + 1
130 NEXT I
140 PRINT "MEAN IS", MEAN
150 PRINT "NUMBER GREATER THAN MEAN IS", K
160 STOP
170 END
```

Note

Variables cannot be declared, are single letters and automatically initialize to zero.

APL

APL (A Programming Language) was originally defined by Iverson as a mathematical language for the concise description of numerical algorithms. In its original form, it contained a large number of operators – the standard operators +, – and × in addition to more exotic ones for operating on arrays. However, when the language was eventually implemented on a computer, several operators were omitted, but it still remained in its programming language form a remarkably 'rich' language.

APL has a large alphabet (52 letters, 10 digits and 52 other characters) and the following unusual characteristics:

- The primitive objects are arrays (lists, tables, or matrices).
- It is an operator-driven language. Although branching operations are possible, they are little used in practice and the power of the language mainly comes from its array operators.
- There is no operator precedence: all statements are parsed from right to left.

APL generally requires a programming technique very different from that used with traditional scientific languages. Indeed, many programmers find the ability to program in a traditional language is more of a hindrance than a help when using APL. To be successful, a programmer needs to envisage what effect different operators, either on their own or in conjunction with other operators, have on arrays. Programs often contain, therefore, a succession of such operators. The designer Iverson recommended beginners to 'play' with the language to get a feel for the effect of the operators, both on their own and in conjunction.

Although there has been a lot of controversy about APL, it nevertheless seems to attract devotees who consider it the only language for the programmer. It has also been suggested that it brings computing and mathematics closer together.

2.7 Special-purpose languages

A large number of programming languages have been developed for a specific purpose; for example, SNOBOL which illustrated string manipulation techniques. This section looks at some of the languages that are important either in their own right or because of their influence on the development of other programming languages.

String manipulation languages

The first effective string manipulation language was COMIT, which provided a means of searching a string pattern and performing transformations when that pattern was found. COMIT was developed at the Massachusetts Institute of Technology (MIT) in the period 1957–61. A more widely used and influential string manipulation language was SNOBOL, which was developed at Bell Laboratories several years after COMIT. The early versions of SNOBOL had several teething troubles and when discussing the language, it is usually SNOBOL4, which came out in 1967, that is considered as the definitive version. These early string manipulation languages were used in areas such as symbolic mathematics, text preparation and natural language applications.

In SNOBOL4, the basic element is the character string. Although there are operations for joining and separating these character strings, the most fundamental operation in SNOBOL4 is the pattern match. This operation examines a string to see if it possesses a particular substring or other property. If a match is found, then various possibilities, such as replacement, can take place.

There are two types of data structure: ARRAY and TABLE. ARRAY is a collection of data items that need not be of uniform type. The items are indexed by numeric subscripts in the normal way. TABLE, on the other hand, is an associative array with each element indexed by a unique associative value that is not necessarily an integer; for example, it could be a string such as COLOUR ['RED'].

Although SNOBOL4 has had little influence on the major general-purpose languages, whose string handling facilities fall far short of those provided by SNOBOL, the ideas embedded in SNOBOL did have an impact on the designers of text editors. It should be remembered that the more sophisticated operations in SNOBOL, such as pattern matching with replacement, can extend the length of the original string, but that to do this satisfactorily requires dynamic storage allocation. However, as this is not something language implementors are keen to provide, string operations in other languages are usually restricted to string comparison, string movement and other operations that do not lengthen the string. The effect of this is that, in these other languages, strings have a fixed maximum length throughout the execution of a program.

SNOBOL, with its emphasis on strings and string manipulation, jumps and labels and with no declarations, is a maverick among modern languages. It shows an alternative way of doing things which, in many cases, is not as bad as 'the structuralists' would have people believe. The main complaint against SNOBOL is its unfortunate habit of making spaces significant in some operations. Once such an error is made it can be very troublesome to find.

List-processing languages

In the early scientific languages (FORTRAN and ALGOL), the only data structure was the array. All of its elements were of the same type and, in the case of FORTRAN, it was of fixed size. Although COBOL had a data structure that allowed elements of different types, in none of these early languages was there scope for altering the basic structure of the array. This is in essence what list processing accomplishes, usually by having an element divided into an information part and a pointer part. The pointer part can, in the case of a linked list, reference the next element in the list, but in tree structures there are usually at least two pointers. In general, the linkage can be as complex as required by the problem although in languages such as LISP the pointers are implicit.

The early list-processing languages were developed to show the value of such processing in the programming environment. The first such language was IPL-V, which was developed at the Carnegie Institute of Technology in the period 1957–1961. IPL-V was really an assembly level set of commands for doing list processing on a hypothetical machine – the commands were interpreted. The significance of IPL-V was to define the concept of a list and to show how it could be implemented, albeit very crudely. It was used mainly by those programming artificial intelligence problems and it pioneered many of the fundamental concepts of list processing – in particular, the idea of a **free space list** from which storage space for new elements of the list could be obtained and to which storage space could be returned when no longer required.

The other early list-processing language, LISP, has had a more lasting effect on programming language design. It was developed by John McCarthy at MIT in the late 1950s and he and his co-workers produced a workable language in the early 1960s.

The principal features of LISP are as follows:

- It performs computations with or on symbolic expressions rather than numbers. This arose mainly because the designers were mainly mathematicians who were particularly interested in applying computing to artificial intelligence problems (game playing, theorem proving, natural language processing).

- It represents symbolic expressions and other information in the form of list structures in computer memory – this idea originated from IPL.

- It uses a small set of constructor and selector operations to create and extract information from lists. These operations are expressed as functions and use the mathematical idea of the composition of functions as a means of constructing more complex functions.

- Control is recursive rather than iterative.

- Data and programs are equivalent forms. Thus, programs can be modified as data and data structures executed as programs.

In addition to these features, LISP was probably the first language to implement storage management by garbage collection. Furthermore, there is an affinity between LISP and Lambda calculus which it seems was not planned by the designers.

LISP as implemented on a computer is somewhat different from the 'pure' LISP of the original definitions. It does, however, come close to being a **functional language** (as pure LISP is). A functional language has as its fundamental operation the evaluation of expressions. This is in contrast to the majority of languages (FORTRAN, Pascal, BASIC, ALGOL), known as **imperative languages**, which use a sequence of commands to carry out the desired operations. Interest in functional languages has increased significantly during the 1980s and their recent development is discussed in Section 2.8.

LISP has survived as a language despite the death of most list-processing languages and there are several reasons for this. It is an elegant mathematical system, with a simple basic functional structure capable of expressing the ideas of the Lambda calculus. These features, together with the fact that LISP systems allow programs to be developed interactively, make LISP well suited to artificial intelligence applications. Finally, the survival of LISP has been helped by the development of modern dialects such as Scheme, and an agreement on a standard version of the language known as COMMON LISP.

The early 1960s saw a rash of list-processing languages: for example, L6, IPL, SLIP, WISP. However, their day was soon over as the general-purpose languages (ALGOL W, ALGOL 68, PL/I, Pascal and Ada) started to include list processing within the language.

Simulation languages

The simulation of discrete systems was one of the first problems that computers were used to solve. These systems are modelled by a series of state changes that often occur in parallel. Complex interactions could arise between the elements of the system as they compete for restricted system resources. The simulation technique itself follows the system elements through their changes of state gathering quantitative information. This information is then used to predict the properties of the system under hypothetical situations. For example, simulation of a traffic system can predict how the proposed model will perform as traffic densities increase and hopefully show where bottlenecks could occur.

The earliest simulation language to be widely used was GPSS (General-Purpose Simulation System). Although it was first described in 1961, it was somewhat later before the system was available to programmers. In GPSS, the system being simulated is described by a block diagram in which the blocks represent the activities and the lines joining the blocks indicate the logical sequence in which the activities can be executed. When there is a choice of activities, this is represented by several lines leaving a block and the conditions under which this choice is made is stated in the block.

GPSS has often been criticized for the slow execution time of its programs. While not denying the slow run time, which is due mainly to the use of interpretive programming to implement the block diagram, the designers point out that the ease of using GPSS means that the overall time for developing the model and obtaining the final results is shorter than that in many other languages.

In Europe in the early 1960s a small group led by Ole-Johan Dahl and Kristan Nygaard at the Norwegian Computer Centre was also constructing a simulation language which eventually became known as SIMULA 67, although this was not the first working version of the language. It was designed for system description and simulation; a system in this case being a collection of independent objects with a common objective. Systems were simulated by examining the life cycle of the elements of the system.

SIMULA was based on ALGOL 60 with one very important addition – the **class** concept. Using this concept, it is possible to declare a class, generate objects of that class, name these objects and form a hierarchical structure of class declarations. Although this concept was only introduced to describe the life cycles of the elements in the discrete simulation, later it was recognized as a general programming tool ideal for describing and designing programs in an abstract way. The basic idea was that the data (or data structure) and the operations performed on it belonged together, and this forms the basis for object-oriented programming and for the implementation of abstract data types.

The class concept has been taken over and used in many modern languages, such as Modula-2, C++, Ada, Smalltalk and Eiffel. It has proved to be particularly useful in concurrent programming. Classes in SIMULA are based on procedure declarations and the block structure of ALGOL 60, but free the latter concept from its inherently nested structure by allowing several block instances to co-exist.

When viewed objectively, SIMULA is more like a general-purpose language of the ALGOL W type rather than a special-purpose simulation language. Indeed, the simulation is usually done by using two supplied classes SIMSET and SIMULATION.

Systems programming languages

In the 1960s there was considerable resistance to the use of any high-level languages on the part of programmers who were writing systems programs (such as compilers and operating systems). They argued that the needs of efficiency dictated the use of assembly-level languages. Gradually, systems programmers moved away (often reluctantly) from low-level programming to high-level languages such as PL/I. However, they still tended to retreat back into low-level code for the 'vital' parts of the system because, basically, the general-purpose languages did not contain the low-level facilities required in systems work. What was really needed was a specialist systems programming language, but unfortunately there seemed to be no agreement on what such a language should contain. Hence, the result was a proliferation of such languages – it almost seemed that you could not be considered an advanced systems programming group if you did not have your own language.

Systems languages is rather a broad term, covering a wide range of applications such as operating systems and real-time systems. Such languages should have facilities for activating several processes simultaneously, synchronizing these processes as appropriate and responding to interrupts. The ideas of concurrent processing (or parallel programming) were developed more intensively in the 1970s and are discussed in Section 2.8.

BCPL and Coral 66, introduced during the late 1960s and early 1970s, were the most popular systems languages in the UK, the latter being more widely used because of the support given to it by the UK Ministry of Defence. In the United States, the situation was less clear as several languages (for example, JOVIAL, BLISS, and XPL) were being used. The most widely used systems programming language is now C, which is examined in more detail in Section 2.8.

An interesting new development is the language occam, which was developed for use with a particular computer – the transputer. The idea is to build powerful computers from a network of transputers operating in parallel. Communication and synchronization are therefore central to the design of both the transputer and of the language occam.

Occam is a simple language that has the process as the central concept. What would be subprograms in a conventional language are processes in occam. Processes communicate with one another by sending messages over channels which correspond closely to the hardware links between transputers. The general approach to communication and synchronization is in fact very similar to that used in Ada and is discussed in Chapter 11.

Packages

Packages are not strictly programming languages at all, but it is sometimes very difficult to tell where a package ends and a language begins. There has been a large increase in the use of packages over the past 15 years, mainly at the expense of specialist languages. Hence, users, instead of learning a specialist language for their field, are provided with a package which often requires very little extra knowledge to use.

Possibly the most widely used package is SPSS (Statistical Package for Social Scientists). SPSS has replaced simulation languages in many applications even though it provides less sophisticated facilities. However, it is much easier to use and can be employed by people with very little knowledge of computers and how they operate. This fact leads many users to treat such a package as a black box, with little idea of how it works, which has dangerous implications and does require such users to take care in checking the validity of what they are doing and the results obtained.

Packages are heavily used in scientific calculations and, as numerical methods become standardized, new and improved algorithms are incorporated. SSP (Scientific Subroutine Package) was the forerunner, but has been superseded by the NAG (Numerical Algorithms Group) library in Britain and Europe and by ISML in the United States. In both these cases, a specialist group keeps the packages up to date by adding new accredited algorithms and improving existing ones.

2.8 Programming languages in the 1970s and 1980s

The 1960s saw the establishment of many programming languages – notably FORTRAN, ALGOL, COBOL, PL/I and BASIC. These languages consolidated their grip on the market and made it exceedingly difficult for any new language to make a major impact. Of the languages that emerged during the 1970s, three are certain to survive throughout the 1990s. These are Pascal, which continues to exert a strong influence as an initial teaching language; C, which is currently the main language for systems programmers and is boosted by the continuing and growing importance of the UNIX operating system; and Ada which arrived at the very end of the 1970s and is more correctly considered a language of the 1980s. Another language that arrived in the late 1970s but made little impact until the 1980s is PROLOG. Modula-2 also emerged in the 1970s from the Wirth stable which was responsible for the design of ALGOL W, PL360 and Pascal.

The 1980s saw a significant increase in interest in functional languages largely because, as functional programs achieve their effect by creating new objects rather than by modifying existing ones, they are easier to reason about than their imperative counterparts. Modern functional languages include Scheme, a dialect of LISP, ML, Miranda and Haskell. Object-oriented programming, which is based on two primitives, objects and messages, is also attracting a lot of attention. Its main representative languages are Smalltalk, Eiffel and C++.

Pascal

Pascal was developed by Professor Niklaus Wirth in the late 1960s and early 1970s. His aims were to produce a language that could be efficiently implemented on most computers and be suitable for teaching programming as a logical and systematic discipline, thus encouraging well-structured and well-organized programs. Pascal was influenced more by ALGOL-like languages than FORTRAN. However, there was a determined effort by Wirth to make his language efficient. He felt that this was the only way to challenge the strong grip FORTRAN had on programming, particularly in the United States. Thus, Pascal contains certain features for efficiency reasons.

The static array is probably the most controversial feature of Pascal. In most ALGOL-like languages, the size of an array does not have to be specified until a block is entered at run time. Although this allows for more flexible programming and a more efficient use of storage, it does usually slow down program execution. Pascal adopted the static array, as used in FORTRAN, where the size is determined at compile time. In addition, the passing of array parameters in procedures also used fixed sized arrays. This was an even more controversial decision because of the restrictions it imposed, particularly on those doing numerical calculations. However, this restriction was removed when the ISO Standard for Pascal was published in 1982 (ISO, 1982).

One of the positive aspects of Pascal is the inclusion of features that encourage well-written and well-structured programs. For example, although **goto** statements are included, they are a restricted and minor feature of the language. Pascal also includes ALGOL-like structured loops with the addition of a **repeat ... until** construct. Data types are a prominent feature of Pascal and they can be built up from the primitive, unstructured types *integer, real, Boolean* and *char*. The unstructured user-defined types are defined either by enumeration of the possible values, as in:

type *suit* = (*clubs, diamonds, hearts, spades, notrumps*);

or by subrange, as in:

type *letter* = 'A' .. 'Z';
       digit = 0 .. 9;

The structured user-defined types include arrays, records, sets and files. In addition, pointer types may be used, usually in conjunction with records, to form linked lists or tree structures. Strings can be declared and manipulated in Pascal, but the rigid size of the string and the lack of suitable string operations make string handling clumsy.

Pascal only started to be widely used in the late 1970s, when many universities adopted it as their initial teaching language for computer science students, and by the mid 1980s it had become the dominant teaching language. The reasons for this movement were the need for a language that provided a comprehensive set of data structures and which encouraged good programming style. Although the switch to Pascal has been slower in industry, there is now considerable interest in the language, particularly at the small computer end of the market. Previously, microcomputer programmers used low-level languages, with BASIC as the common high-level language because of the smallness of its interpreter. However, Pascal compilers are usually small enough to fit comfortably into micros and many users prefer the programming facilities of Pascal to those provided by the unstructured BASIC.

The C language

Historically, C evolved from BCPL through the language B and was the programming language used to implement the UNIX operating system together with most of its commands. C and the UNIX system were developed together at Bell Laboratories. Some aspects of the design of C – for example, the ++ operator – reflect its origins and features that were available on the PDP-11 computer for which the first compiler was written.

The strength of C lies in the fact that it combines the advantages of a high-level language with the facilities and efficiency of an assembly language. The flexibility required by a systems programming language is provided by the lack of type checking and the ability to perform arithmetic on store addresses and operations on bit patterns. This flexibility, combined with the availability of a wide range of operators that may be freely combined, means that it is possible to write very compact and efficient code. However, the major drawback is that the code is often far from readable and the lack of full type checking means that it is much easier to write erroneous programs in C than in a language like Pascal.

Apart from the fact that it does not allow the nesting of subprograms, C has all the facilities expected in a modern imperative language; that is, structured control statements, recursion, records and dynamic data structures. It is also a relatively small language and the existence of a portable C compiler means that it can be implemented relatively easily on a new machine.

An ANSI Standard for C was drafted in the late 1980s, but this has led to the situation that there are now two versions of C in common use: traditional C and ANSI Standard C. Differences between the two versions are discussed at appropriate points in later chapters. One of the main changes is the addition of language features to increase the amount of type checking that can be done.

Although it originated as a systems programming language, the use of C has spread into other areas and so it must now be regarded as a general-purpose language. It is, however, a language for experienced programmers rather than novices.

An object-oriented extension to C, called C++, was developed by Stroustrup in the early 1980s. It uses the class construct of SIMULA to give data abstraction and information hiding, but goes further than Ada and Modula-2 by also supporting inheritance. Various changes to C++ have been made during the 1980s and the present version has ANSI Standard C as a subset. In line with modern thinking, type checking is much stricter than in early versions of C. C++ is discussed in more detail in Chapters 7 and 8.

A C program

A C program to solve the problem of finding the mean of a list of numbers and how many are greater than the mean is as follows:

```
main()
/* this is the C version of the program to find the
    mean and the number of those greater than the mean */

{  float a[100], mean, sum;
   /*the array a has 100 elements – a[0], .. a[99] */
   int n, i, number;
   scanf("%d", &n);
   for(i = 0; i < n; i++) scanf("%f", &a[i]);
   sum = 0.0;
   for(i = 0; i < n; i++)
       sum += a[i];
   mean = sum / n;
   number = 0;
   for(i = 0; i < n; i++)
   {  if (a[i] > mean) number++;
   }
   printf("MEAN = %f\n", mean);
   printf("NUMBER OVER MEAN = %d\n", number);

}
```

Note

The three statements

$$i++; i += 1; i = i + 1;$$

all have the same effect.

Ada

The US Department of Defense, the largest user of computers in the world, decided to sponsor the development of a new programming language in the mid 1970s. The main reason for this was that it was dissatisfied with the conglomeration of different languages used in its computer systems and wanted a standard programming language for embedded computer systems. The latter are computer systems used to control part of a larger system, such as an industrial plant, an aircraft or a hospital life support system. These applications are normally very large, highly complex, contain a high degree of concurrency and change with time. The other important requirement of such systems is high reliability combined with the ability to recover from errors.

The original requirements for this new language were given in a document called 'Strawman' and were further refined in documents called 'Woodenman', 'Tinman', 'Ironman' and 'Steelman'. At the 'Tinman' stage, it was decided there was no suitable existing language and so an international design competition was organized. This was won by a group from CII-Honeywell Bull of France headed by

Jean Ichbiah. The resulting language was called Ada after Ada, Countess of Lovelace, who worked on Babbage's Analytical Engine and was considered by many to be the first programmer.

Although Ada is Pascal based, it is a much larger and more complex language. It not only extends Pascal constructs but contains features that have no analogue in Pascal. One of the key features of Ada is the package, which is designed for the description of large software components. A package has affinities with the class concept of SIMULA 67 and C++ and the module of Modula-2. It contains type definitions and data objects together with the operations for manipulating these objects. Packages aid information hiding because both the representation of data and the implementation of the operations may be hidden from the user. Ada also has the notion of a library of packages, thereby enabling the programmer to create a system from combinations of existing packages, rather than writing a new program from scratch.

Apart from a broad range of built-in data types, there is a powerful set of data typing mechanisms. Ada is a strongly typed language, which means that all type checking can be done at compile time. Sequencing and control statements are similar to those used in Pascal – namely, **if ... then ... else, case, while** and **for** – but the **goto** statement is only given in a restricted form. An interesting feature of Ada is the loop structure which includes an **exit when** construct. This allows general loops with a test at the beginning, like the traditional **while** statement, at the end like the **repeat ... until** statement, or in the middle of the loop. Procedures and functions are again similar to those in Pascal, but the parameter-passing mechanisms using **in, out** and **in out** correspond to ALGOL W's value, result, and value-result.

The task facility in Ada is included to permit parallel processing and there is a *clock* data type to exercise control and allow the programmer to handle real-time applications. Ada also contains an extensive set of features for interrupt and exception handling. These are on the same lines as the PL/I ON-conditions, but are more powerful and somewhat better designed. In the opinion of the authors, the ramifications of these complex facilities were not fully understood by the language designers and the lack of a formal semantics supports this view.

Ada is undoubtedly a very comprehensive language and the support of the US Department of Defense will ensure it has a prominent place in the programming environment. The strongest criticism of the language is Tony Hoare's ACM Turing Lecture entitled 'The Emperor's Old Clothes' (1981). His principal objection to Ada is that it is too big and far too complex, to which the Ada designers reply that large, real-world problems cannot be solved with small simple languages. No doubt this argument will continue to rage for many years.

Modula-2 and Oberon

The language Modula-2 was designed by Wirth. Modula was Wirth's first attempt to extend Pascal with modules and, while not wholly successful, pointed the way forward. Modula-2 is, in effect, Pascal with the module concept and some multi-programming facilities added.

The extensions to Pascal in Modula-2 are:

- The module concept and, in particular, the separation of specification and imple-mentation.

- A more systematic syntax so that each programming structure starts and ends with a keyword.

- The inclusion of low-level facilities for mapping structured data on to storage without structure. This enables Modula-2 to be used as a systems programming language.

- The concept of processes and their synchronization, modified by the notion of coroutines.

- Procedure types, which extend the normal idea of procedure to allow the declaration of types whose values are procedures.

Modula-2 has the advantage of being less complex and hence much easier to implement than Ada, but this has not managed to outweigh Ada's Department of Defense backing.

Oberon is a development of Modula-2 (Wirth, 1988). The principal addition is **extended record types** where a base record may be extended with extra fields. This has many similarities with the *struct* and *class* constructs of C++ described in Chapter 7.

Functional languages

In a very influential paper, Backus (1978) introduced the language FP and made the case that imperative languages were fundamentally flawed because of their reliance on side-effects. As a purely functional language only involves the evaluation of expressions, it is possible to reason formally about the effect of a functional program and to prove that it meets its specification.

FP is too simple to become an effective programming language, but it generated a lot of interest in the functional paradigm. Two other functional languages developed in the late 1970s and early 1980s are ML and Hope, many features of which were combined to produce the language Standard ML. An important feature of ML is its type inference system. ML is strongly typed, but the programmer does not have to declare the types of all identifiers as the system can infer what their type must be by scanning the program text and can report on any inconsistencies.

ML is not a purely functional language, as I/O is performed using side-effects. Purists argue that, as a functional program should contain no side-effects, even I/O should be performed in a purely functional style. This is achieved in the languages Miranda and Haskell by the use of lazy evaluation.

A more detailed description of functional languages is given in Chapter 9.

PROLOG

PROLOG originated at the Groupe d'Intelligence Artificielle at the University of Marseilles in the early 1970s. Its development, including the writing of compilers, was carried out at Marseilles and at the Department of Artificial Intelligence, University of Edinburgh in the mid and late 1970s. However, the first book on PROLOG was not published until 1981 (Clocksin, 1981). Although PROLOG represented the first step towards programming in logic, it is not the complete logic programming language.

PROLOG's approach to programming is quite different from that of conventional languages, perhaps because it started as a language for solving artificial intelligence problems. Using the language of logic, a PROLOG programmer provides a specification for a problem by giving the known facts together with the relationships between the objects and what relationships are true. Unlike the programmer in languages like Pascal and Ada, there is very little explicit control of how the problem is to be solved – the solution to the problem is produced by inference from the given facts and rules.

A PROLOG program consists of a series of clauses, which are of three basic types.

(1) Those declaring facts about objects and their relationships. Such facts are always deemed to be unconditionally true.

(2) Those defining rules about objects and their relationships.

(3) Those asking questions about objects and their relationships. Such questions ask the program whether some statements are true or false.

A more detailed description of PROLOG is given in Chapter 10 together with a simple example showing facts, rules and questions.

Interest in PROLOG grew rapidly throughout the 1980s, particularly since Japan announced that PROLOG would have an important part to play in their fifth-generation computer initiative.

There has been considerable discussion of the merits of logic programming as opposed to functional programming, particularly as regards the use of PROLOG and LISP programs to solve the same problems. It is doubtful whether such detailed comparisons will result in any definite conclusions. (Those who are interested in such comparisons can read the paper by O'Keefe (1983).) In contrast to LISP, which is effective when list processing is required, PROLOG is best used in searching applications with databases and expert systems. PROLOG is not ideally suited for data processing work and the lack of compound expressions in the language can make some applications very clumsy. Furthermore, a strictly logical approach to programming can often lead to severe inefficiencies at run time. Although PROLOG programmers have found ways to avoid some of these difficulties, these methods seem *ad hoc* and represent a move away from the purity of mathematical logic.

Object-oriented languages

Both the package concept in Ada and the *object* in Smalltalk have as their origin the SIMULA class, but whereas a language like Ada has simplified the class concept, Smalltalk has extended it. The fundamental concept in Smalltalk is the object; that is, some local data together with a set of procedures that operate on that data. All calculations are performed by sending messages to objects, and problems are solved by identifying real-world objects and modelling them by Smalltalk objects. This has led to what is known as object-oriented programming, which is discussed in Chapter 8.

The approach taken in Smalltalk is to integrate the language fully with its support tools, thus providing a complete programming environment. Indeed, with Smalltalk, it is impossible to say where the language stops and the environment begins.

The first version of Smalltalk was developed by Xerox at their research centre in Palo Alto in the early 1970s for use with powerful graphics workstations. The current version is known as Smalltalk-80. Its support tools (pop-up menus, windows, icons and mouse input) have led the way in providing a user-friendly interface for both the expert and non-expert user. The Apple Macintosh is currently the best known of the systems that have been influenced by these ideas.

Message passing and the support of a sophisticated environment are both expensive in terms of computer resources. In the early days of computing, computer time was very expensive compared with people's time. Languages and systems were therefore developed so that they made the best use of machine resources. The Smalltalk philosophy, on the other hand, is that computers are cheap and so systems should be developed to make the best use of people's time. The recent developments in computer design and reduction in computer costs have made this approach attainable.

Object-oriented programming took off in a big way in the 1980s and a large number of languages, mostly experimental, have been designed as well as extensions to traditional languages such as the development of C++ from C. A central theme of object-oriented programming is software reuse. The language Eiffel was designed by Bertrand Meyer in the 1980s with the aim of providing a language that would support the creation of large robust systems from existing tried and tested components. An important difference from Smalltalk is that, in order to support the creation of reliable software, type checking is performed at compile time.

Summary

(1) High-level languages (often called third-generation languages) developed from the need to make programming easier for the non-specialist programmer and to make languages independent of specific computer hardware.

(2) FORTRAN was the first widely used high-level language. It was immensely successful when it emerged in the late 1950s and is still widely used today in its FORTRAN 77 and FORTRAN 90 versions for scientific and engineering applications.

(3) ALGOL 60, which appeared a few years after FORTRAN, was not as successful in terms of numbers of users, but it had a much greater influence on subsequent languages, such as Pascal and Ada. It introduced many new concepts into programming languages including recursion, block structure, syntax definition and structured statements.

(4) COBOL was the first effective high-level language for commercial data processing. It is still a major language today although its pre-eminence in the business computing world is under challenge from the many and varied 4GLs.

(5) PL/I attempted to provide a general multipurpose language by combining many of the features of FORTRAN, ALGOL 60 and COBOL. However, it proved to be too large and unwieldy.

(6) The use of terminals attached to a central computer led to the introduction of interactive languages in the 1960s, one of which, BASIC, has become very popular due to its simplicity and the fact that its interpreter will fit into the memory of small machines.

(7) A vast number of special-purpose languages were designed in the 1960s, but often these were only used by the small group who implemented them. The main survivors are SNOBOL4, which is a string manipulation language, and GPSS, which is a simulation language.

(8) LISP is oriented towards the manipulation of symbols, rather than numbers, and for three decades has been the dominant language in artificial intelligence.

(9) LISP is a list-processing language and is close to being a functional language. Functional languages are easier to reason about than their imperative counterparts.

(10) Pascal is now the major teaching language and has had a beneficial influence on programming style.

(11) C has proved to be the most successful systems programming language.

(12) Ada, Modula-2 and C++ are the most important of the modern generation of general-purpose imperative languages. They incorporate the current ideas of modularity and information hiding.

(13) PROLOG has introduced programmers to the delights of logic programming. Its impact has been enhanced by the support it has received from Japan's fifth-generation initiative in intelligent knowledge-based systems.

(14) Object-oriented programming has received increasing attention in recent years, the main object-oriented languages being Smalltalk, Eiffel and C++.

EXERCISES

Some of the following exercises will require further reading.

2.1 What were the original design goals of FORTRAN and how far were they realized? What new concepts did FORTRAN introduce into programming languages and what influence did it have on later languages?

2.2 ALGOL 60 was less successful than FORTRAN, but it has had a much greater impact on the design of later languages. Explain this apparent paradox.

2.3 Consider a text editor known to you and compare its string handling facilities with those typically found in programming languages.

2.4 Apart from LISP, the list-processing languages introduced in the 1960s have disappeared. LISP is still widely used, particularly in artificial intelligence applications. Describe the properties of LISP that have contributed to its longevity.

2.5 How important in the rise or fall of a new programming language is the availability of efficient compilers for a wide range of computers? What factors affect the provision of suitable compilers?

2.6 Identify Ada facilities that:

(a) are similar to those in Pascal,

(b) extend a Pascal construct,

(c) differ significantly from anything in Pascal.

Choose an example from each group and suggest reasons why the Ada construct was designed as it was.

2.7 James Martin (1985) claims that computer science departments have ignored 4GLs. How far do you think his comments are justified? Are universities ignoring languages which are of fundamental importance?

2.8 Discuss how programming in PROLOG differs from programming in conventional languages such as Pascal.

BIBLIOGRAPHY

The development of programming languages are well covered by the following books and articles. Two good starting points are the article by Wegner (1976) and the paper by Knuth entitled 'Early Development of Programming Languages' (Metroplis, 1980), which is excellent on languages up to and including FORTRAN I. Much more detail is provided in the book by Sammet (1969) which gives all the major, and many minor, languages from the 1950s and 1960s. The only criticism is that it is very oriented to languages from the United States. Two further papers by Sammet (1972, 1981) bring the history of languages up to date.

In a Conference in 1981 (Wexelblat, 1981), the designers of the major languages of the 1950s and 1960s were asked to give their view of the language's design and development. The languages covered with the speaker's name in brackets are: FORTRAN (John Backus), ALGOL (Alan Perlis and Peter Naur), LISP (John McCarthy), COBOL (Jean Sammet), APT (Douglas Ross), JOVIAL (Jules Schwartz), GPSS (Geoffrey Gordon), SIMULA (Kristen Nygaard), JOSS (Charles Baker), BASIC (Thomas Kurtz), PL/I (George Radin), SNOBOL (Ralph Griswold), APL (Kenneth Iverson).

The evolution of modern functional languages is described by Hudak (1989).

ANSI (1968), *USA Standard COBOL*.

Backus, J. (1978), 'Can Programming be Liberated from the Von Neumann Style?', *Comm. ACM*, **21**, pp. 613–641.

Clocksin, W. F. and Mellish, C. S. (1981), *Programming in Prolog*, Springer-Verlag.

Dijkstra, E. W. (1968), 'Goto Statement Considered Harmful', *Comm. ACM*, **11**, pp. 147–148.

Hoare, C. A. R. (1981), 'The Emperor's Old Clothes', *Comm. ACM*, **24**, pp. 75–83.

Hudak, P. (1989), 'Conception, Evolution, and Application of Functional Programming Languages', *ACM Computing Surveys*, **21**, pp. 359–411.

Humby, E. (1964), 'ICT COBOL Rapidwrite' in *Introduction to System Programming* (P. Wegner, Ed.), Academic Press, pp. 166–177.

ISO (1982), *Specification for Computer Programming Language Pascal*, ISO 7185–1982.

Martin, J. (1985), 'Excerpts from: An Information Systems Manifesto', *Comm. ACM*, **28**, pp. 252–262.

Metroplis, N., Howlett, J. and Rota, G.-C. (1980), *A History of Computing in the Twentieth Century*, Academic Press.

Naur, P. *et al.* (Eds.) (1960), 'Report on the Algorithmic Language ALGOL 60', *Comm. ACM*, **3**, pp. 299–314.

Naur, P. *et al.* (Eds.) (1963), 'Revised Report on the Algorithmic Language ALGOL 60', *Comm. ACM*, **6**, pp. 1–17.

O'Keefe, R. A. (1983), 'Prolog Compared with Lisp', *ACM SIGPLAN Notices*, **18** (5), pp. 46–56.

Sammet, J. E. (1969), *Programming Languages: History and Fundamentals*, Prentice-Hall.

Sammet, J. E. (1972), 'Programming Languages: History and Future', *Comm. ACM*, **15**, pp. 601–610.

Sammet, J. E. (1981), 'An Overview of High-Level Languages' in *Advances in Computers*, **20**, Academic Press, pp. 199–259.

US Department of Defense (1960), *COBOL, Initial Specification for a Common Business Oriented Language*.

US Department of Defense (1961), *COBOL, Revised Specification for a Common Business Oriented Language*.

Wegner, P. (1976), 'Programming Languages – the First 25 Years', *IEEE Transactions on Computers*, **C-25**, pp. 1207–1255.

Wexelblat, R. L. (1981), *History of Programming Languages*, Academic Press.

Wirth, N. and Hoare, C. A. R. (1966), 'A Contribution to the Development of ALGOL', *Comm. ACM*, **9**, pp. 413–431.

Wirth, N. (1988), 'The Programming Language Oberon', *Software – Practice and Experience*, **18**, pp. 671–690.

Types, objects and declarations

CONTENTS

3.1 **Names**   **52**
3.2 **Declarations and binding**   **53**
3.3 **Type definitions**   **59**
3.4 **Numeric data types**   **61**
3.5 **Logical types**   **65**
3.6 **Character types**   **66**
3.7 **Enumeration types**   **66**
3.8 **Pointers**   **68**

This chapter looks at the declaration of simple variable and constant objects and at the binding time of their various attributes. Objects can be divided into two groups: simple or scalar objects and structured objects. (Structured objects such as arrays and records are built from simpler objects and are the subject of Chapter 6.)

An important attribute of an object is its type. This chapter looks at the numerical types *integer, real*, fixed point and *complex* as well as the logical type *Boolean*, the *character* type, enumeration types and pointers. In addition, it shows how languages have developed so that a programmer can express a solution in terms of the problem to be solved rather than in terms of the computer being used.

The efficiency and flexibility of a language is largely governed by whether the attributes of objects are bound early (for example, at compile time) or whether the binding is delayed until run time. This chapter distinguishes between static and dynamic scope and between the scope (name–declaration binding) and the lifetime (declaration–reference binding) of a variable.

3.1 Names

A program may be regarded as the specification of a series of operations that are to be performed on data objects. Languages vary as to the types of object that are allowed, the operations that can be applied to them and the method of controlling the sequencing of those operations. (Operations are dealt with in Chapter 4.)

The type of an object determines its allowed values together with the set of operations that can be used to manipulate these values. Data objects have a **value** and a **type** and may be stored in what are known as **variables**. Variables have a **name**, various **attributes** and refer to an area of computer store. Although the details of the storage are not usually the concern of the high-level programmer, he or she is very much concerned with the naming of variables and defining their type. It is necessary to keep clear the distinction between:

- the name of a variable (its identifier),
- the area of store (its **reference** or its address),
- the value stored.

The connection between names, references and values is shown diagrammatically in Figure 3.1 using a graphical notation developed by Barron (1977).

The names of variables are often called **identifiers**. Typically, an identifier is a combination of letters and digits with the first character being a letter. As was stated in Chapter 1, spaces are not normally allowed within identifiers except in languages such as ALGOL 60, which ignore spaces wherever they occur. Identifiers such as:

left link, buffer size, customer account

seem quite natural and so languages such as Ada and C have found a compromise by using the underscore character:

left_link, buffer_size, customer_account

Languages differ in their approach to the allowed length of an identifier. FORTRAN, for example, restricts the length to six characters (FORTRAN 90 has extended this to 31) while languages such as Pascal allows identifiers of any length; however, some implementations only treat the first eight characters as significant. The recent trend in languages such as Ada and Modula-2 is to have no limit, while ANSI C guarantees that at least the first 31 characters in an identifier are significant.

No consensus seems to have been reached on whether or not upper and lower case letters should be distinct. In ALGOL 60, C and Modula-2 the case matters, while in Pascal and Ada it does not.

Figure 3.1
Connection between names, references and values.

3.2   Declarations and binding

One of the most important factors controlling the power, flexibility and efficiency of a language is the time at which different language features are associated with, or bound to, one another. This is known as their **binding time**. Binding can take place at compile time, load time, subprogram entry or during statement execution. In general, the ability to bind two features early (for example, at compile time) leads to efficient execution while binding that is delayed until run time leads to more flexibility.

Name–declaration binding

This section looks first at the binding between a variable and its attributes such as its name, its reference (that is, where it is held in store), its current value and its type. In most modern programming languages, variables are introduced into a program by a **declaration**. They can then be used in program statements. The connection between the use of a name in a statement and its declaration is referred to here as **name–declaration binding**. To look at this, consider the following Pascal example:

```
program example(input, output);
var x, y : real;

   procedure inner;
   var y, z : integer;
   begin
      ...
      y := 34;
      y := y + 1;
      x := 27.4;
      ...
   end {inner};

begin
   ...
   x := 3.768;
   ...
   y := x;
   ...
end {example}.
```

Four variables have been declared; *x* and *y* of type *real* in the main program *example* and *y* and *z* of type *integer* in procedure *inner*.

The main program and procedure *inner* are both examples of what are known as **blocks**. Blocks may be nested within other blocks and in this example block *inner* is nested within block *example*. Essentially, a block is a piece of program text, containing both declarations and statements, which is used to control the visibility of identifiers. The rules governing the visibility of identifiers are called the **scope rules**.

Names declared in a block are not visible from outside that block; hence, the integer variables y and z are not visible outside procedure *inner*. They are called **local variables**. On the other hand, blocks inherit names declared in enclosing blocks and so the real variable x can be used within procedure *inner* as well as in the main program. In both cases, its use is bound to the declaration of x in the main program. Variables used in one block, but declared in an enclosing block, are called **non-local variables**. A non-local variable that has been declared in the outermost block is often referred to as a **global variable**.

Consider now the declarations of y as a real variable in block *example* and as an integer variable in block *inner*. Variables are bound to their most local declaration; hence, the use of the identifier y in the statement:

$y := x$

which occurs in the main program is bound to the declaration of the real variable y while the use of y in the statement:

$y := 34$

which occurs in procedure *inner* is bound to the declaration of the integer variable y. It is not possible within *inner* to refer to the real variable y. This is referred to as a 'hole in the scope'. Ada follows the same rules as Pascal, but it would allow the real variable y to be accessed from within a procedure like *inner* by giving it the expanded name of *example.y*; that is, the variable y declared in block *example*.

In languages such as FORTRAN, C, Pascal, Ada and Modula-2, the visibility of identifiers and the binding of names to declarations is determined at compile time. This is called **static scope** and it has the consequence that the binding of names to types (**name–type binding**) is also fixed at compile time. The advantage of static scope is that it allows type checking to be performed by the compiler; that is, it enables the compiler to check that variables are always used in their proper context. Languages with this property are said to be **statically typed**. When the types of all objects can be determined at compile time, that is, there are no loopholes, a language is said to be **strongly typed**. Ada and ALGOL 68 are strongly typed but, as will be seen later, there are loopholes in the type checking of most other widely used languages.

Static scope leads to programs that are:

- more reliable, as type errors are detected at compile time,
- more efficient, as type checks do not have to be made at run time,
- easier to understand, as the connection, or binding, between the use of an identifier and its declaration can be determined from a static scan of the program text.

Dynamic scope, on the other hand, gives more flexibility. In dynamic scope, the binding between the use of an identifier and its declaration depends on the order of execution, and so is delayed until run time. The difference between static and dynamic scope is best seen through an example. Consider the following outline Pascal program:

```
program dynamic(input, output);
var x : integer;

    procedure A;
    begin
        ... write(x); ...
    end {A};

    procedure B;
    var x : real;
    begin
        ... x := 2.0; ... A; ...
    end {B};

begin
    ... x := 1; ... B; ... A; ...
end {dynamic}.
```

As Pascal has static scope rules, the use of the variable x in procedure A is bound to the declaration of the integer variable x in the main program and so the value 1 is output. However, if the name–declaration binding is dynamic, the use of x in procedure A would be bound to the most recent declaration of x. Hence, when procedure A is called from procedure B, the use of x in A would be bound to the declaration of the real variable x in procedure B causing 2.0 to be output, while when A is called from the main program, the use of x would be bound to the declaration of the integer variable x in the main program and the value 1 is output.

With dynamic binding, the type of a non-local variable such as x in procedure A therefore depends on where A has been called from. Type checking at compile time is therefore not possible. Many implementations of LISP use dynamic scope although modern LISP dialects such as Scheme use static scope.

In languages such as APL, SNOBOL4 and LISP, the type of a variable depends on its current value: a value such as 7 has an integer type and a value such as 94.7 a real type. Name–type binding is therefore delayed until run time. This allows little or no type checking at compile time, but it does allow considerable extra flexibility at run time, even if this flexibility is at the expense of running speed. Such languages are said to be **dynamically typed**. When a program is executed under the control of an interpreter, the interpreter is able to perform any required bindings during program execution. Programs written in dynamically typed languages are therefore usually interpreted rather than being compiled.

Although LISP is a dynamically typed language, recent functional languages such as ML have type definitions, and name–type binding occurs at compile time. ML also has a **type inference system**. Although ML is strongly typed, the programmer does not have to declare all the types as the system can work them out for itself from the context of their use. ML also supports what are called polymorphic functions which allow the advantages of early name–type binding to be combined with the flexibility enjoyed by dynamically typed languages. Type inference systems and polymorphic functions are described in Chapter 9.

Declaration–reference binding

A description of the execution of a program in an imperative language is most easily given in terms of the traditional von Neumann computer where a store is composed of individually addressable storage locations. Program variables are allocated to these storage locations and the value of a variable then corresponds to the location's contents.

The **lifetime** (sometimes called the **extent**) of a variable is when, during the execution of a program, that variable has storage space allocated to it. In Pascal and the other ALGOL-like languages, a variable is only allocated storage on entry to the block in which it is declared. Hence, the real variables x and y in program *example* are allocated storage when program execution starts, but the integer variables y and z are only allocated storage when procedure *inner* is called, this space being deallocated when *inner* is left. The lifetime of the real variables x and y therefore lasts throughout the execution of the program whereas the integers y and z have a new incarnation each time *inner* is called. Consequently, the declarations of y and z may be bound to different storage locations (that is, bound to different references) on different calls of procedure *inner*.

Before proceeding further, it is important to be clear about the distinction between the scope and the lifetime of a variable. The scope property is concerned with name–declaration binding and, in languages like Pascal, is a compile-time feature, and so can be discussed purely in terms of the program text. The lifetime of a variable, on the other hand, is concerned with **declaration–reference binding** which occurs at run time. The distinction between these two properties is shown diagrammatically in Figure 3.2.

Binding the declaration of a local variable to a different storage location (or reference) each time a block is entered has the consequence that, on block entry, a local variable does not inherit the value it had when the block was last executed. The value of a local variable is, therefore, undefined on block entry. There are occasions when it is useful for a procedure to 'remember' information from one call to the next. The only way this can be achieved in Pascal is by using global variables, and so to increase the lifetime of a variable its scope must be extended, thereby making it accessible to regions of the program from which we would rather it was hidden.

To handle this problem, ALGOL 60, C and PL/I allow the declaration of **static local variables** in addition to ordinary local variables. In ALGOL 60, these are

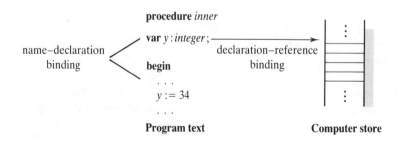

Figure 3.2
Scope and extent.

known as **own variables**. Static local variables obey the same scope rules as ordinary local variables, but declaration–reference binding occurs at the beginning of program execution (that is, at load time) rather than on block entry. This means that a static local variable exists throughout program execution and its declaration remains bound to the same storage location. However, as problems arise with deciding how a static variable is to be initialized the first time a block is entered, such variables have been dropped from recent language designs. Chapter 7 describes how Ada and Modula-2 use modules to solve this problem in an elegant way.

Reference–value binding

The binding of a variable to a value occurs as a result of either an input or an assignment statement. Typically, during the execution of a program, a variable will be bound to a succession of different values. Consider, for example, the statement:

$$y := y + 1;$$

whose effect is to increment the value of y by 1. At first sight, this seems trivial until it is realized that y on the left-hand side refers to a place where a value may be stored (that is, it is a reference) while the y on the right-hand side refers to the current value of y. The binding of a variable to its value, therefore, involves three bindings:

(1) The binding of the variable's name to its declaration (name–declaration binding).

(2) The binding of its declaration to a store location (declaration–reference binding).

(3) The binding of the storage location to a value (**reference–value binding**).

The process of finding the value, given the reference, is known as **dereferencing**. In the assignment statement just given, the y on the right-hand side is dereferenced to find its value so that 1 can be added to it. The resulting value is then assigned to the location whose reference is obtained from the left-hand side. A reference is sometimes called an **L-value** and the value of a variable an **R-value** where L and R stand for left and right.

It is worth noting at this point that it is the assignment operation, with its notion of updating a storage location, that requires store locations and references to be introduced into the computational model. When a language has no assignment statement, names can be directly bound to values as will be seen in Chapter 9 which discusses purely functional languages.

Constants

Some data objects in a program do not change once they have been given an initial value, and these objects should be declared as **constants**. In Pascal, for example, constants are declared in the following way:

Figure 3.3
Name–value binding
for a constant.

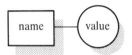

> **const** *pi* = 3.14159265;
>   *lowestprime* = 2;
>   *lastletter* = 'z';

where the type is determined from the value.

The name–value binding for a constant is shown in Figure 3.3. It has a name and a value, but as a constant identifier cannot appear on the left-hand side of an assignment statement, there is no need for a reference. In Pascal, the name–value binding of a constant occurs at compile time while, with a variable, a value is bound to a reference during statement execution.

Ada has generalized Pascal's constant declarations and brought them more in line with variable declarations. In Ada, both variables and constants can be given values within a declaration. Hence, the effect of the Ada declaration:

> *size* : *integer* := 20;

is to declare an integer variable whose initial value is 20 whereas the effect of the declaration:

> *size* : **constant** *integer* := 20;

is to declare an integer constant whose value is always 20. The values in such variable and constant declarations may be given by expressions that cannot be evaluated until run time. Consequently, in Ada, the name–value binding of a constant may have to be delayed until block entry.

Although ANSI C has introduced constant declarations, such as:

> **const int** *size* = 20;

constants are usually introduced into a C program in a very different way. The lines:

> #define PI 3.14159265
> #define LOWESTPRIME 2

are directives to the C **preprocessor** that all occurrences of PI and LOWEST-PRIME (except when they occur within a string or a comment) are to be replaced by 3.14159265 and 2, respectively. This is purely textual substitution and so this feature is really outside the C language.

3.3   Type definitions

The most important attribute of an object is its type. The characteristics of a type are its allowed values together with the set of operations that can be used to manipulate these values. At the lowest level, data is usually just a collection of 1s and 0s, but a collection of such bits can be viewed as an integer or real number, an array of numbers, a character or even (although it is of no concern here) an instruction.

Scalar types that appear in most programming languages are:

- Numeric data types: integer, floating point and sometimes fixed point and complex.
- A logical type (often called Boolean).
- A character type.

Scalar types can be split into two categories: **discrete** (or **ordinal**) types, where each value (except the maximum and the minimum values) has a predecessor and a successor, and others such as *float* for which this is not the case. *integer*, *Boolean* and *character* are discrete types. Hence, the integer 42 has 41 as its predecessor and 43 as its successor, but it does not make sense to talk about the successor of a floating-point number such as 42.734.

A distinction can be made between the **built-in** or **primitive** types, which are immediately available to the programmer, and other types, which can be constructed from the primitive types, although this distinction is becoming less important. In a language like Ada, new types can be added to the set of built-in types in such a way that a user cannot easily distinguish between the two groups.

Table 3.1 gives the principal built-in types of some common languages.

Table 3.1   Built-in data types of some common languages.

FORTRAN 77	Pascal	C	Ada
INTEGER	*integer*	*int*	*integer*
REAL	*real*	*float*	*float*
LOGICAL	*Boolean*		*Boolean*
CHARACTER	*char*	*char*	*character*
DOUBLE PRECISION		*double*	*long_float*

Specifying type information

In most languages, variables can be declared to be either one of the primitive types or a structured type. Some languages also have implicit or default declarations. For example, in FORTRAN, it is assumed that all undeclared variables with names starting with a letter in the range I to N are of type *integer* while those starting with any other letters are of type *real*. Although this method saves the programmer the somewhat tedious task of making declarations at the start of a program, it does suffer from the serious defect that misspelt variable names are taken to be references to new variables.

In ALGOL 60, on the other hand, all variables must be declared before they can be used. Typical declarations are:

integer *a*, *b*;
integer array *c*[1 : 10], *d*[1 : 5];

In Pascal, a variable can be declared to be of a type that is a subrange of another type, such as an integer; for example:

var *a* : 1 .. 10;

However, instead of giving the range constraints as part of the variable declaration, it is possible, and preferable, to define a new named type, as in:

type *index* = 1 .. 10;
var *a* : *index*;

Details of the new type are thus brought together in one place rather than being distributed throughout the program in separate variable declarations. This is necessary when variables with the same constraint are to be declared in different parts of a program or are to be passed as parameters to subprograms. Also, by choosing meaningful type identifiers, the reader can be provided with additional information.

The description of name–declaration binding given earlier in Section 3.2 involved the use and declaration of variables. Here, name–declaration binding involves types with the use of the name *index* in:

var *a* : *index*;

being bound to its declaration in:

type *index* = 1 .. 10;

In Ada, a distinction is made between new types (called **derived types**) and new **subtypes**. The Ada declaration:

subtype *index* **is** *integer* **range** 1 .. 10;
count : *index*;

has a similar effect to the earlier declaration in Pascal. Hence, provided its value does not go out of range, an object of subtype *index* can be used anywhere that an object of type *integer* can be used.

Programs often have objects that are logically distinct although they may be represented in the same way on the computer (for example, as integers). If these objects are declared to be of different types, it is possible to guard against them being combined in ways that are logically inconsistent, and this allows many logical errors to be detected at compile time. The type declaration:

type *new_index* **is new** *integer* **range** 1 .. 10;
new_count : *new_index*;

for example, creates a new integer type called *new_index*. A consequence of this type declaration is that for each operator available on objects of type *integer* there is now a corresponding, but distinct, operator on objects of type *new_index*. Hence, the expression *count* + 1 has the integer addition operator while *new_count* + 1 has the *new_index* addition operator. Integer literals are available with type *integer* and all types derived from type *integer*.

Consider now the expression:

count + new_count

This expression is illegal as the two operands are of different types. Explicit conversion between type *integer* and type *new_index* can be made through the use of what is known as a **type mark**. In the expression:

new_index(count) + new_count

the type mark *new_index* is used to convert the value of *count* from type *integer* to type *new_index*. The type of the expression is, therefore, *new_index* while the expression:

count + integer(new_count)

is of type *integer*.

3.4 Numeric data types

Numeric data types are usually modelled on the machine representation of integer and floating-point (real) numbers. Although this gives the advantage of speed, it does mean that the range and precision of the numbers represented will vary from one machine to the next; thus, a program involving floating point arithmetic may give different answers on different machines.

The arithmetic operators (+, −, *, /) for addition, subtraction, multiplication and division correspond directly to machine code instructions. However, as computers have different machine code instructions for integer and floating-point arithmetic, the effect of these operators depends on the context in which they are used. Hence, the expression 2 + 3 involves integer addition while 6.5 + 3.7 involves floating-point addition. When the effect of an operator depends on the type of its operands, the operator is said to be **overloaded**.

Languages such as ALGOL 60, Pascal and Modula-2 have a separate operator (**div**) for integer division with / being reserved for real division. In ALGOL 60 and Pascal, the result of evaluating 7 **div** 2 is 3 while the result of 7 / 2 is 3.5. In Modula-2, on the other hand, the operation 7 / 2 is illegal as the / operator is only defined for real operands.

Not all languages have two division operators. Both an early language like FORTRAN and later ones like Ada and C make do with a single overloaded division operator. In these languages, 7 / 2 gives the integer result 3 while real division is obtained by writing 7.0 / 2.0.

The exponentiation operator in FORTRAN is ** and in ALGOL 60 it is ↑. As part of the move for simplicity, this operator is not available in Pascal on the grounds that it was used too casually by programmers who did not realize how expensive it was in processing time. When R is a positive number of type REAL, the FORTRAN expression X ** R is actually evaluated as:

```
EXP(R * ALOG(X))
```

where ALOG is the natural logarithm and EXP is the exponential operator. As both these functions are available in Pascal, all that is lost is ease of use. In this way, casual use of exponentiation is discouraged. Ada has restored the operator ** , but has added the restriction that the exponent must be an integer.

Other operators available with numeric types are the relational and equality operators. The result of a relational expression is of type *Boolean*. Most languages use <, <=, >, >= for the relational operators, but there is no agreement about 'not equals'; Pascal uses <>, C uses != and Ada /=. C is unusual in that it uses == as the equality operator with = being used for assignment.

A major difference between integer and real numbers is that integers are always represented exactly while the floating-point representation of a real number is only approximate. This is for the same reason that it is not possible to write down a finite decimal expansion for the number one-third. A consequence of this is that the equality operators do not always give the expected result when dealing with floating-point quantities and their use in this context is bad practice.

Integer

integer is the simplest of the built-in types. The range of possible integers is dependent on the machine hardware and the representation used. With a 32–bit word, integers in the range -2^{31} to $2^{31} - 1$ may be represented when the **two's complement representation** is used.

Integers are used by programmers in two contrasting ways: firstly, in the normal mathematical sense, although with a finite range, and, secondly, as counters in a loop or as an array index. The range of allowable integers is usually excessive for the second application while it can at times be insufficient for the first. This has led to several developments.

Languages such as C have the integer types *short* and *long* to provide integers of different lengths, but the actual length of each of these types depends on the implementation. So, on a 16–bit machine, variables of type *int* typically have the same range as variables of type *short* on 32–bit machines. It is even possible for a C compiler to implement *short, int* and *long* in the same way since it is stated that 'you should only count on short being no longer than long', which seems rather to defeat the object of the exercise.

Subrange declarations in Pascal can reduce storage requirements, but their main advantage to the programmer is in the detection of logical errors. For example, given the declaration:

var *count* : 1 .. 10;

then the following:

for *count* := 0 **to** 10 **do**

will result in the error being picked up at compile time.

Like C, Ada has three predefined integer types; *short_integer, integer* and *long_integer*. The drawback that the allowed range of each is implementation dependent is overcome by not expecting the programmer to use these types directly, but instead to define a derived type. In a declaration such as:

type *my_integer* **is range** 1 .. 20000;

the compiler will select the most appropriate built-in integer type. Hence, although this type may be derived from type *long_integer* on an implementation on a 16–bit machine and from type *integer* on a 32–bit machine, this need not concern the programmer.

Floating-point numbers

Floating-point numbers are the most common type used in mathematical calculations. The name *real* has been used to denote this type in most of the older languages while C and Ada use the term *float*.

The range and precision of floating-point numbers is determined by the implementation. Often, a real number will be represented by 32 bits, as shown in Figure 3.4: one bit for the sign, seven bits for the exponent and the remaining 24 bits for the mantissa. The representation chosen is, essentially, a compromise as more bits for the exponent will increase the range and decrease the precision, since there will be fewer bits for the mantissa.

Real literals may be written with or without an exponent. Examples in Pascal are:

3.75   4.0   2.5E7   0.1786E-5

The literal 2.5E7 is read as 'two point five times ten to the power seven'. The number 4.0 is a real literal while 4 is an integer literal. In ALGOL-like languages, there must be at least one digit after the decimal point, hence 4.0, while in FORTRAN 4. is allowed. There are few other differences between languages except that 3E5 is treated as a real literal in Pascal and as an integer literal in Ada.

sign   7 bit   24 bit mantissa (m)
bit exponent (e)   ($0.5 \leqslant m < 1$)
     (-64 to $+63$)

Real number = sign $\times m \times 2^e$

Figure 3.4
Representation of
a floating-point
number.

Using the representation given above for a 32–bit word, a floating-point number will have about seven decimal places of accuracy. Although this is sufficient for many calculations, there are times when more accuracy is required; for example, in certain algorithms used in numerical analysis where errors can accumulate. Languages intended for scientific use, therefore, usually provide a type which gives more precision. In ALGOL W and ALGOL 68 it is called *long real*, in FORTRAN it is called DOUBLE PRECISION and in C it is called *double*. The normal approach taken is to provide two words of storage for the floating-point number, instead of one. The sign and exponent parts are usually unchanged and the mantissa extended to include the second word. Thus, extending the earlier example to two 32–bit words would give a mantissa with 56 bits and 17 decimal places of accuracy. Unfortunately, this extra accuracy is not without its penalties. Since two words are used, there is an increase in processing time as well as the occupation of extra space.

In Ada, although the built-in floating point type is *float*, other floating point types may be declared. For example, the declaration:

type *real* **is digits** 8;

will define a floating-point type which has at least eight significant decimal digits. At first sight, this appears to give great flexibility, but as it is usually necessary in computer hardware to give an integral number of words to a floating-point number, this flexibility is largely illusory. Futhermore, a maximum precision is often imposed by the implementation.

Fixed-point numbers

Floating-point types are required in scientific calculations where very large and very small fractional numbers need to be represented. Many business calculations also require fractional numbers, but they do not need a large range, and so fixed-point numbers are more appropriate. For example, in PL/I the declaration of a variable X that was accurate to six decimal places, including two after the decimal point, could be written as:

DECLARE X FIXED DECIMAL (6,2);

The number 5.01 is then represented to three decimal places of accuracy while 1005.01 is given to six. This is in contrast to floating-point numbers where the accuracy is relative and so is always to the same number of decimal digits.

Fixed-point numbers are available in Ada and so it might be thought that an Ada type of the same range and accuracy could be defined as:

type *dollars* **is delta** 0.01 **range** 0.0 .. 9999.99;

However, this is not the case. Fixed-point types in Ada are similar to floating-point types in that their representation is approximate. The value after **delta** specifies that all variables of type *dollars* are to be represented within an accuracy of 0.01 – that is, 1/100. The one thing that can be guaranteed is that one hundred times 0.01 does not equal 1. This is misleading, especially for those with experience of fixed-point types in earlier languages.

Complex numbers

The type COMPLEX in FORTRAN consists of a pair of REAL numbers together with suitable predefined operations. However, it does not occur as a built-in type in most languages, and facilities in languages like Ada make it easy to define such a type from its components. Chapter 7 looks at how this can be done.

3.5 Logical types

If a program always obeyed the same series of statements in exactly the same order, it would not be a very flexible or powerful tool. Conditional control statements are, therefore, very important. As such statements depend on logical expressions that may be true or false, most languages have a logical type. In FORTRAN and ALGOL W, this is given the name LOGICAL, but in most languages the name given is *Boolean* in honour of George Boole the Irish mathematician who invented an algebraic approach to logical notation. Theoretically, it is possible to represent Boolean values by a single bit, but this is seldom done as single bits are not usually separately addressable.

In FORTRAN, the logical values are written as .FALSE. and .TRUE.. In more recent languages, the predefined identifiers *false* and *true* are used although in ALGOL 60 and ALGOL 68 these identifiers are reserved words. C does not have logical literals as such. In C, a false logical expression returns the integer value 0 while a true logical expression returns the value 1, although any non-zero value is treated as being true. This is a common source of errors by programmers who convert to C from other languages such as Pascal. As they are used to writing = as the equality operator, rather than ==, it is easy incorrectly to write:

if (a = 3) ...

instead of:

if (a == 3) ...

Both statements are syntactically correct. The expression a == 3 is only true when *a* is equal to 3 while the effect of a = 3 is to assign the value 3 to *a*. Assignments in C have a value. In this case, it is 3, which is interpreted by the **if** statement as the result true!

Examples of the use of the logical operators (**and, or, not**) are given in Chapter 4.

3.6 Character types

The early languages FORTRAN and ALGOL 60 had few facilities for processing strings of characters. The main use of characters was within a string to describe the results being output. The specialist string processing language SNOBOL4, on the other hand, included all the high-level facilities required to manipulate strings. However, the slow running of SNOBOL4 programs highlighted the difficulty involved in attaining both efficiency and ease of programming.

Most high-level languages now include type *character* as a built-in type together with character operations. Character values are usually enclosed by single quotes as in:

'a' 'A' ';' ' ' '3'

Apart from input, output and assignment, the main operations on characters involve the relational and equality operators.

Most languages do not define the character set to be used and so this depends on the implementation. In Pascal, all that can be assumed is that the digits and the lower and upper case letters are in their normal order; that is:

'0' < '1' < '2' ... < '9'
'a' < 'b' < 'c' ... < 'z'
'A' < 'B' < 'C' ... < 'Z'

Ada goes one step further than this and states that type *character* gives the 128 characters of the ASCII character set.

The inclusion of strings of characters in languages such as C, Pascal, Modula-2 and Ada is accomplished by a data structure such as an array of characters. As data structures are the subject of Chapter 6, the discussion of strings will be deferred until then.

3.7 Enumeration types

So far, the types discussed have either been primitive types or they have been derived from primitive types, usually by constraining the range of allowed values. Enumeration types are user-defined types and their use leads to much more readable programs. For example, consider the construction of a program that deals with the days in a week. One way of doing this would be to define an integer subrange type:

type *days* = 1 .. 7;

and remember that 1 represented *Sunday*, 2 represented *Monday*, etc., However, a much better solution would be to define what is known as an **enumeration type**. This can be accomplished, in Pascal, by the declaration:

type *days* = (*Sunday, Monday, Tuesday, Wednesday, Thursday, Friday, Saturday*);

where the possible literal values of type *days* are listed in order. This facility, which was first provided by Pascal, is a good example of the general trend in language design that provides the programmer with facilities to express a solution in terms of the problem to be solved rather than in terms of the computer being used.

The relational and equality operators are available with enumeration types with the relative values of the enumeration literals depending on their order in the declaration; hence:

Sunday < Monday < ... < Saturday

In Pascal, successor and predecessor operations (*succ* and *pred*) are also available. The value of *succ(Monday)* is *Tuesday* while *pred(Monday)* is *Sunday*. *Sunday* has no predecessor and *Saturday* no successor.

In Section 3.1, the characteristics of a type were defined to be its allowed values together with the set of operations that can be used to manipulate these values. One drawback of using:

type *days* = 1 .. 7;

to represent the days of the week is that all the operations on integers are still available, and it does not make sense, for example, to multiply two *days* together. The problem of having too rich a set of operations is removed by using an enumeration type, although the reverse problem now exists; that is, all the necessary operations on *days* are not available. Thus, additional operations such as *daybefore* and *nextday* will be needed so that *daybefore(Sunday)* is *Saturday* and *nextday(Saturday)* is *Sunday*. Similarly, if an *integer* subrange is used to represent days, it is necessary to ensure that the successor of 7 is 1!

In Pascal, the definition of a new type and its associated operations cannot be grouped together in the program text and so it is not obvious to the reader that they are logically related. This problem is resolved by the use of modules and will be discussed in Chapter 7.

Also, in Pascal, enumeration values cannot be input or output. This restriction on their use has been lifted in Ada where it is possible to read them in and write them out. It is also possible in Ada to convert an enumeration literal to its representation as a character string and vice versa; thus:

days'image(Friday) is the string "FRIDAY"
days'value("FRIDAY") is the literal *Friday*

There is no counterpart of this in Pascal.

In Pascal, Ada and Modula-2, type *Boolean* is a predefined enumeration type that is declared behind the scenes as:

type *Boolean* = (*false, true*);

In Pascal, C and Modula-2, the literals in different enumeration types must be distinct. In Ada, however, the following is legal:

type *light* **is** (*red, amber, green*);
type *flag* **is** (*red, white, blue*);

The enumeration literal *red* is said to be **overloaded**. It must always be clear from the context which version of *red* is being used; if it is not, it is necessary to **qualify** the use of *red* and either write *light'(red)* or *flag'(red)*.

The *character* type in Ada is also an enumeration type and this allows other character sets to be defined. Type *character* normally uses the ASCII character set, but if the Extended Binary Coded Decimal Interchange Code (EBCDIC) character set was required instead, it could be defined by listing all the EBCDIC characters in order as the literals of an enumeration type definition. In this way, type hexadecimal could be defined as:

type *hexadecimal* **is** ('0', '1', '2', '3', '4', '5', '6', '7', '8', '9', 'A', 'B', 'C', 'D', 'E', 'F');

In Pascal, C and Modula-2, enumeration literals must be identifiers and so the above is not allowed.

3.8   Pointers

Pointer variables have as their value an address – that is, a reference to another data object. Such data types were not available in early languages such as FORTRAN, ALGOL 60 and COBOL although most later languages have included this facility.

Pointers, or references, may be used as simple variables or as components of a record. Typically, as in Pascal, pointers can be assigned values, used in equality comparisons and dereferenced. They also have a special value **nil** (**null** in Ada and C) which indicates that the pointer variable is currently pointing nowhere. This is used to indicate the end of a linked list and can be thought of as being similar to the zero of ordinary integer arithmetic.

Pointer variables in PL/I can point to objects of any type and so there is no type checking at compile time. Later languages are, however, more restrictive than PL/I and the type of object being pointed at must be given as part of the pointer declaration.

The language C makes extensive use of pointers. The declaration:

int *ci*, **cipoint*;

declares an integer variable *ci* and a variable *cipoint* whose type is 'pointer to integer'. So, after execution of the assignment statements:

ci = 34;
cipoint = &*ci*;

where the operator & can be read as 'the address of', the value of *cipoint* is the address of the variable *ci*. This is shown diagrammatically in Figure 3.5.

Thus, the value of *ci* in an expression can now be referred to in the normal way, as in *ci* + 27, or it can be referred to indirectly by dereferencing *cipoint*, as in **cipoint* + 27. Both these expressions have the value 61. Note that any change to the value of *ci* is reflected in the value obtained by dereferencing *cipoint*. When there is more than one way of referring to an object – that is, when the object has

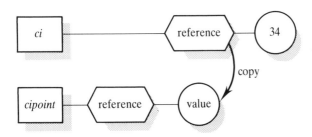

Figure 3.5
Effect of
cipoint = &ci.

more than one name – the object is said to have an **alias**. It is generally regarded as a bad idea to have aliases and so Pascal, Modula-2 and Ada restrict the use of pointers. The only operations available with pointer variables in these languages are dereferencing, assignment and comparison for equality.

A pointer type can be declared in Pascal in the following way:

type *integerpt* =↑*integer*;

Variables may then be declared in the usual way:

var *pipoint, another : integerpt*;
            pi : integer;

As Pascal has no equivalent of the C language's & operator, neither *pipoint* nor *another* can be assigned the address of an existing integer variable such as *pi*.

In Pascal, new objects are created by calls of the predefined procedure *new*. The effect of executing the statement:

new(pipoint);

is to allocate space for a new integer variable and to assign its address to *pipoint*. This is shown in Figure 3.6. The newly created object is known as a **dynamic variable** and can be referred to as pipoint↑. It can be given a value by writing:

pipoint↑ := 17;

It should be noted that:

pipoint   is of type pointer to *integer*
pipoint↑   is of type *integer*

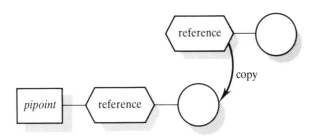

Figure 3.6
Effect of
executing
new(pipoint).

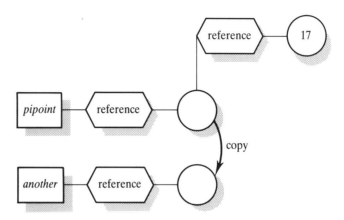

Figure 3.7
Effect of executing
another := pipoint.

Normally, declaration–reference binding occurs on block entry. However, in this case, the binding of pipoint↑ to a reference has occurred during statement execution and is referred to as **dynamic storage allocation**. Other languages use a similar approach although the syntax is different. For example, in Ada, it is written:

pipoint := **new** *integer*;

while in C and Modula-2 the amount of space required must be stated. In C, this is written as:

cipoint = (**int** **) malloc(sizeof(***int**));

The presence of *(***int** **)*, which is known as a **cast**, is to ensure that a pointer of the correct type is assigned to *cipoint*.

Aliasing is possible in Pascal because after execution of:

another := pipoint;

the situation is as shown in Figure 3.7, where *pipoint* and *another* both point to the same integer variable, although we at least have the security of knowing that such aliasing is restricted to dynamic variables. (Aliasing can also be introduced when parameters are called by reference and that is dealt with in Chapter 5.)

If *pipoint* is declared in a procedure, then it is only allocated storage while that procedure is being executed. Consider what happens when a dynamic variable is accessed via *pipoint* and in no other way. On exit from the procedure in which *pipoint* is declared, the dynamic variable will still exist, but it will no longer be possible to access it. In this case, it is said to be **garbage**.

Another way that garbage can be created is by further calls of *new*. After a second call of *new(pipoint)*, the situation will be as shown in Figure 3.8. As *another* is still pointing to the object created by the original call of *new(pipoint)*, no garbage has been created. However, if this is followed by a call of *new(another)*, the situation shown in Figure 3.9 will arise and garbage will have been created.

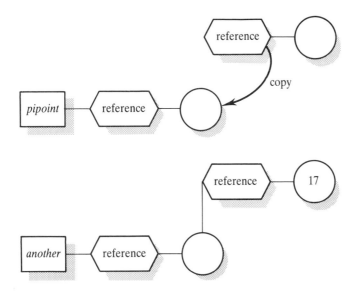

Figure 3.8
Effect of a second
call of *new(pipoint)*.

During the execution of a large program, the amount of garbage can build up. To overcome this problem, languages like Pascal have a *dispose* operation (DEALLOCATE in Modula-2). The effect of:

    dispose(pipoint);

is to deallocate the space allocated to the dynamic variable pointed to by *pipoint*, so that it can be reused in a later call of *new*. Thus, it appears that the build-up of garbage can be avoided by preceding each call of *new* by a call of *dispose*. However, the problem with this is that there may be more than one access path to the dynamic variable, as was shown in Figure 3.7. If the call *dispose(pipoint)* had been executed in these circumstances, it would have resulted in the pointer variable *another* pointing to an area of store that had been returned to the system for reuse. This is known as a **dangling reference** and will normally lead to a program either crashing or giving the wrong results. The *dispose* operation must, therefore, be used with great care.

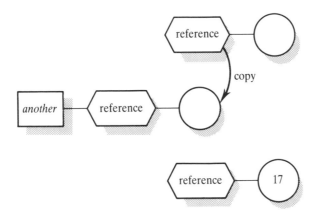

Figure 3.9
Effect of a
subsequent call of
new(another).

The solution to the problem of garbage build-up is to let the system determine which dynamic variables can no longer be accessed and for an automatic **garbage collector** to be invoked when the available space runs low.

The space available for dynamic variables is usually organized in the free space list (also known as the **heap**). A call of *new(pipoint)*, for example, will remove the amount of space required for the dynamic variable from the free space list and assign its address to *pipoint*.

A garbage collector has two functions. It first determines those store locations that have been allocated to dynamic variables and which can no longer be accessed, and then it collects these store locations together and returns them to the free space list. This approach is used in languages like LISP, but as it is time consuming and adds to the complexity of the run-time system, it is unusual in the implementation of imperative languages.

The main use of pointers is with dynamic data structures; these are dealt with in Section 6.4.

Summary

(1) Associated with a variable are attributes such as its name, type, reference and current value.

(2) Early binding time of an object's attributes leads to efficient programs while run-time binding leads to more flexibility.

(3) Static scope is when name–declaration binding occurs at compile time.

(4) The characteristics of a type are its allowed values and the set of operations that can be used to manipulate these values.

(5) When the type of all objects can be determined at compile time, a language is said to be strongly typed.

(6) The lifetime (or extent) of a variable is when, during the execution of a program, that variable has storage space allocated to it.

(7) Integer numbers are represented exactly in a computer while the representation of real numbers is only approximate.

(8) Enumeration types allow the programmer to express a solution in terms of the problem to be solved.

(9) Unlike C, the languages Pascal, Modula-2 and Ada restrict the use of pointers so that they can only refer to dynamic variables.

(10) Dynamic variables are created during statement execution.

(11) When a dynamic variable can no longer be accessed, it is said to be garbage. Inaccessible locations may be returned to the free space list either explicitly, by means of an operation such as *dispose*, or automatically by the system invoking a garbage collection routine.

(12) Most imperative languages use the dispose operation (or its equivalent) while functional languages use garbage collection.

EXERCISES

3.1 What is the difference between a constant and a variable?

3.2 In ALGOL 60 the identifiers *false, true, integer* and *real* are reserved words while in Pascal they are predefined identifiers and may be redefined. Which approach is to be preferred and why?

3.3 Although variables may be initialized as part of their declaration in Ada, this is not possible in Pascal. What advantages and disadvantages would result if a Pascal implementation gave all variables a default initial value? Suggest suitable default values for integer, character and real variables. What, if any, are the drawbacks of the choices you have made?

3.4 Distinguish between:
(a) the lifetime and the scope of a variable,
(b) static scope and dynamic scope,
(c) static typing, strong typing and dynamic typing.

3.5 What advantages result from being able to perform type checking at compile time?

3.6 Why are programs written in dynamically typed languages usually interpreted rather than being compiled?

3.7 When a block is entered at run time, the local variables do not still have the values they had when the block was last executed. Why is this?

3.8 Languages such as ALGOL 60, FORTRAN and PL/I do not have type declarations. What are the advantages of being able to declare new types in languages like Pascal?

3.9 Distinguish between subtypes and derived types in Ada.

3.10 What problems result when the equality operator is used to compare floating-point quantities?

3.11 Define an enumeration type for the months of a year and list a suitable set of operations on objects of type *month*.

3.12 List those situations in Pascal where values of a discrete type may be used, but not values of type *real*.

3.13 COBOL, PL/I and Ada have a predefined fixed-point type. Why is this type absent from the other widely used languages?

3.14 Why can the ability to refer to variables by more than one name (aliasing) lower the reliability of programs?

3.15 Section 3.8 showed how dangling references can be introduced by careless use of *dispose*. What other source of dangling references exist in languages which contain the equivalent of the C language's & operator?

BIBLIOGRAPHY

The description in this chapter has been informal and is based to a large extent on how the features are implemented on present day computers. This is similar to the approach taken by Ghezzi (1987). A more theoretical approach is given in the book by Tennent (1981).

Barron, D. W. (1977), *An Introduction to the Study of Programming Languages*, Cambridge University Press.

Ghezzi, C. and Jazayeri, M. (1987), *Programming Language Concepts* (Second Edition), John Wiley.

Tennent, R. D. (1981), *Principles of Programming Languages*, Prentice-Hall.

Expressions and statements

4

CONTENTS

4.1	**Expressions**	**76**
4.2	**Statements**	**79**
4.3	**Sequencing and control**	**82**
4.4	**Iterative statements**	**85**
4.5	*goto* **statement**	**91**
4.6	**Exception handling**	**91**

The main components of an imperative language are declarations, expressions and statements. Declarations were the subject of the last chapter and this chapter now deals with expressions and statements. An expression yields a value, while a statement is a command to carry out some operation that normally alters the state. (Informally, the state can be considered to be the locations in store and their associated values.)

The order of evaluation of an expression depends on the precedence rules. With the exception of the logical operators, there is broad agreement in different programming languages as to the order of precedence of the operators. There has also been a trend in language design towards compatibility of types in assignment statements and to impose restrictions on mixed-mode expressions.

Structured control statements are an important feature in language design as they have a major impact on how well a language can support structured programming. This chapter discusses such statements in detail with particular attention being given to the development of the **for** statement.

Finally, the advantages of providing exception handling facilities in a language are discussed.

4.1 Expressions

Expressions are composed of one or more operands (that is, variable or constant objects) whose values may be combined by operators. To evaluate the expression:

$a * b + 4.0$

for example, values are substituted for the variables a and b, these values are multiplied together and 4.0 added to the result. At first sight, evaluating an expression appears to be one of the easier operations in computing but there are many subtleties.

For example, the above expression could also be evaluated by adding 4.0 to the value of b and multiplying the result by the value of a. Since these two methods will normally give different values, it is necessary to have precise rules, called the **precedence rules**, to govern the order in which an expression is evaluated. Pascal, which is typical of many languages, has the following evaluation rules:

(1) Evaluate any expressions enclosed within brackets first, starting with the innermost brackets.

(2) Apply the operator precedence shown in Table 4.1 within the brackets.

(3) If the operators in (2) have the same precedence, apply them in order from left to right.

Table 4.1 Pascal operator precedence (highest at the top).

not
*, /, **div**, **mod**, **and**
+, –, **or**
=, <>, >, <, >=, <=, **in**

Rules somewhat similar to these apply in many other languages – for example, FORTRAN, Ada, C, etc. However, some languages have completely different rules; for example, in APL all operators have the same precedence and expressions are evaluated from right to left.

Application of the precedence rules allows a tree structure to be constructed. The tree structure corresponding to the expression:

$a + b * c / d$

is shown in Figure 4.1. Here, the values of b and c are first multiplied together, the result is then divided by d and the result of that operation is added to a.

The evaluation of an expression should produce a value and nothing more; that is, it should not change the state of the program. However, if function calls are used in an expression, there is no guarantee that a side effect of the function will not change the state. This practice is bad programming style and should be strongly discouraged. (A further discussion of this topic is given in Chapter 5.)

The action of an operator and a function is very similar, indeed the syntax analyser can treat them both the same except that an operator obeys precedence rules. This is illustrated by operations like *abs*, which finds the absolute value of its

Figure 4.1
Tree structure.

argument. In a language like Ada, *abs* is an operator while in Pascal *abs* is a standard function.

Most of the simple operators in expressions are **binary** (or **dyadic**); that is, they operate on two operands and produce a single result. A **unary** (or **monadic**) operator, on the other hand, operates on one operand and produces a single result. Some operators, like + and −, can be both unary and binary under different conditions. For example, consider the two expressions:

$$-a * b + c$$
$$+ x / y - z$$

In the first expression, − is used as a unary operator while * and + are binary; however, in the second expression, / and − are binary and + is unary.

Boolean expressions

So far, the expressions used in this chapter have been arithmetic expressions; that is, the operands have been of numeric type and the operators arithmetic. However, expressions can be of different types and one type in nearly every language is Boolean (sometimes known as logical). In a Boolean expression, the value returned must be either true or false. Boolean expressions usually involve relational operators, as in:

$$a + b > 0$$
$$x = y$$

However, a Boolean expression can also contain variables of type Boolean and Boolean operators. The common Boolean operators are **not, and, or**. Ada also includes exclusive or (**xor**) while ALGOL 60 has two extra Boolean operators for implies and equivalence.

The usual convention in recent languages, such as Ada, is to give **not** the highest precedence (above *) with **and** and **or** below the relational operators. This allows Boolean expressions such as:

$$a > b \text{ and } c + 4 < d$$

Pascal and Modula-2, on the other hand, to reduce the number of levels of precedence, give **and** the same precedence as * and **or** the same as +. However, as a result, the above Boolean expression is invalid in Pascal and Modula-2 because it would mean attempting to evaluate *b* **and** *c*. To achieve the same result as Ada, it is necessary to write:

$$(a > b) \text{ and } (c + 4 < d)$$

Boolean operators are often used in **if** and **while** statements to combine relational expressions; for example:

if (*i* = 0) **or** (*a*[*i*] > *a*[*i*+1]) **then** ...

However, in such a case, if *i* = *0* is true, *a*[*i*] may not be inside the array bounds, resulting in a run-time error. Logically, of course, there is no need to evaluate the second relation if the first one is true because the overall result is bound to be true by the definition of the operator **or**. This is known as **short-circuit** evaluation and works as follows:

(1)   Given *a* **and** *b* where *a* is false, *b* is not evaluated.

(2)   Given *a* **or** *b* where *a* is true, *b* is not evaluated.

Some Pascal compilers take advantage of short-circuit evaluation while others do not, which is not a very satisfactory situation for the programmer. Modula-2 uses short-circuit evaluation while Ada provides distinct Boolean operators (**and then, or else**) for cases where short-circuit evaluation is desired. The C logical operators are && and | |. The && operator corresponds to the Ada **and then** operator while | | corresponds to **or else**.

Mixed-mode expressions

A previous section showed how operators like + and − may be overloaded; that is, have different meanings depending on their operands. The evaluation of a + b differs if *a* and *b* are real or *a* and *b* are integer. The advantage of overloading an operator is that it allows its normal use to continue. The alternative, which is to have a different operator for real addition and integer addition, would be clumsy.

A further problem of evaluating such an expression when the operands *a* and *b* are of different types is that languages differ on how they deal with such mixed-mode expressions. Three categories of language can be identified:

(1)   Languages such as Ada and Modula-2 that forbid mixed-mode expressions.

(2)   Languages like Pascal that allow 'sensible' combinations such as adding an integer to a real. The result of such an expression is, as would be expected, of type *real*.

(3)   Languages like PL/I and C that allow 'unusual' combinations such as the ability to add an integer to a character. A major problem with this approach is that it can lead to unexpected results.

Hence, to add an integer to a real in a language like Ada or Modula-2, the type conversion must be done explicitly. For example, if *a* and *b* are of type *integer* and type *real*, respectively, such an expression would have to be written in Ada as:

real(*a*) + *b*

The only disadvantage of this approach is that more has to be written.

4.2   Statements

Statements are the commands in a language that perform actions and change the state. Typical statements are:

*   Assignment statements, which change the values of variables.

*   Conditional statements, which have alternative courses of action.

*   Iterative statements, which loop through many statements until some condition is satisfied.

This section considers assignment statements and compound statements while conditional statements are considered in Section 4.3 and iterative statements are the subject of Section 4.4.

A design aim of ALGOL 68 was that the number of independent language concepts should be reduced. One idea was that there should be no distinction between statements and expressions and so all statements in ALGOL 68 have a value. This idea has not been adopted in many later languages for, although it can lead to shorter and more efficient programs, it can also make programs much more difficult to read and understand, as it encourages the use of side effects within expressions.

Assignment statements

The general form of the assignment statement is:

$EL := ER$

where EL is the expression on the left-hand side of an assignment statement that gives a reference as its result and ER is the expression on the right-hand side of an assignment statement that gives a value as its result. The value of the right-hand expression is then assigned to the reference given by the left-hand expression. Assignment is, therefore, an operation on reference-value pairs.

In ALGOL 68, the value of an assignment statement is the reference EL. In C, where the assignment operator is =, statements do not have a value, although an assignment such as:

$EL = ER$

is an expression and so can be used within other expressions in the same way as in ALGOL 68, with the same advantages and disadvantages.

In many languages, there are restrictions on the expressions EL and ER. For example, many languages only allow a variable name, indexed variable or the field of a record for EL. Languages may also impose restrictions on the compatibility between the type of EL and the type of value given by ER. As an example, consider the typical Pascal or Ada assignment statement:

$x := a + b * c;$

If the type of x is the same as that of the result obtained by evaluating the expression on the right-hand side, then there are no problems. However, some languages state if the two types are not identical, then it is a compile-time error. Such a strict interpretation of assignment compatibility is common in modern languages like Ada.

Languages such as ALGOL 68 and Pascal have adopted a different approach to assignment compatibility by allowing what is known as **widening**. If x is of type *real* and if the right-hand expression has an integer value, then the assignment is valid as, essentially, there is no loss of information in making such an assignment. However, in the reverse situation, where x is of type *integer* and the right-hand expression has a real value, such an assignment causes a loss of information since the real value must be either truncated or rounded to the integer type. Although such assignments were allowed in older languages (ALGOL 60 used rounding while FORTRAN and C use truncation), most later languages like Pascal do not allow assignment when information is lost. In such languages, the programmer is expected to decide what is required and program accordingly, using the standard conversion functions available. To assign the real x to the integer i in Pascal, either of the following statements can be written:

$i := trunc(x)$;
$i := round(x)$;

depending on whether truncation or rounding is required.

C allows conversions when the left-hand and right-hand expressions in an assignment statement have different types. However, not all of these conversions are consistent; for example, *float* $\rightarrow$ *int* causes truncation of the fractional part while *double* $\rightarrow$ *float* results in rounding.

Assignment operators

As statements of the form:

$a := a + expression$

occur frequently in computer programs, languages such as C, ALGOL 68 and Modula-2 provide special short-hand forms. In C, this can be written as:

$a += expression$

Other similar operators in C are ($- =$, $*=$ and $/=$). These assignment operators allow the compiler to generate efficient code without resorting to extensive optimization techniques.

C also has increment (++) and decrement (– –) operators. They can be used in two ways. The effect of executing:

$a = 1; b = ++a$;

is to set a to 1, increment the value of a by 1 and then assign its value to b. The result is that a and b will both have the value 2. The effect of executing:

$a = 1; b = a++$;

is to assign the value of *a* to *b* before *a* has been incremented. Hence, *b* will have the value 1 and *a* the value 2. Although such operators allow very compact code to be written in C, the resulting programs are often difficult to understand.

Multiple assignment statements

Many languages allow multiple assignment statements. For example, in ALGOL 60 the value of the expression in:

   a := b := c := expression;

is evaluated and then assigned to each one of the variables given in the list on the left-hand side.

   In languages that allow assignments to have values, such as ALGOL 68 and C, the assignment operator has very low precedence and is evaluated from right to left. Multiple assignment then comes out naturally. The value of the C assignment:

   a = expression;

is the value assigned to *a*. Hence, in the statement:

   a = b = c = expression;

the expression is evaluated first and its value assigned to *c*. The value of the assignment:

   c = expression;

is then assigned to *b* and that value is then assigned to *a*.

Compound statements

Languages usually have a facility to group several statements together so that they may be considered as one statement. In Pascal, for example, this is done by the use of **begin ... end** brackets, so:

   begin S1; S2; S3; ... **end**

can be treated like a single statement. The language C has a similar construction to the compound statement but uses { } brackets to group statements together.

   As will be seen in the next section, a construction such as the compound statement is vital in languages such as ALGOL 60, Pascal and C when constructing structured control statements. However, more recent languages, such as Ada and Modula-2, have used explicit terminators for conditional and iterative statements, and the necessity for compound statements has disappeared. This is a welcome change to students who often forgot the **begin, end** brackets and were then bemused when the flow of control did not meet their expectations.

4.3 Sequencing and control

As the execution of statements is central to imperative languages, sequencing mechanisms are necessary for routing control from one statement to another and for separating individual statements. As was mentioned in Chapter 1, the end of a line terminates a statement in FORTRAN, BASIC and COBOL while a semicolon is used to either separate statements in Pascal and Modula-2 or terminate them in Ada and C. Conditional and iterative statements are necessary so that the flow of control can vary depending on a program's input data.

Selection

The earliest conditional statements were in FORTRAN and had the form:

```
IF (C1) L1, L2, L3
```

This is the FORTRAN arithmetic IF statement. The expression C1 is evaluated and, depending on whether it is negative, zero, or positive, there is a branch to the statement with the integer label L1, L2 or L3. There is also a similar logical IF statement in FORTRAN 66 which has the syntax:

IF (*logical expression*) *statement*

However, its use is limited as only a single statement can be obeyed if the logical expression is true and that statement cannot be a DO or another IF statement.

Statements containing conditional jumps to statement labels tend not to appear in current languages, even in up-to-date versions of FORTRAN. Instead, most languages use the **if** statement introduced by ALGOL 60 as their basic conditional statement; for example:

if C1 **then** S;
if C2 **then** S1 **else** S2;

where C1 and C2 are conditions and S, S1 and S2 are statements. The structure of these two forms of the **if** statement is shown diagrammatically in Figure 4.2.

Often, in a program, a situation arises where several statements are to be obeyed after finding that a condition such as C1 is true. As the statements S, S1 and S2 can be compound statements, this can easily be achieved in ALGOL 60 without having to resort to explicit jump instructions, as would be necessary in FORTRAN 66. Statements such as the ALGOL **if** statement are called **structured statements** and have the important property that they have only one entry and only one exit point. This property can prove very helpful when trying to reason about a program's effect and in writing well-structured programs.

Although ALGOL's **if** statements have proved relatively straightforward and easy to use, they can result in a problem known as 'the dangling else' because both forms are allowed. For example, in the following statement:

if C1 **then if** C2 **then** S1 **else** S2

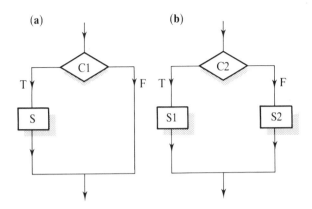

Figure 4.2
Structure of the two
forms of an **if**
statement.

it is not clear whether the single **else** is associated with the first **if ... then** or the
second **if ... then**. Therefore, two interpretations are possible:

   if C1 **then begin if** C2 **then** S1 **end else** S2

or:

   if C1 **then begin if** C2 **then** S1 **else** S2 **end**

Different languages have found different solutions to cope with this ambiguity.
ALGOL 60 forbids conditional statements after a **then** and so extra **begin ... end**
brackets must be used. Pascal and C make the interpretation that the **else** is
associated with the innermost **if**; when the other interpretation is required, a compound statement must be used. In Ada, each **if** is paired with a closing **end if**; for
example:

   if C1 **then**
     if C2 **then** S1;
     end if;
   else S2;
   end if;

or:

   if C1 **then**
     if C2 **then** S1; **else** S2;
     end if;
   end if;

A similar solution is also adopted in ALGOL 68, Modula-2 and FORTRAN 77.

An **if** statement can be nested inside another **if** statement and this nesting
process can be continued as required. In such cases, it is usually better for the
nested **if** statement to follow the **else**, as this corresponds much more closely with
human processing. When the **if** statement follows the **then** part, the human mind
must stack information for later processing and repeated operation will soon
exhaust the stacking ability of most humans. Some languages, notably Ada and

Modula-2, have an **elsif** construction to assist in the presentation and understanding of cascaded conditional statements.

When a selection from many statements is required another construction, called the **case** statement, is best used. This was first implemented in ALGOL W and has been adopted by most subsequent languages. The Pascal version is as follows:

```
case E of
    CL1 : S1;
    CL2 : S2;
      .
      .
      .
    CLn : Sn
end
```

where E is an expression, CL1, CL2, ... CLn are case labels and S1, S2, ... Sn are statements. The case labels must be constant values of the same type as the expression E.

The use of the **case** statement can be illustrated by writing down the number of days in a month as a Pascal **case** statement, where January is the integer 1, February 2, etc.

```
case month of
    1, 3, 5, 7, 8, 10, 12 : days := 31;
    4, 6, 9, 11 : days := 30;
    2 : if years mod 4 = 0 then
            days := 29
        else days := 28
end
```

The expression after the word **case** is often called the **selector** and must be of a discrete type.

More recent languages, notably Ada, have made two changes to the basic case statement. The first is the inclusion of a default condition. In standard Pascal, if the expression value is not one of the constant values in the case lists an error will occur; for example, if *month* had the value zero. Such a default case is covered in Ada by the compulsory inclusion of **others**, so the programmer must explicitly consider what action is required if an unspecified value is encountered. (Note that **others** is unnecessary if all the discrete type alternatives are covered in the **case** statement.) Secondly, Ada allows ranges of values to be used for each constant in the case list while in Pascal each value must be explicitly defined.

The following Ada example illustrates these modifications:

```
case ch is
    when '0' .. '9' => put_line("digit");
    when 'A' .. 'Z' => put_line("letter");
    when others => put_line("special character");
end case;
```

Similar multi-selection statements are included in many languages, such as ALGOL 68, Modula-2 and C. However, S-ALGOL and some other experimental languages are unusual in that the selector in the **case** statement is allowed to be a string, as in:

case name **of**
    "Julia": *write* "It was Julia"
    "Alan" : *write* "It was Alan"
    default : *write* "It was some-one else"

It is assumed that *name* is a string variable and that the S-ALGOL output statement is self-explanatory.

4.4   Iterative statements

The essence of making use of the computer's extraordinary speed of operation is to have loops of statements. Such loops are terminated in one of two ways: either by a condition being fulfilled or by completing a fixed number of iterations.

while statement

This is the most common of the statements controlled by a condition. In its simplest Pascal form it is:

    while C **do** S;

where C is a condition and S is a statement. Its structure is shown diagrammatically in Figure 4.3.

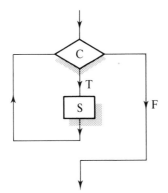

Figure 4.3
Structure of the
while loop.

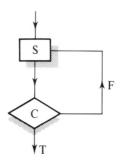

Figure 4.4
Structure of the
repeat loop.

repeat statement

This was introduced by Pascal and is similar to the **while** statement except that the condition is tested at the end of the loop instead of at the beginning. The Pascal form is:

> **repeat** *sequence of statements* **until** C;

Its structure is shown diagrammatically in Figure 4.4. The statements in the loop are always performed at least once, and this can have advantages, for example, when reading in data.

The language C has a traditional **while** statement in addition to a **do ... while** statement, which is similar to the **repeat** statement in that the test is at the end of the loop.

loop statement

This is a more general form of statement and includes both the **while** and **repeat** statements as special cases. In its Ada form it consists of:

> **loop**
>   *sequence of statements*
> **end loop**;

The sequence of statements can include an **exit** statement:

> **exit when** C;

Furthermore, it is possible to have more than one exit from a loop.

The following example shows how an **exit** statement can be used when reading and summing a list of positive numbers where the list is terminated by a negative number:

> *sum* := 0;
> **loop**
>   *get*(*number*);
>   **exit when** *number* < 0;
>   *sum* := *sum* + *number*;
> **end loop**;

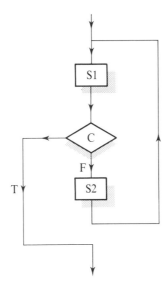

Figure 4.5
Structure of **loop**
statement with one
exit.

This **loop** statement illustrates how a programmer can overcome a common problem in computing; that is, performing *n* and a half loops.

Figure 4.5 shows the structure of a loop with one exit, where S1 and S2 are sequences of zero or more statements. It can be seen from this figure that when S1 is null, it becomes a **while** statement and when S2 is null, a **repeat** statement. Hence, it is not necessary for Ada to include any iterative statement other than the **loop** statement. However, it does include a **while** statement presumably on the grounds that it is part of most programmers' armoury and they would be lost without it.

for statement

This statement differs from the other **loop** statements in that it is used for an iteration that is to be performed a fixed number of times.

Pascal has two forms of the **for** statement:

for *cv* := *low* **to** *high* **do** S;
for *cv* := *high* **downto** *low* **do** S;

where *cv* is the control variable, *low* and *high* are discrete expressions and S is a statement. These two forms of the Pascal **for** statement are simplified forms of the more general ALGOL 60 **for** statement.

for *cv* := *initial* **step** *increment* **until** *final* **do** S;

In the Pascal **for** statement there is an implicit increment. In the first form it is +1 and in the second form it is −1. At first sight, this might appear a major restriction; however, in practice, most **for** statements are used in conjunction with arrays, the control variable being the same as the array subscript. Thus, the majority of cases are covered by step lengths of +1 and −1; the few unusual cases can be treated by special programming techniques.

Ada has adopted a similar approach to Pascal. The two forms of the Ada **for** statement are:

> **for** *cv* **in** *low .. high* **loop**
>
>   ...
>
> **end loop**;

and:

> **for** *cv* **in reverse** *low .. high* **loop**
>
>   ...
>
> **end loop**;

Modula-2, on the other hand, allows an optional increment, as in:

```
FOR cv := initial TO final BY increment DO
    ...
END
```

The structure diagram of the **for** statement shown in Figure 4.6 is constructed on the lines of the Pascal/Ada statement so that the control variable does not go out of range. This is particularly necessary when *cv* is defined as a subrange variable whose values can be in the range *low* to *high*.

As the **for** statement has evolved from the looping statements of early languages, it is instructive to study its development to understand the advantages and disadvantages of the various forms provided by different languages.

- FORTRAN uses a very restricted DO loop with integer counting and positive increments. In FORTRAN 66, the loop was always executed at least once.
- ALGOL 60 provides a very powerful **for** statement. The initial, final and incremental value can all be expressions and can even be of type *real*.
- C has a very complex **for** statement. Its general form is:

> **for** (e1; e2; e3) S;

where each of the expressions e1, e2, e3 are optional. This form is equivalent to:

> e1;
> **while** (e2) {S; e3}

so if the traditional **for** statement is required, this can be written as:

> **for** (*i*=1; *i*<=*n*; *i*++) S;

which is equivalent to:

> **for** *i*:= 1 **to** *n* **do** S;

in Pascal, but is not as obvious to the programmer.

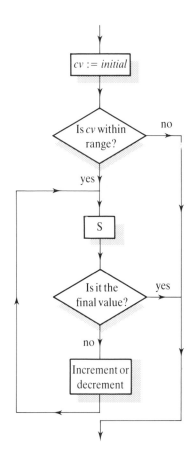

Figure 4.6
Structure of the
Pascal/Ada **for**
statement.

From the use of **for** statements in early languages, several conclusions seem to have been drawn. Firstly, using real values in a counting loop, as ALGOL 60 did, is likely to lead to error. For example:

for $i := 0.0$ **step** 0.1 **until** 6.0 **do**

does not guarantee that the final value 6.0 will be considered within the loop. Its inclusion or non-inclusion depends on the rounding error and how the real numbers are represented in the particular computer. But programs should not be subject to such variations and although programmers could counter such problems (typically by adding a small fraction of the increment to the final value), it is now generally agreed that **for** loops should work with discrete types, since they are counting loops.

It is also better to allow **for** loops to do nothing in certain circumstances rather than to insist, as in FORTRAN 66, that the statements in the loop must be executed at least once. The increment and final value are best evaluated once, when the **for** loop is first encountered, and not re-evaluated each time around the loop, as was the case in ALGOL 60. Furthermore, the control variable should only be changed by the increment; that is, no instruction in S should be allowed to alter its value.

The purpose of the changes just outlined is to make the action of a **for** loop very clear to the programmer. By looking at the first line (no matter how complicated S is), the programmer can see the starting point, the increment and the finishing point. This is, in essence, the purpose of the **for** statement. Other statements such as the **while** statement can carry out the same looping process but, unlike the **for** statement, they do not make the exact range of the looping process, where it starts, what the step is and where it finishes, obvious to the user, and all in the first line of code.

Ada allows an **exit** statement within a **for** loop but this feature should not be used, as the action of the **for** statement is then no longer obvious from the first line.

The scope of the control variable in the **for** statement has also been the subject of some controversy. ALGOL W and Ada take the strong line that the control variable only has scope within the **for** statement and is not available outside it. In Ada, the **for** loop forms a block in which the control variable is implicitly declared.

Earlier languages had the problem of deciding what the value of the control variable should be on leaving the loop. The options were either the value that failed the loop test or the last value that was used in the loop statement S. In Pascal and Modula-2, the loop control variable is undefined on exit from the loop. However, implicitly defining the control variable and making its scope the **for** loop avoids this problem and seems the best solution.

Languages such as Pascal and Ada, which allow discrete types such as characters or enumeration types, also permit the use of these types in **for** statements. Given the type declaration:

type *month* = (*Jan, Feb, Mar, Apr, May, Jun, Jul, Aug, Sep, Oct, Nov, Dec*);

the **for** statement:

for *i*:= *Jan* **to** *Dec* **do** S;

will iterate through the 12 values *Jan, Feb, ... Dec*.

Iterators

In the Pascal **for** statement:

for *i* := *low* **to** *high* **do** S

the control variable *i* takes each value in the discrete range *low* to *high* in turn. In theory, this can be generalized so that the control variable can range over all the members of a structured data type such as a set, sequence, stack or tree.

For example, given a set of names, the meaning of the **for** loop:

for *x* **in** *d* **do** S

would be to execute the statement S for each name *x* in the set *d*. The order in which the names *x* are selected from the set *d* is undefined, but this is not a problem. The requirement is to access each element in the set in turn; the precise order in which this is done is unimportant. **for** statements similar to this occur in CLU and Alphard, but both implementations are more complicated than the structure shown here.

A mechanism for iterating over the elements of a data structure is known as an **iterator**. Section 8.4 shows how such an iterator can be defined and used in the object-oriented language Eiffel.

4.5   *goto* statement

Controversy has raged over the use of the **goto** statement since Dijkstra's letter to the *Communications of the ACM* entitled 'Goto Statement Considered Harmful' (1968). Most programmers in the early days of computing made widespread use of the conditional jump. Indeed, it was one of the important features available for constructing the primitive loops of the 1950s and early 1960s. Of the early high-level languages, FORTRAN and COBOL encouraged the continued use of jumps (**goto** statements) with their associated labels. In ALGOL 60, with somewhat better loop instructions, programs could be written with only a minimal use of **goto** statements, mainly to exit from **for** loops in failure situations.

Since the mid 1970s, the general consensus of opinion has swung strongly against the use of the **goto** statement. Overuse of such conditional jumps in complicated programs can lead to errors that are often obscure and difficult to locate. The reason many teachers argue against the use of BASIC and FORTRAN as the first language for programmers is that they encourage such bad habits.

Modern high-level languages have usually compromised in their approach to the **goto** statement. With the exception of Modula-2, most such languages still include **goto** statements and labels while also providing loops by such methods as **for, while** and **repeat** statements.

Languages such as Pascal, C and Ada have taken this line but have played down the use of the **goto** statement and have placed restrictions on its use. For example, ALGOL 60 permits jumps into and out of **if** statements but Pascal allows no jumps into any structured statement.

Newer languages do allow jumps although they are restricted. The **exit** statement in Ada and Modula-2 is a controlled jump to the end of a loop and Ada goes further than Pascal in not allowing jumps out of procedures. The break instruction in C is also a controlled exit from a loop. Given this current state of affairs, it is probably only a matter of time before the **goto** statement disappears altogether.

4.6   Exception handling

During program execution, 'exceptional' events may occur making normal continuation undesirable or even impossible. Such exceptional occurrences can arise as a result of errors, such as attempted division by zero, erroneous user input or an array subscript going out of bounds, rare conditions like encountering the *end_of_file* marker or as a result of the need for tracing and monitoring in program testing.

Many programming languages leave the onus of dealing with exceptional events completely with the programmer. It is their responsibility to test for the possibility of such events before they occur and to handle them as they see fit. However, such a policy often leads to complex programs and can obscure the underlying structure of the program.

An alternative strategy is to provide exception handling facilities as part of the language. The first language to do this in a systematic way was PL/I, by including features called ON-conditions. ALGOL 68 also included exception and default handling facilities but these were restricted to files, and were not available for general program execution. Of the more recent languages, CLU, Ada and Eiffel are examples of languages that have provided exception handling facilities of a reasonably general nature.

When an exceptional event occurs, an exception is said to be raised. Normal program execution is interrupted and control is transferred to a specially written part of the program, known as the **exception handler**. Normally, different exception handlers exist for each kind of exception. A program written to handle the different exceptional events that might occur is called a **fault-tolerant program**.

Ada exception handling

Ada has both predefined and user-defined exceptions. The predefined exceptions – such as *constraint_error*, which is raised when, for example, subscripts exceed the declared bounds – are essential for an embedded language like Ada so that errors that cannot be checked at compile time are raised as an exception at run time. Exception handlers are associated with a statement sequence in what is called a **frame**, which can be a subprogram body, a package body or a block. Consider execution of the statements in the following frame:

```
begin
   ... if a(i) < 0 then ...
      ...
exception
   when constraint_error => ... ;
end;
```

If the value of the subscript i goes out of bounds, an exception is raised, normal program execution is interrupted and control is transferred to the statements following:

```
when constraint_error =>
```

When the statements in the exception handler have been executed, the frame is left. This is in contrast to PL/I where control is passed back to the point where the exception was raised.

If an exception is raised in a frame that does not have an exception handler for that exception, the exception is propagated to the next level. If the frame concerned is a subprogram body, the exception is passed to the frame containing the subprogram call. If it cannot be handled there, the exception is raised again in the calling frame. A similar mechanism is used for blocks and package bodies. If no exception handler is found, then the system will report a run-time error and stop execution of the program. In analogy with the Ada **case** statement, **others** can be included in the exception handling mechanism to catch the exceptions not specifically mentioned at the end of a frame.

A user can declare exceptions as follows:

overflow, help : **exception**;

User-defined exceptions must be explicitly activated by a **raise** statement, as in:

raise *overflow*;

As well as being automatically raised when an error occurs, the predefined exceptions may also be activated by a **raise** statement. However, it is better not to raise predefined exceptions explicitly, but to declare and then raise a separate user-defined exception so that there is no confusion as to the cause of an error. A predefined exception could, after all, have been raised automatically for some other reason.

An example

As users of computer systems often make mistakes when typing in data, robust programs must be able to respond to such errors in a sensible way and not immediately crash. If, in Pascal, for example, a letter is typed in response to a request for a numerical value, then the program will be terminated with control being passed to the operating system. If a programmer wishes control to remain within the program, then he or she must define special procedures to read the group of characters from which the numerical value is to be constructed character by character. The programmer can then program in the appropriate action that is to be taken when an unacceptable character is encountered. This approach is far from satisfactory in a high-level language.

In Ada, the exception mechanism can handle such errors. If a letter is typed in response to the input statement *get(x)* when a number is expected, a *data_error* exception is raised. Consider the following loop:

```
loop
   begin
      get(x);
      exit;
   exception
      when data_error =>
         skip_line;
         put_line("Error in number, try again");
   end;
end loop;
```

If an error is detected on reading *x*, control is transferred to the exception handler which, in this case, performs the remedial action of skipping the remaining characters on the current line before giving a new prompt. The loop then allows a second attempt to be made to read *x*.

Overuse

Exceptions should be restricted to the handling of abnormal situations. It is bad programming practice to use them to handle unusual, but normal cases. For example, given the definition of *days* in Section 3.7, the function call *days'succ(Saturday)* results in a *constraint_error* exception being raised. Such a situation should always be handled by an explicit check as in:

```
if today = Saturday then
    tomorrow := Sunday;
else
    tomorrow := days'succ(today);
```

rather than with:

```
begin
    tomorrow := days'succ(today);
exception
    when constraint_error =>
        tomorrow := Sunday;
end;
```

Eiffel

Meyer (1988) takes a very strong line on the action to be taken by an exception handler. He takes the view that only two possible actions are appropriate:

- Tidy up the mess, report an error and terminate.

- Attempt to fix what went wrong and then retry the operation that raised the exception.

A function or procedure should therefore always either carry out the requested action or report failure. This view has been put into practice in the exception handling facilities of Eiffel. As in Ada, when an exception is raised, control is transferred to an exception handler which can attempt to recover from the error. However, in Eiffel, there are only two ways in which an exception handler may be left; by executing a **retry** command (which causes the function or procedure in which the exception occurred to be executed again) or by coming to the end of the handler which causes the exception to be raised in the calling routine.

This approach is reasonable in a sequential language where program termination does not lead to a catastrophe. However, in an embedded system, it is often not possible for a program to terminate safely when an exception is raised. It must continue, perhaps with reduced capability, while reporting the error so that remedial external action can be taken. As Ada was designed for use with embedded systems, this justifies its more flexible approach to exception handling.

Summary

(1) An expression yields a value while execution of a statement alters the state.

(2) The order of evaluation of an expression depends on the precedence rules used in the language.

(3) Side effects in the evaluation of an expression should be avoided.

(4) The meaning of an operator can depend on its operands. Such an operator is said to be overloaded.

(5) Structured statements should have only one entry and one exit point. This is important when reasoning about a program's effect and in writing well-structured programs.

(6) There are two kinds of conditional statement in modern imperative languages: the **if** statement and the **case** statement.

(7) A default condition is not allowed in the Pascal **case** statement, but is permitted in C, Ada and Modula-2.

(8) There are three kinds of iterative statement in most modern imperative languages: the **while** statement, the **repeat** statement and the **for** statement.

(9) In Pascal and Ada, the **for** statement is restricted to unit steps.

(10) The control variable in an Ada **for** statement is implicitly declared. In Pascal and Modula-2, the control variable must be declared and its value is undefined on exit from the loop.

(11) When a run-time error occurs in Ada or Eiffel, an exception is raised. Normal program execution is interrupted and control is passed to the appropriate exception handler.

(12) Exception handling is important in embedded systems as they have to be able to recover from errors that occur during program execution.

EXERCISES

4.1 Compare the precedence of the logical operators **and, or, not** in Pascal and Ada. List the drawbacks of the precedence rules adopted by each language and outline your preferred solution.

4.2 Under what circumstances will short-circuit evaluation of logical operations lead to results that differ from those obtained from full evaluation?

4.3 Why do recent languages, such as Ada and Modula-2, not allow mixed-mode expressions and require type conversions to be done explicitly?

4.4 In ALGOL 68, a statement has a value. What are the advantages and disadvantages of this?

4.5 In Pascal, a positive decision was made not to have a default condition in the **case** statement. In contrast, in Ada, a default case must be included unless the full range of the **case** expression is already covered by the case labels. Which approach leads to the more reliable programs?

4.6 As it is desirable for structured statements to have only one entry point and one exit point, do you think that Ada should have been restricted so that **exit** statements were not allowed in **while** and **for** loops?

4.7 Consider the problem of reading and summing a list of positive numbers where the list is terminated by a negative number. An Ada solution, using an **exit** statement, is given in Section 4.4. Compare it with a Pascal solution to the problem.

4.8 (a) Describe how the **for** statement differs in ALGOL 60, Pascal and Ada.

(b) ALGOL 60 allowed the control variable to be changed within a loop. Why was that freedom removed in Pascal?

(c) Is it a major restriction for the increment of the control variable to be restricted to +1 or −1?

(d) What are the advantages of the control variable being implicitly declared, as it is in Ada?

4.9 Why is the presence of exception handling facilities important in a language like Ada?

4.10 Once an exception has been handled in PL/I, control is returned to the statement following the exception, while in Ada the frame containing the exception is left. Compare the effect of these two approaches.

4.11 Compare the Ada and Eiffel approaches to exception handling.

BIBLIOGRAPHY

Structured programming and the design of a suitable set of structured control statements was a major issue in language design in the late 1960s and early 1970s following Dijkstra's letter about the **goto** statement (1968). A special issue of ACM *Computing Surveys* (1974) has an interesting series of articles on the topic.

ACM (1974), 'Special Issue : Programming', *ACM Computing Surveys*, **6**(4).

Dijkstra, E. W. (1968), 'Goto Statement Considered Harmful', *Comm. ACM*, **11**, pp. 147–8.

Meyer, B. (1988), *Object-oriented Software Construction*, Prentice-Hall.

Subprograms

CONTENTS

5.1	**Stepwise refinement**	98
5.2	**Using subprograms**	98
5.3	**Program structure**	102
5.4	**Parameters**	106
5.5	**Functions**	116
5.6	**Storage management**	119
5.7	**Recursion**	123
5.8	**Forward references**	125
5.9	**Subprograms as parameters**	127

One of the most important issues that has to be addressed in the design of a language is the support it gives to the control of complexity. This is achieved by hiding unwanted detail and is implemented by dividing programs into self-contained units that can only interact with one another through small, strictly defined interfaces. This chapter looks at subprograms and how they form a satisfactory unit of decomposition for small programs. For larger programs, a means of grouping subprograms into larger units is needed and this is dealt with in Chapter 7.

Although the subprogram principle varies very little from one language to another, there are major differences in the way subprograms are combined to form complete programs. In FORTRAN, subprograms may be compiled independently. However, this is not possible in languages like Pascal as subprograms are declared within the main program and can be nested within other subprograms.

There are wide variations in parameter-passing mechanisms. This chapter looks at and compares the main mechanisms used and at the effect they each have in promoting the reliability of programs.

The chapter also looks at the various methods of storage allocation and relates this to concepts such as the lifetime of a variable, discussed in earlier chapters.

5.1   Stepwise refinement

The usual approach to program design, with which the reader is assumed to be familiar, is called **programming by stepwise refinement** or **top-down design**. The first step in this process is to produce a top-level algorithm expressed in terms of the problem to be solved. This approach allows the designer to concentrate on the organization and design of the solution without being distracted by implementation details. Although the statements in the top-level algorithm are not capable of being directly implemented on a computer, they can be regarded as the specifications of subproblems. Thus, the next step is to produce a solution to each of the subproblems by expanding the corresponding specification into a series of more detailed statements, each of which can in turn be considered as the specification of an even simpler problem. This stepwise refinement continues until the subproblems produced are simple enough for their solution to be written directly in a programming language.

The language features that help support this approach to design are structured control statements and the subprogram. Structured control statements are described in Chapter 4. The advantage of using subprograms is that, instead of producing the solution to a subproblem by directly expanding a statement in the top-level algorithm, an appropriate subprogram can be defined and then used. In this way, the final main program will not be too different from the original top-level algorithm, since many of the top-level statements will have been implemented by subprogram calls. Furthermore, if meaningful identifiers are used for each of the subprograms, a reasonable idea of the intent of a program can be gained by reading the relatively short main program.

Subprograms are, therefore, a major abstraction mechanism. By using a subprogram, it is possible to concentrate on what the program does without having to bother about how it does it. This ability to hide unwanted detail is the main tool used to control complexity in programming languages.

Chapter 2 described how information hiding can be further promoted by the use of packages in Ada, modules in Modula-2 and classes in SIMULA and C++. A more detailed description of these features is given in Chapter 7 which also shows that the stepwise refinement of data structures is at least as important as the stepwise refinement of commands.

As subprograms are central to the production of structured programs, virtually all programming languages include a mechanism for declaring and calling subprograms. Although there are major differences in what may be passed as parameters to or returned as the value of a function, there is general agreement among languages as to the form of both subprogram declarations and calls.

5.2   Using subprograms

Two kinds of subprogram are commonly used in programming languages; namely, procedures (or subroutines) and functions. A procedure call is a statement in its own right, while a function call is part of an expression and returns a value.

A major idea in language design is that there should be as few distinct concepts as possible. Hence, although languages such as FORTRAN, Pascal and Ada make a clear distinction between functions and procedures, others, such as ALGOL 68 and C, regard a procedure as a special case of a function in which the returned value is void.

The parameters in a subprogram declaration are referred to as formal parameters while the parameters in the call of a subprogram are referred to as actual parameters. When a subprogram is called, each actual parameter is associated with its corresponding formal parameter. To illustrate this, consider the following Pascal example. This swaps the values of two integer variables *higher* and *lower* and then swaps the values of the integer variables *his* and *hers*. It does this by declaring a procedure and having two procedure calls.

```
program exchange(input, output);
var higher, lower, his, hers : integer;

    procedure swap(var first, second : integer);
    var intermediate : integer;
    begin
        intermediate := first;
        first := second;
        second := intermediate
    end {swap};

begin
    ...
    swap(higher, lower);
    ...
    swap(his, hers);
    ...
end.
```

In Pascal, the types of the corresponding formal and actual parameters must match and this check is performed at compile time. In the first call of *swap*, the variable *higher* is associated with the formal parameter *first* and the variable *lower* is associated with the formal parameter *second*. The effect of executing the procedure body is therefore to swap the values of *higher* and *lower*.

Subprograms allow the user to think at a more abstract level. Thus, once a *swap* procedure has been declared, it is no longer necessary to think about how to swap two integer variables (or the need for an intermediate). Such a procedure, in effect, adds a new operation to the language. If a collection of such subprograms is created, it is not necessary for a programmer to have to start from scratch when writing a new program; instead, the subprograms, which have already been written and tested, can simply be incorporated.

The outline programs given in Figure 5.1 show how the declaration and call of a *swap* subprogram are achieved in several different languages. Although the mechanisms used to pass parameters differ considerably, all the subprograms can clearly be seen to be performing the same operation.

(a)
```
PROGRAM EXCHAN
INTEGER HIGHER, LOWER, HIS, HERS
...
CALL SWAP(HIGHER, LOWER)
...
CALL SWAP(HIS, HERS)
...
STOP
END

SUBROUTINE SWAP(FIRST, SECOND)
INTEGER FIRST, SECOND, INTERM
INTERM = FIRST
FIRST = SECOND
SECOND = INTERM
RETURN
END
```

(b)
```
void swap(int *first, int *second)
{   int intermediate;
    intermediate = *first;
    *first = *second;
    *second = intermediate;
}


main( )
{   int higher, lower, his, hers;
    . . .
    swap(&higher, &lower);
    . . .
    swap(&his, &hers);
    . . .
}
```

Figure 5.1
Example programs –
subprograms in:
(a) FORTRAN;
(b) ANSI C;
(c) Modula-2;
(d) Ada.

(c)
```
MODULE exchange;
    VAR higher, lower, his, hers : INTEGER;

    PROCEDURE swap(VAR first, second : INTEGER);
    VAR intermediate : INTEGER;
    BEGIN
        intermediate :=first;
        first := second;
        second := intermediate
    END swap;


BEGIN

    . . .
    swap(higher, lower);

    . . .
    swap(his, hers);
    . . .
END exchange.
```

(d)
```
procedure exchange is
    . . .
    higher, lower, his, hers : integer;

    procedure swap(first, second : in out integer) is
        intermediate : integer;
    begin
        intermediate := first;
        first := second;
        second := intermediate;
    end swap;

begin
    . . .
    swap(higher, lower);
    . . .
    swap(his, hers);
    . . .
end exchange;
```

In FORTRAN and traditional C, the types of the actual and formal parameters are not checked to ensure that they match, while in Modula-2 and Ada they are checked at compile time. The ANSI C function heading:

void *swap*(**int** **first*, **int** **second*)

is written in traditional C as:

void *swap*(*first*, *second*)
int **first*, **second*;

In most languages, the structure of a subprogram and the structure of the main program are very similar. However, instead of the words procedure or subroutine, Pascal and FORTRAN use the word **program**/PROGRAM to denote the main program and Modula-2 uses the word MODULE. C uses a subprogram called *main* while Ada allows an ordinary procedure such as *exchange* to be the main program. The different parameter-passing mechanisms are described in Section 5.4.

Finally, declarations can be made within a subprogram in the same way as they can in a main program. They are then called **local declarations**.

5.3 Program structure

As well as using parameters, subprograms can communicate with one another by sharing access to non-local information. The way in which this is done depends on the program structure adopted by the language.

FORTRAN

In FORTRAN, a program consists of a main program in addition to a series of independent subprograms. The structure of a FORTRAN program is shown in Figure 5.2. Note that the local variable R is only in scope within the main program while S and T are only in scope in the subroutines in which they are declared.

Subprograms in FORTRAN can interact with one another via parameters or through a list of COMMON variables. Although the COMMON list must be repeated in each subprogram, the identifiers do not have to be the same in each case, and the lists do not even have to be of the same length. Variables in corresponding positions in each of the COMMON lists share the same locations in store. Hence, any change to the variable U in subroutine A of Figure 5.2 automatically changes the value of the variable X in the main program and the value of the variable E in subroutine B.

As well as allowing subprograms to communicate with one another, COMMON lists are sometimes used to reduce a program's storage requirements. They do this by enabling variables that have no connection with one another to share the same storage locations. This is called **overlaying** and was important when FORTRAN

```
PROGRAM MAIN
COMMON X, Y, Z
INTEGER R
  .
  .
  .
STOP
END
```

```
SUBROUTINE A ...
COMMON U, V, W
INTEGER S
  .
  .
  .
RETURN
END
```

```
SUBROUTINE B ...
COMMON E, F, G
INTEGER T
  .
  .
  .
RETURN
END
```

Figure 5.2
Structure of a
FORTRAN program.

was first designed as then the main stores of computers were small and space was often at a premium. However, such a concept does not aid in the understanding or improve the reliability of programs!

Independent compilation

As FORTRAN subprograms do not depend on one another, they can be compiled independently and held in libraries of pre-compiled routines. Such an approach allows programmers to incorporate tried and tested routines in their programs. Furthermore, if changes need to be made to a subprogram, then only that subprogram has to be recompiled, which is a major advantage when modifications have to be made to large programs containing many subprograms. However, the drawback of this approach is that full type checking across subprogram boundaries is not possible: as each subprogram is compiled independently, it is not possible to check that the type of the actual parameters in a subprogram call matches the type of the formal parameters in the subprogram declaration. This presents a major problem when trying to produce large, reliable systems consisting of many sub-programs. (The difference between independent and separate compilation is discussed in Section 7.4.)

ALGOL-like languages

In ALGOL 60 and its many successors (for example, Pascal), an alternative approach has been adopted. Such languages have one monolithic program and sub-programs can either be declared within the main program or nested within other subprograms. This is illustrated by the Pascal program skeleton given in Figure 5.3.

Languages that allow the nesting of subprograms are said to be **block struc-tured**. As was described in Section 3.2, each subprogram in Pascal can be regarded as a block and subprograms inherit all the declarations made in enclosing blocks. ALGOL 60, Pascal, Modula-2 and Ada also allow the declarations of subprograms to be nested in this manner while FORTRAN and C do not.

The rules governing the visibility of identifiers are called the scope rules and they were described in Chapter 3. The rule that an identifier is always bound to its most local declaration means that a programmer can concentrate on one procedure at a time and choose the most suitable identifiers without worrying if these identi-fiers are used elsewhere in the program. Hence, within procedure *b* of Figure 5.3, the integer variable *y* can be declared and used without worrying that a real variable *y* has already been declared in an enclosing block.

If identifiers are declared as locally as possible, the number in scope at any particular time is kept to a minimum. To help promote this condition, ALGOL 60,

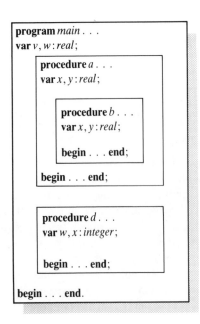

Figure 5.3
Pascal program
skeleton.

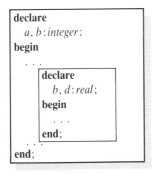

Figure 5.4
Nested blocks in
Ada.

ALGOL 68, C and Ada allow the nesting of blocks that are not subprograms. This is illustrated in the Ada program segment shown in Figure 5.4 where one block is nested within another. As the usual scope rules apply, the integer variable a and the real variables b and d are visible in the inner block while the integer variable b is hidden.

In a block-structured language, subprograms are declared in an environment created by the enclosing blocks. Although this rules out independent compilation, it does make full type checking possible across subprogram boundaries. (Note that several implementations of Pascal do allow independent compilation, but this is usually accomplished in a way that involves the drawbacks found with FORTRAN.)

Reconciling the advantages of being able to pre-compile parts of a program and yet be able to have full type checking has been a major concern of language designers. The way in which this has been achieved in Ada and Modula-2 is described in Section 7.4.

Variables used in a subprogram can be declared in an enclosing block. However, when a subprogram is called there is no indication that such non-local variables may be accessed or, what is worse, may be changed as a result of the call. To be reliable, programs must be easy to read and understand, and a necessary condition for this is that there are no hidden side effects. In addition, procedures are used to help support the decomposition of problems into a series of smaller sub-problems, each of which can be tackled independently. Procedures should therefore be as self-contained as possible. For these reasons, the use of non-local variables is now generally frowned upon.

As an example, the language Alphard has retained block structure, but sub-programs cannot inherit the names of variables declared in enclosing blocks, although they do inherit the names of types. The language Euclid, which was derived from Pascal, has gone even further. In Euclid, subprograms have a **closed scope**. (Another name for the usual scope rules is **open scope**.) In closed scope, declarations are not normally inherited from an enclosing block. Instead, each sub-program has an import list indicating which identifiers in the enclosing blocks may be used in the subprogram. To prevent the import lists becoming too long, constant, subprogram and type identifiers, but not variable identifiers, may be declared to be **pervasive**. Identifiers thus declared are then automatically available in inner blocks without having to be imported.

The C language

The structure of a C program can be thought of as being intermediate between that of FORTRAN and the ALGOL-like languages. A large C program is usually divided into separate parts with each part being held in a separate file. The contents of each file, which may hold several subprograms, may be compiled independently of the rest of the program. Variables, constants and types can be declared outside subprograms in what can be considered as an outer block, but their visibility is restricted to the subprograms in the current file. A file containing part of a program could have the following outline contents:

```
int a;

int y(...)
{ ... /* a is visible and can be used */ ...
}
```

If a subprogram in a part of the program declared in another file needs to access the integer variable a, a must be declared to be an external identifier, as in:

```
int w(...)
{ ... /* a is not visible */ ...
}

int x(...)
{ extern int a;
    ... /* a is visible and can be used */ ...
}
```

C therefore manages to support independent compilation by ensuring that global identifiers are re-declared when they are needed in files other than the one in which they were originally declared. No type checking takes place, however, to ensure that the different declarations match.

5.4 Parameters

Parameters can be classified into three groups or modes. They can be used to:

- pass information to a subprogram,
- receive information from a subprogram, or
- pass information to a subprogram where it is to be updated before being returned.

Ada has three different parameter modes called **in, out** and **in out**, corresponding to each of the three cases, but most other languages manage with fewer modes.

To complicate matters further, each mode can be implemented in different ways. In addition, some languages define the mechanism to be used while others leave it up to the compiler writer. This section considers the following mechanisms:

- Passing information in: call by value, constant-value and reference-constant.
- Passing information out: call by result.
- Updating information: call by value-result, reference and name.

Table 5.1 shows the methods used in several different languages. An asterisk in the table indicates that the mechanism is specified by the language and a question mark that it is a possible mechanism.

Table 5.1   Parameter-passing mechanisms.

Language	Mechanism						
	value	constant-value	reference-constant	result	reference	value-result	name
ALGOL 60	*						*
FORTRAN					?	?	
PL/I					?	?	
ALGOL 68		*			*		
Pascal	*				?		
C	*				*		
Modula-2	*				?		
Ada (scalars)		*		*		*	
Ada (others)		?	?	?	?	?	
Alphard		*	*		*		

Passing information in

In **call by value**, the formal parameter acts as a local variable, which is initialized with the value of the actual parameter. Consider the Pascal procedure:

```
procedure readandwrite(total : integer);
var symbol : char;
begin
    while total > 0 do
    begin
        read(symbol); write(symbol);
        total := total–1
    end
end {readandwrite}
```

If *length* is an integer variable which has been given the value 10, the effect of the procedure call:

```
readandwrite(length);
```

will be to pass a copy of the value of *length* to the formal parameter *total*. Within the procedure, the changes made to *total* are to this local copy, and so they have no effect on the actual parameter *length*. Thus, when the program returns from the procedure, after having read and written 10 characters, the actual parameter *length* will still have the value 10.

In **call by constant-value**, the formal parameter is a local constant rather than a local variable. The following Ada version of the foregoing procedure requires a local variable as the value of *total* may not be changed:

```
procedure read_and_write(total : in integer) is
    symbol : character;
    count : integer := total;
begin
    while count > 0 loop
        get(symbol); put(symbol);
        count := count − 1;
    end loop;
end read_and_write;
```

It is now clearer that the actual parameter is not affected by the procedure call. In both call by value and call by constant-value the actual parameter may be a constant or an expression as only the value of the actual parameter is passed over.

A major drawback of these two methods is that when the parameter is a structured object, such as an array, a copy of the complete structure is created, which is expensive in space and time. To overcome this inefficiency, Pascal and Modula-2 programmers often pass array or record parameters by reference rather than by value, even when the structure is not being updated. In **call by reference**, it is the address of the actual parameter that is passed. However, this method does not have the advantage of call by value: when only a copy is passed to a subprogram, this guarantees that any change to the formal parameter has no effect on the actual parameter.

In Ada, the passing of structured parameters of mode **in** may be implemented by **reference-constant** instead of by constant-value. The difference between call by reference-constant and call by reference is that the formal parameter is a local constant. As a constant cannot be updated, there is no reduction in security.

Figure 5.5 illustrates the three methods discussed here for passing information into a procedure.

Passing information out

Call by result is used in Ada to implement **out** mode parameters for scalar types. The formal parameter acts as an uninitialized local variable which is given a value during execution of the procedure. On leaving the procedure, the value of the formal parameter is assigned to the actual parameter, which must be a variable. This is shown in the following Ada procedure:

(a)

(b)

(c)

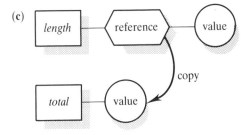

Figure 5.5
Passing information
in a procedure:
(a) call by value;
(b) call by constant-
value; (c) call by
reference-constant.

```
procedure read_negative(neg_number : out integer) is
   number : integer;
begin
   get(number);
   while number >= 0 loop
      put_line("number not negative, try again");
      get(number);
   end loop;
   neg_number := number;
end read_negative;
```

As an **out** parameter may not appear within an expression, it is necessary to have a
local variable called *number*. In the call:

    read_negative(amount);

the value of the integer variable *amount* is not updated to the value of *neg_number*
until procedure *read_negative* is left.

Call by result was originally used in ALGOL W, but with a subtle difference from the mechanism described here. In Ada, the address of the actual parameter is computed on subprogram entry while in ALGOL W it is not computed until subprogram exit. These two approaches only give different answers in rather contrived situations, as will be seen later in this section.

As call by result means that a local copy must be created within the procedure, it suffers from the efficiency drawbacks that occur with structured parameters, as already discussed. For this reason, Ada allows structured **out** parameters to be passed by reference. As languages such as Pascal and Modula-2 do not have a special parameter mode corresponding to the **out** mode of Ada, they use the same mechanism as that for updating information.

Updating information

Call by value-result is, as might be expected from its name, an amalgamation of call by value and call by result. The formal parameter acts as a local variable which is initialized to the value of the actual parameter. Within the procedure, changes to the formal parameter only affect the local copy. It is only when the subprogram is left that the actual parameter is updated to the final value of the formal parameter. For example, given the following Ada procedure to update a bank account by reading and then adding on the next 10 transactions:

```
procedure update(balance : in out integer) is
   transaction : integer;
begin
   for j in 1 .. 10 loop
      get(transaction);
      balance := balance + transaction;
   end loop;
end update;
```

then in the call:

```
update(currentaccount);
```

the actual parameter *currentaccount* is only updated when the procedure is left.

In Ada, **in out** scalar parameters must be passed by value-result although structured parameters may be passed by reference. The definitions of Pascal and Modula-2 do not specify the mechanism to be used, but call by reference is always chosen.

In **call by reference**, the address of the actual parameter (that is, a pointer to the location containing the actual parameter) is passed to the formal parameter. Within the subprogram, any use of the formal parameter is treated as an indirect reference to the actual parameter. Hence, if the parameter in procedure *update* was called by reference, the actual parameter *currentaccount* is automatically changed each time there is an assignment to *balance*.

Figure 5.6 illustrates the two methods discussed here for updating information.

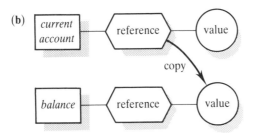

Figure 5.6
Updating
information: (a) call
by value-result; (b)
call by reference.

Call by value-result has the same disadvantages with structured objects as call by value and so in such circumstances call by reference would seem to be the better choice. Call by value-result, on the other hand, has the advantage that all references within the subprogram are to local variables, which is faster than the indirect references to non-locals used in call by reference.

Programs should always be written in such a way that they do not depend on whether the mechanism used is call by value-result or call by reference. In most circumstances, the two mechanisms have the same effect, the exception being when an actual parameter is in scope within the body of the called procedure, and is accessed both directly as a non-local variable and indirectly through the formal parameter. This is known as **aliasing** and an example is shown on pages 113–114 in the call of procedure *whichmode*. Aliasing can lead to errors which are very difficult to find and correct.

Another form of aliasing is when the same actual parameter is passed to two different reference formal parameters. This could happen, for example, with the *swap* procedure with the call:

   swap(*this*, *this*);

Languages such as Pascal have outlawed such subprogram calls, but it is not clear how calls such as:

   swap(*a*[*i*], *a*[*j*]);

should be treated. This call is legal unless the values of *i* and *j* are equal and so erroneous calls can only be detected at run time.

To avoid the problems raised by aliasing, a variable in Euclid may not be passed as a **var** parameter to a subprogram in whose import list it appears. This has the consequence that call by reference and call by value-result always have the same effect.

In Pascal, Modula-2 and Ada, actual parameters passed by reference or by value-result must be variables, but FORTRAN and PL/I allow them to be constants or expressions. At first glance, this does not appear to be possible as the actual parameter must be capable of being updated. In some early implementations of FORTRAN this led to constants being changed as a result of a subprogram call, with the effect that the resulting errors were difficult to track down.

A solution to this problem with call by reference is for the compiler to allocate a location into which the value of the constant or expression may be put when the call takes place. The address of this location is then passed over to the subprogram. When parameter passing in FORTRAN is implemented as call by value-result, the solution is not to generate code for the result part when the actual parameter is not a variable.

Parameters in C

Scalar parameters in C are always passed by value. (Array parameters are discussed in Section 6.2.) The effect of call by reference can be achieved by having formal parameters of a pointer type and passing the address of a variable as the actual parameter. Hence, in procedure, *swap*, shown in the previous section:

```
void swap(int *first, int *second)
{ int intermediate;
  intermediate = *first;
  *first = *second;
  *second = intermediate;
}
```

the parameters *first* and *second* are both value parameters, but the * in their declaration indicates that their type is 'pointer to integer'. The assignment:

```
*first = *second;
```

should be read as 'the value held in the location pointed to by *second* is assigned to the location pointed to by *first*'. A possible procedure call is:

```
swap(&higher, &lower);
```

The & operator means that it is not the values of *higher* and *lower* that are passed, but their addresses. The effect is exactly the same as call by reference, the difference being that the C programmer needs to be more aware of what is going on and how parameter passing is being implemented. It can be argued that one of the aims of high-level languages is to hide implementation details so that the programmer can concentrate on the problem to be solved. Thus, this example shows how C is a lower level language than Pascal or Ada. C++ has reference parameters in addition to value parameters.

Call by name

ALGOL 60 uses call by name as the mechanism for updating information. This involves the equivalent of textual substitution of the actual parameter for each occurrence of the formal parameter. In call by reference, the address of the actual parameter is calculated once at the point of call. In call by name, on the other hand, the actual parameter is passed unevaluated and is recalculated each time the formal parameter is used during the execution of the subprogram. This introduces the possibility of a different address being produced for different uses of the same formal parameter. In fact, this only leads to different results from call by reference where the programmer is being 'overclever'. Thus, as call by name is much more expensive to implement than call by reference, it has not been used in recent languages.

Table 5.2 Results of different parameter-passing mechanisms.

Mechanism	Result		
	a[1]	a[2]	element
call by value	6	2	2
call by value-result (ALGOL W)	6	4	2
call by value-result	4	2	2
call by reference	9	2	2
call by name	6	5	2

Comparison of methods

In the following rather contrived example, the effect of the call *whichmode(a[element])* on *a* and *element* depends on how the parameter is passed. It must be emphasized that this example is only given to highlight the differences between the various methods; such tricky programming is not encouraged.

```
...
var element : integer;
    a : array [1 .. 2] of integer;

procedure whichmode(x : ? mode integer);
begin
    a[1] := 6;
    element := 2;
    x := x + 3
end;

begin
    a[1] := 1; a[2] := 2;
    element := 1;
    whichmode(a[element]);
...
```

If the parameter is passed by result, an error will occur as the value of x in the expression $x + 3$ is undefined. If x was an **out** mode parameter in Ada, this use of x would give a syntax error. The other possibilities are given in Table 5.2.

When the parameter is called by reference, elements of the array a can be accessed in two different ways: either directly as in:

$a[1] := 6;$

or, because the actual parameter is $a[element]$, indirectly as in:

$x := x + 3$

This is an example of aliasing and is the cause of call by value-result and call by reference giving different answers. The reason that call by name gives a different answer from call by reference is that the address of $a[element]$ on procedure entry is different from its address when the statement:

$x := x + 3$

is executed. Similarly, as the address of $a[element]$ computed on procedure entry is different from that on procedure exit, the two variants of call by value-result give different answers.

Overloading

Ada and C++ allow more than one subprogram with the same identifier to be declared in the same scope, but they must have a different parameter profile so that they can be differentiated from one another. Hence, in Ada, the following declarations are allowed:

> **procedure** $P(a, b : $ **in** $real)$ **is**
> **begin** ... **end** P;

> **procedure** $P(a, b : $ **in** $integer)$ **is**
> **begin** ... **end** P;

The call $P(2.0, 5.0)$ is a call of the first procedure while the call $P(2, 5)$ is a call of the second. If it is not possible to tell from the actual parameters which procedure is being called, then a compile-time error results.

A use of this feature is in the library of input/output routines where, for example, different *put* procedures write out values of different types. For example, there is one *put* routine for type *integer*, one for type *real* and one for type *character*. Thus, in the call *put(item)*, the procedure used will depend on the type of the variable *item*. Overloading therefore gives a simple straightforward interface for the input/output routines, which is easy for novices to learn and use.

To achieve a similar effect, Pascal 'cheats'. The *read* and *write* routines in Pascal appear to be ordinary Pascal procedures, but as they may have parameters of different types (and a variable number of parameters), they do not follow the standard Pascal rules.

Input/output routines in Modula-2 do follow the normal rules for procedures, but as overloading is not allowed, separate routines are required for each parameter type: WriteInt is used to write the value of an integer, Write the value of a character and WriteReal the value of a real. However, this is less convenient and more error prone than the Ada approach.

Named parameters

The usual mechanism for pairing actual and formal parameters is by position, with the first actual parameter corresponding to the first formal parameter, and so on. An alternative mechanism, available in PL/I and Ada, is to have **named association**. For example, consider the following Ada procedure:

```
procedure increment(item : in out integer;
                    by : in integer) is
begin
   item := item + by;
end increment;
```

If *number* is a variable of type *integer*, then a possible call is:

```
increment(number, 2);
```

Using named association, the procedure call could be written in one of the three following ways:

```
increment(number, by => 2);
increment(item => number, by => 2);
increment(by => 2, item => number);
```

As can be seen, the names of the formal parameters are repeated in the procedure call to indicate the association between actual and formal parameters. Positional and named associations may be mixed, but in such cases all the positional associations must come first. When the formal parameter identifiers are carefully chosen, named association can lead to clearer code, especially when there are a large number of parameters whose relative positions have no intrinsic meaning.

Default parameters

Another feature of Ada is that **in** mode parameters may be given a default initial value. Hence, the *increment* procedure could be written as:

```
procedure increment(item : in out integer;
                    by : in integer := 1) is
begin
   item := item + by;
end increment;
```

A call such as:

    increment(number, 2);

will increment *number* by 2, but if a second actual parameter is not given, as in the call:

    increment(number);

by is given the default value of 1.

Named association and default parameters are most useful when used together. For example, when real values are written in Ada, parameters are needed to specify the format; that is, the number of digits before the decimal point (*fore*), the number after the decimal point (*aft*) and the number in the exponent (*exp*). A possible statement to write out the value of the real variable *size* is:

    put(size, fore => 2, *aft =>* 5, *exp =>* 3);

which is more understandable than:

    put(size, 2, 5, 3);

as there is then nothing in the procedure call to indicate which actual parameter corresponds to *fore*, which to *aft* and which to *exp*. It is quite easy, on the other hand, to remember that the first parameter represents the value being written. As *fore, aft,* and *exp* have default values, they do not have to be explicitly mentioned in a call of *put*. This allows calls such as:

    put(size, aft => 5);

where two of the format parameters are given their default value. In an earlier use of *put* in procedure *read_and_write*, all three format parameters were in fact given their default values. An advantage of this feature is that a novice user does not have to know about the existence of these extra parameters until he or she becomes more experienced.

5.5 Functions

A function differs from a procedure in that it returns a value. The type of the returned value is usually given in the function heading, as can be seen from the example functions given in Figure 5.7 which return the sum of the values of their two integer parameters.

The value to be returned is given in FORTRAN, ALGOL 60 and Pascal by assigning a value to the name of the function, but this approach has been replaced in more recent languages by the use of an explicit **return** statement. Execution of a **return** statement causes immediate exit from a function, thereby making multiple exit points possible. In contrast, assignment to the name of a function does not cause an exit; such functions are left once their final statement has been executed. Ada, C and FORTRAN also allow the use of a **return** statement with procedures.

(a)
```
INTEGER FUNCTION ADD(A, B)
INTEGER A, B
ADD = A + B
RETURN
END
```

(b)
integer procedure $add(a, b)$;

    value a, b; **integer** a, b;

    $add := a + b$

(c)
function $add(a, b : integer) : integer$;

begin

    $add := a + b$

end $\{add\}$

(d)
int $add(\textbf{int } a, \textbf{int } b)$

$\{ \textbf{return } (a + b)$;

$\}$

(e)
```
PROCEDURE add(a, b : INTEGER) : INTEGER;

BEGIN

    RETURN a + b

END add
```

(f)
function $add(a, b : \textbf{in } integer)$ **return** $integer$ **is**

begin

    return $a + b$

end add;

Figure 5.7
Example programs –
functions in:
(a) FORTRAN;
(b) ALGOL 60;
(c) Pascal;
(d) ANSI C;
(e) Modula-2;
(f) Ada.

Function calls occur as part of an expression, as in the statement:

$j := 3 * add(7, 11)$;

which assigns the value 54 to j. The value returned by a function can be regarded as an extra **out** parameter. Languages differ in what can be returned. ALGOL 60, FORTRAN 77, Pascal and Modula-2 do not allow structured values to be returned while Ada, ANSI C, FORTRAN 90 and ALGOL 68 do. (Languages which allow functions to be returned as the value of a function are discussed in Chapter 9.)

The exact order of evaluation of the operands in an expression is often not specified in the definition of a language so that the compiler writers have a free hand in producing optimal code. Evaluation of the expression:

a + *b* * *c*

in Pascal or Ada, for example, will cause the values of *b* and *c* to be multiplied together and the result added to *a*. However, when *a, b* and *c* are functions, the user has no knowledge of the order in which the three function calls will take place. It is, therefore, even more important than with procedures that functions have no side effects.

Good programming practice suggests that information should only be passed in to a function via its parameters and that the only effect of the function on the rest of the program should be through the returned value. Ada, in fact, does not allow **out** or **in out** parameters with functions, although both it and most other languages (with the exception of experimental languages such as Euclid) do still allow access to, and modification of, non-local variables. Programmers should not normally indulge in this latter freedom.

Operators

Most languages have a set of built-in infix operators such as +, − and * while functions correspond to prefix operators. Thus, a call of *add* is written as:

c := *add*(2, 3);

while the corresponding infix form is:

c := 2 + 3;

To illustrate the use of these two forms of operators, consider an enumeration type called *day* which is declared as:

type *day* **is** (*sun, mon, tues, wed, thurs, fri, sat*);

Consider also a function with two parameters – *today* of type *day* and *n* of type *integer* – that will return the day which is '*n* days after *today*'. In Ada and C++, the names of functions are not restricted to identifiers. An example of operator re-definition in Ada is:

```
function "+"(today : in day; n : in integer) return day is
begin
    return day'val((day'pos(today) + n) rem 7);
    --day'pos converts a day to the corresponding integer in
    --the range 0 .. 6 while day'val converts an integer in
    --the range 0 .. 6 to the corresponding day
end "+";
```

Assuming that *newday* has been defined to be of type *day*, a possible call of the function is:

> *newday* := "+"(*tues*, 6);

although the more natural approach:

> *newday* := *tues* + 6;

shows more clearly that a new operator has been defined and would normally be used. In both cases, *newday* will be given the value *mon*. This new definition of + does not replace the existing definitions, but extends them. It is the overloading property of Ada and C++ that determines, from the type of the parameters (that is, the operands), which of the + operators is intended. If this cannot be decided unambiguously, a compile-time error occurs. All the + operators have the same precedence.

Most languages overload operators like +, − and * thereby allowing them to represent either integer or floating-point operations. What Ada and C++ have done is to incorporate this feature into the language and to use it as the basis for extending the available operations in a natural way. This topic will be discussed further in Chapter 7 when abstract data types are dealt with.

5.6 Storage management

Modern languages are usually implemented in such a way that storage for program code and storage for data items are allocated separately. The area of store set aside to hold the data items used in a call of a subprogram is called its **data area** or **activation record**.

There are two main storage strategies for allocating data areas; static and block-structured dynamic.

Static storage allocation

This method requires that the maximum size of each data item is known at compile time and that no data item can have multiple simultaneous occurrences. As this second requirement rules out languages that allow recursive subprograms − that is, subprograms that can call themselves − FORTRAN is the only one of the languages discussed in this chapter that can make use of this method.

FORTRAN subprograms are compiled independently and are then linked together when the program is loaded into store for execution. With static storage allocation declaration−reference binding − that is, the allocation of data items to their final storage locations − occurs at load time. Although this method is straightforward and allows data items to be accessed efficiently, it does have the drawback that local variables occupy storage locations even when the subprogram in which they are declared has not been called. When a subprogram is entered for a second or subsequent time, all the local variables have the values they had on the previous exit. Programmers must not make use of this effect, for although FORTRAN allows such a storage mechanism, the definition of the language does not insist on it. As an alternative, a more complicated approach such as stack storage management may be used.

Stack storage management

In most modern languages, as was outlined in Section 3.2, declaration–reference binding occurs on block entry. This means that the declaration of a local variable is bound to a different storage location each time a block (that is, a subprogram) is entered. The storage mechanism that is usually used to implement this type of binding is called **stack storage management**. Using this mechanism, storage is allocated to the main program's data area at load time, while storage for a subprogram's data area is only allocated when the subprogram is called. On return from the subprogram, this storage is de-allocated.

To illustrate block-structured storage allocation, consider the following skeleton Pascal program:

```
program main(output);
var b, d : integer;

    procedure z;
    var e, f : integer;
    begin
       ...
    end {z};

    procedure y;
    var g, h : integer;
    begin
       ...
       z;
       ...
    end {y};

begin
   ...
   y;
   ...
   z;
   ...
end.
```

The changes that occur in the allocation of storage to the data areas as the execution of this program progresses are shown in Figure 5.8 When execution begins, space is allocated to the data area of *main*. It is only when procedure *y* is called that space is allocated to its data area – that is, to the variables *g* and *h*. In

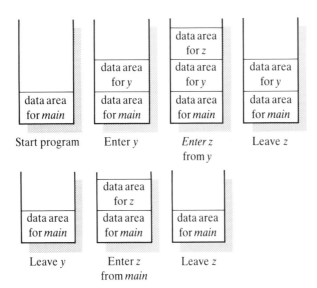

Figure 5.8
Stack storage
allocation.

procedure *y*, there is a call of procedure *z*. On entry to *z*, space is allocated to its data area. On exit from procedure *z* and return to *y*, space for *z*'s data area is de-allocated; at this point, the local variables *e* and *f* cease to exist in the sense that they no longer have storage locations allocated. On return from *y* to the main program, the local variables in *y* cease to exist in the same way

There is now a second call of *z*, this time from the main program. This call results in space being allocated once again to *z*'s data area. However, as the storage locations allocated are different this time, when *z* is entered for this second time, its local variables do not inherit their previous values.

This mechanism just outlined results in a stack of data areas called the **run-time stack**. When a subprogram is entered, space for its data area is allocated; on exit from the subprogram, the data area is popped from the stack. The lifetime of the variables *b* and *d* declared in the main program extends throughout the execution of the whole program, while the lifetime of, for example, *g* and *h* starts when procedure *y* is called and ends when it is left.

An advantage of this type of storage allocation is that space is only allocated when it is needed, which is in contrast to static storage allocation where storage for all data items is allocated at load time. A drawback is that, as the locations allocated to local variables are not fixed, the code generated by the compiler to access them is more complex than in the case of static allocation. However, this approach is so useful that modern computers have special hardware instructions to ease access to variables allocated storage on the run-time stack.

Provided that the size of all local variables is constant, the relative position of an item within a data area is known at compile time and is called its **offset**. The position of the data area, on the other hand, is unknown until the subprogram is entered at run time. When a data area is added to the run-time stack, its base address can be stored in a register as a pointer to the current data area. Local variables may then be accessed using this base address plus the offset determined at compile time.

Data areas

In addition to parameters and local variables, data areas need to hold certain system information, such as the address of the instruction that must be returned to on leaving the subprogram. Also, on leaving a subprogram, the run-time stack must be restored to its position before the subprogram was entered and so each data area must hold a pointer to the data area of the subprogram that called it. This information, which links the data areas together in the reverse order in which the subprograms were called, is known as the **dynamic chain**.

To understand how the information held in the data area is accessed, consider the following Pascal program:

```
program main(output);
var b, d : integer;

    procedure z;
    var e, f : integer;
    begin
        ...
    end {z};

    procedure y;
    var g, h : integer;

        procedure x;
        var j, k : integer;
        begin
            ...
        end {x};

    begin
        ... z; ... x; ...
    end {y};

begin
    ... z; ... y; ...
end.
```

In the main program, only variables b and d can be accessed. When executing procedure z, the local variables e and f and the non-local variables b and d can be accessed. When y is being executed, the local variables g and h and the non-local variables b and d can be accessed. When x is executed, the non-local variables g, h, b and d can be accessed as well as the local variables j and k.

When procedure z is called from procedure y, three data areas will be on the run-time stack, (z, y and *main*), but variables in only two of the data areas will be

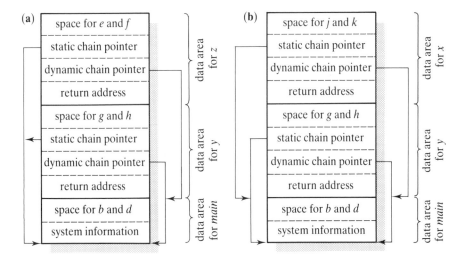

Figure 5.9
Run-time stack:
(a) when z has
been called from y;
(b) when x has
been called from y.

accessible (*z* and *main*). When procedure *x* is called from *y*, three data areas will again be on the run-time stack, but this time variables in all three data areas will be accessible. Thus, a mechanism is needed that allows access to certain non-local items, but which restricts access to others.

The rules governing which data areas may be accessed and which cannot are the scope rules, and so this information is known at compile time. A solution is to hold in each data area a pointer to the data area of its textually enclosing block. As that data area will, in turn, contain a pointer to its textually enclosing block, this forms a chain, known as the **static chain**, which links together the accessible data areas.

The contents of the run-time stack when procedure *z* has been called from procedure *y* is shown in Figure 5.9(a). As *z* and *y* are both declared in the main program, their static chain pointers both point to the data area of *main*. Figure 5.9(b) shows the run-time stack when procedure *x* has been called from procedure *y*. As *x* has been declared locally to *y*, its static chain pointer points to the data area of *y*.

Space is allocated for parameters in the data area in the same way as for local variables. For value parameters, the value of the actual parameter is copied into the appropriate location in the data area on procedure entry. With reference parameters, it is the address of the actual parameter that is held in the data area.

5.7   Recursion

Stack storage management is capable of dealing with recursive subprograms – that is, subprograms that may call themselves. Each time a subprogram is called, its data area is added to the run-time stack. With a recursive subprogram, this means that there will be several data areas in existence simultaneously, one for each recursive call.

This can best be illustrated by considering the following recursive program which calculates factorials. It is written in Pascal, although programs written in ALGOL 60, ALGOL 68, C, Ada and Modula-2 all behave in essentially the same way.

```
program fact(input, output);
var number : integer;

    function factorial(n : integer) : integer;
    begin
      if n > 1 then
        factorial := n * factorial(n – 1)
      else
        factorial := 1
    end {factorial};

begin
    read(number);
    if number < 0 then
      writeln('error: negative number')
    else
      writeln('factorial is', factorial(number))
end.
```

Before looking at the execution of this program, it is important to note that the definition of the factorial function in the program uses the property that factorials can be defined in terms of a simpler version of themselves. In general, $n!$ is $n *$ $(n – 1)!$. This can be illustrated by considering the value of four factorial (written as 4!), which is $4 * 3 * 2 * 1$ or, to put it another way, $4 * 3!$.

Consider now, the execution of program *fact* when *number* has been given the value 3. This leads to the call *factorial(3)*. The function *factorial* is entered and, as *n* has been given the value 3, the expression:

$3 * factorial(2)$

is to be evaluated. This involves a recursive call of function *factorial*. In this second call of *factorial*, *n* has the value 2 and this leads to evaluation of the expression:

$2 * factorial(1)$

Function *factorial* is entered for a third time, but as *n* has the value 1, the execution of this call is completed, returning the value 1. The program now completes execution of:

$2 * factorial(1)$

and so returns from the call *factorial(2)* with the value 2. Finally, the program completes execution of:

$3 * factorial(2)$

and returns to the main program with the answer 6.

| data area for the call *factorial* (1) |
| data area for the call *factorial* (2) |
| data area for the call *factorial* (3) |
| data area for the main program |

Figure 5.10
Data areas for a
recursive function.

The structure of the data areas for the recursive function *factorial* is shown in Figure 5.10. In each data area, a location is set aside for the value parameter *n*. When function *factorial* is entered for the third time, three data areas for *factorial* are in existence simultaneously. Therefore, three 'incarnations' of *n* can be considered to be in existence simultaneously with the respective values of 3, 2 and 1. (Note that such a situation does not cause any problems as any reference to *n* is always to the one in the current data area.) When the program returns from the function calls, the data areas are removed from the stack in the reverse order to that in which they were added.

Recursive subprograms are most effective when the solution to a problem can be expressed in terms of a simpler version of itself. Such solutions often involve data structures such as linked lists and trees, which can also be defined recursively. This class of problem is discussed in Section 6.4, which deals with dynamic data structures, and in Chapters 9 and 10 which deal with functional and logic programming.

5.8   Forward references

Pascal was designed so that it can be translated by a one-pass compiler. To make this possible, the scope of an identifier extends from its declaration to the end of the block in which it is declared, rather than throughout the whole block. As a consequence, all identifiers, including subprogram identifiers, must be declared before they can be used. However, this is not always possible when two subprograms are **mutually recursive** – that is, when each calls the other. To get round the problem, **forward declarations** are used in Pascal, as illustrated in the following two procedures *S* and *F*. The effect of calling procedure *S* is to read and validate an arithmetic expression consisting of a series of zero or more additions where the operands are either *a* or are bracketed arithmetic expressions with the same form as the overall expression. An example valid expression is:

$a+(a+(a)+((a+a)+a))$

Procedure *S* calls procedure *F* which in turn may call procedure *S*.

```
procedure F(var ca : char); forward;

procedure S(var cb : char);
begin
  F(cb);
  while cb = '+' do F(cb)
end {S};

procedure F;
begin
  read(ca);
  if ca = '(' then
  begin
    S(ca);
    if ca <> ')' then writeln('missing bracket')
  end else
  if ca <> 'a' then writeln('missing operand');
  read(ca)
end {F};
```

The compiler can deal with the call of procedure F from within procedure S as it knows the number and type of the parameters of F from the forward declaration. The actual body of F is given later in the program although the parameters are not repeated.

In C, any subprogram called before it has been declared is assumed to be an integer function. When this is not the case then, as in Pascal, a forward declaration (called a **function prototype** in ANSI C) such as:

```
void F(char *);
```

must be given before the first call of F. In traditional C, the type of the parameter is not given and this would be written as:

```
void F();
```

This is an example of how ANSI C has increased the amount of type checking done at compile time compared with traditional C.

Ada differentiates between the specification and the body of a subprogram. The declaration:

```
function a(b : integer) return real;
```

is of a function specification while:

```
function a(b : integer) return real is
begin ... end a;
```

is a function body.

Normally only a subprogram body is declared, although it is always possible for a subprogram specification to be declared as well. This allows subprogram specifications to be used in the same way as forward subprogram declarations in Pascal. The one difference is that the parameters are given in the forward declaration in Pascal, and are not repeated in the actual body, while with Ada they must be given in both situations. Although this requires more writing, it makes programs easier to read.

In ALGOL 60, ALGOL 68, FORTRAN and Modula-2 the order of declaration of the subprograms does not matter and so there is no need for forward declarations.

5.9 Subprograms as parameters

So far, this chapter has shown how constants, expressions and variables can be passed as subprogram parameters. In most languages, it is also possible to pass functions and procedures as parameters. These are referred to as **formal functions** or **formal procedures**.

The ability to pass subprograms as parameters is of central importance in functional languages and is discussed in Chapter 9. It is less widely used in imperative languages, although it is useful in numerical analysis where it allows general mathematical routines to be written. For example, to calculate the value of:

$$\frac{f(x2) - f(x1)}{x2 - x1}$$

for any function f and any value of $x1$ and $x2$, the following Pascal function could be used:

```
function slope(f(y : real) : real; x1, x2 : real) : real;
begin
  if x1 = x2 then
    slope := 0
  else
    slope := (f(x2) - f(x1)) / (x2 - x1)
end {slope};
```

A call of this function requires three parameters, the first of which is a real function with one real parameter. Given the functions:

```
function straight(x : real) : real;
begin
  straight := 2 * x + 1
end {straight};

function tan(x : real) : real;
begin
  tan := sin(x) / cos(x)
end {tan};
```

then possible calls of *slope* might be *slope(straight,* 3.8, 3.85*)* and *slope(tan,* 3.8, 3.85*)*. Both of these calls will return real values.

In FORTRAN, ALGOL 60, traditional C and in the original definition of Pascal, the type of the parameters in the formal subprograms does not have to be specified and this leads to a loophole in the type checking rules. This omission was rectified for Pascal and C when their standards were produced.

Modula-2 goes further than Pascal and allows procedure types and procedure variables. Thus, it is possible, for example, to have the type declaration:

```
TYPE realfunc = PROCEDURE(REAL) : REAL;
```

and the variable declaration:

```
VAR fx : realfunc;
```

The variable fx can take as values functions which have one real value parameter and which return a real value. Given a function similar to *straight*, the assignment can then be:

```
fx := straight;
```

The function *slope* would be written in Modula-2 as:

```
PROCEDURE slope(f : realfunc; x1, x2 : REAL) : REAL;
BEGIN
   IF x1 = x2 THEN
      RETURN 0
   ELSE
      RETURN (f(x2) − f(x1)) / (x2 − x1)
   END
END slope;
```

The call *slope*(*straight*, 3.8, 3.85) is still possible in this case, but it is also possible to have the call *slope*(*fx*, 3.8, 3.85) where the function passed depends on the current value of *fx*. In Modula-2, therefore, subprograms are much closer to becoming objects which can be manipulated in the same way as variables. It is permissable, for example, to have arrays of subprograms. ALGOL 68 and the functional languages go further than Modula-2 and allow functions to be returned as the value of a function.

Subprograms may not be passed as parameters in Ada, although a similar effect is achieved by what are called **generics**. Instead of *slope* having three parameters, one of which is a formal function, the Ada equivalent is a **generic subprogram** with two parameters. First, the generic subprogram specification is declared:

```
generic
   with function f(y : real) return real;
function slope(x1, x2 : real) return real;
```

and then the subprogram body:

```
function slope(x1, x2 : real) return real is
begin
   if x1 = x2 then
      return 0;
   else
      return (f(x2) − f(x1)) / (x2 − x1);
end slope;
```

A generic subprogram is a **template** from which an actual subprogram may be obtained by what is called **instantiation**. If two Ada functions *straight* and *tan* are assumed, two possible instances of the generic function *slope* are one in which calls of *f* are replaced by calls of *straight* and one in which they are replaced by calls of *tan*. These instances may be produced by the two generic instantiations:

> **function** *straight_slope* **is new** *slope*(*f* => *straight*);
> **function** *tan_slope* **is new** *slope*(*f* => *tan*);

Generic instantiation occurs at compile time and results in two completely different *slope* functions being created; one called *straight_slope* and the other called *tan_slope*. In the case of Pascal, on the other hand, there will be a single *slope* function. The equivalent of the Pascal calls of *slope*(*straight*, 3.8, 3.85) and *slope*(*tan*, 3.8, 3.85) are *straight_slope*(3.8, 3.85) and *tan_slope*(3.8, 3.85). The subject of generics will be discussed further in Section 7.5.

Summary

(1) The ability to hide unwanted detail is the main tool for controlling complexity. By using a subprogram, it is possible to concentrate on what the program does rather than on how it does it.

(2) A procedure call is a statement in its own right, while a function call is part of an expression and returns a value.

(3) A FORTRAN program consists of a main program in addition to a series of independent subprograms.

(4) In a block-structured language such as Pascal, subprograms are declared in an environment created by the enclosing blocks.

(5) In Pascal, C and Modula-2, the parameter-passing mechanism of call by value is used to pass information into a subprogram.

(6) In call by value, the formal parameter acts as a local variable, while in call by constant-value (used in Ada) it acts as a local constant.

(7) Call by value can be expensive in terms of space and time when the parameter is a structured object.

(8) In the absence of aliases, call by reference and call by value-result have the same effect.

(9) The only effect of a function call on the rest of a program should be through its returned value.

(10) Ada and C++ allow the redefinition of operators such as +.

(11) Stack storage management is required to support recursive subprograms.

(12) If the amount of storage required by all local objects can be determined at compile time, it is possible to implement a language so that the relative position of each object within a data area is known at compile time. This was a major goal in the design of Pascal.

(13) Pascal was designed so that it can be translated by a one-pass compiler.

(14) Subprograms can be passed as parameters in Pascal and in Modula-2, but not in Ada. Ada uses generic subprograms to achieve a similar effect.

EXERCISES

5.1 Subprograms in FORTRAN may not be nested and can be compiled independently of one another. Pascal procedures and functions may be nested, but cannot be compiled independently. Discuss the advantages and disadvantages of these two approaches and any possible compromises between the two.

5.2 Compare the approach to type checking across subprogram boundaries adopted in FORTRAN, Pascal, C and Ada.

5.3 Compare the program structure of C with that of Pascal and FORTRAN. Which features do you consider are closer to FORTRAN and which are closer to Pascal?

5.4 Ada is unusual in having **out** parameters. Is the addition of this extra concept worthwhile or are **in out** parameters sufficient to cover this case?

5.5 Compare the parameter-passing mechanisms call by value, call by constant-value and reference-constant for both simple and structured parameters.

5.6 Assuming that j has the value 1, $a[1]$ the value 2 and $a[2]$ the value 3, what would be the effect of the call $swap(j, a[j])$ when the parameters are passed (a) by value-result, (b) by value-result (ALGOL W), (c) by reference and (d) by name? Would any of the parameter-passing mechanisms give a different answer if the call was $swap(a[j], j)$?

5.7 Ada is based on Pascal, but is much larger. Compare the parameter-passing facilities in the two languages with particular regard to the question of whether the introduction of default parameters and named association is worth the added complexity.

5.8 Good programming practice indicates that procedures should be free from side effects. Why is this even more important with functions? As it is generally agreed that changing non-local variables is undesirable, why is this feature permitted in almost all languages including those that have only recently been defined?

5.9   In Exercise 3.11 of Chapter 3, you were asked to list a suitable set of operations on objects of type *month*. Give implementations of these operations in Pascal and in Ada.

5.10   Describe the advantages of being able to overload procedure and function identifiers. Why is this facility particularly useful with operators?

5.11   Why is static storage allocation not able to support the implementation of recursive procedures?

5.12   Describe how stack storage management can be used in the implementation of procedure entry and exit in a block-structured language. What is the purpose of the static and dynamic chains?

5.13   How has the addition of function prototypes in ANSI C allowed more type checking to be done at compile time compared with traditional C?

5.14   Compare the facility of passing procedures and functions as parameters in Pascal and Modula-2 with the use of generic subprograms in Ada.

BIBLIOGRAPHY

The bibliography at the end of this book gives a list of textbooks on the main programming languages. They all give further information on the structure of subprograms and how parameters are passed in their particular language. A discussion of parameter passing in several languages has been given by Tai (1982). Details of the implementation of subprograms, parameter passing and data areas are given in books on compiling such as that by Aho (1986). A more general description is given by Pratt (1984).

Aho, A. V., Sethi, R. and Ullman, J. D. (1986), *Compilers: Principles, Techniques and Tools*, Addison-Wesley.

Pratt, T. W. (1984), *Programming Languages: Design and Implementation* (Second Edition), Prentice-Hall.

Tai, K.-C. (1982), 'Comments on Parameter Passing Techniques in Programming Languages', *ACM SIGPLAN Notices*, **17**(2), pp. 24–27.

Data structures

CONTENTS

6.1 **Introduction**   134
6.2 **Arrays**   135
6.3 **Records**   143
6.4 **Dynamic data structures**   148
6.5 **Strings**   152
6.6 **Sets**   156
6.7 **Files**   158

Chapter 3 looked at simple types. This chapter now looks at structured types, which have simpler types as components. The two basic data structures of modern languages are the array and the record.

All the components (elements) of an array have the same type and the elements are accessed using a computable index. The components (fields) of a record may have different types and are referred to by name. An important use of records is in the construction of dynamic structures, such as linked lists and trees, where one or more of the fields of the record are of a pointer type.

Strings in many imperative languages are implemented as arrays of characters, which restricts the available set of string operations. In SNOBOL4, on the other hand, the character string is a basic type in the language and a full set of string operations are available.

Pascal is unusual in having a *set* data type. Pascal also introduced a *file* data type which has been used as the basis for files in Modula-2 and Ada.

6.1   Introduction

A data object that is constructed from other data objects is called a **data structure** (or, more rarely, a structured data object). The objects from which it is composed are called components and they may be simple data objects or other structured objects.

The early languages, FORTRAN and ALGOL 60, had only one kind of data structure, called the **array**, whereas most modern languages have both arrays and records. Figures 6.1 and 6.2 show the major features of arrays and records, respectively. The richness of data structures in most languages is obtained by combining the two basic data structures in various ways. At the simplest level, such combinations are arrays of records, and records some of whose fields are arrays. Both these combinations are useful in computing applications, but probably the most

---

Example

type *list* = **array** [1 . . 20] **of** *real*;
var *a* : *list*;

Component type

Homogeneous–all elements are of the same type.

Access to components

This is accomplished by knowing the position of the components in the array; for example, the fourth element in the array given above is referred to as *a* [4]. The array index may be an expression.

Efficiency

Efficient access at run time although not as efficient as simple variables due to the computable index.

Use

If the position of the required components (elements) of a structure has to be computed at run time, then arrays are an appropriate data structure. They are usually used in conjunction with loops and are very important in the solution of scientific and engineering problems.

Figure 6.1
Array features.

Example
type *person* =
  record
    name : *string*;
    age : 0 . . 99;
    sex : (*male, female*)
  end;
var *john* : *person*;

Component type

Heterogeneous–mixed types

Access to components

Access is by name of the component field of the record; for example, *john.age*.

Efficiency

As the field selectors are fixed at compile time, the components of a record may be accessed as efficiently as simple variables.

Use

They are used to group together data items, which are components of a single item in the problem domain.

Figure 6.2
Record features.

interesting and useful extension of the basic data structures is that in which records are used in conjunction with pointers to form **dynamic data structures**.

The judicious selection of the appropriate data structures is as important as top-down design in the production of a well-structured program.

6.2   Arrays

Arrays have been widely used as data structures since the earliest programming languages. To specify an array, its attributes must be known, which are:

- The type of its elements: this is a single type since all elements are of the same type.

- The number of components: usually this is given as the number of dimensions with an upper and lower bound for each dimension.
- The type of the subscripts: in early languages this was always integer.

In imperative languages, the specification of the attributes of an array are given in the declaration. In Pascal, this declaration might be:

type *matrix* = **array** [1.. 10, 0.. 15] **of** *real*;
var *a* : *matrix*;

The name of this array variable is *a*, its elements are all of type *real*, it is two dimensional with bounds 1 and 10 for the first dimension and 0 and 15 for the second dimension, and the subscripts are of type *integer*. The elements of an array are accessed using a computable index – that is, by evaluating the subscripts that can, in general, be expressions. Hence if *i* and *j* are integer variables with values 3 and 5 respectively, $a[i-1, j+1]$ refers to the element at position row 2, column 6.

Array elements can normally be used in a language wherever a variable of that type is allowed. The only major exception to this rule is that most languages do not allow a subscripted variable as the control variable of a **for** statement.

Implementation

As the elements of an array are normally referred to frequently, they need to be accessed quickly and easily, as otherwise a considerable inefficiency will result. There are several ways in which this can be achieved, but the commonest is the **mapping function**. This is a formula that allows a direct calculation of the address of the element required. An array is normally stored with the array elements in contiguous storage locations. For the example of Figure 6.3, the array elements are stored in row order, and so the address of element $a[i,j]$ is:

Base address + component_size *
    (row_length * (*i* – first_lower_bound)
    + *j* – second_lower_bound)
= Base address + 1 * (16 * (*i* – 1) + *j* – 0)

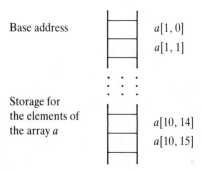

Figure 6.3
Possible storage for elements of the array *a*.

Base address $a[1, 0]$
                $a[1, 1]$

Storage for
the elements of
the array *a* $a[10, 14]$
                $a[10, 15]$

Arrays in C

In C, the declaration:

    int $a[10]$;

declares an array of integers whose subscripts are in the range 0 to 9. The elements of a can be accessed in the usual way, that is as $a[i]$, but an alternative using pointers, is also available.

    If the identifier b is declared as:

    int $*b$;

then the assignment:

    $b = \&a[0]$;

will assign the address of $a[0]$ to b. This assignment can also be written as:

    $b = a$;

since, in C, the identifier a is a constant integer pointer whose value is the address of $a[0]$. The array element $a[i]$ can now be referred to, using pointer arithmetic, as $*(a + i)$ or as $*(b + i)$ and it is possible to step through the elements of an array by incrementing the value of the integer pointer b.

    Hence, instead of:

    $sum = 0$;
    for$(i = 0; i < 10; i{+}{+})$
        $sum\ {+}{=}\ a[i]$;

it is possible to write:

    $sum = 0; b = a$;
    for$(i = 0; i < 10; i{+}{+})$
        $sum\ {+}{=}\ {*}b{+}{+}$;

and this gives very fast access to array elements.

    In C, parameters are always passed using call by value, but as an array identifier is a pointer, this is equivalent to arrays being passed by reference.

Name–size binding

More important than the details of the storage of an array is the time at which the required amount of storage is determined. The binding of the name of an array variable to its required amount of storage is referred to here as **name–size binding**, and there are three possibilities.

Static arrays (compile-time binding)

In this case, the size is fixed when the array variable is declared and it cannot change at run time. The major languages using this method are FORTRAN, Pascal, Modula-2 and C. It is simple to compile and is fast at run time. This method is used in Pascal as, for reasons of efficiency, a design decision was made that the size of all objects should be known at compile time. Chapter 5 showed how storage can be allocated to data areas on block entry and how it is important that the relative position of all items within the data area is known at compile time. With static arrays, this is indeed the situation.

There are disadvantages of this method, however: it is inflexible and arrays must be declared the maximum size they can ever attain, which can lead to considerable wastage in storage space.

Semi-dynamic arrays (binding on block entry)

In this case, the size of an array is not determined until block entry. As this method was introduced into language design in ALGOL 60, a typical piece of code from that language will be used to illustrate the idea.

```
begin integer m, n;
    read(m, n);
    begin real array x[1 : m, 1 : n];
        ...
    end;
    ...
end
```

With this method, the relative position of all of the items in a data area is no longer known at compile time as the size of x is not known until values for m and n are read at run time. A solution is only to hold a pointer to the array x in the data area and to allocate storage to the actual array elements on the heap. As the relative position in the data area of the pointer is known at compile time, it can be used to provide indirect access to the array elements.

Many other languages, such as SIMULA 67, ALGOL W, ALGOL 68 and Ada, have followed ALGOL 60 in allowing semi-dynamic arrays. The advantage of using this method is that arrays can be created to exactly the size required by the particular problem.

Dynamic arrays (binding during statement execution)

The amount of storage used by a dynamic array can be changed at any time during the array's lifetime. This is a very flexible arrangement for the programmer and ideally suited to interactive languages where it may be required to add new array elements at any time. It is not surprising, therefore, that an interactive language like APL should feature such arrays. Another language that makes use of dynamic arrays is SNOBOL4 and, as will be seen in Section 6.5, there is a close connection between dynamic arrays and strings of variable length. Dynamic arrays also occur in ALGOL 68 which has, in addition to semi-dynamic arrays, a construction called a **flex**. In ALGOL 68, a dynamic integer array d with initially no space can be declared by:

flex [1:0] **int** d;

The assignment:

   $d := (1,2,5,9);$

then makes the bounds from 1 to 4 and puts the four values into the elements $d[1]$, $d[2]$, $d[3]$ and $d[4]$.

     The flexibility of dynamic arrays has to be set against their slow run-time performance due to the need to allocate storage space on the heap.

Array parameters

Consider the problem of finding the sum of the elements of an array of 20 reals. In Pascal, this could be declared as:

   type *list* = **array**[1 .. 20] **of** *real*;

and a suitable function would be:

```
function sum(a : list) : real;
var i : integer;
    total : real;
begin
   total := 0.0;
   for i := 1 to 20 do
      total := total + a[i];
   sum := total
end {sum};
```

However, if the problem is extended to find the sum of the elements in an array of 40 reals, a completely new function must be written as the size of an array is part of its type. This was a major problem in early versions of Pascal although it did not occur in earlier languages such as FORTRAN, ALGOL 60 and C where the size of the array could be passed as a parameter.

     The ISO Pascal standard has solved this problem by introducing what are known as **conformant array parameters**. Function *sum* now becomes:

```
function sum(a : array[low .. high : integer] of real) : real;
var i : integer;
    total : real;
begin
   total := 0.0;
   for i := low to high do
      total := total + a[i];
   sum := total
end {sum};
```

If *b* is of type *list*, the function call *sum(b)* will cause *low* and *high* to be given the values 1 and 20, respectively. The function *sum* is, therefore, now able to accept one-dimensional arrays of reals of any size.

If the parameter *a* is a variable parameter then, when the function *sum* is called, only a pointer to the actual parameter is passed together with values for *low* and *high*. The size of all objects is therefore still known at compile time. When the parameter *a* is a value parameter, on the other hand, a copy of the actual parameter is passed. As there can be several calls of *sum*, each with an actual array parameter of a different size and, indeed, the actual parameter may itself be a conformant array parameter, the amount of space to be reserved within the data area of *sum* can no longer be fixed at compile time. Value conformant array parameters must therefore be implemented in a similar way to semi-dynamic arrays.

Ada has **constrained** and **unconstrained** array types. The declaration:

type *list* **is array**(*integer* **range** <>) **of** *real*;

declares an unconstrained array type *list*. An array variable *b* can then be declared as:

b : *list*(1 .. 20);

The size of a particular array can be found by using what are called its attributes. Hence, *b'first* is 1, *b'last* is 20 and *b'range* is the range 1 .. 20. These attributes can be used in the body of a function so that arrays of differing sizes can be dealt with. The Ada function for *sum* is:

```
function sum(a : list) return real is
   total : real := 0.0;
begin
   for i in a'range loop
      total := total + a(i);
   end loop;
   return total;
end sum;
```

Type equality

Chapter 5 explained that when a function or procedure is called, the types of the actual and formal parameters must match. This leads to the question of when two arrays are of the same type. Consider the following Pascal declarations:

```
type first = array[1 .. 10] of integer;
   second = array[1 .. 10] of integer;
var a : first;
   b : second;
   c : array[1 .. 10] of integer;
   d, e : array [1 .. 10] of integer;
   f : first;
```

As can be seen, there are six array variables all of which have 10 elements of type *integer*. Structurally, these six array variables are all the same, but are they all the same type? In the original definition of Pascal, this problem was not addressed and so the answer was left up to the compiler writers.

Two approaches can be taken to this problem. If **structural equivalence** is assumed, as in C, then all six variables are of the same type. An alternative approach, known as **name equivalence**, assumes that two variables only have the same type if they have the same type name. The ISO Pascal standard adopts name equivalence as the criterion and so *a, b, c* and *d* all have different types while *a* and *f* are of the same type as are *d* and *e*.

Name equivalence is also used in Ada, but as the Ada declaration:

   d, e : **array**(1 .. 10) of *integer*;

is equivalent to:

   d : **array**(1 .. 10) of *integer*;
   e : **array**(1 .. 10) of *integer*;

the variables *d* and *e* are of different types, which seems rather counter-intuitive.

The question of name and structural equivalence in Pascal was first discussed in a paper by Welsh (1977) and interested readers might like to consult this document.

Operations on complete arrays or slices of arrays

With the exception of some operations on strings and array assignment, Pascal does not allow operations on complete arrays although other languages, notably PL/I and APL, do. Thus, in PL/I, it is possible to write:

```
X = 0;
```

which will make all the elements of the array X zero.

Similar operations on complete arrays are available in APL although there are problems when assignment is to the array that is being altered. For example, consider:

```
X = X / X(I,J); in PL/I
X ← X ÷ X[I,J]  in APL
```

Both of these statements seem to be carrying out the same operations, that is, updating each element of an array X so that it becomes equal to the value obtained by dividing its previous value by the value of X(I,J). The question is what happens when X(I,J) itself is altered. Is the new value immediately used as the divisor or not? In PL/I, as soon as X(I,J) is changed, the new value is used as the divisor. In APL, on the other hand, the operation is carried out on a copy of X and so the same value of X[I,J] is used throughout the operation.

Ada allows the specification of array values, called **array aggregates**, which are especially useful in cases where it is necessary to initialize an array. Given the Ada declaration:

   type *vector* **is array** (1 .. 6) **of** *integer*;
   a : *vector*;

the following assignments are allowed, each having the same effect:

$a := (7, 0, 7, 0, 0, 0);$
$a := (1 => 7, 2 => 0, 3 => 7, 4 .. 6 => 0);$
$a := (1 | 3 => 7, \textbf{others} => 0);$

Many languages allow operations on **slices** of an array. The commonest situation is in a two-dimensional array where a row or a column is to be used as the slice. Again, the notation varies somewhat between languages: for example, the third row of a two-dimensional array would be denoted A(3,*) in PL/I and A[3;] in APL, while the fourth column would be A(*,4) in PL/I and A[;4] in APL. These slices may also be used as one-dimensional arrays in a quite natural way. It is particularly convenient to use such a slice as an actual parameter of a procedure whose equivalent formal parameter is a one-dimensional array.

In Pascal and Ada, a two-dimensional array is an array of arrays and so the concept of a row slice is a natural one. A row of a two-dimensional array can be passed as a one-dimensional array parameter to a procedure or function, but it is not possible to treat a column as a slice. In Ada, a slice can be part of a one-dimensional array. For example, given the declaration:

$a, b : vector;$

an assignment such as:

$a(1 .. 3) := b(4 .. 6);$

sets the first three elements of a to the values of the fourth, fifth and sixth elements of b, respectively.

In Pascal and Modula-2, functions may only return scalar values or pointers. In Ada and ANSI C, arrays or records may also be returned. As an example, consider the problem of adding two vectors together. In Ada, this can be accomplished by the function:

```
function add(left, right : vector) return vector is
   total : vector;
begin
   for i in left'range loop
      total(i) := left(i) + right(i);
   end loop;
   return total;
end add;
```

If a, b and c are all of type $vector$, a possible function call is:

$c := add(a, b);$

However, if the function is called "+" instead of add, the following statement could be written:

$c := a + b;$

which gives a much more natural way of dealing with vector arithmetic than is possible in most other languages.

Array notation

Languages have varied in their notation for array elements. In FORTRAN and Ada, the subscripts are contained in round brackets as in A(I), while other languages such as Pascal, Modula-2 and C have followed ALGOL 60's lead and have used square brackets as in $a[i]$. The argument in favour of square brackets is that arrays and their subscripts can clearly be distinguished from those parts of a program that use round brackets – that is, in expressions and function calls. The counter argument for round brackets is that they make arrays look like functions, and this is not unreasonable as they are both mapping functions: an array selects a particular element from a table whereas a function performs the same process using an algorithm.

6.3   Records

A **record** type is a structured type that is composed of heterogeneous elements of data – in fact, in languages such as PL/I and ALGOL 68 it was called a *structure* and in C it is called a *struct*. The declaration of a record type specifies the name and the type of the various fields of the record. Implicit in the declaration of a record is its tree structure. This is because the fields of a record can themselves be records and this introduces a hierarchical structure similar to that of a tree.

A typical example of how a record can be used in data processing is given in Figure 6.4(a) for a PL/I structure and in Figure 6.4(b) for the equivalent Pascal record. The equivalent tree structure is shown in Figure 6.4(c). There are 10 different elements in this record and the type of each needs to be declared. This must be done explicitly in languages like Pascal but in PL/I it can be done explicitly or by default. These 10 different elements are the terminal nodes (or leaves) of the equivalent tree structure in Figure 6.4(c).

The tree structure of the record is perhaps clearer in the declarations in languages like PL/I (which was based on COBOL records) where the level numbers are given and these can conveniently be made the same as the level numbers of the equivalent tree. Languages like Pascal, on the other hand, use records and sub-records, and this makes the tree structure less evident.

Complicated records are not commonly used in Pascal where the prime use of records is not in the solution of data processing problems, but to allow logically related data items to be grouped together as one structured variable. Being able to structure data in this way is central to the construction of understandable programs. Given the definition of type *student* in Figure 6.4(b), for example, it is possible to define procedures and functions which deal with items of type *student*. This enables users of these subprograms to be able to think in terms of type *student* rather than be concerned with the details of the components out of which type *student* has been composed.

(a)

```
DECLARE
    01 STUDENT,
        02 NUMBER FIXED,
        02 NAME,
            03 FIRST NAME CHARACTER(10),
            03 INITIAL CHARACTER(4),
            03 SURNAME CHARACTER(10),
        02 DEGREE,
            03 COURSE CHARACTER(4),
            03 YEAR DEC FIXED(1),
        02 DEPARTMENT,
            03 DEPT NAME CHARACTER(10),
            03 ADVISOR LIKE NAME;
```

Figure 6.4(a)
A PL/I structure.

(b)

```
type string = packed array [1 . . 10] of char;
     shortstring = packed array [1 . . 4] of char;
     namestring =
        record
            firstname : string;
            initial : shortstring;
            surname : string
        end;
     degreetype =
        record
            course : shortstring;
            year = 1 . . 4
        end;
     dept =
        record
            deptname : string;
            advisor : namestring
        end;
     student =
        record
            number : integer;
            name : namestring;
            degree : degreetype;
            department : dept
        end
```

Figure 6.4(b)
A Pascal record.

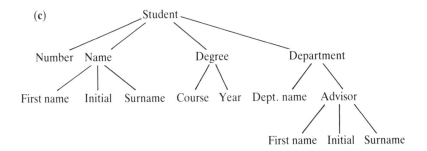

Figure 6.4(c)
The equivalent tree
structure.

The individual items in a record or structure are referred to by name and not by computable index as in an array. The name needs to be qualified. For example, in the PL/I structure given in Figure 6.4(a), the name:

```
STUDENT.DEPARTMENT.ADVISOR.SURNAME
```

could be used to refer to one particular element. This is a fully qualified name but it can be abbreviated, provided it is not ambiguous. The problem of very long names is common to records in most languages. Another method of reducing their length is to use, as in Pascal and Modula-2, the **with** statement. Assuming that *st* has been declared to be of type *student*, the Pascal code:

```
read(st.degree.year);
if st.degree.year = 4 then
    writeln('Final year student')
else
    st.degree.year := st.degree.year + 1;
```

can be written as:

```
with st.degree do
begin
    read(year);
    if year = 4 then
        writeln('Final year student')
    else
        year := year + 1
end;
```

Ada has **record aggregates** and so values can be assigned to complete records. Given an Ada record variable *person* with the same structure as the Pascal record *namestring* of Figure 6.4(b), this can be written:

```
person := (firstname => "Alan     ",
           initial => "P       ",
           surname => "Clark    ");
```

Arrays and records combined

As was shown in the example of a record in Figure 6.4, it is quite legitimate in most languages to have fields of an array type. In the example given, this was simply to provide strings, but it often has more sophisticated uses. Consider, for example, the problem of providing a simple stack structure in Pascal. This can be done as follows:

```
type stacklist =
   record
      a : array [1..20] of real;
      head : 0 .. 20
   end;
var stack : stacklist;
```

The two fields of the record *stacklist* represent the elements of the stack in the array *a* and the pointer to the top of the stack in the integer *head*. Thus, the representation of the stack is contained wholly within the record. More complex representations of tree and graph structures can be similarly contained within a single record.

Returning to the Pascal definition of *stacklist*, the stack must be initialized before items can be added to it. Thus, after the assignment:

```
stack.head := 0
```

the stack is initialized and is empty. In Ada, on the other hand, default initial values can be specified in type definitions and so a separate initialization stage is not required. The Ada definition of type *stacklist* would be:

```
type reallist is array (1 .. 20) of real;
type stacklist is
   record
      a : reallist;
      head : integer range 0 .. 20 := 0;
   end record;
```

The alternative way of combining data structures – that is, of having arrays of records – is also a useful feature. An example in Pascal is:

```
studentlist : array [1..3000] of student;
```

where *student* is defined by the record given in Figure 6.4(b). An individual field in any of the 3000 student records can be picked out. For example, *studentlist[i].number* selects the student number of the *i*th student in the array of student records.

Variant records

Static typing supports reliability at the expense of flexibility. Consider a problem in which there is a need for a list containing both postgraduate and undergraduate students. In a dynamically typed language, there is no difficulty; some of the components of the list will be of type *undergraduate* and others of type *postgraduate* and type checks are made at run time to ensure that the components are always used correctly. This is not possible in a statically typed language as all the components of a list must have the same type.

Languages, such as Pascal, Modula-2 and Ada, solve this problem by means of **variant records**. In Pascal, a variant record has a fixed part, with fields as in a normal record, followed by a variant part, in which there are alternative fields. For example:

```
type status = (undergraduate, postgraduate);
     student =
record
  {fixed part}
  name : string;
  studentno : integer;
  {variant part}
  case kind : status of
     undergraduate : (advisor : string);
     postgraduate : (course : string;
                     supervisor : string)
end;
```

The field *kind* is called the **tag field** and in this example there are two alternatives. The tag field determines whether there is a single field, *advisor*, in the variant part or two fields, *course* and *supervisor*.

Given the declaration:

```
studentlist : array[1 .. 3000] of student;
```

and assuming that the array has been suitably initialized, the following code will print out the name and advisor of the *i*th student when the student is an undergraduate and the name, course and supervisor when the student is a postgraduate.

```
with studentlist[i] do
begin
  write(name);
  if kind = undergraduate then
    writeln(advisor)
  else
    writeln(course, supervisor)
end;
```

Pascal's method of using variant records can unfortunately lead to insecurities and inconsistencies. These arise if the tag field is changed without changing the variant fields that depend on the tag.

Ada allows similar variant records, although with some syntactic differences, and the insecurities of the Pascal construction are removed by not allowing the tag field to be changed independently of the dependent fields in the variant part. Variant records are still, however, a rather untidy feature. Chapter 8 describes the C++ solution, where the definition of a record (a *struct* or a *class*) can extend the number of fields that it inherits from a base record.

6.4   Dynamic data structures

A very different kind of data structure is obtained by using records in conjunction with pointer variables. Fields in a record can be specified to be of pointer type and data structures in which individual records are linked to others can be built up by means of pointer fields. Thus, in Pascal, a simple linear linked list can be written as follows:

```
type ptr = ↑node;
     node =
         record
             data : char;
             next : ptr
         end;
var p, listhead : ptr;
    ch : char;
```

Note that the above type declaration is one of the few places in Pascal where an identifier (*node*) can be used before it has been declared.

Procedure *new* was introduced in Chapter 3. The effect of a call of *new(p)* is to create a record of type *node* which is pointed at by the pointer variable *p*. This is shown in Figure 6.5. The value 'A' can be assigned to the *data* field and **nil** to the *next* field by writing:

```
p↑.data := 'A'; p^.next := nil
```

A list can be read in and linked as follows:

```
listhead := nil;
read(ch);
while ch <> ' ' do
begin
    new(p); p↑.data := ch;
    p↑.next := listhead;
    listhead := p;
    read(ch)
end;
```

Figure 6.6 shows the state of the linked list after each cycle round the loop as the characters A, B and C followed by a space are read in.

Languages differ in the restrictions they put on pointers. Pascal is quite rigid in this respect and a pointer variable may only point to an object of one particular type. In the example just given, *listhead* is of type *ptr* and therefore can only be used to point to objects of type *node*.

Figure 6.5
Creating a record.

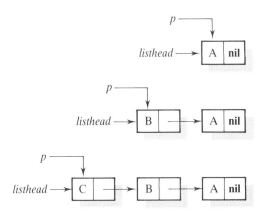

Figure 6.6
Stages in building a
linked list.

PL/I has a much looser system as regards pointers, allowing them to be used with different record types (called **areas** in PL/I). However, this makes it difficult to do any type checking of records at compile time.

Ada follows much the same pattern as Pascal although the syntax is different. As a name cannot be used before it has been declared in Ada, it is necessary to write:

> **type** *node*;
> **type** *ptr* **is access** *node*;
> **type** *node* **is**
>   **record**
>   *data* : *character*;
>   *next* : *ptr*;
>   **end record**;

Dynamic variables in Ada can be given initial values when they are created. Thus, instead of the Pascal:

> *new(p)*; $p\uparrow.data := ch$; $p\uparrow.next := listhead$

the following can be written:

> $p :=$ **new** *node'(data => ch, next => listhead)*;

C and C++

In C, a linked list can be defined as:

> **struct** *node* {
>   **char** *data*;
>   **struct** *node* * *next*;
> };

A declaration in C can, therefore, be **self-referential** which is not allowed in languages such as Pascal and Ada.

The type of the structure is *struct node* with the identifier *node* being known as a **tag name**. It is now possible to define a type *node* as:

typedef struct *node node*;

which can be rather confusing to the reader. In C++, the definition:

```
struct node {
    char data;
    node * next;
};
```

introduces a type *node* rather than a type *struct node*. The **typedef** is therefore no longer required. As the parameters and the returned value of a function in C and C++ can be referred to as being of type *node* *, it is not necessary to define a type such as *ptr* as was required in the Ada and Pascal definitions.

A pointer to type *node* can be declared as:

node * *p*;

and, in C, space for the node is allocated by the call:

p = (*node* *) *malloc*(*sizeof*(*node*));

which is equivalent to *new(p)* in Pascal. In C++, the operator **new** can be used instead of *malloc* as in:

p = **new** *node*;

The elements of a C or C++ struct are called **members**. The struct pointed to by *p* can be referred to as **p* and so, using the normal dot notation, the value 'A' can be assigned to the *data* member by:

(**p*).*data* = 'A';

As pointers to members of a struct are a common feature of C and C++, a more meaningful syntax is provided and the assignment can be written as:

p–>data = 'A';

Trees

Dynamic data structures can be considerably more complicated than simple linked lists. One structure that they model in a particularly appropriate way is the tree. In a tree structure there is more than one pointer field in each record. A type declaration in Pascal for a binary tree could be:

```
type ptr = ↑node;
     node =
         record
             data : char;
             left, right : ptr
         end;
```

The effect of *new(root)*, where *root* is of type *ptr*, is shown in Figure 6.7.

Figure 6.7
Creating a node.

Both lists and trees can be conveniently defined recursively. For example, a binary tree can be defined as follows:

> A binary tree is either null or it consists of a special node, called the root, which has a value and two descendants, called the left subtree and the right subtree. The left subtree and the right subtree are themselves binary trees.

As trees can be defined recursively, they are most easily manipulated using recursive procedures. To illustrate how this may be done, consider the problem of printing out a binary tree representing an algebraic expression in what is known as **reverse Polish notation** where an operator follows its two operands. This can be achieved by using the following recursive Pascal procedure:

```
procedure revPolish(p : ptr);
begin
  if p <> nil then
  begin
    revPolish(p↑.left);
    revPolish(p↑.right);
    write(p↑.data)
  end
end;
```

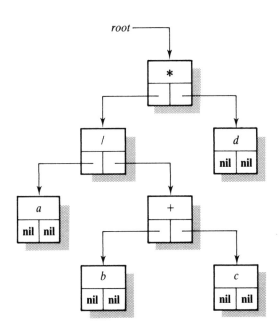

Figure 6.8
A binary tree.

Assuming that *root* points to the tree shown in Figure 6.8, the procedure call *revPolish(root)* will cause the contents of the tree to be printed out in the order:

*a b c + / d ***

Tracing through the execution of *revPolish(root)* is left as an exercise for the reader.

The use of records and pointers does entail a good deal of detailed programming on the part of the programmer. Some of this can be reduced by the judicious use of modules or packages with their associated data structures, procedures and functions. The detailed building of dynamic data structures from records and pointers is a feature of the more sophisticated imperative languages such as ALGOL 68, C, Pascal, PL/I, Ada, Modula-2. The alternative method of approaching such dynamic data structures is with functional languages and this issue is taken up again in Chapter 9.

6.5   Strings

Character strings and their manipulation only played a very minor role in the early scientific languages and it was SNOBOL4 that actually showed how character strings could be manipulated in a programming language. However, it was soon realized that the unrestricted manipulation of strings brings with it considerable penalties in the slowness of the run-time program.

String operations are best divided into two categories. The first category consists of string comparisons, the selection of a component (a character or group of characters) and the moving of strings. The second category of operations includes the construction of new strings, the concatenation of strings (joining two strings together), the replacement of substrings within a string and the decomposition of a string into substrings.

The operations in the first category cause few problems for the compiler writer as strings remain the same length throughout. Operations in the second category, on the other hand, have the potential of altering the length of the strings or giving strings whose length cannot be predicted at compile time, and thus require to be implemented on the heap.

In Pascal, Ada, Modula-2 and C, strings are simply arrays of characters and since arrays are not dynamic in these languages, the length of a string cannot be changed once it has been declared. In Pascal, a string is typically declared as:

type *name* = **packed array** [1..8] **of** *char*;

The reserved word **packed** used in this declaration indicates that the compiler should allocate the minimum amount of space possible for objects of type *name*, even though this may increase the time required to access individual array elements. The need to declare this requirement explicitly has not been carried over into Modula-2 and Ada.

In Pascal, the length of an array is part of the type and so any attempt to assign or compare strings of different lengths gives an error at compile time. This means that trailing blanks must always be inserted in string constants. Hence, if *person* is of type *name*, four trailing blanks are required in the assignment:

  person := 'Alan   '

A similar assignment is necessary in Ada although strings of different length may be compared. Hence, the expression:

  person < "James"

is legal in Ada while in Pascal three trailing blanks are needed, as in:

  person < 'James   '

Trailing blanks do not have to be inserted in Modula-2 string assignments and so:

  person := 'Alan'

is legal. A null character is automatically inserted after the four characters of 'Alan'. When the string constant fits exactly, as in:

  person := 'Margaret'

no null character is inserted. Although string assignment has been made easier to use, it is not possible in Modula-2 to use the relational operators to compare strings, as it is in Pascal and Ada.

  The language C also uses the null character as an explicit string terminator but, unlike Modula-2, space must be set aside for it in all strings. The null character is represented in a C program as the character '\0'. Assuming *str* has been defined as an array of characters, *ch* as a character and *i* as an integer, a line of characters could be read in by the C statements:

```
i = 0;
while ((ch = getchar ()) != '\n')
    str[i++] = ch;
```

This reads characters into the array *str* until the newline character is encountered, when it is necessary to add the statement:

  str[i] = '\0';

to append the null character to the end of the string. The null character can be used to recognize the end of the string and so C strings are in effect variable up to a maximum defined length.

  In C, there is a distinction between character constants and string constants. For example, 'x' is a character constant but "x" is a string of length two, the first character of which is x and the second is the null character. Similarly 'x' and "x" in Ada are character and string constants, respectively. As Pascal uses single quotes for both characters and strings, string constants of length one are not possible.

COBOL also has strings of fixed declared length and the Pascal string given at the beginning of this section would be declared in COBOL as:

```
NAME PIC X(8)
```

This gives a character string variable called NAME containing exactly eight characters. However, in contrast to Pascal, a string value can be adjusted during assignment either by truncating the excess characters or by padding out the string with additional blanks on the right, if it is not long enough.

Since these languages have fixed length strings, only the first category of string operations is allowed, although Ada does permit some second category operations provided that the length of the string is not changed. Examples are:

person := "James   ";
person(2 .. 5) := "immy";

Ada also has the catenation operator &. This can be useful in constructing a string with a constant and a variable part, as in:

put_line("Hello " & *person*);

At the other extreme are languages such as SNOBOL4 that have the character string as a basic type and it can vary arbitrarily in length. No bounds are placed on the string's length and so, if strings get longer, extra storage has to be allocated. ALGOL 68 was another language that allows strings to have a dynamic length. As was seen in Section 6.2, it does this by having the mode *string* predefined as a flexible array of characters, as in:

mode *string* = **flex** [1:0] *char*;

This is an array with dynamic bounds that will automatically expand or contract to accommodate the length of string required.

All the string operations in the first and second category are potentially available to languages such as SNOBOL4 and ALGOL 68 although, of course the methods vary. In ALGOL 68, for example, substrings are selected by subscripting whereas in SNOBOL4 this is done by pattern matching. The SNOBOL4 statement:

```
TEXT 'programme' = 'program'
```

will find the first occurrence of 'programme' in the string TEXT and replace it by 'program'. To replace all occurrences, the statement could be written:

```
LAB1 TEXT 'programme' = 'program' :S(LAB1)
```

The S here stands for success and so if a successful replacement is made in TEXT, a jump is made to the statement labelled LAB1. The statement:

```
TEXT 'programme' = 'program'
```

is therefore repeated until no more replacements can be made.

Between the two extremes of fixed declared length and variable strings is a compromise position adopted by PL/I – that is, to have a variable length up to a declared upper bound. PL/I does this by the following declaration:

```
DECLARE NAME CHARACTER VARYING(15);
```

The variable NAME will hold a character string up to a maximum length of 15 characters. However, unlike COBOL, if the string is less than 15 characters in length, PL/I holds exactly the correct number of characters and does not need to add trailing blanks. PL/I also allows fixed length strings and these are declared in a similar way, although the word VARYING is omitted.

Strings of the PL/I type can be represented in Pascal, Ada or Modula-2 as a record. An example in Pascal is:

```
type varstring =
    record
        string : packed array[1 .. 80] of char;
        currentlength : 0 .. 80
    end;
```

To manipulate such varying strings and to convert to and from ordinary strings, a series of procedures and functions is needed. Ada and Modula-2 have better facilities for doing this than Pascal, as will be seen in the next chapter, although some dialects of Pascal have such a string type built in.

Most languages, exceptions being Modula-2 and C, allow relational operations to apply to strings: thus, operators such as equal, not equal and greater than can be used with string variables. A collating sequence is used to decide the outcome of a comparison of two strings. For example, to evaluate $a > b$, where a and b are two character string variables, the collating sequence starts with the leftmost characters of a and b and compares them. If a decision can be made, the sequence stops and no more comparisons are made. If a decision cannot be made – for example, if the first character of a is the same as the first character of b – then the sequence proceeds to compare the second characters of a and b. This sequence continues in this manner until either a decision is reached or both strings are exhausted. Normally, if the strings being compared are not the same length, the shorter one is padded out with null characters on the right. In Pascal, when the strings are not the same length, a syntax error results.

String implementation

The implementation of strings depends on which of the three methods of string handling has been adopted. The easiest method to implement is the fixed length method, where each character is normally held in a byte, with four characters per 32–bit word. The PL/I method requires in addition two integer descriptors, one for the maximum length and the other for the current length. There is no need in this case for trailing characters to be made blank.

(a) In Pascal this reflects the declaration:

st : **packed array** [1 . . 10] **of** *char*;

(b) This reflects the PL/I declaration:

```
DECLARE ST CHARACTER VARYING(10);
```

Figure 6.9
String storage
implementation:
(a) fixed
declaration length;
(b) variable length
up to a maximum
bound;
(c) unbounded
length (SNOBOL4
method).

(c)

This assumes that a pointer uses one word

The least efficient implementation is that involving dynamic strings of unbounded length. One possible implementation is an integer descriptor for the current length together with a linked list of characters. Another possible implementation is a pointer to a contiguous series of characters on the heap. Operations such as concatenation then require a new extended string and disposal of the old version. The various storage implementations are shown diagrammatically in Figure 6.9 where each character occupies a byte and a word is four bytes or 32 bits.

6.6 Sets

A **set** is an unordered collection of distinct elements (objects) of the same type. This is in contrast to both lists and arrays which are ordered collections of possibly non-distinct elements.

Very few of the major languages have included the set as a standard data structure. The notable exceptions are Pascal and Modula-2, where sets are basically implemented as a packed array of *Boolean*. This is, in essence, the bit string method of implementing sets. If a set consists of days of the week, the following declarations can be written in Pascal:

type *day* = (*sun, mon, tues, wed, thur, fri, sat*);
     weekset = **set of** *day*;
var *w1, w2* : *weekset*;
     d : *day*;

At some stage, the set *w1* might be [*mon, thur, sat*]. This could be represented as the bit string 0100101. To illustrate the Pascal set operations, suppose that *w2* = [*mon .. fri*]. (Similar operations are available in Modula-2.)

- Membership: is the value *d* a member of set *w1*?

    if *d* **in** *w1* **then** ...

- Insertion: the expression *w1* + [*mon*] inserts *mon* into the set *w1* unless it is already present.

- Deletion: the expression *w1* − [*mon*] deletes *mon* from the set *w1* if it is a member of that set.

- Union: the expression *w1* + *w2* gives the set [*mon .. sat*]; that is, the set of those values that are in either *w1* or *w2*, or in both.

- Intersection: the expression *w1* * *w2* gives the set [*mon, thur*]; that is, the set of those values that are members of both *w1* and *w2*.

- Difference: the expression *w1* − *w2* gives the set [*sat*]; that is, the set of those values in *w1* that are not also in *w2*.

- Inclusion: the expression w1 <= w2 is true if *w1* is a subset of *w2*. As *sat* is a member of the set *w1*, but not of *w2*, the expression w1 <= w2 gives the value false. The set operations >=, <> and = are also available and have their obvious meanings.

    In addition to these operations, there is also straightforward assignment, as in:

w2 := [*mon, thur, sat*];

The empty set is represented by [].

The bit string method of implementing sets is satisfactory if the number of possible elements in the set is small, as in the Pascal example given at the beginning of this section when it was 7. This usually implies in Pascal implementations a restriction on the overall set size, which often is hardware dependent.

When this is not the case, more elaborate storage methods such as hashing have to be resorted to. This is particularly necessary when a set can contain a large number of different integers or character strings. Nevertheless, some of the set operations can be performed very efficiently using hashing methods. Membership, insertion and deletion can all be done quickly provided the amount of storage for the hashing table is sufficient. Problems arise when the number of elements in the set approaches the size of the scatter storage table used by the hashing method. The operations of union, intersection and difference are not carried out as efficiently by hashing as they are by bit string methods.

Pascal is unusual in having sets although several languages allow bit strings and operations on bit strings. In essence, such bit strings (with their operations) can be manipulated like sets. Systems programming languages are prime examples of languages that need to be able to manipulate bit patterns. In Modula-2, sets are primarily used for this purpose. Of the earlier languages, PL/I and ALGOL 68 had similar types with names like BIT and *bits*. The approach taken in Ada is to represent a bit pattern as a *Boolean* array. The Boolean operators **and, or** and **xor** can be applied to such arrays. For example, given the declarations:

```
type bytestring is array (1 .. 8) of Boolean;
a, b, c : bytestring;
t : constant Boolean := true;
f : constant Boolean := false;
```

the execution of the statements:

```
a := (f, f, f, t, t, t, t, t);
b := (t, f, t, f, t, f, t, f);
c := a and b;
```

will result in *c* being assigned the value (*f, f, f, f, t, f, t, f*), which can be used to represent the bitstring 00001010.

6.7 Files

Files are large collections of data that are kept on secondary storage devices. They are liable to have an extensive lifetime, which will normally be longer than the run of the computer program that created them. In data processing applications, the logical structure of a file is usually considered to be a collection of records. Hence, in languages such as COBOL and PL/I the primary purpose of records (structures) is to describe information held in files.

Files were not explicitly represented in early scientific languages. Pascal was, therefore, unusual in having a file type defined in the language, although this approach has been followed by most of its successors. A file in Pascal can be thought of as an ordered collection of homogeneous data. A typical Pascal file definition is:

```
type stream = file of entities;
```

where entities can be of any type except another file.

There are two main differences between a Pascal array and a Pascal file. Firstly, the size of an array is given as part of its declaration while a file is unbounded. Secondly, the access to arrays is random – that is, the time to access an element in an array is independent of its position – whereas with Pascal files the access is sequential, mirroring the way that sequential files are accessed on backing store.

In Pascal, file variables usually correspond to external disk files. In such cases, the variable must be listed as a parameter in the program heading as well as being declared as a variable, as in:

```
program ex(old, new);
type stream = file of ...;
var old, new : stream;
```

Local files may also be declared both within the main program and within a procedure. The normal rules governing the lifetime of an object apply to files and so a file declared within a procedure will come into existence when the procedure is entered and will cease to exist when the procedure is left. The main use of local files is in the temporary storage of information of unknown size. When the maximum size is known an array is more commonly used.

Operations on files are usually given by a set of predefined functions and procedures. Operations are required to open files for reading and writing, to determine the current position within a file, and to read and write information. As files are, therefore, primarily associated with the input and output of data, a detailed discussion of files is delayed until Chapter 13, which discusses input and output.

Summary

(1) The judicious selection of appropriate data structures is as important as top-down design in the production of a well-structured program.

(2) All components of an array have the same type and are accessed using a computable index.

(3) In Pascal and C, the size of an array is fixed at compile time. In Ada, fixing the size of an array can be delayed until block entry.

(4) In C, pointers can be used to access elements of an array.

(5) In Pascal and its derivatives, a two-dimensional array is an array of arrays.

(6) The components of a record can have different types and are accessed by name.

(7) Pascal is strongly typed except in the case of variant records. This problem is overcome in Ada.

(8) Dynamic data structures are built from records that have one or more fields of a pointer type.

(9) The representation and manipulation of strings is determined by whether the language design allows operations that potentially increase the string length.

(10) Sets and files are rarely included in languages as first-class objects.

EXERCISES

6.1   Arrays and records are both aggregates of data. How do they differ? What information would you expect in the declaration of (a) an array and (b) a record?

6.2   Describe how a mapping function can be used to find the storage location of an array element. What is meant by the base address in such a situation and how is it used by the compiler? Given the following Pascal array declarations, what would be suitable mapping functions?

> **var** x : **array**[2 .. 10] **of** *real*;
> a : **array**[1 .. 7, 0 .. 5] **of** *integer*;

In what locations, relative to the base address, would you expect to find $x[7]$ and $a[3, 2]$?

6.3 Why was a decision made in the design of Pascal that the size of all objects should be known at compile time?

6.4 Discuss the concept of dynamic bounds in an array explaining the meaning of the terms static array, semi-dynamic array and dynamic array. Give examples of languages that implement arrays in each of these ways. What are the advantages and disadvantages of each method to the programmer and to the implementor?

6.5 In Pascal, a two-dimensional array can be regarded as a one-dimensional array, each of whose elements is itself a one-dimensional array. What advantages does this give? How is the concept extended to three and higher dimensional arrays?

6.6 Give an example of a Pascal procedure with a one-dimensional array as a formal parameter together with a call of the procedure in which the corresponding actual parameter is a slice of a two-dimensional array. Definitions of appropriate one- and two-dimensional array types should also be given.

6.7 What additional information must be available at run time in the implementation of semi-dynamic arrays, as compared with static arrays?

6.8 How could the definition of Pascal variant records be improved so that type insecurity does not arise?

6.9 Show how a queue can be represented by a record with three fields, one of which is an array whose elements are the items in the queue and the other two are used to indicate the front and rear of the queue. Use this structure to define two operations, one to add a new element to the rear of the queue and the other to delete an element from the front of the queue.

6.10 Lists may be implemented as arrays or as linked lists. Which is to be preferred when solving:

(a) a problem that requires the elements of the list to be accessed in a random order,

(b) a problem that requires the elements of the list to be accessed sequentially,

(c) a problem that requires the ordering of a list of ordered elements to be retained during the insertion and deletion of elements.

6.11 Modify procedure *revPolish*, given in Section 6.4, so that it will print the algebraic expression in forward Polish notation, where the operator precedes its two operands.

6.12 Why are recursive algorithms particularly appropriate for the manipulation of structures such as lists and trees?

6.13 Given the Ada declaration:

a : **array**(1 .. 7) **of** *character*;

the effect of the assignment:

$a(4 .. 6) := a(3 .. 5)$;

is to make a copy of the value of $a(3 .. 5)$ before the assignment takes place. If a initially has the value "CORECAT", what will its value be after the assignment?

6.14 (a) Discuss the facilities that programming languages have provided for string handling. Contrast a language like Pascal, which has relatively primitive string operations, with a language like SNOBOL4.

(b) Why are string handling operations divided into two categories and what are the operations in each category? How did PL/I try to reach a compromise between primitive and sophisticated string handling?

6.15 Describe how a linked list could be used in the implementation of a set. Outline procedure declarations for the insert and delete operations.

BIBLIOGRAPHY

There are a large number of textbooks on the representation and manipulation of data structures, several of which are given below. The first volume of Knuth's *The Art of Computer Programming* (1968) was the earliest book to make a systematic approach to data structures. It is a pity that only three volumes of this monumental series were published.

Another influential book was *Algorithms + Data Structures = Programs* by Wirth (1976) which emphasized that data structures are at least as important as algorithms in the construction of programs.

Many recent books take all their examples from one particular language, usually Pascal. The other recent trend is to emphasize the importance of data abstraction as is done, for example, in the book by Lings (1986).

Aho, A. V., Hopcroft, J. E. and Ullman, J. D. (1983), *Data Structures and Algorithms*, Addison-Wesley.

Hoare, C. A. R. (1972), 'Notes on Data Structuring' in *Structured Programming*, Academic Press, pp. 83–174.

Knuth, D. E. (1968), *The Art of Computer Programming, Volume 1 : Fundamental Algorithms*, Addison-Wesley.

Lings, B. J. (1986), *Information Structures : A Uniform Approach Using Pascal*, Chapman and Hall.

Page, E. S. and Wilson, L. B. (1983), *Information Representation and Manipulation Using Pascal*, Cambridge University Press.

Welsh, J., Sneeringer, M. J. and Hoare, C. A. R. (1977), 'Ambiguities and Insecurities in Pascal', *Software Practice and Experience*, **7**, pp. 685–696.

Wirth, N. (1976), *Algorithms + Data Structures = Programs*, Prentice-Hall.

Modules

CONTENTS

7.1 **Large programs** 164
7.2 **Information hiding** 168
7.3 **Abstract data types** 172
7.4 **Separate compilation** 179
7.5 **Generics** 182
7.6 **Object-oriented development** 183

As was discussed in Chapter 5, complex problems are best solved by decomposition into smaller subproblems. Similarly, the design, implementation and maintenance of large programs is usually handled by dividing such programs into self-contained units called modules, where each module is itself divided into two parts: a small strictly defined interface through which it can interact with other modules and a hidden implementation part.

Modules enable type and subprogram declarations to be grouped together. This chapter looks at the way in which modules are implemented in Modula-2 and Ada, which support both full type checking across module boundaries and separate compilation. As long as the interface part of a module is unaffected, recompiling the implementation part of a module does not require the recompilation of any other modules.

The chapter then looks at how Ada packages are used in the definition of abstract data types. The type name and the operations on the type are made visible while the representation of the type and the implementation of the operations remain hidden. The approach used in C++, where the module (class) is a type, is then described.

The chapter finally looks at generic packages that allow the definition of parameterized abstract data types and at how abstract data types can be used in the object-oriented development of large systems.

7.1 Large programs

As a result of their size and complexity, large problems must be solved by a team of programmers rather than by a single individual. Each member of the team is set a well-defined task by a team leader, who alone may know the overall design of the system. For this approach to be possible, there must be some mechanism for dividing the problem into separate parts which only interact with one another through small strictly defined interfaces.

Large systems, by their nature, are usually in use for many years and during this time they may undergo substantial modification. Some of the changes will be due to the discovery of errors, but others will be due to changes in the system requirements, which could not be foreseen when the original system was designed. As it is not practicable to redesign large systems from scratch, due to their high cost and the time involved, the systems should be designed and written so that they can be easily modified. The best way of achieving this is for the programs to be written in such a way that the effect of any change is localized. This again points to a solution where the program is designed and implemented in separate parts (modules), each with a clearly defined external interface.

As solutions to different large problems often require solutions to similar subproblems, modules should be capable of being reused. In this way, a library of software components can be made available 'off the shelf' for use in the construction of new programs. Modules allow a large system to be designed by specifying what each module is to do and what its interface with the rest of the system is to be. Once this has been done, different users may implement each of the modules without any need for consultation.

Chapter 5 discussed how problems can be solved using stepwise refinement and how subprograms can be used to hide detail, so the user need only be concerned with 'what' a subprogram does and not with 'how' it does it. Subprograms can be considered to be modules that can be joined together to form complete programs. Their parameters act as small well-defined interfaces. However, as will be seen in Section 7.2, this type of module has a limitation on its ability to hide information. Newer programming languages such as Modula-2, Ada, Euclid and C++ use a more powerful form of module.

Instead of a single subprogram, such a module consists of a collection of related subprograms, types and objects. It is possible to decide what information is to be visible from outside the collection and what information is to be kept hidden. This can be achieved in several ways. One method is to have an **export list**; for example, in a Euclid module, information is hidden unless explicitly listed for export.

Another method is to divide a module into two parts. The part that tells the user 'what' the module does then acts as the interface with the user while the part containing the details of 'how' the operations are carried out is hidden from the user. An Ada module is called a **package**. The interface with the outside world is called the **package specification** and the implementation details are held in a separate **package body**. In Modula-2, these two parts are known as the **definition module**

and the **implementation module**, respectively. Package specifications and definition modules should always be as small as possible, since they form the interfaces
between what are otherwise self-contained units. A large interface is often a sign that
the decomposition of the problem could be improved.

As an example of a module, consider the following Ada package:

```
package days_in_week is
    type day is (sun, mon, tues, wed, thurs, fri, sat);
    function next_day(today : day) return day;
    function day_before(today : day) return day;
end days_in_week;

package body days_in_week is

    function next_day(today : day) return day is
    begin
        if today = sat then
            return sun;
        else
            return day'succ(today);
        end if;
    end next_day;

    function day_before(today : day) return day is
    begin
        if today = sun then
            return sat;
        else
            return day'pred(today);
        end if;
    end day_before;

end days_in_week;
```

As identifiers declared in a package specification are visible from outside the package, users of the module can declare variables of type *day* and call the functions
next_day and *day_before*. The only information about *next_day* and *day_before*
that is given in the package specification is that needed by the user to call the subprograms properly; namely, the number and type of the parameters and the type of
the returned function values. Details of the implementation of the subprograms (the
subprogram bodies) are hidden in the package body, since there is no need for a
user to have access to this information.

A package specification is an example of an Ada **program unit** while its
accompanying body is called a **secondary unit**. An Ada program consists of a
series of program and secondary units. One of the program units, the main program,
must be a procedure. Variables declared in a program or secondary unit are allocated space at load time, which allows the separation of the scope and extent of a
variable in a way not possible in languages such as Pascal.

```
package days_in_week is
  -- visible information that may
  -- be accessed by other units
end days_in_week;
```

```
package body days_in_week is
  -- hidden implementation details
end days_in_week;
```

```
with days_in_week;
procedure main is
  -- information exported by
  -- days_in_week is accessible
end main;
```

Figure 7.1
Structure of a
simple Ada
program.

To make the items in the visible part of a package available to another program or secondary unit, the unit is prefixed with what is called a **context clause**, as in:

with *days_in_week*; **use** *days_in_week*;
procedure *main* **is**
   ...
   holiday, working_day : day;
   ...
begin
   ...
   holiday := sat;
   working_day := day_before(holiday);
   ...
end *main*;

The context clause:

with *days_in_week*; **use** *days_in_week*;

enables the user to refer to type *day* and to the functions *next_day* and *day_before* within procedure *main*. A context clause consists of a **with** clause and an optional **use** clause. If the optional **use** clause is omitted, as in:

with *days_in_week*;

it would still be possible to use the visible information from package *days_in_week*, but the items would have to be referred to by their full names: *days_in_week.day*, *days_in_week.next_day* and *days_in_week.day_before*. The structure of this simple Ada program is shown in Figure 7.1.

Modula-2

The Modula-2 definition and implementation modules corresponding to the Ada package are as follows:

```
DEFINITION MODULE DaysInWeek;
    EXPORT QUALIFIED Day, NextDay, DayBefore;

    TYPE Day = (Sun, Mon, Tues, Wed, Thurs, Fri, Sat);
    PROCEDURE NextDay(Today : Day) : Day;
    PROCEDURE DayBefore(Today : Day) : Day;
END DaysInWeek.

IMPLEMENTATION MODULE DaysInWeek;

    PROCEDURE NextDay(Today : Day) : Day;
    BEGIN ... END NextDay;

    PROCEDURE DayBefore(Today : Day) : Day;
    BEGIN ... END DayBefore;

END DaysInWeek.
```

As with Ada, all identifiers in a definition module are automatically available in the corresponding implementation module, but unlike Ada, where identifiers in a package specification are visible by default outside the package, identifiers in a definition module must be explicitly exported by means of an export list. Also, like Ada, the contents of the implementation module are hidden and cannot be accessed by users of the module. Information on how to call a subprogram is given in the definition part while the implementation of the subprogram is hidden in the implementation part.

In the definition module just given, the reserved word QUALIFIED indicates that Day, NextDay and DayBefore must be referred to as DaysInWeek.Day, and so on, outside module DaysInWeek although, as will be seen later, this requirement can be superseded in an importing module by the use of a FROM clause. As qualified export is virtually always used, it really should be the default.

A possible Modula-2 main program is:

```
MODULE main;
    FROM DaysInWeek IMPORT
        Day, NextDay, DayBefore;
    ...
    VAR Holiday, WorkingDay : Day;
BEGIN
    ...
    Holiday := Sat;
    WorkingDay := DayBefore(Holiday);
    ...
END main.
```

The identifiers declared in the definition module DaysInWeek that are to be used in main are given in the import list. As it is normal for all identifiers in a definition module to be exported, the export list is usually redundant, and it is not clear whether it adds much to the understanding or clarity of programs. In contrast, the import list serves an important function: only the identifiers actually used in main are imported and the import list clearly states what they are and where they come from.

Such a useful checklist is not given by an Ada context clause as all identifiers in the specification are automatically imported. As a procedure or package can import variables and types from several different packages, it can be far from clear where a particular identifier has been declared. It is therefore advisable to give the full name of infrequently used identifiers rather than the abbreviated form, made possible by a **use** clause.

7.2 Information hiding

In large programs, it is often desirable for information to be visible to several sub-programs and yet be hidden from the rest of the program. As an example, suppose that part of the solution to a problem required a table of 100 elements, a procedure to initialize the table, a procedure *insert* to add new items to the table and a function *lookup* to search the table for an item, either returning its position if it is in the table or zero if it is not.

In Pascal, this might be written:

```
program ...
type item = ...
     table = array[1 .. 100] of item;
...
var data : table;
...
procedure initialize(var info : table);
begin ... end {initialize};

procedure insert(x : item; var info : table);
begin ... end {insert};

function lookup(x : item; info : table) : integer;
begin ... end {lookup};


...


begin ... end.
```

To ensure the integrity of the table, all access should be through *initialize*, *insert* or *lookup*. Unfortunately, for the table to be accessed by all three subprograms, it must be declared in the main program, which means that it could be accessed or even changed by commands elsewhere in the program.

Many implementations of Pascal have introduced a module facility to deal with this problem in a similar way to that described below for Ada and Modula-2, but as modules are not part of ISO Pascal, these additions are not discussed here. A possible Ada package specification to deal with this problem is:

```
package retrieve is
    type item is ...
    type table is private;
    procedure initialize(info : in out table);
    procedure insert(x : item; info : in out table);
    function lookup(x : item; info : table) return integer;
private
    type table is array(1 .. 100) of item;
end retrieve;
```

while the associated outline package body is:

```
package body retrieve is
    procedure initialize(info : in out table) is
    begin ... end initialize;

    procedure insert(x : item; info : in out table) is
    begin ... end insert;

    function lookup(x : item; info : table) return integer is
    begin ... end lookup;

end retrieve;
```

The identifiers *item, table, initialize, insert* and *lookup* declared in the package specification of *retrieve* are visible outside the package. Type *table* has however been declared to be what is called a **private type** and information about its structure is given in what is called the **private part** of the package specification. This means that no information about the structure of *table* is available to users of the package. The only built-in operations available with a private type are equality and assignment.

Consider now how *retrieve* can be used in the program:

```
with retrieve; use retrieve;
procedure main is

    ...
    data : table;

    ...
begin
    ...
end main;
```

As the type identifier *table* is visible, variables of type *table* can be declared in procedure *main*, but as the structure of *table* is private, and therefore hidden, nothing is known in *main* about the structure of *data*. Hence, it can only be accessed through the subprograms *initialize*, *insert* and *lookup*.

A reasonable question to ask at this point is why Ada package specifications have a private part. Why, for example, can *table* not be declared private in the specification and its structure given in the package body? The reason is that an Ada package specification and the units that depend on it may be compiled without the compiler having any knowledge of the package body, but to achieve this the compiler must know from the specification alone how much space is required for each visible object and type.

The disadvantage of this set-up is that to change the implementation of *table*, both the package specification and the body must be modified. This problem can be overcome by the following alternative specification for *retrieve* in which *table* is an access (pointer) type rather than an array:

```
package retrieve is
    type item is ...
    type table is private;
    procedure initialize(info : in out table);
    procedure insert(x : item; info : in out table);
    function lookup(x :item; info : table) return integer;
private
    type actual_table;
    type table is access actual_table;
end retrieve;
```

As the size of all access values (pointers) is the same, the compiler knows how much space to reserve for variables of type *table*. The structure of *actual_table* can be hidden in the package body as knowledge about its size is not required either in the specification of *retrieve* or by any program unit which depends on *retrieve*.

A definition module in Modula-2 may be compiled separately from its implementation module but, as there is no equivalent of a private part in a definition module, the only way a type such as *table* can be exported, while keeping its structure hidden, is to give the type name in the definition module and put the full declaration in the implementation module. For the reason just given, this is only possible with pointer types. This leads to the following outline Modula-2 program:

```
DEFINITION MODULE Retrieve;
    EXPORT QUALIFIED Item, Table, Initialize, Insert, Lookup;

    TYPE Item = ...
        Table;
    PROCEDURE Initialize(VAR info : Table);
    PROCEDURE Insert(x : Item; VAR info : Table);
    PROCEDURE Lookup(x : Item; info : Table) : INTEGER;
END Retrieve.

IMPLEMENTATION MODULE Retrieve;
```

```
TYPE ActualTable = ARRAY[1 .. 100] OF Item;
     Table = POINTER TO ActualTable;

PROCEDURE Initialize(VAR info : Table);
BEGIN ... END Initialize;

PROCEDURE Insert(x : Item; VAR info : Table);
BEGIN ... END Insert;

PROCEDURE Lookup(x : Item; info : Table) : INTEGER;
BEGIN ... END Lookup;

END Retrieve.

MODULE main;
    FROM Retrieve IMPORT
        Item, Table, Initialize, Insert, Lookup;

    ...
    VAR Data : Table;
    ...
BEGIN
    ...
END main.
```

The module structure developed so far allows more than one table to be declared. However, if only one table is required, there is no need for type *table* to be visible. Both *data* and *table* could be hidden in the package body or implementation module, respectively. A possible Ada package is, therefore:

```
package retrieve_2 is
    type item is ...
    procedure insert(x : item);
    function lookup(x : item) return integer;
end retrieve_2;

package body retrieve_2 is
    type table is array(1 .. 100) of item;
    data : table;

    procedure insert(x : item) is
    begin ... end insert;

    function lookup(x : item) return integer is
    begin ... end lookup;

begin
    --possible code to initialize the data table
end retrieve_2;
```

Normally, the use of non-local variables is discouraged so that a subprogram can be regarded as a black box and does not produce unexpected side effects. In this example, *lookup* accesses *data* as a non-local variable while *insert* changes its value. A parameter of type *table* cannot be passed to these subprograms because the type *table* would not then be hidden from users of the package. The hiding of information has thus taken precedence over the usual advice on the use of non-local variables. But this does not, in fact, conflict with the general view of side effects since the variable *data* is hidden within the package, and so changes to it are not visible from outside. The subprograms *insert* and *lookup* therefore remain black boxes to users of the package.

Moving the declaration of *data* from the main program to the body of package *retrieve_2* has had the effect of providing a straightforward solution to the earlier problem with static variables: the scope of *data* is now restricted to the package body while its extent is unchanged and, if *retrieve_2* is a program unit, *data* remains in existence throughout the execution of the program. A module with the same effect as *retrieve_2* can also be written in Modula-2 and this is left as an exercise for the reader.

A package body in Ada or an implementation module in Modula-2 may contain an optional sequence of statements that is executed as soon as space has been allocated to the variables in the module. This can be used to initialize the table.

7.3 Abstract data types

Most programming languages have a set of built-in or primitive types such as *integer, real, character* and *Boolean*, each of which is characterized by an allowed range of values together with a set of operations.

Calculations with integers, for example, take place in terms of arithmetic operators (+, −, *, etc.), relational operators (<, =, >, etc.) and the assignment operator. When solving a problem involving integers, it does not usually help to consider how integers are represented on a computer (for example, in two's complement notation) or how operations such as addition are implemented. In fact, for most purposes, it would be a positive hindrance, as it would introduce unwanted detail.

Problems whose solutions are easily expressed in terms of the built-in types can be tackled in a straightforward manner. Hence, most conventional imperative languages are good at carrying out scientific calculations involving integer and real arithmetic while they are less good at, for example, list processing. LISP, on the other hand, is excellent at list processing because lists and operations on lists are part of the language. This suggests that the power of a language can be enhanced by extending the number of primitive types. Unfortunately, the number of types required for all possible problems is open-ended, and so a better approach is to have a mechanism through which new types can be created.

Such a mechanism must provide the facilities to:

- declare a new type, give it a name and specify which operations are available to manipulate objects of the type, and

- hide the details of how the objects and the operations on the objects are to be implemented.

By clearly distinguishing between how an object may be used and how it is implemented, users can consider the object from an abstract point of view.

To illustrate this concept, consider a stack of items. It does not really matter what the items are, but for the moment assume that they are characters. The aim is to be able to declare stack variables and to define operations for pushing items on, and popping items off, a stack and for examining the top item. Once this has been done, the stack can be regarded as an abstraction and so it is possible to declare stack objects and perform stack operations without considering implementation details.

Conventional languages such as Pascal allow the definition of new types and the declaration of procedures and functions to perform operations on objects of these types. However, such languages do not have a mechanism, like the Ada package or Modula-2 module, that allows types and operations to be declared together as a unit and that enables the representation of a type and the implementation of the operations to be hidden while allowing the type name and the specifications of the operations to remain visible. It is only when the implementation of a type is hidden that it is possible to guarantee that it will only be manipulated through the defined operations, and that users will not take 'efficient' short cuts by manipulating internal details.

In the definition of a stack type in Ada, the type name and the specification of the associated operations are given in a package specification with how the stack is to be represented being hidden in the private part. The following package specification declares a new type called *char_stack* together with the three operations *push, pop* and *top*. How objects of type *char_stack* are to be represented is private information not available to users of the type.

```
package stacks is
    type char_stack is private;
    procedure push(x : character; st : in out char_stack);
    procedure pop(x : out character; st : in out char_stack);
    function top(st : char_stack) return character;
private
    type values is array(1 .. 100) of character;
    type char_stack is
        record
            val : values;
            top_of_stack_ptr : natural := 0;
        end record;
end stacks;
```

The implementations of *push, pop* and *top* are given in the package body. An abstraction of a stack has thus been created. Such user-defined types are usually referred to as **abstract data types** or **encapsulated data types**.

As the name of the type is visible to users of the package, objects of type *char_stack* may be declared. However, as the type is private, the only way such objects may be examined or changed is through the defined operations, as in:

```
with stacks; use stacks;
procedure main is
    a, b : char_stack;
    ch : character;
begin
    ...
    push('f', a); push('g', b);
    pop(ch, a);
    ...
end main;
```

As the value of *top_of_stack_ptr* is set to zero by default, both *a* and *b* initially represent empty stacks.

As *char_stack* is a private type, the only built-in operations available on objects of type *char_stack* are equality and assignment. However, the predefined equality operator cannot be used to compare two stacks for equality as it would compare elements beyond the current top of stack pointer, as well as the elements that are currently on the stack. To deal with such situations, Ada has **limited private types**. When a variable such as *char_stack* is declared to be limited private, neither predefined equality nor assignment is available. If required, a new function =, which only compares the relevant elements in the array of characters, can be defined, but the assignment operator := cannot be redefined, and so if assignment is still required a special *assign* procedure must be declared.

In this example, the stack has been represented as an array. An alternative representation would be a linked list. This can be achieved by changing the hidden representation of the stack and the implementation of the operations. Users of the package will see the stack abstract data type in exactly the same way as before and do not need to be aware that the representation has been changed.

A stack abstract data type can be defined in a similar way in Modula-2 although, as described in Section 7.2, this requires the use of a pointer type in the definition module as there is no equivalent of the Ada private part.

Classes

The Ada package and Modula-2 module provide a packaging mechanism that enables types and their associated operations to be defined together and allows the implementation of the operations and the representation of the types to be hidden. In C++, the equivalent of the package or module is called a **class**. Here the emphasis has changed as the definition of a new type is the central concept and a class is a type. This is a central feature of the object-oriented programming languages discussed in the next chapter.

A class definition in C++ consists of **data members** which define the internal representation details, and **member functions** through which the internal details may be accessed. Consider, for example, the definition of a stack of characters in C++:

```
class char_stack {
    char val[100];
    int top_of_stack_ptr;
public:
    char_stack() {top_of_stack_ptr = −1;}
    void push(char);
    void pop(char *);
    char top();
};
```

A new class, called *char_stack*, with operations *push, pop* and *top* has been defined. As information in a class is private by default, the representation of the stack, given by the data members:

```
char val[100];
int top_of_stack_ptr;
```

is hidden from users and may only be accessed through calls of member functions such as *push, pop* and *top*. Classes may include a member function whose name is the same as the class name. This is called a **constructor** and is used to initialize variables of a class when they are created. After the declaration:

```
char_stack a;
```

for example, the variable *a* will have its data member *top_of_stack_ptr* initialized to −1.

It is possible for member function bodies to be declared within a class definition, but it is more usual only to give the function prototypes and declare the function bodies separately, as follows:

```
void char_stack :: push(char x)
{ val[++top_of_stack_ptr] = x;}

void char_stack :: pop(char * x)
{ *x = val[top_of_stack_ptr−−];}

char char_stack :: top()
{ return val[top_of_stack_ptr];}
```

The **scope resolution operator** :: is used to associate the member function names with the appropriate class. For simplicity, the definitions have not dealt with adding items to a full stack or removing items from an empty stack.

Users of the information declared in a class are known as **clients**. Variables of class *char_stack* may be declared and manipulated by a client as follows:

```
main()
{
  char_stack a, b;
  char ch;
  ...
  a.push('f'); b.push('g');
  ch = a.top();
  ...
}
```

The declaration:

```
char_stack a, b;
```

causes two objects (that is, variables) of class *char_stack* to be created. They are both empty stacks as the value of each of their *top_of_stack_ptr* members is initialized by the constructor to –1.

The notation used in calls of member functions such as:

```
a.push('f'); b.push('g');
```

is the same as that used to access fields of a record in a language like Pascal. In fact a C++ class can be considered to be a record whose fields (members) may be function definitions. The C *struct* has been extended, in C++, so that its members can be function definitions. The only difference between a C++ *struct* and a class is that, in a *struct*, members are public by default while, in a class, they are private.

It is possible to modify the definition of class *char_stack* so that stacks of different sizes may be declared. The class definition now becomes:

```
class char_stack {
  char *val;
  int top_of_stack_ptr;
public:
  char_stack(int size) {val = new char[size];
                        top_of_stack_ptr = -1;}
  ~char_stack() {delete val;}
  void push(char);
  void pop(char *);
  char top();
};
```

The implementations of functions *push, pop* and *top* do not have to be changed. The member function:

```
~char_stack() {delete val;}
```

in the class definition is known as a **destructor**. It ensures that whenever the function in which a *char_stack* has been declared is left, the allocated storage will be reclaimed.

Two stacks, one with 50 elements and the other with 100 elements, can now be declared as:

   char_stack a(50), *b*(100);

and used in exactly the same way as before.

Complex numbers

As a second example of an abstract data type, consider the complex numbers. Complex arithmetic is available in FORTRAN, PL/I and ALGOL 68, but not in most other languages. A complex number has a real and an imaginary part. In the number:

```
2.7 + 5.6i
```

2.7 is the real part, i is the square root of minus one and 5.6 is the imaginary part. The following statements are legal FORTRAN:

```
      COMPLEX X, Y
      X = (2.7, 5.6)
      Y = X + (0.1, 2.1)
C     Y HAS THE VALUE 2.8 + 7.7I
      X = X * Y
```

Type *complex* can be introduced into Ada through the following package:

package *complex_type* **is**
   type *complex* **is private**;
   function "+"(*a, b : complex*) **return** *complex*;
   function "–"(*a, b : complex*) **return** *complex*;
   function "*"(*a, b : complex*) **return** *complex*;
   function *make_complex*(*rea, ima : float*) **return** *complex*;
   function *real_part*(*a : complex*) **return** *float*;
   function *imagin_part*(*a : complex*) **return** *float*;
private
   type *complex* **is**
     record
       re, im : float;
     end record;
end *complex_type*;

package body *complex_type* **is**

   function "+"(*a, b : complex*) **return** *complex* **is**
   begin
     return (*a.re* + *b.re, a.im* + *b.im*);
   end "+";

   function "–"(*a, b : complex*) **return** *complex* **is**

```
begin
    return (a.re – b.re, a.im – b.im);
end "–";

function "*"(a, b : complex) return complex is
begin
    return (a.re * b.re – a.im * b.im,
                a.re * b.im + a.im * b.re);
end "*";

function make_complex(rea, ima : float) return complex is
begin
    return (rea, ima);
end make_complex;

function real_part(a : complex) return float is
begin
    return a.re;
 end real_part;

function imagin_part(a : complex) return float is
begin
    return a.im;
end imagin_part;

end complex_type;
```

The functions *make_complex, real_part* and *imagin_part* are necessary as users of
package *complex_type* have no knowledge of how type *complex* has been implemented. They can be regarded as type conversion functions. As the operators + , –
and * have been redefined and overloaded, complex arithmetic can now be used as
naturally in Ada as in FORTRAN, where it is part of the language. Thus:

```
with complex_type; use complex_type;
procedure main is
    ...
    x, y : complex;
    ...
begin
    ...
    x := make_complex(2.7, 5.6);
    y := x + make_complex(0.1, 2.1);
    --y has the value 2.8 + 7.7i
    x := x * y;
    ...
end main;
```

Abstract data types such as *complex* cannot be defined as cleanly in languages such
as Modula-2, which do not allow the redefinition of operators.

It would have been possible to have defined other operators in package *complex_type* such as:

> **function** "+"(*a* : *complex*; *b* : *float*) **return** *complex*;

Although this would have allowed expressions such as:

> *x* + 0.1

as a shorthand for:

> *x* + *make_complex*(0.1, 0.0)

it would have been against the normal use of the + operator in Ada, where both operands have to be the same type. Abstract data types should always be defined so that their use is compatible with the use of the primitive types.

7.4   Separate compilation

The discussion on modules has so far concentrated on the logical subdivision of a program into its components. Another important feature of programs is their physical decomposition into separate files whose contents may be compiled separately. Chapter 5 showed how FORTRAN programs are organized so that each subprogram can be compiled independently. The disadvantage of this approach is that it is not possible to check that the types of the actual parameters in a subprogram call match the type of the formal parameters in the subprogram declaration. Block-structured languages such as Pascal, on the other hand, allow full type checking, but not independent compilation.

When dealing with large systems composed of hundreds of subprograms, it is important to ensure that a change in one subprogram does not necessitate the recompilation of all other subprograms while, if the system is to be secure and reliable, it is important to have full type checking. Ada and Modula-2 solve this problem by replacing *independent* compilation by *separate* compilation. As an example, consider the following outline Ada program:

```
package low is
   ...
end low;

package middle is
   ...
end middle;

with low;
package body middle is
   ...
end middle;
```

```
with middle;
package high is
    ...
end high;

package body high is
    ...
end high;

with high, middle;
procedure main is
begin ... end main;
```

The packages *low, middle* and *high*, the package bodies *middle* and *high*, and the procedure *main* can all be compiled separately and, together with their context clauses, are called **compilation units**. These units are not totally independent, since some depend on information specified in others and their interdependence is given by the context clauses. A package body is always dependent on its specification as identifiers declared in a specification are available in the corresponding body. Similarly, items in package *middle* imported into the specification of *high* are also imported into the body of *high*. The dependencies are shown diagrammatically in Figure 7.2 where the arrows show the direction in which information is passed.

No unit may be compiled before any of the units on which it depends. As the package specifications of *middle* and *low* do not depend on the others, they may be compiled first. The body of *middle* cannot be compiled until both its specification and the specification of *low* have been compiled. Note that the package body of *middle* depends on *low* while the specification of *middle* does not. This is quite a common occurrence as an implementation often requires more facilities than its specification.

Associated with each Ada program is a library file, called the **program library**, which contains information on the compilation units, including the time at which they were compiled. The compilation of the specification of package *high*, for example, is not done independently, but 'in the context of package *middle*' and the compiler uses the information in the library file to ensure strict type checking across the package boundaries.

To illustrate the effect of program modifications on compilation, consider the effect of changing and then recompiling the specification of package *middle*. In this case, the body of *middle*, the specification and body of *high* and procedure *main* all have to be recompiled, since they all depend on *middle* either directly or indirectly. This is shown in Figure 7.3. Not much has been gained, therefore.

Figure 7.2
Package
dependencies.

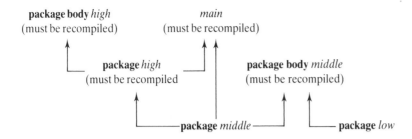

Figure 7.3
Effect of
recompiling
package *middle*.

If, on the other hand, it was the body of *middle* that was changed and recompiled, then no other unit would need to be recompiled, as units only depend on the specification of a package, not on the body. As most errors and modifications occur in package bodies, with the specifications being fixed at the design stage, the amount of recompilation required in practice is kept to a minimum. This also means that the implementation of a module can be completely changed without affecting the program units that use the module, as long as the interface stays the same. Localizing the effects of changes in this way is of paramount importance in the maintainance and enhancement of large programs. As an example, the effect of recompiling package *low* is shown in Figure 7.4. As it is only used by the body of *middle*, the effect is localized.

The approach taken in Modula-2 is essentially the same as that just outlined for Ada. Information can only be imported from a definition module and so an implementation module may be recompiled without requiring further recompilations.

The C++ language does not support separate compilation with full type checking, but a convention is used which, when followed, achieves this aim. Consider, for example, class *char_stack* given in Section 7.3. The class definition is held in a **header file** with a name such as *stacks.h* while the definition of the function bodies is held in file *stacks.c*. File *stacks.c*, and any file containing code which uses the *char_stack* class, must contain the directive:

```
#include "stacks.h"
```

In that way, the different files all access exactly the same interface information and full type checking is achieved. A similar approach is used with C programs. It is, however, much better if checking is controlled by language rules rather than being left to conventions that cannot be enforced.

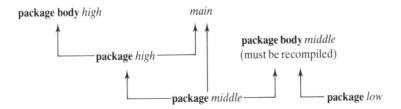

Figure 7.4
Effect of
recompiling
package *low*.

7.5 Generics

Algorithms for the stack operations do not depend on the type of the stack elements. A package that implements a stack of characters is essentially the same as a package that implements a stack of integers or some other type. To implement stacks of different types in Modula-2 and C++, it is necessary to declare separate modules that are essentially copies of one another. In Ada, however, a single **generic package** can be defined which has the type of the stack element as a parameter. Such a generic package gives an abstraction of a stack that is independent of the element type. This has the advantage of making the program text shorter and hence easier to read. Also, as the stack operations are independent of the type of the element, once the package has been shown to be correct for an element of one type, it can be guaranteed to work for elements of any other type.

Generic subprograms were discussed briefly in Chapter 5. Generic subprograms and packages are templates that have to be instantiated to produce actual subprograms or packages. As an example, consider the following generic Ada stack package:

```
generic
   type item is private;
package stacks is
   type stack is limited private;
   procedure push(x : item; st : in out stack);
   procedure pop(x : out item; st : in out stack);
   function top(st : stack) return item;
private
   type values is array(1 .. 100) of item;
   type stack is
     record
       val : values;
       top_of_stack : natural := 0;
     end record;
end stacks;
```

The implementations of *push, pop* and *top* are given in the package body in the normal way. Package *stacks* has a generic parameter and that gives the element type. Hence, a package with the properties of the earlier stack of characters can be produced by the following instantiation:

```
package stk_char is new stacks(item => character);
```

while a stack of integers would be produced by:

```
package stk_int is new stacks(item => integer);
```

As instantiation takes place at compile time, strong type checking is not compromised in any way.

Packages *stk_char* and *stk_int* may now be used as follows:

```
with stk_char, stk_int;
use stk_char, stk_int;
procedure main is
    a, b : stk_char.stack;
    d : stk_int.stack;
    ch : character;
begin
    ...
    push('f', a); push('g', b);
    pop(ch, a);
    push(42, d);
    ...
end main;
```

The identifiers *push* and *pop* are overloaded, but their parameters make it clear which version is being employed.

In this example, the size of the stack was fixed. To have stacks of differing sizes, a second generic parameter can be introduced, as in:

```
generic
    type item is private;
    size : integer;
package stacks is
    type stack is limited private;
    ...
private
    type values is array(1 .. size) of item;
    ...
end stacks;
```

An integer stack with, say, 50 elements can then be created by writing:

```
        package stk_int is new stacks(item => integer, size => 50);
```

7.6   Object-oriented development

When tackling a large problem, an important question is to decide how to identify the components into which the problem is to be divided. The approach taken in **object-oriented development** is to build a model. This is accomplished by identifying the real-world objects involved and then designing a high-level solution, expressed in terms of these objects and their associated operations. Although there is seldom a simple correspondence between the real-world objects and the types built into a programming language, it is possible to model the objects by means of suitable abstract data types. These abstract data types are the components into which the problem is to be decomposed.

To illustrate how such a model can be built up, consider the example of automating a library catalogue. The objects might be books (represented by their title, author's name, library catalogue number, ISBN number and publisher), journals (represented by their title, volume and part numbers, library catalogue number and publisher) and the catalogue, which would hold information about the books and journals. The catalogue operations would include the ability to add a book or journal to the catalogue together with the ability to search the catalogue with different book or journal attributes as the key. Note that the catalogue object has book and journal objects as components.

This approach separates the problem of writing programs to use the catalogue from the more difficult task of implementing the catalogue and its operations, and so allows these two parts of the problem to be tackled independently.

In Ada, a package is used to hold the definition of an object such as *book*. A possible package specification is:

```
package books is
    type book is private;
    function mk_volume(ti, au, cat_no, isbn_no, pub : string)
        return book;
    function title(bk : book) return string;
    function author(bk : book) return string;
    function catalog_no(bk : book) return string;
    function isbn(bk : book) return string;
    function publisher(bk : book) return string;
private
    type book is ...
end books;
```

Type *book* and the necessary operations on *book* objects are exported by the package while the representation of a *book* and the implementation of the operations are hidden. A *journal* can be defined in a similar way.

```
package journals is
    type journal is private;
    function mk_volume(ti, cat_no, pub : string;
                       vol, part : integer) return journal;
    function title(jour : journal) return string;
    function publisher(jour : journal) return string;
    function catalog_no(jour : journal) return string;
    function volume(jour : journal) return integer;
    function part_no(jour : journal) return integer;
private
    type journal is ...
end journals;
```

Consider now the library catalogue. If the catalogue is to be held on a computer, it might be decided that only a single copy of the current catalogue need be held. The catalogue package will therefore export not a catalogue type, but operations that can examine or modify a hidden variable defined in the package body and which represents the catalogue object. This is similar to the hiding of the variable *data* and the type *table* in package *retrieve_2*. Part of a possible package specification is:

```
with books; use books;
with journals; use journals;
package catalog is
    procedure add(bk : book);
    procedure add(jl : journal);
    procedure delete(bk : book);
    procedure delete(jl : journal);
    function item_in(bk : book) return Boolean;
    function item_in(jl : journal) return Boolean;
    function book_with_title(ti : string) return book;
    function journal_with_title(ti : string) return journal;
    ...
end catalog;
```

The procedures *add* and *delete* modify the *catalog* object by adding or deleting a *book* or *journal* while the functions *item_in*, *book_with_title* and *journal_with_title* examine its current state. Procedure identifiers such as *add* are overloaded. The particular *add* procedure called is determined at compile time by the type of the actual parameter as we saw in Chapter 5. For example, assuming that *bk1* is of type *book*, a book can be added to the catalogue by the procedure call:

```
catalog.add(bk1);
```

There are therefore two ways in which the objects identified during object-oriented development can be implemented in a language like Ada. When a large number of objects of the same type is required, as in the case of a book or a journal, the objects are implemented as abstract data types with each type being defined in a separate Ada package. The alternative, used in the catalogue example, is to implement an object as an Ada package containing a hidden variable.

If, instead of a single catalogue, a small number of catalogue objects is required, the second approach can be generalized by the use of a generic package as in:

```
with books; use books;
with journals; use journals;
generic
package gen_catalog is
    procedure add(bk : book);
    ...
end gen_catalog;
```

This is not the normal use of a generic package. It does not contain any generic parameters as its only purpose is to provide a template from which several instances can be created by instantiation as in:

```
package catalog_a is new gen_catalog;
package catalog_b is new gen_catalog;
```

The book *bk1* can now be added to *catalog_a*, for example, by the call:

   catalog_a.add(bk1);

   Using a generic Ada package in this way has some similarities with the use of classes in C++. An Ada generic package and a C++ class are both definitions of an object which may only be accessed through its exported operations. Several instances of the object may be created with package instantiation in Ada corresponding to the declaration of a class variable in C++. However, the analogy cannot be pushed too far, for although it is possible to create instances of an Ada generic package, a generic package such as *gen_catalog* is not a type and the objects *catalog_a* and *catalog_b* cannot be manipulated as variables or used as subprogram parameters. This greatly restricts the situations in which they can be used. It is also an expensive approach, as the code for the operations in the generic package will typically be duplicated rather than shared in the different instantiations. When several instances of an object are required in Ada, they are therefore usually implemented as abstract data types.

Sharing common behaviour

As books and journals have many features in common, as well as differences, it would be beneficial to define a package called *publications*, containing their common attributes, rather than to define a completely new package for each kind of object in the library. Package *books* and package *journals* can then be constructed from package *publications* by the addition of different sets of more specialized operations while re-using the software (declared in package *publications*) that they have in common.

   The representation of type *publication* could be given as a variant record with a tag field indicating whether a *book* or a *journal* was being represented. However, this approach is rather messy and, if it was later decided that a third kind of publication was to be held in the catalogue, the definition of type *publication* would have to be modified and package *publications*, in addition to all packages which depend on it, would have to be recompiled.

   Object-oriented development as used in a language like Ada can therefore be seen to be a useful approach to the decomposition of a large problem into meaningful smaller components. It uses the powerful data abstraction, information hiding and operation overloading facilities of the language, but there is a lack of language support for the idea that different abstract data types can **inherit** information from a common ancestor.

   How this is dealt with in object-oriented languages is discussed in the next chapter.

Summary

(1) To solve a large problem, it must be possible to divide it into separate parts that only interact with one another through small strictly defined interfaces.

(2) To ensure that a program can be easily modified, it must be designed so that the effect of any change is localized.

(3) Modules consist of a collection of related subprogram, type and object declarations.

(4) A module is usually divided into two parts. The interface part describes 'what' the module does while the implementation part gives details of 'how' the operations are to be carried out and is hidden from the user.

(5) In Ada, these two parts are called the package specification and body while in Modula-2 they are called the definition and implementation modules.

(6) Modules support information hiding. Identifiers declared in the interface part can be used in other modules while identifiers declared in the implementation part are hidden.

(7) Modules are compiled separately, but in the context of the other modules from which they import information. In this way, type checking can be performed across module boundaries.

(8) If the interface part stays the same, changing and then recompiling the implementation part of a module does not require any other module to be recompiled.

(9) A type is characterized by its range of values and the operations that can be performed on objects of that type. Ada packages, Modula-2 modules and C++ classes can be used to extend the range of types available in the language. The allowed operations are given in the interface part while the implementation of the operations and the representation of the objects are hidden. Types defined in this way are called abstract data types.

(10) A class (module) in C++ is a type.

(11) Generic packages in Ada allow the implementation of parameterized abstract data types.

(12) Abstract data types are central to the design method known as object-oriented development. To solve a problem using this method, the real-world objects concerned are identified and then a high-level solution designed, which is expressed in terms of these objects and their associated operations.

(13) Object-oriented development in Ada uses the data abstraction, information hiding and operation overloading features of the language.

EXERCISES

7.1 Large programs are usually implemented as separate modules. In early languages, subprograms were used as modules. What were the deficiencies of this approach?

7.2 What is meant by information hiding and why is it important in the construction of large programming systems?

7.3 The two principles of information hiding given by Parnas (1972a) are:

(a) The intended user must be provided with all the information needed to use the module correctly, and nothing more.

(b) The implementor must be provided with all the information needed to complete the module, but should be given no information about the structure of the calling program.

Describe how packages in Ada, modules in Modula-2 and classes in C++ support these two principles.

7.4 How have the problems that arise with the use of ALGOL 60 own variables been tackled in Ada and Modula-2?

7.5 Distinguish between independent and separate compilation.

7.6 What are the essential features of an abstract data type? What language facilities to support the implementation of abstract data types are available in Ada, but are absent from ISO Pascal.

7.7 A queue differs from a stack in that items are added at one end and are deleted from the other. A generic Ada package specification for a stack is given in Section 7.5. Give a generic package specification for a queue.

7.8 Construct an Ada package, a Modula-2 module and a C++ class that will implement a rational number abstract data type. Compare the solutions. Is being able to overload operators important?

7.9 In Chapters 3 and 5, you were asked to define a type *month* together with a suitable set of operations on objects of type *month*. Construct an Ada package and/or a C++ class to implement a *month* abstract data type.

7.10 Discuss the advantages and disadvantages of the notation used to define an abstract data type in C++, where a module definition introduces a new type, compared with the notation used in Ada.

7.11 Distinguish between a *class* and a *struct* in C++. Is it helpful, or confusing, to have two language constructs which are so similar? What is the difference between a *struct* in C and C++?

7.12 What are the features of generic packages in Ada that allow full type checking to be carried out at compile time?

7.13 In Section 7.2, package *retrieve* was defined to deal with a table of items. Write a generic version of this package in which *item* is a generic parameter.

7.14 Consider how you would go about designing a generic *sort* procedure.

7.15 Describe the object-oriented approach to software development.

BIBLIOGRAPHY

The implementation of modules in modern programming languages is a modification of the SIMULA class concept (Birtwistle, 1975). A very influential paper that discusses the way systems should be designed using modules is 'On the Criteria To Be Used in Decomposing Systems into Modules' by Parnas (1972b). Further details on how modules are used in Ada, Modula-2 and C++ are available from the standard language texts.

The design of abstract data types in Ada and their use in object-oriented development is described by Booch (1992). Also recommended is a general article on abstraction by Shaw (1984).

Birtwistle, G. M., Dahl, O.-J., Myhrhaug, B. and Nygaard, K. (1975), *Simula Begin*, Auerbach.

Booch, G. and Bryan, D. (1992), *Software Engineering with Ada* (Third Edition), Benjamin/Cummings.

Parnas, D. L. (1972a), 'A Technique for Software Module Specification with Examples', *Comm. ACM*, **15**, pp. 330–336.

Parnas, D. L. (1972b) 'On the Criteria To Be Used in Decomposing Systems into Modules', *Comm. ACM*, **15**, pp. 1053–8.

Shaw, M. (1984), 'Abstraction Techniques in Modern Programming Languages', *IEEE Software*, **1**(4), pp. 10–26.

Object-oriented programming languages

CONTENTS

8.1 **Object-oriented programming**   192
8.2 **Inheritance**   193
8.3 **Dynamic binding**   196
8.4 **Eiffel**   198
8.5 **Concluding remarks**   206

Modularity, data abstraction and information hiding were discussed in the last chapter. This chapter deals with the additional object-oriented concepts of inheritance and dynamic binding.

The chapter starts by introducing the concept of inheritance which is central to object-oriented programming systems. It shows how a derived class may extend or modify the representation information and the public operations that it inherits from a base class by adding specialized representation information and operations of its own. Dynamic binding, where the decision about which version of an operation is to be used is delayed until run time, is then examined.

After looking at C++, which is a hybrid between a traditional imperative language and an object-oriented language, Eiffel is examined as an example of an object-oriented programming system. The use of generic classes and multiple inheritance is introduced and described by means of an example which shows how an iterator over a data structure can be defined. Throughout the section on Eiffel, differences between the approaches taken in C++ and Eiffel are discussed.

8.1 Object-oriented programming

A language like Ada is often described as being **object based** as it supports data abstraction and information hiding. This chapter is concerned with the extra features that distinguish an object-oriented language from an object-based language.

An object has a hidden local state and exports operations that can act on this state, while an object-oriented program consists of a set of objects that communicate with one another through calls of these exported operations. As an object is an instance of a class, an object corresponds to a variable in a conventional language while a class corresponds to a type.

This definition of class corresponds to the C++ classes described in Chapter 7. C++ is, in fact, a hybrid between a conventional imperative language and an object-oriented programming language. The assumption is that the object-oriented approach is useful for some, but not all, parts of the software development process. By having a single language that combines conventional imperative and object-oriented features, programmers can get the best of both worlds. The object-oriented approach has been taken much further in a group of languages that have the object as their central concept. The best known of these languages are Smalltalk and Eiffel. In Smalltalk everything is an object.

Objects, as defined so far, are not significantly different from the instances of abstract data types described in Chapter 7. However, a central feature of object-oriented programming is that new classes are not created from scratch, but by **inheriting** information from existing classes which they can then modify or extend. The new class is said to be a **subclass** and the class from which it was derived, a **superclass**.

An object of a subclass can always be used when an object of its superclass is expected. When an operation originally defined in a superclass is redefined in a subclass, the decision as to which operation is applicable in a given situation can be delayed until run time, that is, we have dynamic binding. Inheritance and dynamic binding are the subjects of the next two sections.

Another important feature of languages such as Smalltalk and Eiffel is that they are not just languages; they are complete systems designed to support **object-oriented programming**. Software reuse is central to the object-oriented philosophy. Object-oriented systems typically provide several hundred predefined classes for concepts such as linked lists, sets and trees which can be enhanced or specialized to give the particular class required. In addition, facilities are usually available for the user to *browse* through the collection of available classes. When solving a problem, a programmer will use the *browser* software tool to find classes from which the solution can be constructed. It will often be the case that a class will *almost*, but not quite, meet the requirements. In such a case, inheritance can be used to construct a new class which inherits the desired features from the existing class and then extends or modifies them to produce what is required. This is known as **specialization**.

Although the origin of the object-oriented approach lies with SIMULA, the ideas were carried forward into Smalltalk which is the original object-oriented programming system. Smalltalk was designed to be used with powerful personal computers complete with windows, pop-up menus, icons and mouse pointing devices, and a large part of the Smalltalk system is devoted to supporting this environment. This, together with the fact that it uses dynamic type checking, has meant that Smalltalk programs execute relatively slowly. However, with the continued drop in the price of hardware, this is no longer the barrier it was in the past and so the Smalltalk approach is becoming increasingly attractive.

8.2   Inheritance

The idea of how a package *books* and a package *journals* could be constructed from a package *publications* by the addition of different sets of new operations, while reusing the code already defined in *publications*, was discussed at the end of Chapter 7. What is needed is language support for the concept of inheritance. The following example shows how this is provided in C++.

In C++, a *publication* class can be defined as:

```
#include <string.h>
#include <stream.h>

class publication {
protected:
    char the_title[255], the_cat_no[20], the_pub[40];
public:
    publication(char * ti, char * cat_no, char * pub)
    { strcpy(the_title, ti);
      strcpy(the_cat_no, cat_no);
      strcpy(the_pub, pub);
    }

    void title(char *);
    void catalog_no(char *);
    void publisher(char *);
    void do_print()
    { cout << the_title << '\n';}

    void cont_print()
    { cout << "Contents are : ";
      do_print();
    }
};

void publication::title(char * s)
{ strcpy(s, the_title);}

void publication::catalog_no(char * s)
```

```
{ strcpy(s, the_cat_no);}
```

void *publication::publisher(char * s)*
```
{ strcpy(s, the_pub);}
```

The directives:

```
#include <string.h>
#include <stream.h>
```

respectively, make available string operations, such as *strcpy* which copies a string, and the C++ I/O routines. The statement:

```
cout << the_title << '\n';
```

causes the value of *the_title*, followed by a newline character to be printed.

Variables (objects) of class *publication* may be declared and given values as follows:

```
publication apub("Computer Journal", "CS", "BCS");
```

In C++, a superclass such as class *publication* is known as a **base class**. The subclasses *book* and *journal* may now be **derived** from class *publication* using **inheritance**. They inherit the representation of a *publication* together with public operations such as *title* and *publisher* from the base class and each adds more specialized representation information and operations of their own. Inheritance therefore provides a mechanism for software reuse.

It will often be the case that a derived class will need to have access to members of a base class that should be hidden from clients of the base class. That is the reason for the reserved word **protected** in the *publication* base class. It indicates that the identifiers *the_title*, *the_cat_no* and *the_pub* are to be visible to member functions of a class that is directly derived from class *publication*. Apart from that, protected members have the same visibility as private members. Class *journal* is derived from class *publication* as follows:

```
class journal : public publication {
   int the_vol, the_part;
public:
   journal(char * t, char * c, char * p, int vol, int part)
     : publication(t, c, p)
   { the_vol = vol;
     the_part = part;
   }

   int volume() { return the_vol;}
   int part_no() { return the_part;}

   void do_print()
   { cout << the_title << ", "<< the_vol << '\n';}
};
```

Note that the constructor in class *journal* uses the constructor of class *publication* to initialize that part of the representation of a journal which is being inherited from class *publication*. The use of *public* in the heading of the definition of class *journal* indicates that all public members of the base class are public in class *journal*. If *private* had been written instead of *public*, then the public members of *publication* would have been private to class *journal*.

Variables of class *journal* may be declared as:

journal ajournal("Comm ACM", "CS", "ACM", 27, 3);

In a similar way class *book* can be derived from class *publication*:

```
class book : public publication {
    char the_authors[255], the_isbn[20];
public:
    book(char * t, char * c, char * p, char * au, char * isbn_no)
        : publication(t, c, p)
    { strcpy(the_authors, au);
      strcpy(the_isbn, isbn_no);
    }

    void author(char *);
    void isbn(char *);

    void do_print()
    { cout << the_title << ", " << the_authors << '\n';}
};

void book::author(char * s)
{ strcpy(s, the_authors);}

void book::isbn(char * s)
{ strcpy(s, the_isbn);}
```

Overloading

As well as extending a base class by the addition of new members, a derived class may redefine existing member functions. In the example, *do_print* is defined in class *publication* and redefined in *journal* and *book*.

Consider the following program fragment:

```
journal ajournal("CACM", "CS", "ACM", 30, 6);
publication * ptr = &ajournal;
journal * jptr = &ajournal;
ptr->do_print();
jptr->do_print();
```

As has already been stated, in an object-oriented language, an object of a subclass can always be used when an object of its superclass is expected. Hence, a pointer such as *ptr*, which is of type ''pointer to a base class'', may be used to point to objects of a class derived from that base class. In this case, *ptr* points to an object of class *journal*. In the function call *ptr–>do_print*(), the version of *do_print* selected depends on the type of *ptr*. As the type is "pointer to publication", the version of *do_print* defined in class *publication* is selected and only the title is printed. The fact that *ptr* is currently pointing to an object of class *journal* has no effect. Which function is called is therefore determined at compile time, that is, the binding is static. Similarly, as *jptr* has the type "pointer to journal", the version of *do_print* selected in the call *jptr–>do_print*() is that defined in class *journal* and so both the title and volume number are printed.

The output from the program fragment is, therefore:

```
CACM
CACM, 30
```

8.3   Dynamic binding

Consider again the function call:

```
ptr–>do_print();
```

when *ptr* is pointing to an object of class *journal*. To make full use of the flexibility that comes from a variable of type "pointer to a base class" being able to point to objects derived from the base class, the version of *do_print* which is selected should depend on the class of the object at which *ptr* is currently pointing, that is, the selection of the version of *do_print* should be delayed until run time. This is achieved when a function in the base class is prefixed by the reserved word *virtual*. Consider that the definition of *do_print* in class *publication* is changed to:

```
virtual void do_print()
{ cout << the_title << '\n';}
```

The output from the program fragment given in the previous section now becomes:

```
CACM, 30
CACM, 30
```

As both *ptr* and *jptr* are pointing to an object of class *journal*, the version of *do_print* which is selected is that defined in class *journal*. This is an example of dynamic binding.

As a further example, consider the effect of executing the program:

```
main()
{
    int i;
    publication apub("Computer Journal", "CS", "BCS");
    journal ajournal("CACM", "CS", "ACM", 30, 6);
```

```
book abook("Pride and Prejudice", "Lit", "Penguin",
          "Jane Austen", "0–14–043–072–5");
publication * ptr;
for (i = 0; i < 3; i++)
{
   if (i == 0)
      ptr = &apub;
   else if (i == 1)
      ptr = &ajournal;
   else
      ptr = &abook;
   ptr->cont_print();
}
}
```

In the three iterations of the loop, *ptr* points, in turn, to an object of class *publication*, *journal* and *book*. Each time round the loop, the member function *cont_print* defined in class *publication* is called. This function, in turn, calls function *do_print*. As *do_print* is defined, in class *publication*, as a virtual function, the version of *do_print* which is selected is determined dynamically at run time and depends on the class to which the pointer *ptr* is currently pointing. The output from the program is therefore:

```
Contents are : Computer Journal
Contents are : CACM, 30
Contents are : Pride and Prejudice, Jane Austen
```

Hence, when *ptr* is, for example, pointing to *ajournal*, the version of *do_print* that is selected during the execution of *cont_print* is the one defined in class *journal* and so the volume number is printed as well as the title.

Finally, it should be noted that type checking is still performed at compile time. An expression such as:

```
ptr->volume();
```

is picked up as an error by the compiler as *volume* is not one of the member functions of class *publication*. This guards against possible run-time errors since, although the statement has a valid interpretation when *ptr* is pointing at a *journal* object, it does not have a valid interpretation when *ptr* is pointing at either a *book* or *publication* object.

Message passing

Programming in an object-oriented style requires a different approach to problem solving and, to emphasize the central position of the object and the dynamic nature of object interaction, the object-oriented community has developed a new vocabulary. The object-oriented view is that objects send **messages** to one another and, on receiving a message, an object decides (at run time) which of the available

methods (that is, operation bodies) should be used in response. An object may send a message to itself. The call of *do_print* in the definition of *cont_print*, for example, can be written as:

this–>*do_print*();

where *this* is a C++ reserved word indicating the current object.

Consider execution of the statement:

ptr–>*cont_print*();

when *ptr* is pointing to an object of class *book*. The message *cont_print* is sent to the *book* object. As class *book* has no method for handling a *cont_print* message directly, when the *book* object receives the message, it is the method defined in the base class (*publication*) that is selected. Execution of the method for *cont_print* involves sending the message *do_print* to the current object, that is, the *book* object. As the *book* class has a method for *do_print*, that is the one selected and so the author is printed as well as the title.

8.4 Eiffel

In Smalltalk, everything is an object; even a class is an object. An aim of Eiffel is to produce an object-oriented system that is simpler and more efficient than Smalltalk and which can be used in the production of high quality and reliable production-level software. Eiffel, unlike Smalltalk, therefore uses static type checking so that any type inconsistencies can be picked up at compile time. The method used by an object when it receives a message is still, however, decided at run time. Eiffel also makes a clear distinction between a class and an object. Classes in Eiffel correspond to types in a traditional language while an object is an instance of a class and exists at run time.

Although objects are an excellent way of handling structured entities, they do entail a certain overhead. Evaluation of the expression 3 + 6, for example, in a pure object-oriented system, involves sending the message + with parameter 6 to the object 3. The result is the object 9. In Eiffel all objects are accessed indirectly through a reference, that is, a pointer. For efficiency reasons, instances of simple types such as integer, character, real and Boolean are not treated as objects and are accessed directly.

The text of an Eiffel program consists of a set of class definitions. At run time, objects are created dynamically. All actions involve performing an operation on some object which can cause other objects to be created or the attributes of objects to be changed. As in Smalltalk, garbage collection is automatic and so the destructor operator of C++ is not required. The argument is that storage management is properly the responsibility of the system and leaving the destruction of objects to the programmer is inherently unsafe.

An Eiffel example

In Eiffel, the definition of class *publication* can be written as:

```
class PUBLICATION
export
    title, catalog_no, publisher, do_print, cont_print
feature
    the_title, the_cat_no, the_pub : STRING;

    title : STRING is
    do
        result := the_title.duplicate
    end; - - title

    catalog_no : STRING is
    do
        result := the_cat_no.duplicate
    end; - - catalog_no

    publisher : STRING is
    do
        result := publisher.duplicate
    end; - - publisher

    do_print is
    do
        io.putstring(the_title);
        io.putstring("\n")
    end; - - do_print

    cont_print is
    do
        io.putstring("Contents are : ");
        do_print
    end; - - cont_print

    Create(ti, cat_no, pub : STRING) is
    do
        the_title := ti.duplicate;
        the_cat_no := cat_no.duplicate;
        the_pub := pub.duplicate
    end - - Create
end - - class PUBLICATION
```

Instead of having public, private and protected members (known as **features** in Eiffel), features which are to be visible to the clients of a class must be explicitly exported. There are two kinds of feature: data items, which are called **attributes** in Eiffel, and correspond to **instance variables** in Smalltalk, and **routines** which correspond to methods. The constructor is the special feature *Create*. The call of *do_print* in the *cont_print* feature can be written as:

Current.do_print

that is, send the message *do_print* to the current object. This corresponds to the use of *this* in C++. Functions return values by an assignment to *result* as in:

result := the_title.duplicate

In this case a copy (duplicate) of the string attribute *the_title* is returned.

In Eiffel, an attribute of an object may be made directly visible to a client. In Smalltalk, on the other hand, instance variables are hidden and may only be accessed through one of the object's methods. Allowing the representation of an object only to be accessed by a client through a procedural interface has much to recommend it. The decision to allow Eiffel attributes to be visible was made purely on efficiency grounds, that is, to save the overhead of a routine call.

The Eiffel version of the derived class *journal* is:

```
class JOURNAL
export
    volume, part_no, repeat PUBLICATION
inherit
    PUBLICATION rename Create as Publication_Create
                        redefine do_print
feature
    the_vol, the_part : INTEGER;
    volume : INTEGER is
    do
        result := the_vol
    end; – – volume

    part_no : INTEGER is
    do
        result := the_part
    end; – – part_no

    do_print is
    do
        io.putstring(the_title);
        io.putstring(", ");
        io.putint(the_vol);
        io.putstring("\n")
    end; – – do_print
    Create(ti, cat_no, pub : STRING; vol, part : INTEGER) is
    do
        Publication_Create(ti, cat_no, pub);
        the_vol := vol;
        the_part := part
    end – – Create
end – – class JOURNAL
```

In Eiffel terminology, class *JOURNAL* is a **descendant** of class *PUBLICATION* which is known as the **parent** class. Eiffel does not have the scope resolution operator of C++ and so identifiers have to be renamed in a descendant class if there is any possibility of a name clash. As a constructor is always called *Create*, to use the constructor of class *PUBLICATION* in class *JOURNAL*, it must be renamed.

In C++, the fact that an operation such as *do_print* can be redefined, and the version used chosen at run time, is flagged by the inclusion of the word *virtual* in the base class. No mention of this fact is required in a derived class. The opposite is the case in Eiffel. The feature *do_print* is not flagged in the parent class, as dynamic binding is available by default, but when *do_print* is redefined this must be mentioned in the descendant class.

Information hiding and inheritance

The presence of **repeat** *PUBLICATION* in the export list is to state that all items exported from class *PUBLICATION* are also to be exported from class *JOURNAL*. Although the export list restricts the features that are visible to the clients of a class, all features of a parent class are automatically available to its descendants. This means that it is possible for a descendant to export features that are not exported by its parent class.

Inheritance is about making information available to descendant classes so that software can be reused. It therefore conflicts, to some extent, with the concept of information hiding which is about restricting access. In Eiffel, inheritance seems to be the more important of the two concepts. The designer of a parent class may decide that a certain feature is to be hidden from its clients as, for example, it is concerned with implementation detail. The feature *the_title* is not, for example, exported by class *PUBLICATION*. It cannot therefore be used by a client of *PUBLICATION*. However, it is available to the descendant class *JOURNAL* and, if it is added to the export list of *JOURNAL*, it becomes available to clients of *JOURNAL*. Allowing a feature hidden in a parent class to be exported to the clients of a descendant is against the idea of data encapsulation and information hiding. In C++, information hiding has higher priority. A base class can have private members which are not visible to a derived class. Furthermore, protected members of a base class cannot become public members of a derived class.

Another drawback with inheritance in Eiffel is that the number of identifiers that are in scope can become very large and, as a parent class will typically be descended from its parent, it can be difficult to determine where exactly an identifier has been declared. As was discussed in Section 7.1, a similar problem can arise with Ada and it was recommended that the full name of infrequently used identifiers should be used rather than making use of a **use** clause.

The Eiffel approach to problems of this nature is to provide software tools. For example, the effect of applying the tool *flat* to a class is to expand all inherited features to give one flattened class. The class in which each inherited feature is declared is given as a comment.

Reference variables

In C++, a constructor function is automatically invoked during the declaration of an object. This is not the case in Eiffel where an explicit call of *Create* is required. In Eiffel, objects are always accessed indirectly through reference variables, which correspond to variables of a pointer type in a language such as Ada or C++. For example, the declaration:

> *ptr* : *PUBLICATION*

declares a reference to a *PUBLICATION* object. This declaration is therefore equivalent to:

> *publication * ptr*;

in C++. Initially, *ptr* is said to be *void*, which is equivalent in a traditional language to it being given the value of the NULL pointer. An object of class *PUBLICATION* is created, given a value and attached to *ptr* by executing an Eiffel statement such as:

> *ptr.Create*("CACM", "CS", "ACM")

The *Create* operation is therefore similar to **new** in languages such as Ada and C++.

The equivalent of a main program is the **root class**. When an Eiffel system is executed, the *Create* operation of the root class is invoked. Its execution typically causes other objects to be created. A possible root class to be used with classes *PUBLICATION* and *JOURNAL* is:

```
class SESSION
feature
    Create is
        local
            i : INTEGER;
            apub, ptr : PUBLICATION;
            ajour : JOURNAL;
    do
        apub.Create("Computer Journal", "CS", "BCS");
        ajour.Create("CACM", "CS", "ACM", 30, 6);
        ptr := apub;
        from i := 0 until i > 1 loop
            ptr.cont_print;
            ptr := ajour;
            i := i + 1
        end
    end -- Create
end -- class SESSION
```

The first time round the loop, *ptr* refers to an object of class *PUBLICATION* and so the version of *do_print* called from the feature *cont_print* is that defined in class

PUBLICATION. Hence, only the title is printed. The second time round the loop, *ptr* refers to an object of class *JOURNAL* and so the version of *do_print* which is called is that defined in class *JOURNAL*. Hence, the volume number is printed in addition to the title. The output from executing this Eiffel program is:

    Contents are : Computer Journal
    Contents are : CACM, 30

The result is therefore similar to that obtained from the C++ program in Section 8.2.

Deferred classes

Operation *do_print* was defined in class *PUBLICATION* and redefined in class *JOURNAL*. It is often the case that it is not possible to write meaningful code for an operation such as *do_print* in the base class and so it is necessary to leave the body of the operation undefined. In such a case, the operation and the class containing it are said to be **deferred**. A class in which *do_print* is deferred could be written as:

deferred class *D_PUBLICATION*

    ...
    do_print **is**
        deferred
    end; – – do_print
    ...
end – – class D_PUBLICATION

The reserved word **class** is preceded by the word **deferred** and the definition of *do_print* is left undefined. The only other change is that, as it is not possible to create an instance of a deferred class, the definition of *D_PUBLICATION* must not include a *Create* operation. However, a variable of a deferred class such as *D_PUBLICATION* may be declared and refer to an instance of a (non-deferred) descendant of *D_PUBLICATION*. All non-deferred descendants of a deferred class must contain a definition for all the deferred operations.

Eiffel allows assertions to be attached to operations. This is especially useful with deferred operations as, although it may not be possible to define an operation, there will often be certain preconditions and postconditions that all later definitions must satisfy. These conditions may be included in the deferred operation and must then be satisfied by all the implementations in the descendant classes.

Whether or not assertions are checked at run time is usually an option. If they are being checked, and an assertion is not satisfied, then an exception is raised.

The C++ equivalent of a deferred operation is a **pure virtual function**. A pure virtual function version of *do_print* is:

    virtual void *do_print*() = NULL;

The fact that the body is left undefined is indicated by the value NULL.

Generics and multiple inheritance

Eiffel supports generic classes in a similar way to Ada. It is therefore possible to define, for example, a linked list class which has the class of the list element as a parameter. As might be expected, such a generic class exists in the Eiffel library. It has the heading:

class *LINKED_LIST*[*T*]

and a linked list of integers may be declared as:

list : *LINKED_LIST*[*INTEGER*]

The features exported by class *LINKED_LIST* include:

put_right – to add an item to the front of the list,
item – to return the item at the current position,
put – to put an item at the current position,
off – to test if the end of a list has been reached.

C++ does not support generic classes although they might be introduced in a later version of the language (Stroustrup, 1989).

In the examples given so far in this chapter, a descendant class has had a single parent. In both Eiffel and C++, **multiple inheritance**, where a descendant class has more than one parent, is allowed. This can lead to the problem of name clashes which, in Eiffel, must be resolved by renaming while, in C++, the scope resolution operator can be used.

To show the use of both a generic class and multiple inheritance, consider iteration over all the elements of a linked list. Chapter 4 described **for** loops which are commonly used to iterate over all the elements of an array. Eiffel has a library of **iteration classes** which allow iteration over arbitary structures. The following class uses two iterators, one to print all the elements in a list and the other to multiply all the elements by 10. Both iterators are created by inheriting from the same iterator class, *CHAIN_ITER*, defined in the Eiffel library. Multiple inheritance normally involves inheriting from different classes, while in this example inheritance is from the same class twice.

First consider printing the elements in the list. Class *CHAIN_ITER* contains a deferred feature *item_action* which is used to define what is to happen when each element in the list is visited. This feature is defined below in class *SESSION* by first renaming it *pr_item*, and then giving a definition for *pr_item*. Class *CHAIN_ITER* also contains a deferred feature *item_test* which returns a *BOOLEAN* value. In class *SESSION*, it is renamed *pr_test* and is then defined. This feature is used to control the iteration. In a *do_while* iteration, for example, iteration stops when a list element fails to satisfy the test.

Now consider multiplication by 10. In this case, elements in the list are to be modified. To define how an element is to be modified, the deferred feature *action* of class *CHAIN_ITER*, must be given a definition in class *SESSION*. It is first renamed *mul_action*. In a similar way, feature *test* is renamed and defined to give control of the multiplication iteration.

The code for class *SESSION* is :

```
class SESSION
inherit
   CHAIN_ITER[INTEGER]
      rename item_action as pr_item,
             item_test as pr_test,
             do_all as pr_do_all,
             do_while as pr_do_while
      redefine pr_item, pr_test;

   CHAIN_ITER[INTEGER]
      rename action as mul_action,
             test as mul_test,
             do_if as mul_do_if
      redefine mul_action, mul_test

feature
   list: LINKED_LIST[INTEGER];

   mul_action(li : TRAVERSABLE[INTEGER]) is
   do
      list.put(li.item * 10)
   end; -- mul_action

   mul_test(li : TRAVERSABLE[INTEGER]) : BOOLEAN is
   do
      Result := li.item < 10
   end; -- mul_test

   pr_item(i : INTEGER) is
   do
      io.putint(i);
      io.putstring ("\n")
   end; -- pr_item

   pr_test(i : INTEGER) : BOOLEAN is
   do
      Result := i < 70
   end; -- pr_test

   Create is
   do
      list.Create();
      list.put_right(8);
      list.put_right(6);
      list.put_right(12);
      io.putstring("Print all the list\n");
      pr_do_all(list);
```

```
        io.putstring("Multiply certain elements by 10\n");
        mul_do_if(list);
        io.putstring("Print all the list \n");
        pr_do_all(list);
        io.putstring("Print while element less than 70 \n");
        pr_do_while(list)
    end; – – normal_test
end; – – SESSION
```

The list is created and three items are inserted. Feature *pr_do_all* performs the action defined in feature *pr_item* on all the elements of the list – that is, they are printed. Feature *mul_do_if* performs the action defined in feature *mul_action* on the elements that satisfy the test defined in feature *mul_test* – that is, all elements which are less than 10 are multiplied by 10. All elements in the modified list are then printed and, finally, feature *pr_do_while* performs the action defined in feature *pr_item* while the condition defined in feature *pr_test* is satisfied, that is, 12 and 60 are printed, but the loop terminates when 80 is encountered. The output from executing the program is:

```
Print all the list
12
6
8
Multiply certain elements by 10
Print all the list
12
60
80
Print while element less than 70
12
60
```

A large number of library classes for lists, sets and tree structures are descended from generic class *TRAVERSABLE*. The use of class *TRAVERSABLE* in the definition of *action* and *test* defined in class *CHAIN_ITER* means that the iterator can be used in conjunction with all descendants of *TRAVERSABLE* such as, in this example, *LINKED_LIST*.

8.5   Concluding remarks

There is general agreement that modularity, data abstraction and information hiding are important tools in the creation of large and reliable systems. The addition of inheritance and dynamic binding is certainly an interesting development which, it is claimed, will soon become the dominant approach to programming. There is little doubt that it does provide a practical solution to the problem of being able to reuse existing software in the construction of new systems.

Object-oriented programming languages do require a different approach to be taken by their users and this has proved to be a barrier to their adoption. This situation has not been helped by supporters who continually emphasize differences rather than look for similarities with languages such as Ada and Modula-2 which have a module structure and support the implementation of abstract data types. The all-or-nothing approach, where a language is considered to be of no use unless it is purely object oriented, oversells the advantages. Traditional languages have shown a remarkable ability to adapt and it is likely that object-oriented features will play an increasingly prominent role in the next generation of imperative languages. In this, C++ has shown the way ahead and the proposed Ada 9X revisions (1992) would result in Ada becoming much more object oriented.

Summary

(1) A language like Ada is object based as it supports data abstraction and information hiding. Object-oriented languages also support inheritance and dynamic binding.

(2) A class may inherit representation information and operations from a parent (base) class and add more specialized representation information and operations of its own.

(3) In C++, a derived class may access protected information in the base class which is not visible to clients of the base class.

(4) In dynamic binding, the decision about which version of an operation is to be used is delayed until run time.

(5) Eiffel and C++ combine type checking at compile time with dynamic binding.

(6) The object-oriented terminology is that objects send messages to one another. On receipt of a message at run time, an object decides which method it will use in response.

(7) Garbage collection is automatic in Eiffel and Smalltalk, but not in C++.

(8) Object-oriented systems typically have a large number of predefined classes from which new classes may be created.

(9) Software reuse is central to the object-oriented approach.

(10) There can be a conflict between the aims of inheritance and information hiding.

(11) The definition of an operation may be deferred in a parent class and only given a definition in each of the descendant classes.

(12) The language C++ attempts to combine the advantages of object-oriented and conventional imperative languages.

EXERCISES

8.1 Distinguish between an object-based and an object-oriented language. Why is Ada described as an object-based rather than an object-oriented language?

8.2 Discuss the importance of inheritance in object-oriented programming.

8.3 As one is concerned with exporting information and the other with hiding information, is there a conflict between the ideas of inheritance and those of information hiding?

8.4 Why do C++ classes have both private and protected members?

8.5 Modify the C++ class *publication* so that it also holds information about the year of publication and the C++ class *journal* so that it holds information about the month and year of publication. Define a member function *date* which prints the year in which an object of class *publication* or *book* was published and the month and year in which an object of class *journal* was published. Repeat this exercise with Eiffel.

8.6 In Section 8.4, class *JOURNAL* was defined as a descendant of class *PUBLICATION*. Define an Eiffel class *BOOK* which corresponds to the C++ class *book* defined in Section 8.2.

8.7 Compare the overloading facilities of Ada , C++ and Eiffel.

8.8 Describe how C++ and Eiffel manage to combine dynamic binding with compile-time type checking.

8.9 What are the advantages and disadvantages of using an iteration class compared with explicitly programming a loop which accesses all elements of a data structure?

8.10 Using the Eiffel class defined in Section 8.4 as a guide, redefine features *action, test, item_action* and *item_test* so that iterators can be used to :

(a) change all negative elements in a list to zero,

(b) print all elements in the list until a zero is encountered.

8.11 Give arguments for and against automatic garbage collection in the languages C++ and Eiffel.

BIBLIOGRAPHY

The main text on Smalltalk is by Goldberg (1983) and the original text on C++ is by Stroustrup (1986). An introduction to C++ for programmers already familiar with Pascal is by Pohl (1991). A more general introduction to object-oriented programming has been given by Cox (1991) while object-oriented software construction using Eiffel is described by Meyer (1988). The Eiffel language continues to evolve. The system used to test the examples in this chapter is Eiffel Version 2.3. A recent book by Meyer (1992) describes Eiffel Version 3.

Object-oriented programming is an active research area and a large number of languages have been developed. Many, such as Flavors, are based on LISP. An article by Wolf (1989) compares Flavors with C++.

Ada 9X (1992), *Ada 9X Mapping Document*, US Department of Defense.

Cox, B. J. and Novobilski, A. (1991), *Object-Oriented Programming* (Second Edition), Addison-Wesley.

Goldberg, A. and Robson, D. (1983), *Smalltalk-80: The Language and Its Implementation*, Addison-Wesley.

Meyer, B. (1988), *Object-Oriented Software Construction*, Prentice-Hall.

Meyer, B. (1992), *Eiffel: The Language*, Prentice-Hall.

Pohl, I. (1991), *C++ for Pascal Programmers*, Addison-Wesley.

Stroustrup, B. (1986), *The C++ Programming Language*, Addison-Wesley.

Stroustrup, B. (1989), 'Parameterized Types in C++', *Journal of Object-Oriented Programming*, **1**(5), pp. 5–16.

Wolf, W. (1989), 'A Practical Comparison of Two Object-Oriented Languages', *IEEE Software*, **6**(5), pp. 61–68.

Functional languages

9

CONTENTS

9.1 **Von Neumann influence** 212
9.2 **LISP** 218
9.3 **LOGO** 226
9.4 **FP systems** 229
9.5 **ML** 232
9.6 **Concluding remarks** 238

Up till now, the discussion has concentrated on imperative languages with only passing references to languages such as LISP. This chapter looks at languages that achieve their effect by the evaluation of expressions, rather than by changing the value of existing objects through assignment.

It starts by introducing the concepts of functional programming using a functional subset of Ada. This approach has been taken in an attempt to pinpoint and discuss features, such as the absence of side effects, the presence of higher order functions and operations on structured objects, that are absent from many imperative languages without the issues being confused by the introduction of the syntax of a new language.

LISP is described in some detail and it is shown that although LISP contains all the necessary features of a functional language, it also contains imperative features such as assignment. The principal differences between LISP and its dialect Scheme are then discussed. LOGO, which can also be regarded as a dialect of LISP and is best known in connection with turtle graphics, is also discussed and although it too is not a purely functional language, its mode of use is much closer to the functional paradigm than it is to that of traditional imperative programming.

The chapter then goes on to consider FP, the main impact of which has been in exploring new ideas in functional programming rather than as a practical system. The chapter concludes with an examination of ML as a representative of a modern functional language and compares constructs in ML with their counterparts in Scheme.

9.1   Von Neumann influence

The languages discussed so far in this book are often referred to as imperative or procedural languages. A program written in an imperative language achieves its effect by changing the values of variables by means of assignment statements. The design of imperative languages has been closely tied to the design of conventional computers, which follow what is known as the von Neumann design, where a store has individually addressable locations. Since machine code programs achieve their effect by changing the contents of store locations, a variable in an imperative programming language can be regarded as an abstraction of the von Neumann computer store location.

Machine code programs are executed by carrying out machine code instructions in sequence with conditional and unconditional jump instructions being used to alter the flow of control. Similarly, the execution of a program in an imperative language is carried out by executing statements in sequence with conditional and loop statements being used to alter the sequence of control. The influence of the von Neumann computer on the design of imperative languages is therefore clear. As imperative languages are closely tied to the design of conventional computers, they can be implemented efficiently.

With the decreasing cost of computer hardware, radically different designs have become possible. One likely outcome of this is that multiprocessor systems will become the norm. It is even possible that conventional machines of the future will have as many processors as store locations or that the whole concept of the store location will disappear.

It is therefore clear that using currently available hardware as a model is not the only way to design a computer language. Other computational models can be used and if they are found to provide a successful way of describing computations, it may be possible to design computer hardware to fit the computational model rather than the other way round.

Functional languages

An alternative model on which to design a programming language is the mathematical function. A function definition such as:

$$f(x) = 10 * x$$

gives a rule showing how each element in the **domain** of the function f can be mapped to an element in the **range** of the function by multiplying it by 10. If the domain of this function is the set of all integers, then the range will also be the set of all integers. For example, $f(1) = 10$, $f(2) = 20$ and $f(30) = 300$; so the **application** of the function f to the integer 2 results in the integer 20. This corresponds closely to function calls in imperative languages. Languages based on mathematical functions are said to be **functional** or **applicative** as they achieve their effect by the application of functions.

What then are the significant differences between a functional and an imperative programming language? The most important is the concept of assignment: this is fundamental to imperative languages while it does not exist in a purely functional language. Assignment causes a change in the value of an existing object. Application of a function, on the other hand, causes a new value to be returned.

The problem with assignment is that when it is used in conjunction with reference parameters or non-local variables in subprograms it can lead to side effects and aliasing. As a simple example of this, consider the following Ada function that modifies a non-local variable:

```
function strange return integer is
begin
  a_global := a_global + 1;
  return a_global;
end strange;
```

Different calls of *strange* return different results and so the relational expression:

> *strange = strange*

gives the value false! Side effects of this nature make it difficult to reason about the correctness of programs and therefore to ensure that they are reliable.

By doing away with assignment, it is possible to ensure that functions do not have side effects and behave like mathematical functions. The precise order in which functions are called then no longer matters; calling a function with a certain parameter will always give the same answer. This is called **referential transparency** and makes it possible for different expressions to be evaluated concurrently on a multiprocessor system. Determining which parts of an imperative program may be executed concurrently is, on the other hand, very difficult due to the interaction of their various parts via shared store locations.

Language structure

The main components of a functional language are a series of primitive functions together with a mechanism for defining new functions from existing ones. A functional program usually consists of a series of function definitions followed by an expression that involves application of the functions. To illustrate the structure of a functional program, consider the problem of finding the difference between the largest and the smallest of three integer numbers. A solution to this problem can be written in a functional subset of Ada:

```
function max(a, b : integer) return integer is
begin
  if a > b then
    return a;
  else
    return b;
  end if;
end max;
```

```
function min(a, b : integer) return integer is
begin
   if a < b then
      return a;
   else
      return b;
   end if;
end min;
```

```
function difference(a, b, c : integer) return integer is
begin
   return max(a, max(b, c)) − min(a, min(b, c));
end difference;
```

with a possible call being:

put(difference(10, 4, 7));

A function definition that only contains function calls does not specify an order in which the calculation must be carried out. The calls of *min* and *max* can therefore occur in any order or they may be carried out concurrently. Synchronization, which is often a problem in concurrent systems, is automatically dealt with. Consider that in the execution of:

max(a, max(b, c))

both calls of *max* were taking place concurrently. When the value returned by the inner call is required by the outer call, execution of the outer call is suspended until the inner call is completed. Execution of the outer call is then reactivated.

As programs in functional languages state 'what' is to be done rather than 'how' it is to be done, they are at a higher level than imperative languages, and this makes it possible to produce simpler solutions for many problems, especially problems involving symbolic manipulation. Another major reason for this is the central position of the list data structure. Languages like LISP are list-processing languages while most imperative languages can be considered to be scalar-processing languages, since their built-in operations act on scalar rather than on structured objects.

Operations on lists

Objects in most functional languages can either be atoms, lists or functions. There are usually two kinds of atoms: symbolic atoms that correspond to identifiers and numeric atoms that correspond to numbers. The elements of a list are either atoms or they are other lists. Lists, in LISP, are written in brackets with the elements separated by a space or a new line. Hence:

```
(ALPHA BETA GAMMA)
(12 14 16)
((A B) (HELLO THERE) 94)
```

are all lists with three elements. A diagrammatic representation of these lists is

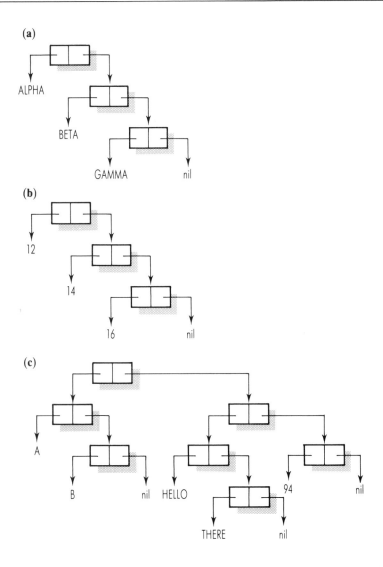

Figure 9.1
List representation.

shown in Figure 9.1. Lists allow the straightforward representation of hierarchical symbolic information and, as they can be defined recursively, they are ideally suited to being taken apart and constructed by recursive functions.

　　Most modern imperative languages such as Pascal, Modula-2, C and Ada allow linked-list structures to be created but, as list processing in such languages involves the direct manipulation of pointers, it is largely concerned with details of 'how' linked lists can be represented and manipulated rather than the higher level of 'what' they represent.

　　In imperative programs, structured objects are usually declared and then given initial values. Then, during program execution, the values of individual elements of a structured object are changed. In functional programs, in contrast, where the concept of modifying store locations does not exist, new copies of an object (that is, new values) are created, rather than an existing object modified. This results in run-time overheads and the need for garbage collection, but leads to conceptually simpler solutions.

As lists are of such importance in functional languages, it is important to have functions to extract elements from a list and to construct a list from its components. Two important functions are *head*, which gives the first element in a list and *tail*, which returns the list containing all elements except the first. Hence, the **head** of the list:

(ALPHA BETA GAMMA)

is the atom ALPHA while the **tail** of the list is:

(BETA GAMMA)

Note that the head of the list:

((A B) (HELLO THERE) 94)

is the list (A B).

Another important function is *cons* which will put back together a list which has been taken apart by *head* and *tail*. Hence, if *x* is the name of a list, the function call:

cons(*head*(*x*), *tail*(*x*))

produces the original list. The functions *head* and *tail* can be defined in terms of *cons*. Assuming an item *a* and a list *x*, the definitions can be written as:

head(*cons*(*a*, *x*)) = *a*
tail(*cons*(*a*, *x*)) = *x*

If the empty list is represented by **nil**, the following function will test if an integer is a member of a list of integers. (It is assumed here that the type *integer_list* has already been suitably declared.)

```
function is_a_member(x : integer; a : integer_list)
        return Boolean is
begin
  if a = nil then
    return false;
  elsif x = head(a) then
    return true;
  else
    is_a_member(x, tail(a));
  end if;
end is_a_member;
```

Function *is_a_member* is an example of a recursive function. If the list *a* is empty, the value *false* is returned as *x* cannot be a member. If the first element in the list is *x*, then *true* is returned. If neither of these conditions holds, *is_a_member* is applied to the tail of the list. In this way, either *x* is found or the number of elements is exhausted and *is_a_member* is eventually applied to the empty list. Where imperative languages use loops to achieve repetition, functional languages use recursion.

Dynamically typed languages

Most modern imperative languages are statically typed. Although this reduces the flexibility of a language, it allows many logical errors to be picked up at compile time. Early functional languages opted for flexibility rather than reliability and are dynamically typed. This approach is illustrated in the following example.

Using type-free notation, function *is_a_member* could be rewritten as:

```
function is_a_member(x, a) is
begin
   ...
end is_a_member;
```

The body of the function is unchanged. In a call of the function the actual parameter corresponding to *a* must be a list. If an atom was passed over instead, this would lead to an error when the function was called. The cost of the increased flexibility is, therefore, that some errors, which would be picked up in a statically typed language at compile time, are not picked up in a dynamically typed language until the program is executed.

Dynamically typed languages usually include Boolean functions which enable run-time checks to be made on the current type of an expression. This can prevent type errors although at the expense of run-time efficiency.

Higher order functions

An important feature of functional languages that is missing from many imperative languages (with the notable exception of ALGOL 68) is that functions can accept functions as parameters and return functions as results. Functions with this property are called **higher order functions** and the languages **higher order languages**. As an example of a higher order function, consider the problem of applying a function *f* to each element in the list (*x1 x2 ... xn*) so that the new list (*f(x1) f(x2) ... f(xn)*) is produced. Using the type-free notation, this could be achieved by the function:

```
function map(f, x) is
begin
   if x = nil then
      return nil;
   else
      return cons(f(head(x)), map(f, tail(x)));
   end if;
end map;
```

map has two parameters, a function *f* and a list *x*. If there is a function:

```
function timesten(x) is
begin
    return 10 * x;
end timesten;
```

then if *a_list* is the list:

(17 24 59)

the effect of the call:

map(timesten, a_list)

would be to produce the list:

(170 240 590)

Execution of a purely functional program

Due to the absence of side effects, the execution of a functional program can be viewed as replacing a function call by the corresponding body in which formal parameters have been replaced by actual parameters. This process is called **reduction** and can be shown by tracing the execution of the function call given in the previous example:

```
map(timesten, (17 24 59))
=> cons(timesten(17), map(timesten, (24 59)))
=> cons(170, cons(timesten(24), map(timesten, (59))))
=> cons(170, cons(240, cons(timesten(59), map(timesten, nil))))
=> cons(170, cons(240, cons(590, nil)))
=> cons(170, cons(240, (590)))
=> cons(170, (240 590))
=> (170 240 590)
```

Replacing a function call by the corresponding body is referred to as the **application of a rewrite rule**.

9.2   LISP

To most people outside the functional programming community, the language regarded as the archetypal functional programming language is LISP, and so it comes as a surprise to find that LISP is not a purely functional language. It does have a functional core and this is considered before some of its imperative features are examined.

One striking difference between LISP and imperative languages is the simplicity of its syntax. In place of a large number of language constructs, LISP has function application.

Objects to be manipulated by a LISP program are known as **symbolic expressions** or **S-expressions**. An S-expression is an atom or a list where a list is written as a sequence of atoms or lists, separated by spaces and enclosed in brackets. The S-expression:

(TIMES 10 2)

is interpreted as applying the built-in function TIMES to the two numerical atoms 10 and 2.

Certain atoms in a LISP system represent predefined functions while others represent what are called **special forms**. Special forms do not follow the usual rules of function application and, indeed, their effect often differs from one system to the next.

New functions can be defined using the special form LAMBDA. The function to multiply a value by 10 can, for example, be written as:

(LAMBDA (X) (TIMES 10 X))

An S-expression whose first element is LAMBDA is called a **LAMBDA expression**. The LAMBDA special form takes two parameters, in this case the lists (X) and (TIMES 10 X). The first parameter gives the parameters of the function being created while the second parameter gives the function body.

To give a function a name, the special form DEF is used, as in:

(DEF TIMESTEN (LAMBDA (X) (TIMES 10 X)))

DEF has two parameters. The first is an atom representing the new name and the second is a LAMBDA expression indicating the function to which the name is to be bound. The value of TIMESTEN is, therefore, a function. In some LISP implementations, DEF takes as its parameter a list of functions to be defined. However, for the purposes here, it is assumed that DEF can only deal with one function at a time.

LISP systems are normally interactive with functions being defined and then applied. For example, once TIMESTEN has been defined, either of the following two S-expressions could be used to multiply the number 2 by 10.

(TIMESTEN 2)
((LAMBDA (X) (TIMES 10 X)) 2)

A typical LISP session will continue with the definition and application of other functions. As the definition of a function can use any existing function, complex new functions can be built up in a hierarchical manner.

In most imperative languages, expressions are written using infix notation. In LISP, prefix notation is used. Hence, instead of $A + B$, the built-in function PLUS is used to add two numbers and it is written as (PLUS A B). The S-expression:

(PLUS A (TIMES B C))

corresponds to the infix expression $A + B * C$. There is no need in LISP to define an order of evaluation of operators as all expressions are fully parenthesized. In the purely functional subset of LISP, there is no assignment. Hence, once parameters such as X have been bound to a value in the call of a function, that value may not be changed.

The S-expression is central to LISP. It is the only data structure in the language and a LISP program is itself an S-expression. This allows LISP functions to be manipulated or even created by other LISP functions. Although it is a powerful feature of LISP, this facility is not available in all functional languages, and so is not a central feature of functional programming.

Due to the importance of lists, quite a few of the predefined functions manipulate lists; for example, CAR and CDR are the head and tail functions, and CONS is the list constructor function. The names CAR and CDR are not meaningful and are a hangover from the machine code instructions used to implement these functions in the first implementation of LISP! The names *head* and *tail* are much more expressive.

When an S-expression such as (A B C) is written, it is interpreted as a request to apply the function A to the arguments B and C. To treat (A B C) as a list that can be passed as an argument to a function, the special form QUOTE must be used, as in:

```
(CAR (QUOTE (A B C)))
```

No attempt is now made to apply the function A and the function CAR is applied to the list (A B C). The result of the application is the atom A.

The use of QUOTE in this way allows a parameter to be passed over unevaluated and so is similar to call by name. The default mechanism in LISP is call by value. Strictly speaking, numbers should also be quoted, as in:

```
(TIMESTEN (QUOTE 2))
```

but most LISP systems do not insist on this. They also usually allow (QUOTE X) to be abbreviated to 'X.

The empty list is referred to by the special form NIL. Other predefined functions are the predicates or Boolean functions. ATOM tests if its argument is an atom, NULL tests if its argument is NIL, EQ compares two atoms for equality and NUMBERP tests if its argument is a numeric atom. The special form T represents true while NIL can be used to represent false.

Instead of the notation **if ... then ... else**, LISP has the special form COND. This takes a list of pairs where the first element of each pair is a Boolean expression. COND is evaluated by evaluating the first element of each pair in turn until one is true. The result is the value of the corresponding second element of the pair. The following function to test for membership of a list of atoms makes use of COND:

```
(DEF ISMEMBER (LAMBDA (X A)
  (COND ((NULL A) NIL)
     ((EQ X (CAR A)) T)
     (T (ISMEMBER X (CDR A)))
  )
))
```

If the list A is empty, NIL (false) is returned, while if the head of the list is X, T is returned. If neither of these conditions is true the third condition T, which is always true, is evaluated and this leads to a recursive call of ISMEMBER where X is tested to see if it is a member of the tail of the list. The effect of evaluating:

    (ISMEMBER 24 '(17 24 59))

will therefore be T.

The predefined function MAPCAR corresponds to the function *map* defined earlier. The effect of evaluating:

    (MAPCAR 'TIMESTEN '(17 24 59))

is the list (170 240 590). An advantage of using higher order functions such as MAP-CAR is that they reduce the need to program recursion explicitly. Another useful function is LIST which takes a list of expressions and returns a new list, each of whose elements is the result of evaluating the corresponding element in the original list. The effect of evaluating:

    (LIST (TIMESTEN 17) (TIMESTEN 24) (TIMESTEN 59))

is the same list as we obtained from our MAPCAR example.

Having looked at the functional core of LISP, consider now the LISP solution to a simple problem. Given an S-expression such as:

    (TIMES 4 (POWER X 3))

the aim is to produce the S-expression that represents its derivative with respect to X, that is, in this case, to produce the list:

    (TIMES 12 (POWER X 2))

The program should also be able to handle expressions in the form (POWER X 3), but to keep the program simple it is assumed that it only has to deal with correctly formed expressions and that special cases are dealt with normally. Hence the result of differentiating:

    (TIMES 3 (POWER X 1))

will be:

    (TIMES 3 (POWER X 0))

which when differentiated gives:

    (TIMES 0 (POWER X -1))

The proposed solution in LISP uses two functions, the first of which selects the third element from a list:

    (DEF THIRD (LAMBDA (Y)
                (CAR (CDR (CDR Y))))
    ))

The main function DERIVE consists primarily of an example of the COND special form and carries out different actions depending on whether the first atom in the list Y is

POWER or TIMES. The DERIVE function is given below followed by an explanation of its action through an example call.

```
(DEF DERIVE (LAMBDA (Y)
  (COND
    ((EQ (CAR Y) 'POWER)
    (LIST 'TIMES (THIRD Y)
        (LIST 'POWER 'X (DIFFERENCE (THIRD Y) 1))
    ))
    ((EQ (CAR Y) 'TIMES)
    (LIST 'TIMES (TIMES (CAR (CDR Y))
        (THIRD (THIRD Y))) (THIRD (DERIVE (THIRD Y)))
    ))
    (T 'ERROR)
  )))
```

Consider the call:

```
(DERIVE '(POWER X 4))
```

As the first element in the list is the atom POWER, this results in the evaluation of:

```
(LIST 'TIMES (THIRD Y)
    (LIST 'POWER 'X (DIFFERENCE (THIRD Y) 1)))
```

This gives a list whose first element is the evaluation of 'TIMES (that is, the atom TIMES), whose second element is the result of evaluating (THIRD Y), which is 4, and whose third element is the list obtained by evaluating:

```
(LIST 'POWER 'X (DIFFERENCE (THIRD Y) 1))
```

As (THIRD Y) is 4, the value of:

```
(DIFFERENCE (THIRD Y) 1)
```

is 3 and so the final result is the list:

```
(TIMES 4 (POWER X 3))
```

The reader should now trace the effect of the function application:

```
(DERIVE '(TIMES 4 (POWER X 3)))
```

Scope rules

Most imperative languages have static scope where the association of the use of an identifier with its declaration can be seen from the program text. Many versions of LISP, on the other hand, have dynamic scope where the use of an identifier is bound to its most recent definition during program execution.

In most circumstances in LISP, static and dynamic scope have the same effect, but they can give different results with higher order functions. For example, consider the following two definitions:

```
(DEF BASE (LAMBDA (F A)
    (PLUS (F 10) A)
))
(DEF TWODIGIT (LAMBDA (A B)
    (BASE '(LAMBDA (C) (TIMES A C)) B)
))
```

In the function definition:

```
(LAMBDA (C) (TIMES A C))
```

the atom A is what is called a **free variable**. As it is declared within function TWODIGIT, it might be expected to be bound to the value of the first parameter in a call of TWODIGIT. The effect of the function call:

```
(TWODIGIT 2 3)
```

would then be 23. However, this is not the result obtained. Application of the function TWODIGIT in fact gives:

```
(TWODIGIT 2 3)
=> (BASE '(LAMBDA (C) (TIMES A C)) 3)
=> (PLUS ((LAMBDA (C) (TIMES A C)) 10) 3)
```

It is only now that the LAMBDA expression is evaluated and the free variable A is associated with the most recent occurrence of A, that is, its appearance as a parameter of function BASE. As this A has been bound to the value 3, the effect of the function application is 33 not 23, giving:

```
=> (PLUS (TIMES 3 10) 3)
=> (PLUS 30 3)
=> 33
```

This problem would not have arisen if the atom A had not been used in two different contexts; for example, if BASE had been defined as:

```
(DEF BASE (LAMBDA (F X)
    (PLUS (F 10) X)
))
```

This shows that care must be exercised in writing higher order functions in a language with dynamic binding if unexpected results are to be avoided.

Scheme

Scheme is a popular dialect of LISP which has been very influential in the development of LISP systems in general. Scheme programs are more readable than their LISP counterparts as Scheme makes use of more meaningful identifiers and special forms are replaced by reserved words. The reserved word DEFINE, for example, replaces the special form DEF, operators such as + and * replace PLUS and TIMES, the empty list is written as (), true and false are written as #T and #F respectively, and the convention with predicates is that the identifiers always end with ? as in ATOM?, NULL?, EQ? and NUMBER?.

Hence, the function TIMESTEN is defined in Scheme as:

```
(DEFINE TIMESTEN (LAMBDA (X) (* 10 X)))
```

The reserved word ELSE can be used in conditional expressions which leads to a more readable construct. The ISMEMBER function in Scheme becomes:

```
(DEFINE ISMEMBER (LAMBDA (X A)
    (COND ((NULL? A) #F)
          ((EQ? X (CAR A)) #T)
          (ELSE (ISMEMBER X (CDR A)))
    )
))
```

Two important features of Scheme are that it has a block structure, allowing the declaration of local identifiers, and that the scope rules are static.

Although LAMBDA expressions can be treated as ordinary values in LISP and higher order functions are possible, the full use of such features requires static scope rules since, as has been shown, dynamic scope can lead to unexpected results. A full discussion of higher order functions is delayed until the section on ML, as Scheme and ML deal with higher order functions in essentially the same way.

Imperative features of LISP

As has already been indicated, LISP is not a purely functional language. It has, for example, two assignment operators SET and SETQ. The function call:

```
(SETQ A 'B)
```

will assign the symbolic atom B to A while:

```
(SET A 'C)
```

will assign the symbolic atom C to the value of A. When the value of A is the symbolic atom B, the effect of the function call (SET A 'C) is to assign the symbolic atom C to B. Note that the immediate effect of assignment is that the order of function application becomes important.

The connection between SET and SETQ is that the effect of:

```
(SET 'A 'B)
```

is the same as the earlier use of SETQ.

SET and SETQ are often used in conjunction with the PROG special form which has an arbitrary number of parameters. The first parameter is a list that defines local variables while the other parameters correspond to the statements of an imperative language. There is even a GO function which causes transfer of control to a label!

The following function uses the PROG feature to calculate the sum of the elements in a list X. It can be seen to have more in common with an imperative Pascal solution (with a rather unhelpful syntax) than with a functional solution. Writing the equivalent (and simpler) recursive function is left as an exercise.

```
(DEF SUMLIST (LAMBDA (X)
    (PROG (TOTAL)
        (SETQ TOTAL 0)
        LOOP
        (COND ((NULL X) (RETURN TOTAL))
            (T (SETQ TOTAL (PLUS TOTAL (CAR X))))
        ))
        (SETQ X (CDR X))
        (GO LOOP)
    )))
```

Concluding remarks

For programmers brought up in the imperative style, LISP programs are not easy to read. This has led to the suggestion that LISP really stands for Lots of Infuriating Superfluous Parentheses. However, this situation has been ameliorated by modern LISP systems providing an editor to help ensure that the proper matching of brackets is achieved, and a pretty printer which lays out programs in a readable form. Modern dialects such as Scheme are also more readable due to their use of reserved words.

LISP systems are interactive and support a development environment where new functions can easily be constructed, tested and modified. This gives many advantages, but one of the central themes in the construction of large reliable programs is that they should be easy to read, even if this means that they are more difficult to write. This is evident in both the design of recent imperative languages such as Ada and in how the languages are used. LISP programs have the advantage of being much shorter than their equivalent imperative programs, but ease of understanding is not helped by many LISP programmers who give mathematical conciseness a higher priority than software engineering concerns of ease of understanding.

Having an acknowledged language standard is another area where LISP falls short. There are almost as many dialects of LISP as there are of BASIC, although there has been an attempt to make COMMON LISP the standard. However, COMMON LISP is very large and seems to combine the features of all other LISP dialects rather than be selective.

Many LISP systems treat function calls at the outermost level differently from inner calls. Hence, instead of writing (TIMES 10 2), it is possible to write TIMES(10 2) or use the predefined function EVAL and write:

```
EVAL (TIMES 10 2)
```

Before using a LISP system, a programmer must discover how that particular system deals with such features. Although the differences may be minor they are offputting to the novice or casual user.

9.3 LOGO

The LOGO language has been implemented on many microcomputers. It is best known in connection with turtle graphics where some of the primitive functions are used to draw lines on a VDU screen with a representation of a turtle being used to indicate the current position of the cursor.

Most of the publicity surrounding LOGO has been about its use as a vehicle to help children think about problem solving. As quite complex patterns can be drawn relatively easily using turtle graphics, this can give children a sense of achievement and they are encouraged to learn while having fun.

LOGO can, in fact, be regarded as a dialect of LISP and a child whose first exposure to computer programming is with LOGO may well assume that the normal programming style is a functional one. In the long term, therefore, it may be LOGO that has the greatest impact on functional programming. Like LISP, LOGO is an interactive language and a LOGO session consists of defining procedures and then applying them. In the language:

- there is a set of built-in procedures,
- new procedures are created from existing ones,
- data objects are words (atoms) and lists,
- words may be either symbolic or numeric,
- parameters are passed by value,
- the scope rules are dynamic, and
- recursion is a major tool.

There is no clear distinction between programs and data and it is possible to create a list and then treat it as a series of commands to be executed.

Some procedures return a value while the purpose of others is to achieve a side effect, such as moving a turtle on the screen. Procedures that return a value are called **operations** and procedures whose purpose is to achieve a side effect are called **commands**. The term function is not usually used in LOGO. A LOGO procedure usually consists of a series of commands and consequently has many similarities with the PROG feature of LISP, although all the commands are procedure calls.

LOGO always comes as a complete system with a built-in editor. Although this makes it easier for novices to learn and to use, it results in the disadvantage that no two LOGO systems are the same.

At the start of a LOGO turtle graphics session, the turtle is at the centre of the screen facing towards the top of the screen. To move the turtle forward, say, 50 units the command is FD 50 and to make it turn 90 degrees to the right it is RT 90. FD and RT are both built-in procedures. Hence the sequence:

```
FD 50
RT 90
FD 50
RT 90
```

```
FD 50
RT 90
FD 50
RT 90
```

returns the turtle to its starting point after it has drawn a square of length 50 units.

The sequence of commands just given can be replaced by a repeat command which has two parameters. The first parameter indicates the number of iterations and the second is a list giving the commands to be repeated. Hence:

```
REPEAT 4 [FD 50 RT 90]
```

Lists in LOGO are written in square brackets with empty lists being represented by [].

The LOGO interpreter executes a list of commands by working from left to right and associating parameters with commands. Each non-numeric word is assumed to be the name of a procedure and when it is encountered an attempt is made to call it. If there is no procedure corresponding to a name an error will result. Given the list of commands:

```
FD SUM 20 30 RT 90
```

there is first a call of procedure FD, which expects one parameter. The next word is SUM which is a procedure which takes two parameters and returns their sum. The call of procedure SUM takes the numeric words 20 and 30 as parameters. This gives the result 50, which becomes the parameter for FD. The actual parameter in the call of FD is, therefore, the result obtained by evaluating SUM 20 30. This mechanism is equivalent to call by value. The interpreter then proceeds to execute RT 90.

A list of LOGO commands can be quite difficult to follow, but additional round brackets can be inserted to indicate to the human reader the grouping of procedures and parameters. Also, as alternatives to the prefix operators SUM and PRODUCT, LOGO provides infix operators such as + and *.

To define a new procedure SQUARE, the TO command can be used as follows:

```
TO SQUARE :SIZE
REPEAT 4 [FD :SIZE RT 90]
END
```

The SQUARE command has :SIZE as its single parameter. To show that they are not the names of functions, parameters are prefixed by a colon. The effect of the call:

```
SQUARE 60
```

is to draw a square with sides of length 60 units.

The assignment operator is MAKE and this is quite widely used because the set of primitive functions is not as powerful as the set in an implementation of LISP. The effect of:

```
MAKE "TEMP 1
```

is to give the variable TEMP the value 1. The symbol " is required for the same reason as QUOTE in LISP although, unlike LISP, lists are automatically quoted.

As LOGO deals with lists it has, as one might expect, a series of built-in operations to decompose and construct lists. FIRST and BUTFIRST correspond to CAR and CDR, and FPUT corresponds to CONS. The LIST operation takes two parameters and returns a list which has the two parameters as its elements. The following examples show the differing effect of LIST and FPUT:

LIST "A [B] produces the list [A [B]]
FPUT "A [B] produces the list [A B]

A map procedure can be written in LOGO as:

```
TO MAP :F :PARAM
IF EMPTYP :PARAM [OUTPUT []]
OUTPUT FPUT (RUN LIST :F FIRST :PARAM)
            (MAP :F BUTFIRST :PARAM)
END
```

The OUTPUT command used here has a similar effect to **return** in other languages and the effect of the RUN command is to execute a list of LOGO commands. Normally, a LOGO command must be typed all on one line; however, this rule has not been obeyed here to make the program easier to read.

Assuming a LOGO version of the TIMESTEN procedure:

```
TO TIMESTEN :X
OUTPUT 10 * X
END
```

the effect of executing:

```
PRINT MAP "TIMESTEN [17 24 59]
```

is as follows. If the list is not empty, the value returned by MAP is a list whose first element is constructed by executing the command:

```
RUN LIST :F FIRST :PARAM
```

while the rest of the list is produced by applying the MAP function to the tail of the original list. The effect of the RUN command is to construct the list:

```
[TIMESTEN FIRST [17 24 59]]
```

and then to execute it. Application of MAP returns a list. In LISP, the list would then be printed out, but in LOGO an explicit call of the PRINT procedure is required.

As a final example of the similarity between LISP and LOGO, here is a LOGO version of the program to differentiate a simple expression with respect to X:

```
TO THIRD :Y
   OUTPUT FIRST BUTFIRST BUTFIRST :Y
END
TO DERIVE :Y
   IF (FIRST :Y) = "POWER
      [OUTPUT FPUT "TIMES (LIST (THIRD :Y)
         FPUT "POWER (LIST "X (THIRD :Y) - 1))]
```

```
    IF (FIRST :Y) = "TIMES
        [OUTPUT FPUT "TIMES (LIST (FIRST BUTFIRST :Y) *
            (THIRD THIRD :Y) (THIRD DERIVE (THIRD :Y)))]
    OUTPUT "ERROR
END
```

Execution of the following two commands takes place in a similar way to the corresponding LISP function applications:

```
PRINT DERIVE [POWER X 4]
PRINT DERIVE [TIMES 4 [POWER X 3]]
```

9.4   FP systems

The FP language or, more correctly, group of languages have been proposed by Backus as an alternative to the LISP style of functional programming. The intention behind FP is that it is a vehicle for new ideas rather than a language that is to be implemented and used.

Data objects in FP are either atoms or sequences and the elements of a sequence can themselves be a sequence. Sequences are written in angular brackets with the elements separated by commas. A sequence in FP is therefore the counterpart of a list in LISP.

FP systems are purely functional languages and so the only operations are the definition and application of functions. Application of a function G to an object X is written as $G : X$. Higher order functions are replaced by what are known as **functional forms** which provide the main mechanism of creating new functions from existing ones. Functions themselves may not be higher order.

As an example of the use of a functional form, consider the following FP alternative to the LISP MAPCAR higher order function. (It is assumed that function TIMESTEN has already been defined.) Instead of:

```
(MAPCAR 'TIMESTEN '(17 24 59))
```

the functional form APPLYTOALL is used in FP to create a new function from the existing TIMESTEN. This new function can be given a name such as TIMESTENALL in a function definition:

```
DEF TIMESTENALL = APPLYTOALL TIMESTEN
```

The effect of the function application:

```
TIMESTENALL : <17, 24, 59>
```

is to apply the function TIMESTEN to each element in the sequence. Hence:

```
APPLYTOALL TIMESTEN : <17, 24 59>
=> <TIMESTEN : 17, TIMESTEN : 24, TIMESTEN : 59>
=> <170, 240, 590>
```

An interesting point to note in the definition of a function in FP is that there is no mention of parameters or variables. There is only the combination of functions. In fact, FP programs do not contain any variables.

Once all the elements have been multiplied by 10, the sequence containing all but the first element could be produced by using the above function combined with the tail function TAIL. The combination is performed by the **composition functional form** o.

```
DEF TAILTENS = TAIL o (APPLYTOALL TIMESTEN)
```

The effect of applying the function H o G to X is the same as first applying G to X and then applying H to the result. Hence, the effect of:

```
TAILTENS : <17, 24, 59>
```

is the same as:

```
TAIL : (APPLYTOALL TIMESTEN : <17, 24, 59>)
```

Thus, an FP system contains a set of primitive functions together with a set of functional forms. Existing functions can be combined using functional forms to create new functions, but it is not possible to define new functional forms. The idea behind this is that an FP system will have a large number of primitive functions rather than a small number out of which useful ones can be created.

A function may only have one parameter, but as that parameter may be a sequence, this is not a restriction. The function +, for example, takes as its parameter a sequence of two numbers and returns their sum as a numeric atom.

To create interesting functions, the ability to make choices must exist. This is achieved in FP systems by the **condition functional form** which is written as →. Assuming that the function P is a predicate, the effect of:

```
(P → H; G) : X
```

is that if P : X is true, H is applied to X, otherwise G is applied to X. Another important functional form is **construction**. The result of the function application:

```
[F1, F2, ..., FN] : X
```

is the sequence:

```
<F1 : X, F2 : X, ..., FN : X>
```

These functional forms can be used to define, for example, a function ISMEMBER, which accepts a sequence consisting of a number and a sequence and determines if the number is a member of the sequence. Hence:

```
ISMEMBER : <3, <7, 3, 9>>
```

will give the value true as 3 is a member of the sequence <7, 3, 9>. The definition of ISMEMBER is:

```
DEF ISMEMBER = (NULL o SEC → F;
(EQ o [HEAD, HEAD o SEC] → T;
    ISMEMBER o [HEAD, TAIL o SEC]))
```

The function SEC selects the second element of a sequence while HEAD selects the first element. T is a function which always returns the value *true* and F is a function which always returns the value *false*. The primitive function NULL tests if its argument is the empty sequence while EQ takes a sequence of two elements as its argument and tests if they are equal. Note again that the function definition consists solely of functions and functional forms.

The effect of the function application:

```
ISMEMBER : <3, <7, 3, 9>>
```

is to first evaluate:

```
NULL o SEC : <3, <7, 3, 9>>
```

to determine if the sequence being examined is empty. This evaluates to:

```
NULL : (SEC : <3, <7, 3, 9>>)
=> NULL : <7, 3, 9> => false
```

As the value is *false*, the following is now evaluated:

```
EQ o [HEAD, HEAD o SEC] : <3, <7, 3, 9>>
=> EQ : ([HEAD, HEAD o SEC] : <3, <7, 3, 9>>)
=> EQ : <HEAD : <3, <7, 3, 9>>,
         HEAD o SEC : <3, <7, 3, 9>>>
=> EQ : <3, HEAD : (SEC : <3, <7, 3, 9>>)>
=> EQ : <3, HEAD : <7, 3, 9>>
=> EQ : <3, 7> => false
```

As this also has the value *false*, the value of the function is obtained by evaluating:

```
ISMEMBER o [HEAD, TAIL o SEC] : <3, <7, 3, 9>>
=> ISMEMBER : ([HEAD, TAIL o SEC] : <3, <7, 3, 9>>)
=> ISMEMBER : <HEAD : <3, <7, 3, 9>>,
               TAIL o SEC : <3, <7, 3, 9>>>
=> ISMEMBER : <3, TAIL : (SEC : <3, <7, 3, 9>>)>
=> ISMEMBER : <3, TAIL : <7, 3, 9>>
=> ISMEMBER : <3, <3, 9>>
```

ISMEMBER is now applied to this new sequence and as the second Boolean expression gives the value *true* this time, the value returned by ISMEMBER is *true*.

The advantage of FP systems is that they are amenable to formal mathematical reasoning due to their regular and simple structure. On the other hand, they are perhaps too simple to be effective programming languages and their primary interest may be as a vehicle for the radical re-examination of what languages need to contain. Their major impact is therefore likely to be on the design of more conventional functional languages.

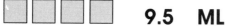

9.5   ML

ML is presented here as an example of a modern functional language. A continuing debate in computing science is over the importance of strong typing. As has been shown, LISP, Scheme and FP are dynamically typed, but there has been a move in recent functional languages, such as ML, towards strong typing.

In ML, the definition of a function such as *Timesten* can be written as:

fun Timesten (n : int) : int = 10 * n;

When a function is defined, the ML system responds with its functionality which in this case is:

val Timesten = fn : int → int

that is, *Timesten* is a function that takes one integer parameter and returns an integer result.

Brackets are not necessary in function application and so the application of *Timesten* to the number 2 can either be written as *Timesten*(2); or as *Timesten* 2; which results in:

20 : int

being typed out – that is, both the the result and its type are given. As function application has higher precedence than addition, the result of *Timesten* 2 + 3; is 23. Brackets can, as usual, be used to alter precedence and so the result of *Timesten*(2 + 3); is 50.

An important feature of ML is that it has a **type inference system**. It is strongly typed, but the programmer does not always have to give the types as the system can work them out for itself. In the case of *Timesten*, the function can be written as:

fun *Timesten* (*n*) = 10 * *n*;

As 10 is an integer, the type of *n* and the type of the returned value must be *int* and so the ML system will respond, as before, with the functionality:

val Timesten = fn : int → int

Names are bound to values in **value declarations** as in:

val *ten* = 10;

which causes the system to respond with:

val ten = 10 : int

A function is a value just as an integer constant is a value. An alternative way of defining *Timesten* is therefore:

val *Timesten* = **fn** *n* => 10 * *n*;

where:

fn *n* => 10 * *n*

is an example of a **function expression** which corresponds to a LAMBDA expression in Scheme. In this case, the function expression defines an anonymous function which takes an integer parameter *n* and returns an integer result whose value is *10 * n*. In the value declaration, the function expression is bound to the name *Timesten*. The reason why the system described the functionality of *Timesten* as:

   val Timesten = fn : int → int

should now be clear.

   A function or LAMBDA expression can be used anywhere a function name can be used. Hence the calls in ML and Scheme:

   (fn *n* => 10 * *n*) 2;

   ((LAMBDA (N) (* 10 N)) 2)

both give the result 20.

Lists

As one might expect, ML has lists as a built-in data structure together with operations such as *hd*, *tl* and *cons* (written as the right associative infix operator ::). Lists are written in square brackets and the elements are separated by commas as in [7, 3, 9] which is syntactic sugar for 7 :: 3 :: 9 :: *nil*. All the elements in a list must have the same type.

   An *IsMember* function to check whether or not an integer is in a list of integers can be defined as:

   fun *IsMember* (*x* : *int*, *y* : *int list*) : *bool* =
      if *y* = *nil* **then** *false*
      else if *x* = *hd*(*y*) **then** *true*
      else *IsMember*(*x*, *tl*(*y*));

The functionality of *IsMember* is:

   val IsMember = fn : (int * (int list)) → bool

showing that the function takes two parameters, an integer and a list of integers (an *int list*) and returns a value of type *bool*. (Strictly speaking, functions in ML have only one parameter which, in the case of *IsMember*, is a pair consisting of an integer and a list of integers. It can, however, be convenient to refer informally to a function having more than one parameter.)

   The above definition is not the usual way of defining a function in ML. Instead **pattern matching** is used. Lists can be classified as being empty or non-empty and *IsMember* can be defined using separate definitions for each of the two cases:

   fun *IsMember* (*x* : *int*, *nil* : *int list*) : *bool* = *false*
   | *IsMember* (*x* : *int*, *first* :: *rest* : *int list*) : *bool* =
         if *x* = *first* **then** *true*
         else *IsMember*(*x*, *rest*);

The appropriate definition is selected by **pattern matching** of the parameters. The symbol *nil* is the pattern representing the empty list and so if the list being examined is empty, the result of the function is *false*. The pattern *first* :: *rest* represents a non-empty list as it has at least one element, namely *first*. Due to the properties of the :: operator, the parameter *first* must represent the head and *rest* must represent the tail of the list.

Consider now the function call:

IsMember(3, [7, 3, 9]);

The second definition is selected with the head of the list, 7, being matched with *first* and the tail, [3, 9], with *rest*. As the value of x = *first* is then *false*, *IsMember* is applied to the tail of the list. In this second call of *IsMember*, the head of the list is 3 and so *true* is returned. If the call had been:

IsMember(3, [7, 6, 9]);

then the first definition would eventually be selected giving the result *false*.

In our earlier definitions of *IsMember* in dynamically typed languages, the function was defined for lists of any type. For full type checking, the only concern with *IsMember* is that the type of the item being searched for is the same as the type of the elements in the list. The type inference system of ML can infer this requirement from the definitions, allowing a general *IsMember* function to be written as:

fun *IsMember* (*x*, *nil*) = *false*
 | *IsMember* (*x*, *first* :: *rest*) =
        if *x* = *first* **then** *true*
        else *IsMember*(*x*, *rest*);

The functionality is now:

val IsMember = fn : ("*a* * ("*a list*)) →*bool*

indicating that if the first parameter is of type "*a*, then the second parameter must be a list of "*a*, where "*a* is what is known as a **type parameter**. There are two kinds of type parameter in ML, written with a single or with two quotes. The difference is that a type parameter of the form "*a* can only be substituted by a type for which equality of values can be tested.

Functions which can take parameters of more than one type are said to be **polymorphic**. Although generic functions in Ada are similar, they have to be instantiated with an actual type before they can be applied, as we saw in Chapter 7. This is not necessary in ML as *IsMember* can be applied directly. Therefore, the test whether a character is present in a list of characters would be written:

IsMember("a", ["a", "e", "i", "o", "u"]);

Higher order functions

Higher order functions are central to ML which, like Scheme, has static scope rules. As an example of a higher order function, consider:

fun *map* (*f*, *nil*) = *nil*
 | *map* (*f*, *first* :: *rest*) =
        f(*first*) :: *map*(*f*, *rest*);

The functionality of *map* is:

val map = fn : (('*a* → '*b*) * ('*a list*)) → ('*b list*) that is, the first parameter of *map* is a function which has a '*a* parameter and returns a '*b* result while the second parameter is a '*a list* and the returned value has type '*b list*.

The effect of the application:

map(Timesten, [17, 24, 59]);

is to print out:

[170, 240, 590] : *int list*

As has already been stated, functions in ML take only one parameter. Consider now the function:

fun *Times m n : int = m * n;*

Its functionality is:

val Times = fn : int → (int → int)

that is, *Times* takes one integer parameter and its result is a function which takes an integer and returns an integer. The structure of this function may be more clearly seen using a functional expression:

fun *Times m =* **fn** *n : int => m * n;*

The result of the function call *Times 10;* is the function:

fn n : int => 10 * n

This function can, in turn, be applied to an integer as in:

(Times 10) 2;

which gives the result 20. Function *Timesten* may now be defined as:

val *Timesten = Times* 10;

The equivalent definitions of TIMES and TIMESTEN in Scheme are:

```
(DEFINE TIMES (LAMBDA (M) (LAMBDA (N) (* M N))))
(DEFINE TIMESTEN (TIMES 10))
```

Function *map* can be re-written in this notation:

fun *map f nil = nil*
   | *map f (first :: rest) =*
      f(first) :: map f rest;

Its functionality is now:

val map = fn : ('a → 'b) → (('a list) → ('b list))

that is, its parameter is a function which takes a '*a* and returns a '*b* and its returned value is a function which takes a '*a list* and returns a '*b list*.

A function to multiply all the elements in a list by 10 can now be defined as:

val *Timesten_all = map Timesten;*

The result of *Timesten_all([17, 24, 59]);* is the list [170, 240, 590].

In the section on FP, functions were composed using the functional form o. This is also allowed in ML, where we have the compose operator o. Function *Tailtens* can be defined as:

val *Tailtens* = *tl* o *Timesten_all*;

The result of *Tailtens*([17, 24, 59]); is the list [240, 590] that is, the result of first applying *Timesten_all* to the list and then applying *tl* to the result.

Data types

The ability to construct data types is a powerful feature of ML. Objects are not defined by how they can be represented, but by the constructor operations used to construct them, together with the definitions of selector operations used to manipulate and examine them.

This is best illustrated by looking at the standard example of a stack. A new type is defined by having a *datatype* declaration where a type is defined in terms of its constructors. For a stack with items of an unspecified type, this might be written:

datatype '*a stack* = *new_stack*
            | *push* **of** ('*a* * '*a stack*);

Here, a stack has been defined in terms of the constructors *new_stack*, which represents a new empty stack, and *push*, which has two parameters and is the means of constructing a new stack from an item and an existing stack. The functionality is given as:

datatype '*a stack* = *new_stack* | *push of* '*a* * ('*a stack*)
con push = *fn* : ('*a* * ('*a stack*)) → ('*a stack*)
con new_stack = *new_stack* : '*a stack*

The definition of the stack is completed by defining *top*, which returns the top element of a stack, *pop*, which returns the stack obtained by removing the top element, and *is_empty*, which tests to see if the stack is empty. The definitions are:

exception *top_err*;

fun *pop* (*new_stack*) = *new_stack*
    | *pop* (*push*(*a*, *b*)) = *b*;

fun *top* (*new_stack*) = **raise** *top_err*
    | *top* (*push*(*a*, *b*)) = *a*;

fun *is_empty* (*new_stack*) = *true*
    | *is_empty* (*push*(*a*, *b*)) = *false*;

The two patterns to be matched are: *new_stack*, which represents an empty stack and *push(a, b)*, which represents a stack with at least one item. Consider the definition:

top (*push*(*a*, *b*)) = *a*

This states that if we have a stack constructed by pushing *a* onto an existing stack, then the top element of the resulting stack is *a*.

A stack value can be bound to a name as in:

val *s1* = *push*(29, *push*(4, *new_stack*));

The result of *top*(*s1*); is then 29. It is an error to try to find the top element of an empty stack. ML allows exceptions to be declared and then raised as was shown in the definitions of the exception *top_err* and the function *top*. The effect of calling *top*(*new_stack*) is that the system reports an error with the message:

Failure: *top_err*

The definitions of *pop*, *top* and *is_empty*, together with the constructors *push* and *new_stack*, fully define a stack without giving any representation information. Such an approach can be difficult for imperative programmers to get used to, as the definition of a stack and its associated operations in a language like Ada or Modula-2 can only be given in terms of some concrete representation. The above set of definitions can be considered as the specification of a stack. The power of ML is that once the full specification has been given, then that is the solution.

Lazy evaluation

In ML and LISP, parameters are called by value, that is, the parameters are evaluated before being passed to a function. It can, at times, be useful for parameters to remain unevaluated until they are required. This is called **lazy evaluation** and is similar to call by name in ALGOL 60.

With lazy evaluation, infinite data structures become possible. Consider the following function definitions:

```
fun generate100 (m) =
    if m <= 100 then m :: generate100(m + 1)
    else nil;

fun lowsquares (nil) = nil
  | lowsquares (first :: rest) =
      if first <= 5 then first * first :: lowsquares(rest)
      else nil;
```

Function *generate100* generates a list of the integers from *m* to 100 inclusive. Function *lowsquares* takes a list of integers and generates a list of squares, stopping when either the end of the list is reached or when an integer greater than 5 is encountered. Using call by value, the function application:

lowsquares(*generate100* 1);

is very inefficient as it first generates a list of 100 integers and then only uses the first few in producing the list of squares.

Using lazy evaluation, function *generate100* only generates those integers required by *lowsquares*, the rest of the list remains unevaluated. Consider now the function:

```
fun generate (m) = m :: generate(m + 1);
```

which generates an *infinite* list of integers. With lazy evaluation this is no problem and the call:

> *lowsquares*(*generate* 1);

works, producing the list of the first 5 squares while, of course, using call by value, it leads to infinite recursion.

Lazy evaluation allows interactive I/O to be implemented in a purely functional language. Data to be input can be considered as a list. The current input is the head of the list while the rest of the list (which has not yet been input) is left, as yet, unevaluated.

The language described in this chapter is referred to as Standard ML and it does not support lazy evaluation. A lazy version of ML, called LML has been produced (Johnsson, 1984).

Summary

In summary, the main differences between ML and the other functional languages considered in this chapter are:

- Strong typing: this gives the advantage that many errors are found at compile time instead of run time. As such errors are often logical errors, debugging is made much easier. Furthermore, the existence of polymorphic functions removes many of the problems that arise with strong typing in conventional imperative languages.

- Pattern matching: using pattern matching as an alternative to conditional expressions allows the different parts of a function definition to be given separately. This both makes it easier to construct the definitions and leads to a layout which is much easier to read and understand than LISP's nested parentheses.

- Data types: there are similarities in the definition of data types in ML, Ada and Modula-2 but their definition in ML is at a much higher and abstract level.

9.6 Concluding remarks

Functional languages have two features that could lead to them becoming increasingly important:

(1) As they are at a higher level, they can be used to produce a program more quickly than is possible with imperative languages, although the program may run much more slowly on conventional computers.

(2) Their lack of side effects, due to the omission of the assignment operator, means that they are more amenable to mathematical reasoning.

These two features allow functional languages to be used in rapid prototyping, where the aim is to provide an initial solution that has the correct effect and can be used to test a design. The experience gained in producing the prototype can then be used to help in the design of an efficient full implementation.

Another consequence of their lack of side effects is that functional languages are much more amenable to having their different parts executed in parallel. If the computers of the future are highly parallel, functional programs could become more efficient than their imperative counterparts due to their ability to exploit parallelism.

Summary

(1) A program written in an imperative language achieves its effect by changing the values of variables by means of assignment statements. A functional program, on the other hand, achieves its effect by creating new values by the evaluation of expressions.

(2) As side effects cannot occur in a purely functional language, calling a function with a certain parameter will always give the same answer. This is called referential transparency.

(3) A functional program consists of function definitions and expressions that involve application of the functions.

(4) Functional languages are much better at dealing with structured objects, such as lists, than are imperative languages.

(5) Most functional languages allow functions to accept functions as parameters and to return functions as results. Such functions are said to be higher order functions.

(6) Objects manipulated by a LISP program are known as S-expressions. An S-expression is an atom or a list of S-expressions.

(7) Many of the predefined functions in LISP are used to manipulate lists.

(8) Expressions in LISP are fully parenthesized and prefix notation is used rather than conventional infix notation.

(9) LISP is not a purely functional language as assignment is possible.

(10) LOGO was derived from LISP and is normally used with turtle graphics on a microcomputer.

(11) FP is a purely functional language and was designed as a vehicle for trying out new ideas in functional programming. Functional forms are used to create new functions.

(12) FP function definitions contain neither parameters nor variables. It is only possible to have a combination of functions.

(13) An advantage of FP systems is that they are amenable to formal mathematical reasoning. This is due to their regular and simple structure.

(14) ML and Scheme have static binding which means that they can make full use of higher order functions.

(15) ML differs from LISP and FP in that it is strongly typed. The programmer does not, however, have to specify all the types as ML has a type inference system that determines what the types must be.

(16) Functions are defined in ML by a set of alternative definitions that cover all possible cases. The appropriate definition is chosen by means of pattern matching.

(17) Instead of the generics of Ada, ML supports polymorphic functions.

(18) Lazy evaluation allows interactive I/O to be implemented in a purely functional language.

EXERCISES

9.1 It is possible to write programs in a functional subset of Ada. What features would have to be added to Ada to make it a useful functional language?

9.2 What properties of functional languages make them better able to exploit the parallelism that results from multiprocessor systems than is possible with imperative languages?

9.3 What is the difference between predefined functions and special forms in LISP?

9.4 Evaluate by reduction, the function applications:

```
(ISMEMBER 24 '(17 24 59))      (LISP)
```

IsMember(24, [17, 24, 59])   (ML)

9.5 Describe the difference between static and dynamic scope rules. Under what circumstances will they lead to different results?

9.6 Why are languages like LISP and ML better able to solve problems which require the manipulation of lists than languages such as Pascal and Ada?

9.7 Using the definition of DERIVE given in section 9.3, evaluate the LOGO operation:

```
DERIVE [POWER X 4]
```

by reduction.

9.8   Compare functional forms in FP with higher order functions in LISP.

9.9   What are the differences between polymorphic functions in ML and generic functions in Ada?

9.10 Write ML and Scheme functions to:

(a) sum the elements in a list of integers,

(b) determine the length of a list,

(c) take a list of integers and return the list from which the negative numbers have been removed.

What is the functionality of each of these functions?

9.11 Construct a higher order function *filter* which takes a list and returns the list containing only those elements for which a certain condition holds. Hence, if *ge*0 was a Boolean function to determine if an integer was greater than or equal to 0, the function *filter ge*0 would be an answer to question 9.10(c). What is the functionality of *filter*?

9.12 Using the ML definition of a stack as a guide, define a queue data type where elements join the queue at one end and leave the queue at the other end.

9.13 LISP and LOGO programs to differentiate a simple expression have been given. Give an implementation in ML.

9.14 Define an ML function *generate*10 which generates a list of integers from *m* to 10 inclusive. Evaluate by reduction, the function application :

   lowsquares(*generate*10 1);

(a) without lazy evaluation,

(b) using lazy evaluation.

BIBLIOGRAPHY

Detailed descriptions of functional programming are given by Henderson (1980) and by Reade (1989). In *Functional Programming: Application and Implementation*, Henderson uses a purely functional subset of LISP (with static scope) called LISPKIT, while *Elements of Functional Programming* uses ML as the main language.

There are many textbooks on LISP. The book by Winston (1988) uses the Common LISP dialect which is the nearest there is to a standard version of the language. A very influential book on the teaching of programming using Scheme is by Abelson (1985). The Revised Report on Scheme was edited by Rees (1986).

Most books on LOGO concentrate on its use with turtle graphics. An interesting alternative is the book by Harvey (1985).

The paper by Backus (1978) has been very influential. As well as introducing FP, it gives a critique of the advantages of the functional style over imperative von Neumann based languages. A description of modern functional languages, including purely functional languages such as Haskell and Miranda, is given by Hudak (1989). The version of ML described in this chapter is known as Standard ML (Wikström, 1987).

The use of functional languages in prototyping has been described by Henderson (1986).

Abelson, H. and Sussman, G. J. (1985), *Structure and Interpretation of Computer Programs*, MIT Press.

Backus, J. (1978), 'Can Programming be Liberated from the Von Neumann Style?', *Comm. ACM*, **21**, pp. 613–641.

Harvey, B. (1985), *Computer Science Logo Style*, MIT Press.

Henderson, P. (1980), *Functional Programming: Application and Implementation*, Prentice-Hall.

Henderson, P. (1986), 'Functional Programming, Formal Specification and Rapid Prototyping', *IEEE Trans. in Software Engineering*, **12**, pp. 241–250.

Hudak, P. (1989), 'Conception, Evolution, and Application of Functional Programming Languages', *ACM Computing Surveys*, **21**, pp. 359–411.

Johnsson, T. (1984), 'Efficient Compilation of Lazy Evaluation', *ACM SIGPLAN Notices*, **19**(6), pp. 58–69.

Reade, C. (1989), *Elements of Functional Programming*, Addison-Wesley.

Rees, J. and Clinger, W. (1986), 'Revised Report on the Algorithmic Language Scheme', *ACM SIGPLAN Notices*, **21**(12), pp. 37–79.

Wikström, A. (1987), *Functional Programming Using Standard ML*, Prentice-Hall.

Winston, P. H. and Horn, B. K. P. (1988), *LISP* (Third Edition), Addison-Wesley.

Logic programming

CONTENTS

10.1 **The PROLOG approach**   **244**
10.2 **The basics of PROLOG**   **244**
10.3 **Data objects**   **250**
10.4 **Efficiency in PROLOG**   **252**
10.5 **A PROLOG example**   **253**
10.6 **The future of PROLOG**   **255**

Logic programming is almost synonymous with PROLOG. Indeed, the name PROLOG stands for PROgramming in LOGic. This chapter is, therefore, mainly concerned with the PROLOG language.

The chapter opens with a discussion of the goal-oriented approach of PROLOG. The basics of PROLOG are then illustrated by means of an example program that defines family relations. This example is then extended to show how unification, backtracking, recursion, negation, data abstraction and information hiding are handled in PROLOG.

Backtracking is an important feature of PROLOG and the use of the cut operation to control this process is examined.

Finally, a PROLOG program that performs simple symbolic differentiation is presented.

10.1   The PROLOG approach

The majority of programming languages concentrate on how operations are carried out. PROLOG, on the other hand, is **goal oriented**; that is, the programmer defines the problem to be solved – the goal. The programmer is not expected to give a detailed solution of how such a goal can be achieved; this is left to the PROLOG system itself. Such a design feature has evolved in part because PROLOG was developed in an artificial intelligence environment where practitioners are encouraged to think in terms of the goals rather than the means of satisfying such goals.

A PROLOG program describes how a goal can be satisfied by giving a list of subgoals whose achievement will result in the fulfillment of the goal. As alternative subgoals can be provided, there may be more than one way in which a goal may be achieved. A subgoal may be an assertion, which evaluates to either true or false, or, alternatively, achieving a subgoal may require the PROLOG system to generate and then try to achieve further subgoals.

Execution of a PROLOG program, therefore, amounts to trying to satisfy a goal. It starts by trying to satisfy the list of subgoals and if failure occurs, it **backtracks** and tries an alternative set of subgoals. If the system runs out of alternatives, then it has failed to achieve the goal. The power of PROLOG lies in the fact that the selection of goals and backtracking are built in, while in most other languages such operations would have to be explicitly programmed.

PROLOG programs have both a *declarative* and a *procedural* meaning. The declarative (or descriptive) meaning is concerned with the objects and their relationships, as defined by the program. The procedural meaning is concerned with how and in what order such relationships are evaluated to obtain a solution. Ideally, programmers would prefer to restrict their attention to the declarative meaning and leave the matter of the efficiency of the search processes to the implementation. Such an approach tends towards pure logic programming, but has as yet not proved very effective.

PROLOG programs are significantly slower than programs written in traditional imperative languages, but it is possible that, in the future, efficient PROLOG implementations will be provided by re-examining basic computer architecture. Just how successfully a new computer architecture can be designed to support logic languages like PROLOG is, however, still a matter for speculation.

10.2   The basics of PROLOG

This section gives an overview of PROLOG, looking at its basic mechanisms and illustrating them by an example. As with most programming languages, problems can be solved in PROLOG in many different ways and no definitive PROLOG style has, as yet, emerged that has had general approval, such as structured programming for imperative languages.

Problem solving in PROLOG is achieved by identifying the basic objects to be manipulated and describing the relationships between these objects. This is accomplished by **facts** and **rules**.

* The facts about objects are declared to be always true.
* The rules about objects and their relationships state that a statement is true if certain stipulated goals and subgoals are satisfied.

Finally, a PROLOG program can be asked **questions**. These questions are about objects and their relationships and are concerned with the satisfying of goals. A question may be concerned with a single goal or a series of goals. In some circumstances, more than one answer will satisfy the goals and PROLOG can be programmed to find as many solutions as the programmer desires, and are available.

To illustrate how PROLOG programs are written, here is an example that defines family relations. The details of the family can be described by the following facts:

```
male(philip).
female(elizabeth).
male(charles).
female(anne).
male(andrew).
male(edward).
female(diana).
male(william).
male(harry).
parents(charles, elizabeth, philip).
parents(anne, elizabeth, philip).
parents(andrew, elizabeth, philip).
parents(edward, elizabeth, philip).
parents(william, diana, charles).
parents(harry, diana, charles).
```

where **parents(A, B, C)** means the parents of **A** are mother **B** and father **C**. Such facts can be represented in many different ways. For example, instead of:

```
parents(charles, elizabeth, philip).
```

the following two binary relationships could be used:

```
mother(charles, elizabeth).
father(charles, philip).
```

Similarly **male(philip)** could be expressed as the binary relationship:

```
sex(philip, masculine).
```

The information on this family can be extended by adding new facts and also by adding rules. For example, the concept of a person being someone's brother can be introduced. This could be defined by the following rule:

```
brother(X, Y):– male(X),
               parents(X, M, F),
               parents(Y, M, F).
```

This rule should be interpreted as stating that if it is the case that the result of evaluating all three subgoals:

male(X),
parents(X, M, F),
parents(Y, M, F).

which make up the **body** of the rule is true, then it is the case that the result of evaluating the **head** of the rule:

brother(X, Y)

is also true. Note that the commas between the conditions are the same as the logical *and*. Note also that PROLOG has the convention of starting variables with capital letters and values with lower case letters. As there is no assignment, variables in PROLOG are different from variables in an imperative programming language like Pascal. They correspond more closely to Pascal parameters than to Pascal variables.

Questions, unification and backtracking

A PROLOG program can be asked questions at any stage. Writing:

?– parents(william, diana, charles).

asks the question 'Is it the case that the parents of **william** are **diana** and **charles**?'. In this case, the answer to the question is 'yes' as the question can be matched to one of the set of facts.

Facts, rules and questions are examples of **clauses** in PROLOG. A PROLOG program consists of a set of clauses with each clause being terminated by a full stop. A clause is considered to have a **head** and a **body**. Facts are clauses with a head but no body; questions have no head only a body; and rules have both a head and a body. The body part of a clause gives a list of the subgoals. If it is a question, then it asks if such goals are true; if it is a rule, then it is defining the goals that can be satisfied to make the clause head true.

Here is a slightly more complicated question:

?– brother(edward, anne).

The PROLOG proof process involves generating subgoals and instantiating (that is, replacing) PROLOG variables by values. Using the rule:

brother(X, Y) :– male(X),
parents(X, M, F),
parents(Y, M, F).

the substitutions **X ← edward** and **Y ← anne** are made and the following subgoals attempted:

male(edward),
parents(edward, M, F),
parents(anne, M, F).

The first subgoal is true, as it matches one of the facts. The program must now find values for **M** and **F** so that it can match:

parents(edward, M, F)

Matching this subgoal to the fact:

parents(edward, elizabeth, philip)

causes the substitutions **M ← elizabeth** and **F ← philip**. The same substitutions for **M** and **F** must be made in the third subgoal giving:

parents(anne, elizabeth, philip)

which can be seen to match one of the facts. As the three subgoals have been satisfied, so has the original goal. The process of finding a suitable set of values which can be substituted for variables, so that a goal can be matched to a fact or to the head of a rule, is called **unification**. The matching used by PROLOG systems does not exactly correspond to unification in logic. However, the differences are minor and subtle and interested readers are referred to *PROLOG for Programmers* (Kluzniak, 1985).

Straightforward questions such as the one just examined would be of little interest in a general problem-solving situation and the questions asked would almost certainly contain variables. Thus, a question like:

?– brother(X, anne).

would require a slightly more complex matching process, since it requires a value for X that satisfies the goal. After making the substitution **Y ← anne**, the subgoals are:

male(X),
parents(X, M, F),
parents(anne, M, F).

The first fact with which **male(X)** can be matched is **male(philip)**. Therefore, the substitution **X ← philip** is made and the following goal attempted:

parents(philip, M, F)

As there is no fact that matches this goal, it fails. The program must now backtrack and attempt an alternative way of achieving the goal **male(X)**. This time, the substitution **X ← charles** is tried, which satisfies both the subgoals **male(charles)** and **parents(charles, M, F)** as one of the facts is:

parents(charles, elizabeth, philip)

As the third subgoal matches the fact:

parents(anne, elizabeth, philip)

the PROLOG system will respond with something like:

X = charles

If a semicolon is typed in response to this answer, the system will attempt to find further matches for the original question by backtracking to find other ways of matching the subgoals. In this case, the other answers are **andrew** and **edward**. The semicolon is the logical *or* and can be used elsewhere in PROLOG with this meaning.

An alternative to asking 'Who is the brother of **anne**?' is 'Who is **edward** the brother of?'.

    ?– brother(edward, X).

The matching process will again give the answer:

    X = charles

If the system is asked for further matches, it will eventually give the match **edward**. Such a result means that the original rule for **brother(X, Y)** was insufficiently specified, and it must be redefined to exclude people being considered brothers of themselves.

As backtracking is such an intrinsic part of PROLOG, here is a more complicated example to show how the backtracking process operates. Suppose that the facts are:

    mother(jane, george).
    father(john, george).
    brother(bill, john).

and the rules are:

    parent(X, Y) :– mother(X, Y).
    parent(X, Y) :– father(X, Y).
    uncle(Z, Y) :– parent(P, Y), brother(Z, P).

If the goal is:

    ?– uncle(X, george).

the steps in the solution process are as follows.

(1)   The substitutions **Y ← george** and **Z ← X** result in the subgoals:

        parent(P, george), brother(X, P).

(2)   Using the rule:

        parent(X, Y) :– mother(X, Y).

        the goal **mother(P, george)** is attempted and, as this is matched by the fact **mother(jane, george)**, the substitution **P ← jane** takes place.

(3)   The subgoal **brother(X, jane)** is now attempted, but it fails as there is no fact with which it can be matched.

(4)   The system must now backtrack to **parent(X, Y)** and try the alternative rule:

        parent(X, Y) :- father(X, Y).

        The goal is now **father(P, george)** and this is matched by the fact **father(john, george)** and so **P ← john**.

(5) The goal **brother(X, john)** is now attempted, which is matched with the fact **brother(bill, john)** giving **X ← bill**.

(6) The goal in the original question is now satisfied since both its subgoals are satisfied. The PROLOG system will respond with something like:

   X = bill

An important factor in all backtracking techniques is the ordering; in PRO-LOG's case, the ordering of the subgoals and the facts. Order is necessary so that the search can be carried out systematically and to prevent the occurrence of infinite loops. Ordering also influences the speed of the searching process and good choices can have a considerable effect on the efficiency. For example, a good heuristic is to place those subgoals that are liable to be most difficult to satisfy as early as possible since this will normally reduce the amount of backtracking.

Recursion in PROLOG

Recursion plays a central role in PROLOG, as it does in functional languages. As with all recursive situations, there must be a rule to halt the recursion in addition to a recursive rule. For example, the rule:

   child(X, Y) :– mother(Y, X).
   child(X, Y) :– father(Y, X).

says that **X** is a child of a parent **Y**. Such a relation can be generalized to **X** is a descendant of **Y**, and this can operate over as many generations as necessary. In PROLOG, **descendant** could be defined as follows:

   descendant(X, Y) :– child(X, Y).
   descendant(X, Y) :– child(X, Z),
   **   descendant(Z, Y).**

This defines both the recursive definition and the definition which halts the recursion. Both of these definitions are needed, since without the first one, the recursion will be infinite, while the first one alone is an incomplete and restricted definition of descendant. The two definitions are often considered together to form a *procedure*.

Negation

Some PROLOG implementations provide **not** as a built-in procedure. If such a facility is available, it is used as a prefix operator, as in:

   ?– not typhoid(bill).

However, care must be taken in interpreting the answer to this question, as negation is not the same as in mathematics.

PROLOG uses the **closed-world assumption** and thus assumes that all the facts about the world are included in the model. Anything not derivable is therefore false. When PROLOG has to process **not typhoid(bill)**, it tries to prove that **bill** has typhoid and it then negates the result. The **not** goal therefore succeeds in two situations:

(1)   When **bill** has definitely not got typhoid.

(2)   When it cannot prove **bill** has typhoid.

The problem of using the closed-world assumption with negation is that the negation of anything not derivable is considered true.

10.3   Data objects

As in most languages, both simple and structured data objects are allowed in PROLOG. Simple data objects are numbers and character strings (also known as **atoms**).

Chapter 6 showed how records in Pascal can be represented by a tree. Structured data objects in PROLOG are also of this nature. The Pascal record:

```
type name = packed array [1 .. 12] of char;
     fullname =
        record
           forename : name;
           surname : name
        end;
     student =
        record
           person : fullname;
           age : integer
        end;
```

could be represented in PROLOG as an object with the structure:

student(fullname(Forename, Surname), Age)

The name part of a structure in PROLOG is called a **functor**. Hence, **student** and **fullname** are functors. The components of a structure are given in brackets.

A structure can be used in facts and rules, as in:

attends(student(fullname(mary, smith), 20), stirling).
attends(student(fullname(joe, brown), 25), stirling).
maturestudent(Surname) :–
    attends(student(fullname(Forename, Surname), Age),
      University), Age > 23.

PROLOG can then be asked questions like:

?– maturestudent(X).

to which the answer is:

   X = brown

Figure 10.1
The structure of
a list.

A database can be built up from a collection of PROLOG facts and the questioning facility used to query the database and the matching mechanisms used to retrieve structured information.

An important structure in PROLOG is the list. It is defined using the special functor . as is shown in the following list representation, which is built from the four atoms **p**, **q**, **r** and **s**:

.(p, .(q, .(r, .(s, []))))

where [] represents the empty list. As lists are used so frequently in PROLOG, a special notation is available. The above list can be written as:

[p, q, r, s]

As is the case in functional languages, a PROLOG list consists of a head, which may be any PROLOG object, in this case **p**, and a tail which must be a list, in this case **[q, r, s]**. A list with the head **X** and the tail **Y** can be written as **[X | Y]**, which allows pattern matching operations on lists in the same way as is done with the :: operator of ML. PROLOG considers lists to be binary trees and the list **[p, q, r, s]** is represented as the tree shown in Figure 10.1.

PROLOG can be used to support the ideas of data abstraction and information hiding by means of what are called **selector relations**. Such relations are used to access components of a structure as illustrated in the following example which selects the **forename** of a **student**. The selector **forename** can be defined by means of the clause:

forename(student(fullname(Forename, Surname), Age), Forename).

although, as the definition of **forename** does not depend on the values of **Surname** and **Age**, this would normally be written as:

forename(student(fullname(Forename,_),_), Forename).

where each occurrence of the underscore character represents a different (anonymous) variable. In PROLOG, the scope of a variable is restricted to the clause in which it is used. Hence, both occurrences of **Forename** refer to the same variable, but the identifier **Forename** has no significance outside this clause, and of course it has no connection with the functor **forename**. Conventional software engineering wisdom would suggest that it is inadvisable to use two identifiers that only differ in the case of their first letter. Such usage does, however, seem to be common practice in PROLOG.

The result of asking the question:

?– S1 = student(fullname(john, smith), 18), forename(S1, X).

will be:

X = john

while the answer to:

?– attends(Person, stirling), forename(Person, mary).

is:

Person = student(fullname(mary, smith), 20)

This illustrates that once selectors such as **forename** have been defined, the user no longer needs to know about the structure of **student**. If, during the development of a program, the structure is changed, then all that is needed is a change to the definitions of selectors such as **forename**. Their use could continue unchanged. Hiding the representation of a structure in this way does, however, remove some of the advantages of pattern matching.

10.4   Efficiency in PROLOG

From a theoretical standpoint, all the user needs to know about the execution of a PROLOG question clause is that it terminates. It is not too difficult for logic languages to attain this goal in theory, but if they wish to be considered seriously as practical programming languages, they must do more than guarantee termination – they must search reasonably efficiently.

When PROLOG is asked a question, a simple backtracking strategy is instituted which is normally **depth-first tree search** with subgoal evaluation from left to right. It is, therefore, of some importance to think about the order in which the goals are listed, as the ordering of the subgoals in a rule is likely to have a considerable bearing on its speed of execution. Such considerations are far from trivial and in complex search problems of the type likely to be encountered in an Expert System, the ordering and methods of searching are often the crux of the solution process.

Allowing automatic backtracking relieves the programmer of the problems of designing a detailed search algorithm. This is satisfactory in small problems or when the searching is not too deep. However, it soon becomes clear to a programmer that complete reliance on the PROLOG search mechanisms produces some very inefficient programs. PROLOG gives the programmer some control of the backtracking process by the **cut** facility. The cut operation, indicated in a PROLOG program by !, is used to stop backtracking. For example, consider the rules:

R :– G1, G2, !, G3.
R :– G4.

where **G1, G2, G3** and **G4** are goals and ! is a cut (or pseudo-goal). When the cut is encountered, **G1** and **G2** will have already been satisfied. The cut ensures that they are frozen in that state, since no further backtracking is allowed. If goal **G3** fails, we will not therefore try to achieve either **G1** or **G2** in some other way. Furthermore, it will not consider the other rule for **R**; that is, it will not try to achieve goal **G4**.

One example where cuts are useful is in rules that have mutually exclusive clauses. A function which is –1, 0, +1 when its argument is negative, zero or positive, respectively, can be expressed in Pascal as:

if $x < 0$ **then** $F := -1$
else if $x = 0$ **then** $F := 0$
else $F := +1;$

The PROLOG rules without cuts could be:

f(X, –1) :– X < 0.
f(X, 0) :– X = 0.
f(X, 1) :–X > 0.

but this could lead to unnecessary inefficiencies and backtracking due to the exclusive nature of the three clauses. A more efficient PROLOG implementation would be:

f(X, –1) :– X < 0, !.
f(X, 0) :– X = 0, !.
f(X, 1).

Here, the use of cuts prevents the program from trying alternatives that cannot succeed. Hence, if the condition **X < 0** is satisfied, neither of the alternatives will ever be tried.

The objection to cuts is that they can change the nature of a PROLOG program. Provided that it terminates, a PROLOG program without cuts has the same declarative and procedural meaning. As has been seen, the procedures may be slow, but they will arrive at the correct answer. When cuts are included, there is no longer a guarantee that the declarative and procedural meanings are the same. When the use of cuts does not affect the declarative meaning, they are called **green cuts**. In other words, if the cuts are removed the answers will be unchanged, and so the cuts are achieving improved efficiency without any disadvantages. Cuts that affect the declarative meaning are called **red cuts**. The use of these types of cuts is more dangerous and they can easily lead to errors since the program's meaning cannot be deduced from the program without cuts.

10.5 A PROLOG example

Chapter 9 looked at LISP and LOGO programs that performed simple symbolic differentiation. This section looks at a PROLOG solution to this problem.

Suppose that an expression such as:

4 * power(x, 3)

is to be converted into **12 * power(x, 2)** and:

power(x, 3)

to be converted into **3 * power(x, 2)**. To differentiate an expression **Y** with respect to **X** giving the result **E**, the heads of the rules will have the form **derive(Y, X, E)**. A first attempt at the rules might be:

> **derive(A * F, X, A * C) :– integer(A), derive(F, X, C).**
> **derive(power(X, N), X, N * power(X, N–1)) :– integer(N).**

where the goal **integer(N)** succeeds when **N** is instantiated to an integer number. The first rule defines the derivative of **A * F** with respect to **X** (where **A** is an integer) to be **A** times the derivative of **F** with respect to **X**. The second rule defines the derivative of **power(X, N)** with respect to **X** to be **N * power(X, N – 1)**. These rules deal with the differentiation, but do not carry out the necessary arithmetic. Using these rules, the result of:

> **?– derive(4 * power(x, 3), x, E).**

is:

> **E = 4 * (3 * power(x, 3 – 1))**

> Arithmetic is performed by means of the **is** operator. The effect of:

> **P is N – 1**

is to evaluate the expression **N – 1** and associate its value with **P**. The **is** operator is used in the following two modifications to the rules for **derive**:

> **derive(A * F, X, G * B) :–**
> **integer(A), derive(F, X, D * B), G is A * D.**
> **derive(power(X, N), X, N * power(X, P)) :–**
> **integer(N), P is N – 1.**

The required PROLOG program is therefore short, although its effect is not immediately obvious. Consider the matching process for the question:

> **?– derive(4 * power(x, 3), x, E).**

The aim here is to match this with:

> **derive(A * F, X, G * B)**

which means that after the substitutions:

> **A ← 4, F ← power(x, 3), X ← x**

the three subgoals to be achieved are:

> **integer(4), derive(power(x, 3), x, D * B), G is 4 * D**

The first subgoal is achieved, but the second subgoal:

> **derive(power(x, 3), x, D * B)**

does not match with the first rule for **derive** and so PROLOG tries to match it with the second:

> **derive(power(X, N), X, N * power(X, P))**

On making the substitutions:

X ← x, N ← 3, D ← 3, B ← power(x, P)

the new subgoals are:

integer(3), P is 3 – 1

The goals **integer(3)** and **P is 3 – 1** (yielding **P ← 2**) are achieved. PROLOG has, therefore, succeeded in matching **D * B** to:

3 * power(x, 2)

The third of the original three subgoals is:

G is A * D

and so **G** is 12. **E** has, therefore, been matched with:

12 * power(x, 2)

The PROLOG program to solve this problem is much shorter than either the LISP or LOGO solution, which are in turn much shorter than a solution in an imperative language like Pascal. This is because much more of the processing is carried out behind the scenes by the PROLOG system.

10.6 The future of PROLOG

Although PROLOG has been available for many years, it was only in the mid 1980s that large numbers of users started to use it for programming. Fortunately, PROLOG is an attractive language and is not offputting to the beginner. However, the newcomer does face problems in trying to acquire a PROLOG programming style and technique.

The book by Bratko (1990) includes a chapter on the subject and suggests that clauses should be short with only a few goals in their body. The more general guidance in Bratko's book is not dissimilar from the advice on structuring a program that would be given to a new programmer using any language. PROLOG does support the implementation of top-down design principles with the subgoals acting as subdivisions of the tasks. Each subgoal can then be subdivided again if further refinements are required.

Case analysis can be implemented conveniently by alternative rules or clauses for the same predicate. Since there is no such thing as a global variable in PROLOG, the ideas of information hiding are easier to implement than in many imperative languages.

For many programmers, PROLOG often poses readability problems, which is partly due to the fact that it can be highly recursive. Although recursion is a powerful and useful programming tool, it does not always aid the transparency of the code. Large PROLOG programs can also lack structure and indeed there is nothing in the language to match the module facilities of Modula-2 and Ada, which impose form and structure on the programmer. This seems an area where improvements are required.

Objections to PROLOG have mainly come from three types of programmer. Firstly, the users of imperative languages have attacked its inefficiencies and claimed that it is unrealistic to consider PROLOG as a serious language for the practical programmer. However, the speed of modern hardware means that PROLOG, although still slower than other languages, is fast enough for many applications. Also, some of the inefficiency caused by the von Neumann architecture of traditional computers may be removed by new hardware configurations.

The second group of objectors are the orthodox mathematicians and logicians who find that the use of cuts and negation (based on the closed-world assumption) take PROLOG away from the realm of a pure logic language. Their objection is valid but misplaced, since programming languages are not pure mathematical objects, but practical tools for solving problems, and a pure logic language can never be that.

Finally, there have been a lot of objections to PROLOG from the artificial intelligence community. This is ironic because it is in AI that many of the most suitable applications for the language exist. The reason for such objections is probably due to the strong hold that languages like LISP have for AI practitioners. It does seem that in the last few years there have been serious attempts to look at both functional and logic languages objectively and examine their strengths and weaknesses. Such moves are welcome and will help to remove the attitude of mind that sees PROLOG and LISP as competitors. These two languages take different approaches to problem solving and should be viewed as alternatives rather than rivals.

Summary

(1) Logic programming is almost exclusively carried out in PROLOG.

(2) PROLOG is a declarative language and is goal oriented.

(3) A program in PROLOG consists of clauses, which can be of three types: facts, rules and questions.

(4) Facts about objects are declared to be always true.

(5) A rule about objects and their relationships gives the goals and subgoals that must be satisfied to make the head of the rule true.

(6) Questions require a goal or series of goals to be satisfied and invoke a process of matching. If a goal fails, an alternative is tried by backtracking.

(7) The operations of selecting goals and backtracking are carried out by the PROLOG system itself. However, the efficiency of these operations can be influenced by the ordering of the subgoals in a rule.

(8) Recursion is an important feature of many PROLOG rules.

(9) PROLOG is well suited to applications involving database queries.

(10) Efficiency in PROLOG can be improved by cuts, which are used to limit backtracking.

(11) PROLOG uses the closed-world assumption and assumes that anything not derivable is false.

EXERCISES

10.1 Using the facts and rules given at the beginning of Section 10.2 for family relations:

(a) Explain in detail how the goals in the following PROLOG questions are achieved:

```
?– brother(william, harry).
?– brother(X, william).
```

(b) Define a rule for **sister** and show the steps in answering the questions:

```
?– sister(X, edward).
?– sister(X, william).
```

(c) How can the brother and sister rules be altered so that a person is not considered to be their own brother or sister?

10.2 Given the facts:

```
loves(john, jane).
loves(bill, jane).
loves(james, jane).
loves(mary, bill).
loves(jane, james).
```

and the rule:

```
goodmatch(X, Y) :– loves(X, Y), loves(Y, X).
```

show the backtracking involved in answering the question:

```
?– goodmatch(A, B).
```

10.3 Given the facts:

```
district(stirling, dunblane).
region(central, stirling).
country(scotland, central).
continent(europe, scotland).
```

define a rule whose head is **within(X, Y)** and which expresses the fact that **Y** is within the geographical region **X**. Show how this can be done using **district**, **region**, **country** and **continent**. How can the facts be redefined and recursion used to simplify the definition of **within**?

10.4 An object **X** is a member of a list **L** if **X** is the head of **L** or if **X** is a member of the tail of **L**. Use this definition of membership to define **member(X, L)** and then trace the actions required by the PROLOG question:

```
?– member(X, [john, bill, fred, peter]), X = fred.
```

10.5 Compare and contrast functional languages, logic languages and object-oriented languages as exemplified by ML, PROLOG and Eiffel, respectively. Discuss areas in which they each have particular strengths and weaknesses.

10.6 Give an example to show how the ordering of the subgoals in a PROLOG rule can make a significant difference in the efficiency of processing of a question.

10.7 Define the minimum function as two rules whose head is **minimum(X, Y, Minval)**. Give an initial definition without a cut and then show how its efficiency can be improved by using a cut.

10.8 Discuss the difference between green and red cuts and give an example of each.

10.9 Compare the use of pattern matching in ML and PROLOG.

BIBLIOGRAPHY

An introduction to the use of logic in problem solving has been given by Kowalski (1979), whose ideas were a major influence in the development of PROLOG. For many years, the only book on PROLOG was Clocksin (1984), although several user manuals were also available. In the last few years many books have appeared, one of the most interesting being that by Bratko (1990).

Bratko, I. (1990), *PROLOG Programming for Artificial Intelligence* (Second Edition), Addison-Wesley.

Clocksin, W. F. and Mellish, C. S. (1984), *Programming in PROLOG* (Second Edition), Springer-Verlag.

Kluzniak, F. and Szpakowicz, S. (1985), *PROLOG for Programmers*, Academic Press.

Kowalski, R. (1979), *Logic for Problem Solving*, North Holland.

Concurrency

CONTENTS

11.1 **Introduction**   260
11.2 **UNIX pipes**   264
11.3 **Monitors**   265
11.4 **The rendezvous**   268
11.5 **Real-time programming**   276

This chapter looks at the language features that are used to support concurrent programming. It starts with a description of the concepts involved and how processes can pass information to one another and synchronize their actions.

The two main methods of communication are through shared variables and by message passing. This chapter looks at how the problems associated with shared variables can be overcome using critical regions and monitors and how this is implemented in Modula-2. As an example of message passing, Ada and occam are discussed and it is shown how the rendezvous mechanism achieves both communication and synchronization.

Finally, the chapter considers the problems encountered in real-time systems and the facilities that Ada provides in this area.

11.1 Introduction

During the execution of a sequential program, statements are executed one at a time in some predefined order. In a concurrent system, several sequential programs or program fragments are viewed as being executed in parallel. Each of the sequential programs or program fragments is usually called a **process** or a **task**.

An obvious use of concurrency is to make a program run faster. Often, the precise order in which certain program statements are to be executed is unimportant. For example, if a, b, c and d refer to different variables, and it is assumed that there is no aliasing, the order in which the assignments:

$$a := a + 5; b := d * 6; c := d - 94$$

take place does not matter; so, if three processors are available, the three statements could be performed in parallel. An optimizing compiler can be used to determine which statements do not interfere with one another or, alternatively, this decision could be left to the programmer using a notation like the ALGOL 68 **collateral** statement. When statements in ALGOL 68 are separated by commas instead of semicolons, the order of execution is not specified. Hence, the statement:

begin
    $a := a + 5, b := d * 6, c := d - 94$
end

can be used as an indication to the compiler that code can be generated for parallel execution. However, care must be taken when using such constructs. As the statements in:

begin
    $a := a + 5, b := d * 6, c := b - 94$
end

are not independent of one another, the result depends on the precise order in which the assignments are carried out.

In the language occam, each statement is considered to be a process and indentation is used to show program structure. The construction:

```
SEQ
    a := a + 5
    b := d * 6
    c := d - 94
```

indicates that three processes are to occur in sequence while:

```
PAR
    a := a + 5
    b := d * 6
    c := d - 94
```

indicates that they may occur in parallel.

In general, identifying the components of a sequential program that can be correctly executed in parallel is far from easy due to the possibility of side effects.

This problem does not, of course, arise with purely functional languages as, due to referential transparency, the order in which expressions are evaluated does not matter.

Parallel hardware

A common situation in programming is a loop in which the same calculations are performed in turn on the different elements of an array as in:

for $i := 1$ **to** 100 **do**
  $a[i] := 3 * b[i]$

Although languages like Pascal impose an order on the processing of the elements in arrays a and b, the order does not in fact matter: given 100 processors, each of the 100 assignment statements could be performed in parallel.

High-performance computers sometimes include what are known as **array processors**, which allow the same operation to be applied simultaneously to different pieces of data – for example, array elements. In applications where a large amount of time is spent processing arrays, the use of an array processor can therefore significantly speed up the processing.

Several extensions to FORTRAN have been designed to aid the identification of loops in which an array processor can be used, but the simplest language solution is to allow complete arrays as operands. The above loop would then reduce to the single statement:

  $a := 3 * b$

which can be evaluated using a loop on a single processor machine, while it is clear that it is safe to perform the operations on each of the elements in parallel when an array processor is available. APL, which has many operations that act on complete arrays, is well suited for use with an array processor.

Other parallel architectures include **multiprocessor systems**, where a set of processors all share the same memory, but where each processor can act independently, and **distributed systems** where the processors do not share memory, but communicate over a **communications network**. An example of a distributed system is a network of diskless workstations under the control of a distributed operating system. In a more **loosely coupled** distributed system, the processors could be many miles apart. Distributed systems introduce extra problems; as the processors become more distant, there is an increase in communication delays and in the possibility of communications failure. They do, however, support the creation of fault-tolerant systems as, if one processor in the network fails, work can be transferred to another.

Process scheduling

A major area in which concurrency is important is in the design and implementation of operating systems. Modern operating systems allow many users to interact with a computer simultaneously, or for a single user at a workstation to have programs running in different windows. When several processors are available, this is called **multiprocessing**; when there is only one CPU, and so there is only pseudo-concurrency, this is called **multiprogramming**. In a multiprogramming system only one process may be active at any given moment while all others are suspended. However, the speed of the computer allows each program to be given sufficient slices of time for it to appear to have sole control of the system.

As it is often the case that there are more processes ready to run than there are available processors, a scheduling algorithm is needed to decide which processes are to be chosen. In the multiprogramming case, only one processor is available and so the scheduling algorithm has to choose one process. Simple approaches to this problem include:

- allowing the process that has been waiting longest to go next, or

- attaching a priority to each process and allowing the process with the highest priority to be the one to proceed.

Whichever method is used, it is important that it allows what is called **fair scheduling** to operate, where all waiting processes are eventually given a chance.

Process synchronization and communication

As the processes in a concurrent system need not be independent, there must be some means through which they can pass information to one another and through which their actions can be **synchronized**. For example, one process may have to wait for results to be produced by another process before it is able to continue. A simple way of achieving synchronization is for a process to execute an instruction (often called a **wait instruction**) so that the process is suspended until another process sends a signal to wake it up. However, care must be taken to avoid a situation where two processes are each waiting for a signal from the other and so neither is able to continue. Such a situation is called a **deadlock**.

There are two main ways in which processes communicate with one another. The simpler method is to have **shared variables**. The problem with this method is that one process may update a shared variable while another process is examining it. This problem can be overcome by the notion of **critical regions** of programs within which any access to shared variables takes place. At any one time only one process may be within a particular critical region. If a second process wishes to enter the region, it is suspended until the first process has left the critical region. This is called **mutual exclusion** and is often implemented by means of a **monitor module**, which provides procedures for the safe updating of shared variables. An important feature of a monitor is that the critical regions are collected together in a module rather than being distributed throughout a program. (Monitors are discussed in detail in Section 11.3.) Communication using shared variables is obviously best suited to systems in which the processes physically share store.

The other method of communication is for the processes to pass **messages** to one another and this method is suited to distributed as well as to shared memory systems. There are two approaches to message passing; synchronous and asynchronous.

In **synchronous message passing**, synchronization is achieved as well as communication because a sending process has to wait for its message to be accepted and a receiving process may have to wait for a message to be sent. Synchronous message passing was proposed by Hoare (1985) in the experimental language CSP (Communicating Sequential Processes) and is the basis for both the Ada **rendezvous** mechanism and for communication in occam. (This mechanism is described in Section 11.4.)

In **asynchronous message passing**, the sending process continues execution after sending a message. Asynchronous message passing is more flexible, but gives the programmer less control over the order of events. It can be constructed from synchronous message passing primitives by the introduction of a buffer process to de-couple the two communicating processes.

Concurrency in design

So far, the discussion has concentrated on how concurrency can be used to improve efficiency when parallel hardware is available. There are, however, situations in which the solution to a problem is most easily expressed in terms of a set of communicating processes. A good example of this is simulation, which attempts to model a real-life situation in which several activities occur in parallel and interact with one another. When used in simulation, concurrency is not being used to promote efficiency; rather, it is being used because it leads to a more natural representation of the solution to a problem. Writing a solution as a concurrent program may be the best approach even when the execution of the program is carried out on a computer with a single processor and each of the processes is executed in turn. The first language designed to support this approach to simulation was SIMULA.

As a set of communicating processes has many similarities with a set of concurrent objects, where each object has a local state, local processing ability and communicates with other objects by message passing, it is not surprising that several experimental concurrent object-oriented languages, such as Emerald, have been developed. Considering a concurrent system as a set of concurrent objects can also be of use in the specification and design phases of software development when the resulting implementation language is not object oriented, but is a language such as Ada. The approach of object-oriented development can, therefore, be used with concurrent as well as with sequential systems.

Problems

Concurrency and process interaction introduce many new problems into programs, such as the management of shared resources and the possibility of deadlocks. Another major problem is that when several processes are executing concurrently, it is not always possible to predict their relative speeds or, on a single processor system, the order in which they may be scheduled, and this may change with the system load. Running the same program with the same data may not, therefore, always give the same results. Such programs are said to be **non-deterministic** and are clearly very difficult to debug.

Ways in which process synchronization and communication can be implemented in a safe and efficient way are still being actively researched. The usual assumption is that processes normally proceed independently and only interact with one another infrequently. That is the origin of ideas such as that of **communicating sequential processes**.

11.2   UNIX pipes

The next three sections use the standard producer/consumer problem to illustrate how the passing of information and process synchronization can be implemented in C, Modula-2, Ada and occam. A consumer process must wait for a piece of information to be produced, while a producer process cannot pass a new piece of information until the previous piece has been consumed. The standard solution is to have a buffer between the two processes.

C is a sequential language. Separate sequential C programs can, however, run concurrently and their effect combined by the use of the UNIX **pipe** mechanism, where the output from one program becomes the input to another. Consider the UNIX command:

A1 | A2 | A3

where *A1, A2* and *A3* are three programs and | represents a pipe. The output from program *A1* becomes the input to program *A2*, and the output from *A2* becomes the input to program *A3*. The pipe is a very powerful feature of UNIX which allows complex actions to be performed by linking together a series of simple programs.

The solution to the producer/consumer problem is to have two sequential programs, representing the producer and the consumer respectively, linked by a pipe which acts as the buffer, as in:

producer | consumer

The C code for the producer program is:

```
#include <stdio.h>
main ()
{
    char c;
    int more = 1;
    while (more)
    {
        /* code to generate next item */
        putchar(c);
    }
}
```

while the C code for the consumer is:

```
#include <stdio.h>
main ()
{
    char c;
    int more = 1;
    while (more)
    {
        c = getchar();
        /* code to consume next item */
    }
}
```

Communication is achieved through the normal I/O commands. Program *consumer* cannot read information until it has been output by program *producer*, although there is no explicit synchronization between the two programs.

In writing programs *producer* and *consumer*, the programmer does not have to take into account the fact that they are to be run in parallel. Concurrency has therefore been left completely in the hands of the operating system, rather than being explicitly catered for in the program code.

11.3 Monitors

In Modula-2, processes communicate with one another through shared variables with monitors being used to guarantee mutual exclusion. Signals may be used to synchronize processes. A process may SEND a signal to wake up another process and it may WAIT until another process SENDs a signal to it. Processes WAITing on a signal are outside of the mutual exclusion provided by the monitor.

Signals are not part of the language, but are defined in a special library module called Processes. This module is used to implement the abstract data type SIGNAL together with the operations SEND, WAIT and Init which initializes a signal. Another exported procedure StartProcess is used to start a new process running. A possible implementation of Processes using **coroutines** is described by Wirth (1982). Coroutines are a simple way of simulating concurrency when only a single CPU is available. A coroutine can suspend itself and transfer control to another (named) coroutine. When a coroutine is re-activated by another coroutine, it continues execution at the point, and in the same state, at which it last relinquished control. Coroutines in Modula-2 are implemented in the predefined SYSTEM module.

Monitors are part of Modula-2 and are implemented as modules. They differ from ordinary modules in that they have a number in the heading that can give a priority to the monitor. Although the number must be present, it has no effect in many implementations of Modula-2! The important point about a monitor is that it guarantees that only one process may be actively executing a procedure in the monitor at any one time.

A possible Modula-2 program to implement the producer/consumer problem is given below:

```
MODULE ProduceConsume;
    FROM Processes IMPORT
        StartProcess, SEND, WAIT, SIGNAL, Init;

    TYPE Item = ...;
    ...

    MODULE Buffer[1];
        IMPORT SEND, WAIT, SIGNAL, Init, Item;
        EXPORT Give, Take;

        VAR TheBuffer : Item;
            Empty, Full : SIGNAL;
            BufferFull : BOOLEAN;

        PROCEDURE Give(x : Item);
        BEGIN
            IF BufferFull THEN
                WAIT(Empty)
            END;
            TheBuffer := x; BufferFull := TRUE;
            SEND(Full)
        END Give;

        PROCEDURE Take(VAR x : Item);
        BEGIN
            IF NOT BufferFull THEN
                WAIT(Full)
            END;
            x := TheBuffer; BufferFull := FALSE;
            SEND(Empty)
        END Take;

    BEGIN
        Init(Empty); Init(Full);
        BufferFull := FALSE
    END Buffer;

    PROCEDURE Producer;
        VAR Info : Item;
    BEGIN
        LOOP
            (*Code to produce an item*)
            Give(Info)
        END
    END Producer;
```

```
PROCEDURE Consumer;
   VAR NewInfo : Item;
BEGIN
   LOOP
      Take(NewInfo);
      (*Code to consume an item*)
   END
END Consumer;


BEGIN
   StartProcess(Producer, 300);
   StartProcess(Consumer, 300);

   ...

END ProduceConsume.
```

The monitor Buffer[1] guarantees mutually exclusive access to the shared variable TheBuffer as only one of the procedures Give and Take may be being executed at any one time.

Although, in most implementations, the execution of this Modula-2 program would not be carried out using true concurrency, when designing programs of this nature it is better to consider that processes such as Producer and Consumer actually run in parallel. In this way, the problem can be considered at an abstract level and implementation details can be ignored.

Consider the execution of this program. The body of module Buffer is first executed and this causes the variables Empty and Full of type SIGNAL to be initialized and the variable BufferFull to be set to FALSE. The Consumer and Producer processes (procedures) are then explicitly started by calls of StartProcess. The number in the call of StartProcess specifies how much workspace is required by the process. This is a surprisingly low level feature and ideally the compiler should be able to determine a suitable figure rather than leaving it to the user.

Now consider what happens if the Consumer process executes first. It calls procedure *Take* and is suspended at WAIT(Full) waiting for a Full signal to be sent. Once it has been suspended, process Consumer relinquishes exclusive access to the monitor and so a call of Give may now take place. After executing the code to produce an item, the Producer process calls procedure Give. As BufferFull is FALSE, the WAIT statement is not executed and execution proceeds.

Before the Producer process leaves Give, the statement SEND(Full) is executed. The Consumer process is now ready to regain exclusive access to the monitor. Therefore, once the Producer process has left Give, the Consumer process may resume execution of Take. The two processes are now able to proceed in parallel with Producer producing the next item while Consumer is consuming the last one. The use of WAIT together with the Boolean BufferFull is to provide synchronization and means that Producer cannot give a new item until Consumer has removed the previous one, and that Consumer cannot attempt to take an item which has not yet been produced.

Monitors have been found to be an effective way of implementing mutual exclusion. A major advantage is that, as they are implemented as a module, their internal details are hidden and protected from the processes that use them. However, as they are concerned with protecting access to shared variables, they are not well suited to systems where the processors do not physically share memory.

11.4 The rendezvous

Unlike Modula-2, Ada and occam have built-in features to support true concurrency involving processors with no shared memory. In Ada, each process is described by means of a task and, like packages, tasks have both a specification and a body.

As two Ada tasks can be declared within the same procedure, they can share access to non-local variables and, therefore, communicate through shared variables. However, the preferred method of inter-task communication in Ada is to avoid the use of shared variables and to use the rendezvous mechanism.

A task is entered by means of an **entry call**. An entry is similar to a procedure, the difference being that an entry call cannot proceed until the called task is ready to accept the call – that is, when there is a rendezvous. An entry call is, therefore, used both for inter-task communication and for synchronization.

A similar method operates in occam, but instead of a rendezvous consisting of an entry call and an accept statement, processes in occam communicate through named **channels**. One process writes information to a channel and the other process reads information from that channel. For example, one process may execute the occam command:

    link ! val

to put the value of val on channel link, while a second process reads the value into variable info by executing the command:

    link ? info

Communication is synchronized since neither process can proceed until the information transfer has taken place. This is the only way in which two processes can communicate in occam as modifying a shared variable is not permitted. The type of item carried on a channel has to be defined. If link is to carry integers, it would be declared as:

    CHAN OF INT link:

The rendezvous mechanism can be illustrated by looking at an Ada solution to the producer/consumer problem. The buffer monitor in the Modula-2 solution is replaced by a buffer task in Ada. This task has two entries, *give* and *take*, which, as they are given in the specification, are visible from outside the task and so may be called by other tasks. The bodies of the *give* and *take* entries are written as **accept** statements in the task body. The tasks *producer* and *consumer* closely parallel the two processes of the Modula-2 solution.

```
procedure produce_consume is
   type item is ...;

   task buffer is
      entry give(x : in item);
      entry take(x : out item);
   end buffer;

   task body buffer is
      the_buffer : item;
   begin
      loop
         accept give(x : in item) do
            the_buffer := x;
         end give;
         accept take(x : out item) do
            x := the_buffer;
         end take;
      end loop;
   end buffer;

   task producer;

   task body producer is
      info : item;
   begin
      loop
         --code to produce an item
         buffer.give(info);
      end loop;
   end producer;

   task consumer;

   task body consumer is
      new_info : item;
   begin
      loop
         buffer.take(new_info);
         --code to consume an item
      end loop;
   end consumer;

begin
   ...
end produce_consume;
```

Tasks are automatically started when the procedure in which they are declared is called. Hence, tasks *buffer, producer* and *consumer* are started by calling procedure *produce_consume.* If three processors are not available, then a decision must be made about which task is to be scheduled for execution first. As the three tasks have equal priority, the scheduling order is not defined by the Ada language, although in circumstances where it is important, it is possible to allocate different priorities to different tasks. The order in which the tasks are executed in this case does not matter.

First, consider task *buffer*. The entry *give* and the entry *take* are given in the specification of *buffer* and can be called by other tasks. An entry is called in the same way as a procedure with information being passed by parameters. The statements to be executed when an entry is called are given by an **accept** statement in the task body.

In the execution of the body of task *buffer*, the first statement in the loop is:

```
accept give(x : in item) do
    the_buffer := x;
end give;
```

This indicates that *buffer* is ready to accept a call of the *give* entry. As no such entry call has been made, the execution of task *buffer* is suspended.

Next, consider execution of the task *consumer*. After entering the loop, the first statement is:

```
buffer.take(new_info);
```

Task *consumer* therefore wishes to make a call of entry *buffer.take*, but as *buffer* is not ready to accept this call, task *consumer* has to be suspended.

Meanwhile the *producer* task will have been executing the code to produce an item before eventually executing the statement:

```
buffer.give(info);
```

As *buffer* is sitting waiting to accept this call, a rendezvous exists between the tasks *buffer* and *producer*. Task *producer* is suspended while the body of the **accept** statement is executed. This ensures that the body of the **accept** statement acts as a critical region where access to shared variables can take place. If this critical region did not exist, the value of *info* might be changed by subsequent execution of instructions in *producer*, before the parameter passing had been successfully completed.

To ensure that the execution of *producer* is not delayed for too long, the critical region should be kept as short as possible. Once the body of the **accept** statement has been executed, the rendezvous is over and both tasks are free to continue in parallel.

Task *producer* starts producing the next item while task *buffer* proceeds to accept the call of *take* from *consumer*. As the *consumer* task is suspended while the body of the *take* **accept** statement is executed, this guarantees that the value of the actual parameter *new_info* is updated before execution of *consumer* resumes. Once that rendezvous has been completed, *consumer* executes code to consume the item while *buffer* waits for the next call of *buffer.give*.

Thus, Ada uses the rendezvous mechanism to achieve both communication and synchronization with messages being passed as the parameters of an entry call. Message passing can be implemented on distributed systems as well as on systems involving shared memory.

A much shorter implementation of the producer/consumer problem can be given in occam. This implementation requires three processes each with a channel

parameter and a local variable. Each process consists of an infinite loop. The occam
process definitions are as follows:

```
PROC buffer(CHAN OF INT give, take)
    WHILE TRUE
        INT thebuffer:
        SEQ
            give ? thebuffer
            take ! thebuffer
:


PROC producer(CHAN OF INT tobuff)
    WHILE TRUE
        INT info:
        SEQ
            - - code to produce info
            tobuff ! info
:


PROC consumer(CHAN OF INT frombuff)
    WHILE TRUE
        INT newinfo:
        SEQ
            frombuff ? newinfo
            - - code to consume newinfo
:
```

A fourth process is now required to show that the three processes are to be executed in
parallel and to declare the channels through which the processes are to interact.
Hence:

```
CHAN OF INT in, out:
PAR
    producer(in)
    buffer(in, out)
    consumer(out)
```

Information is passed from producer to buffer via channel in and from buffer to consumer
via channel out. Interaction between the three processes is very similar to the Ada
inter-task communication described earlier although there is no need for the
concept of a critical region.

Ada versus occam

This section compares the approaches of Ada and occam to inter-process communication. A process initiates communication by making an entry call in Ada or by
putting information on a channel in occam. In the case of Ada, the called task does
not know the identity of the caller and an **accept** statement can accept entry calls
from several different tasks. This is not possible in occam where a channel only
enables communication to take place between two processes.

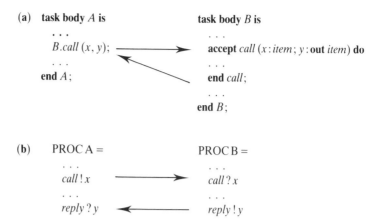

(a)   task body *A* is
           . . .
           B.*call* (*x*, *y*);
           . . .
           end *A*;

           task body *B* is
           . . .
           accept *call* (*x* : *item*; *y* : out *item*) do
           . . .
           end *call*;
           . . .
           end *B*;

(b)   PROC A =
           . . .
           call ! *x*
           . . .
           reply ? *y*
           . . .

           PROC B =
           . . .
           call ? *x*
           . . .
           reply ! *y*
           . . .

Figure 11.1
Data transfer
between processes
in Ada and occam.

Also, in occam, it is the initiating process which transfers information. There is no equivalent of the Ada **out** parameter where an initiating process receives information. Two-way transfer of information between occam processes requires a second rendezvous, as is shown in Figure 11.1. The occam approach is, therefore, at a lower level, but has the advantage that it can be implemented more efficiently.

The main disadvantage of the rendezvous approach is that it often requires a larger number of processes than that required when monitors are used. In the producer/consumer example, a passive buffer monitor in the Modula-2 solution was replaced by an active buffer process in the Ada and occam solutions. Therefore, although the Ada and occam solutions are simpler, they would seem to lead to higher run-time overheads when insufficient processors are available.

The approach in occam is that inter-process communication should be simple and fast and that having a large number of processes is not a problem. Indeed, this idea is central to the occam programming style. In Ada, however, the tasking overhead is high as the language is much more complex and is implemented on general-purpose computers, unlike occam which is implemented on an 'occam machine' (the **transputer**).

Because a source program describes a solution in terms of three processes, this does not mean that it must be implemented in that way. It is possible for an optimizing Ada compiler to remove processes, such as an active buffer, and to move the code to the calling tasks. This gives the advantage of being able to view a solution as if it involved separate processes without this necessarily leading to slower execution.

Larger buffers

When the Ada buffer can contain only one item, the *give* and *take* entries must be accepted alternately, but this is not the case when the buffer is larger. The buffer can then be filled by a sequence of *give* entries or emptied by a series of *take* entries, as long as there are safeguards against adding an item to a full buffer or taking an item from an empty buffer.

To implement this, *buffer* must be modified so that it is capable of accepting either a *give* or a *take* entry. This is achieved by what is known as a **select** statement, which in this case contains two **select alternatives**. Only the body of task *buffer* needs to be changed; the task specification and tasks *producer* and *consumer* remain the same. Hence:

```
task body buffer is
    size : constant integer := 10;
    the_buffer : array(1 .. size) of item;
    no_of_items : integer range 0 .. size := 0;
    in_index, out_index : integer range 1 .. size := 1;
begin
    loop
        select
            when no_of_items < size =>
                accept give(x : in item) do
                    the_buffer(in_index) := x;
                end give;
                no_of_items := no_of_items + 1;
                in_index := in_index mod size + 1;
            or when no_of_items > 0 =>
                accept take(x : out item) do
                    x := the_buffer(out_index);
                end take;
                no_of_items := no_of_items – 1;
                out_index := out_index mod size + 1;
        end select;
    end loop;
end buffer;
```

The buffer acts like a queue with the first item inserted in the buffer being the first item to be removed. Each of the **select** alternatives is *guarded* by a **when** condition to ensure that items cannot be added to a full buffer or removed from an empty one. Statements guarded in this way are called **guarded commands**.

To execute the **select** statement, the guards are first evaluated. If the value of a guard is 'false', the select alternative is said to be 'closed' and the corresponding **accept** statement is not considered further. If the value of a guard is 'true', the select alternative is said to be 'open'. When only a *give* entry call has been made and *no_of_items* is less than *size*, then the *give* entry is accepted. Similarly, when only a *take* entry call has been made and *no_of_items* is greater than zero, the *take* entry is accepted. In the situation when both entry calls have been made and both guard conditions are satisfied, one of the calls is selected arbitrarily (that is, in a non-deterministic manner) and the other has to wait. If no *give* or *take* entry call corresponding to an open **select** alternative has been made, the *buffer* task is suspended until one is.

Occam has an ALT construct that allows guarded alternatives in a similar way to the Ada **select** statement and this makes it possible to write an occam process to implement the larger buffer. Hence:

```
PROC buffer(CHAN OF INT give, take, signal)
    VAL INT size IS 10:
    INT inindex, outindex, noofitems:
    [size]INT thebuffer:
    SEQ
        noofitems := 0
        inindex := 0
        outindex := 0
        WHILE TRUE
            ALT
                noofitems < size & give ? thebuffer[inindex]
                    SEQ
                        noofitems := noofitems + 1
                        inindex := (inindex + 1) REM size
                noofitems > 0 & signal ? ANY
                    SEQ
                        take ! thebuffer[outindex]
                        noofitems := noofitems - 1
                        outindex := (outindex + 1) REM size
    :
```

Arrays in occam are like arrays in C: the subscripts start at zero. The operator REM is the remainder operator.

The guards used in the occam example are a combination of Boolean expressions and an input from a channel. In the guard:

```
noofitems < size & give ? thebuffer[inindex]
```

when the value of noofitems is less than size and information has been sent from process producer and is waiting on channel give, the guard is satisfied and the information can be read into thebuffer[inindex].

A problem arises with the second alternative as in this case it is the buffer process that initiates the action and sends information to process consumer, but it must be known when consumer is ready to take this information. The solution is for the consumer process to first send a message along another channel to indicate that it is ready. This requires the consumer process to be changed to:

```
PROC consumer(CHAN OF INT frombuff, signal)
    WHILE TRUE
        INT newinfo:
        SEQ
            signal ! ANY
            frombuff ? newinfo
            -- code to consume newinfo
    :
```

The reserved word ANY indicates that the nature of the information being passed is unimportant – it is merely a signal.

Guarded commands

Although guarded commands have been introduced in the context of process synchronization, and that is their only use in Ada and occam, in the original proposal (Dijkstra, 1975), they were used to introduce non-determinism to sequential computations.

In the construct:

if
    exp1 → *stat1*
[]
    exp2 → *stat2*
...
[]
    expn → *statn*
fi

all the Boolean guards *exp1, exp2, ... expn* are evaluated and a statement corresponding to an open guard is chosen, non-deterministically, to be executed. It is an error if all the guards are closed. The loop:

do
    exp1 → *stat1*
[]
    exp2 → *stat2*
...
[]
    expn → *statn*
od

terminates when all the guards evaluate to false.

As a deterministic solution can over-specify the order in which events are to occur, certain algorithms can be expressed more abstractly using guarded commands. An example is the algorithm to partition a list into two sublists in which the elements in the first list are less than or equal to the elements in the second.

Assuming a list *a* with subscripts in the range *low* to *high*, and with *x*, *i* and *j* initialized to:

$x := a[(low + high) \textbf{ div } 2];$
$i := low; j := high;$

a possible Pascal program fragment is:

```
repeat
    while a[i] < x do
        i := i + 1;
    while a[j] > x do
        j := j - 1;
    if i <= j then
    begin
        swap(a[i], a[j]);
```

```
        i := i + 1;
        j := j - 1;
    end
until i > j;
```

After execution of this loop, all elements in the list *a* with subscripts in the range *low* to *j* will be less than or equal to elements whose subscripts are in the range *i* to *high*. Using guarded commands, the same effect can be achieved in a single loop:

```
do
    a[i] < x → i := i + 1
[]
    a[j] > x → j := j - 1
[]
    a[i] >= x and a[j] <= x and i <= j →
    begin
        swap(a[i], a[j]);
        i := i + 1;
        j := j - 1;
    end
od
```

As non-determinism introduces extra problems, guarded commands have not been incorporated into any mainstream sequential language. They are, however, important in concurrent systems where non-determinism is inherent and necessary.

11.5 Real-time programming

The central feature of a real-time system is that it must respond to external inputs or events such as **interrupts** sufficiently quickly so that an appropriate response can be made and no information is lost. What is meant by the phrase 'sufficiently quickly' depends on the application, and the response time could be required to be within microseconds, seconds or even days. An example of a real-time system is a computer system controlling a chemical process. If the input from its sensors showed that pressure was building up to an unacceptable level, then the computer system would have to initiate action such as opening valves or lowering the temperature within a very short time period. It is therefore essential that the input of information and the resulting calculations are completed sufficiently quickly so that a suitable response can be made before the chemical plant blows up.

Real-time programming is one of the last bastions of the assembly language programmer as it usually requires access to low-level machine facilities. This includes the ability to access absolute memory locations, such as those used in handling external devices and in processing interrupts. Few high-level languages, with the notable recent exceptions of Ada and occam, have these facilities although several others, such as C and Coral 66, achieve some of the effects through calls to special system routines. A further problem occurs in multiprocessor systems when trying to define what exactly is meant by time – each processor is likely to have its own internal clock and they may all 'tick' at different rates.

When a computer is embedded in, and used to control, non-computer equipment, the system is known as an **embedded system**. An example of such a system is process control in a chemical plant where the computer system is part of a much larger control system. Most embedded systems are also real-time systems and, indeed, some writers treat the two words synonymously. Ada was specially designed for use in real-time embedded systems.

In general, real-time programming has all the problems of concurrent programming with the added problem of time. To help solve such problems, Ada and occam allow different processes to be given different priorities, for clearly the process handling an emergency situation such as the one described for the chemical plant must be given top priority and must not be suspended to make way for routine processing.

To give a specific example of real-time programming, suppose that when a sensor in the chemical plant detects abnormal pressure levels, it sends an interrupt to the computer system. This interrupt appears to a running Ada program as an entry call. Each possible hardware interrupt is associated with a memory address and this association is shown in the specification of the task which is to handle the interrupt by a **for** ... **use at** ... definition. This allows hardware interrupts to be dealt with in exactly the same way as an entry call. Such a task specification has the form:

```
task pr_interrupt_handler is
    entry pressure_warning;
    for pressure_warning use at allocated_location;
end pr_interrupt_handler;
```

In occam, a channel can be associated with a memory address:

```
PLACE pressurewarning AT allocatedlocation
```

giving a similar effect. So that the interrupt can be handled in Ada, there must be a task body waiting to make a rendezvous with the *pressure_warning* entry call. The Ada task body will have the form:

```
task body pr_interrupt_handler is
begin
    accept pressure_warning;
    --appropriate action
end pr_interrupt_handler;
```

There must be a waiting **accept** statement for each interrupt which may be received by the system. By using a **select** statement, one task can be used to handle several interrupts. The occam equivalent is to have a process waiting to receive information on channel pressurewarning.

Time can be introduced into an Ada program through the **delay** statement. Execution of the statement:

```
delay 4.0;
```

will delay a task by at least four seconds. Note that there is no guarantee that the task will be started immediately after four seconds have elapsed for, in a multiprogramming environment, some other task may be chosen by the scheduler. A similar delay in a C program is achieved by the library routine call *sleep*(4).

In occam, the current time can be found by interrogating a channel of the special type TIMER. Given the declaration:

```
TIMER theclock;
```

execution of:

```
theclock ? now
```

sets now to the current value of the processor clock. The command:

```
theclock ? AFTER expression
```

suspends execution until the current time is after the value of expression.

To guarantee that some operation is carried out every four seconds, a simple solution in Ada would seem to be:

```
loop
    --code to carry out some operations
    delay 4.0;
end loop;
```

The problem with this solution is that the time to go round the loop is:

4 seconds + time for operations + delay due to scheduler

which together could be considerably more than four seconds.

The answer to this problem is to use *absolute* rather than *relative* time. Absolute time is provided in Ada by the predefined package *calendar*, which defines the abstract data type *time*. The representation of type *time* is implementation dependent and is hidden, but functions in package *calendar* allow the extraction from values of type *time* of the components *year, month, day* and the time within a day in *seconds*. Absolute time is provided by the function *clock*, which returns the current value of *time*. The package also provides overloaded definitions of +, – and the relational operators, so that *time* arithmetic may be carried out.

With *start_time* having been declared as a variable of type *time*, the problem of carrying out an operation every four seconds may now be programmed as:

```
start_time := clock;
loop
    --code to carry out some operations
    start_time := start_time + 4.0;
    delay start_time – clock;
end loop;
```

The value of the expression:

```
start_time – clock
```

will be less than four seconds as it takes into account the time spent in carrying out the operations. It has, of course, been assumed that the operations in the loop are executed in less than four seconds.

delay statements may be incorporated into **select** statements. Hence, in the process control example, the action to be taken by the interrupt handler when the pressure is too high might be to reduce the temperature knowing that when the process returns to normal a second interrupt will be received. If this interrupt is not received within twenty seconds, the task will initiate emergency action. This could be programmed as the task body:

```
task body pr_interrupt_handler is
begin
   loop
      accept pressure_warning;
      reduce_temperature;
      select
         accept pressure_ok_signal;
      or
         delay 20.0;
         emergency_shut_down;
      end select;
   end loop;
end pr_interrupt_handler;
```

The loop ensures that once this body has finished handling a *pressure_warning* interrupt, it is ready to handle a similar subsequent interrupt.

Delay guards are also possible in occam. The Ada **select** statement translates into:

```
theclock ? start
ALT
   pressureoksignal ? ANY
      SKIP
   theclock ? AFTER start PLUS (20 * second)
      - - emergency shutdown action
```

If a signal is not received on channel pressureoksignal within 20 seconds, the second guard is satisfied and emergency action can take place. The value of second is the number of clock ticks in a second and is implementation dependent, SKIP is the null process and the PLUS operator differs from + in that it cannot cause integer overflow; the value of the largest integer in an implementation PLUS 1 is the most negative integer in the implementation. This property of PLUS is taken into account by the AFTER operator.

Summary

(1) In a concurrent program, several sequential program fragments (processes) are viewed as being executed in parallel. The processes are not independent of one another and so a mechanism is needed through which they can communicate and through which their actions can be synchronized.

(2) Many concurrent programs run on single processor machines and so only pseudo-concurrency exists. In such circumstances, concurrency is not being used to promote efficiency, but because it leads to a more natural solution.

(3) Processes can communicate through shared variables or by message passing.

(4) To get round the problem of one process updating a shared variable while another process is examining it, critical regions are used. In languages like Modula-2, such regions are implemented by means of a monitor module. Only one process may be executing a procedure in a monitor module at any one time.

(5) In Ada, processes are implemented by tasks. A task is entered by means of an entry call which must then be accepted by means of an **accept** statement.

(6) Two Ada processes can only communicate when one process executes an entry call which the other is ready to receive. If one process is not ready to take part in this rendezvous, the other process must wait. Synchronization is thereby achieved. Communication between processes is achieved by passing messages as the parameters of an entry call.

(7) In occam, processes communicate through named channels. Communication is synchronized as neither process can proceed until the information transfer has been completed.

(8) The Ada **select** statement enables a task to be in a position to accept alternative entry calls. The **select** alternatives may have Boolean guards. The ALT construct of occam has a similar effect.

(9) The central feature of a real-time system is that it must respond to external inputs sufficiently quickly so that an appropriate response can be made.

(10) Hardware interrupts are dealt with in Ada programs as entry calls.

(11) Delay statements delay a process by a least the stated time. There is, however, no control over how quickly the process will be re-activated after the delay has expired.

EXERCISES

11.1 Should a language include constructs to indicate that certain program segments may be executed in parallel or should such decisions be left up to the compiler?

11.2 Identify the features of languages such as Pascal, FORTRAN and Ada that make it difficult to determine which parts of a program are independent of one another and so may be executed in parallel.

11.3 Outline the problems associated with shared variables and indicate how they may be overcome.

11.4 Section 11.4 gives the definition of an Ada task for a single item buffer which gives a solution to the producer/consumer problem. What changes would have to be made to the definition of task *buffer* if:

   (a) The same item can be read several times, but a new item cannot be put in the buffer until the previous one has been read at least once.

   (b) Items can be read several times, and new items can be inserted before the previous one has been read.

11.5 The hardware of some existing computers may be able to handle the Ada rendezvous efficiently while others may not. Is it therefore sensible to have notions of concurrency as part of a high-level language?

11.6 Is it reasonable to expect computer design to change to fit high-level languages or should high-level languages always be designed to fit existing hardware?

11.7 Design two outline Ada tasks, one for an alarm and one for a person. The sleeping person task should be ready to receive a call from the alarm task and will either return the value *off* and get up or return the value *snooze* and go back to sleep. The alarm task will terminate when the value *off* is returned. If *snooze* is returned, it will delay for two minutes before calling the person task again. This is repeated until the alarm task is switched off.

11.8 How many channels would be required in an occam solution to the problem in Exercise 11.7?

11.9 Compare inter-process communication in Ada and occam from the point of view of efficiency, flexibility and ease of use.

BIBLIOGRAPHY

An important early synchronization primitive was the semaphore which was introduced by Dijkstra (1968). Monitors were introduced and developed by Brinch Hansen (1973) and Hoare (1974) and are based on the SIMULA class concept (Birtwistle, 1975). Guarded commands were introduced by Dijkstra (1975) and a full description of CSP is given by Hoare (1985).

The survey by Andrews (1983) is recommended for those readers who want a more detailed introduction to the concepts of concurrency. Processes in Modula-2 are described by Wirth (1982), and the rendezvous concept and buffering between producers and consumers are described in most Ada texts, including the reference manual (Ichbiah, 1983). There have been various versions of the language occam. The version given in this book is occam 2 (Burns, 1988). A good description of

Ada's real-time features is given by Burns (1990), while a survey of languages for distributed systems, including object-oriented languages, is given by Bal (1989).

A description of the concurrent object-oriented language Emerald is given by Black (1986) and the use of concurrent objects in design by Clark (1992). There has recently been a lot of research interest in concurrent logic languages, and a number of different languages have been developed. As they are all still experimental, they are not discussed in this book. The interested reader is referred to the survey by Shapiro (1989).

Andrews, G. and Schneider, F. (1983), 'Concepts and Notations for Concurrent Programming', *ACM Computing Surveys*, **15**, pp. 3–43.

Bal, H. E., Steiner, J.G. and Tanenbaum, A. S. (1989), 'Programming Languages for Distributed Computing Systems', *ACM Computing Surveys*, **21**, pp. 261–322.

Birtwistle, G. M., Dahl, O.-J., Myhrhaug, B. and Nygaard, K. (1975), *Simula Begin*, Auerbach.

Black, A., Hutchinson, N., Jul, E. and Levy, H. (1986), 'Object Structure in the Emerald System', *ACM SIGPLAN Notices*, **21**(11), pp. 78–86.

Burns, A. (1988), *Programming in occam 2*, Addison-Wesley.

Burns, A. and Wellings, A. (1990), *Real-Time Systems and their Programming Languages*, Addison-Wesley.

Brinch Hansen, P. (1973), *Operating System Principles*, Prentice-Hall.

Clark, R. G. (1992), 'Using LOTOS in the Object-Based Development of Embedded Systems' in *The Unified Computation Laboratory* (C.M.I. Rattray and R.G.Clark, Eds.), Oxford University Press, pp. 307–319.

Dijkstra, E. W. (1968), 'Cooperating Sequential Processes' in *Programming Languages* (F. Genuys, Ed.), Academic Press.

Dijkstra, E. W. (1975), 'Guarded Commands, Nondeterminacy and Formal Derivations of Programs', *Comm. ACM*, **18**, pp. 453–457.

Hoare, C. A. R. (1974), 'Monitors: An Operating System Structuring Concept', *Comm. ACM*, **17**, pp. 549–557.

Hoare, C. A. R. (1985), *Communicating Sequential Processes*, Prentice-Hall.

Ichbiah, J. *et al.* (1983), *Reference Manual for the Ada Programming Language*, ANSI MIL-STD-1815A-1983.

Shapiro, E. (1989), 'The Family of Concurrent Logic Programming Languages', *ACM Computing Surveys*, **21**, pp. 412–510.

Wirth, N. (1982), *Programming in Modula-2* (Second Edition), Springer-Verlag.

Syntax and semantics

CONTENTS

12.1 **Syntax**   **284**
12.2 **Semantics**   **290**

This chapter describes the use of Backus-Naur form and syntax diagrams in the definition of language syntax. Examples are given of how sentences in a language can be derived from its grammar and how a BNF grammar imposes a phrase structure on the derived sentences.

Although the syntax of a programming language is always defined formally using a notation such as BNF, the semantics are still usually defined in English. Methods do, however, exist for formally describing the semantics of programming language constructs, and brief outlines of two approaches, denotational and axiomatic semantics, are given. As these methods require a higher level of mathematical sophistication than is assumed, they have not been used in this book.

12.1 Syntax

The **syntax** (or **grammar**) of a programming language describes the correct form in which programs may be written, while the **semantics** denotes the meaning that may be attached to the various syntactic constructs. Finding methods and notations to express the formal syntax of a language is a much simpler problem than formalizing the semantics. Therefore, in the definition of a programming language, the syntax is usually expressed formally in a variant of BNF, which stands for Backus-Naur Form or Backus-Normal Form, while the semantic description is given in English.

BNF is an example of a **metalanguage**; that is, a language used to define other languages. The first language whose description used the combination of a syntax description in BNF and a semantic description in English was ALGOL 60 (Naur, 1960), and the same approach was used in the definition of Ada (Ichbiah, 1983) showing how little things had changed in 23 years. When the syntax of a language is expressed in a simple and unambiguous notation such as BNF, it is clear to the language user and implementor alike which constructs are legal and which are not.

A BNF definition consists of a set of **nonterminals**, a set of **terminals** and a series of **production rules** (also known as **productions** or **rewrite rules**). A nonterminal is defined in a production rule, while a terminal is a symbol in the language being defined. In a production rule, the nonterminal on the left-hand side, known as the **left part**, is defined in terms of a sequence of nonterminals and terminals on the right-hand side, known as the **right part**.

Some example production rules are:

```
<digit> ::= 0|1|2|3|4|5|6|7|8|9
<letter> ::= a|b|c|d| ... x|y|z
<identifier> ::= <letter>
             | <identifier><digit>
             | <identifier><letter>
```

In BNF, a nonterminal is written within diamond brackets <>, the symbol ::= means 'is defined as' and the symbol | means 'or'.

These definitions define *<digit>* to be one of the symbols 0, 1, ... 9, *<letter >* to be a lower case letter and *<identifier>* to be either a single letter, an identifier followed by a letter or an identifier followed by a digit. Hence, *ch1* is an identifier as it can be **derived** from *<identifier>* as follows:

```
<identifier>
<identifier><digit>
<identifier><letter><digit>
<letter><letter><digit>
c<letter><digit>
ch<digit>
ch1
```

At each stage, the leftmost nonterminal has been replaced by the right part of one of its defining production rules. The sequence of terminals and nonterminals produced

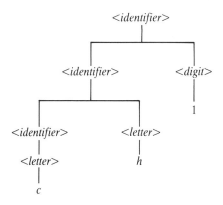

Figure 12.1
Derivation tree for
an identifier.

at each stage in a **derivation** are known as **sentential forms**. The final sentential form, which does not contain any nonterminals, is known as a **sentence**. The structure of a derivation is best shown by what is known as a **derivation tree**. The tree showing how *ch1* is derived from *<identifier>* is given in Figure 12.1.

A complete programming language is defined by starting with a nonterminal such as *<program>*, known as the **start symbol**, and from which all possible programs can be derived by replacing left parts of production rules with one of their corresponding right parts. In practice, derivation trees are created in one of two ways. In the **top-down** approach, the required sentence is derived from the start symbol as was done in the derivation of *ch1*. In the **bottom-up** approach, the starting point is the required sentence which is reduced to the start symbol by replacing right parts by their corresponding left parts. Both approaches are used in the **syntax analysis** phase of modern compilers.

A grammar defining a programming language always has a finite number of production rules, but the use of recursion in, for example:

<identifier> ::= *<identifier><digit>*

allows an infinite number of possible programs. When recursion is included in production rules, the same care must be exercised as would be necessary in a recursive procedure. There must, for example, be a non-recursive alternative so that the recursion can terminate. A production rule such as:

<identifier> ::= *<identifier><letter>*

is said to be **left-recursive** because the nonterminal being defined – that is, *<identifier>* is the leftmost symbol in the right part. Similar definitions exist for **right-recursive** and **self-embedding** production rules.

A BNF grammar is said to be **context-free** as the left part always consists of a single nonterminal. This means that the left part can always be replaced by one of its alternative right parts irrespective of the context in which the left part appears.

As a further example of the use of BNF, consider:

<exp> ::= *<exp>* + *<term>*
              | *<exp>* – *<term>*
              | *<term>*
<term> ::= *<term>* * *<factor>*
              | *<term>* / *<factor>*
              | *<factor>*
<factor> ::= (*<exp>*)
              | *<identifier>*

which defines algebraic expressions. The derivation for the expression:

  a * (*b* + *c*)

is:

<exp>
<term>
<term> * *<factor>*
<factor> * *<factor>*
<identifier> * *<factor>*
a * *<factor>*
a * (*<exp>*)
a * (*<exp>* + *<term>*)
a * (*<term>* + *<term>*)
a * (*<factor>* + *<term>*)
a * (*<identifier>* + *<term>*)
a * (*b* + *<term>*)
a * (*b* + *<factor>*)
a * (*b* + *<identifier>*)
a * (*b* + *c*)

and the corresponding derivation tree is shown in Figure 12.2.

From the derivation tree in Figure 12.2, it can be seen that a structure, known as a **phrase structure**, has been imposed on the sentence *a* * (*b* + *c*). Subtrees of the main tree define **phrases**. Hence, for example, *b* + *c* and (*b* + *c*) are phrases. It should be noted that the phrase structure imposed by the grammar mirrors the grouping of symbols normally expected in an algebraic expression, as evaluation of *a* * (*b* + *c*) takes place by first adding together the values of *b* and *c* and then multiplying the result by *a*.

As the definition of *<exp>* and *<term>* are left recursive, the grammar defines evaluation of *a* + *b* + *c* to take place by first evaluating *a* + *b* and then adding *c* to the result. The grammar also defines multiplication and division to have a higher precedence than addition and subtraction. To convince themselves that this is the case, readers are encouraged to produce the derivation trees for *a* + *b* + *c* and for *a* + *b* * *c* and to examine the phrase structure which has been imposed on these two sentences.

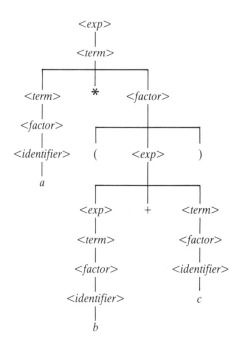

Figure 12.2
Derivation tree for
an expression.

Ambiguity

A problem arises when a BNF definition defines an **ambiguous** grammar, that is, a grammar that allows different interpretations for the same sentence. The classic example of ambiguity in programming languages is the so-called 'dangling else' problem. This occured in the original definition of ALGOL 60 as conditional statements were defined so that the **else** part was optional. Consider the definition:

<statement> ::= *<conditional statement>*
    | **begin** *<statement>* **end**
<conditional statement> ::= **if** *<condition>* **then** *<statement>*
   | **if** *<condition>* **then** *<statement>* **else** *<statement>*

Two different derivation trees exist for the conditional statement:

 if *<condition>* **then if** *<condition>* **then** *<statement>* **else** *<statement>*

and they are given in Figure 12.3. The problem is knowing to which **then** the **else** belongs. As there are two interpretations, the grammar is ambiguous. The approach taken with the revised version of ALGOL 60 was to insist that only unconditional statements could follow the reserved word **then** and so the above statement would have to be written as either:

 if *<condition>* **then**
 begin
  if *<condition>* **then** *<statement>* **else** *<statement>*
 end

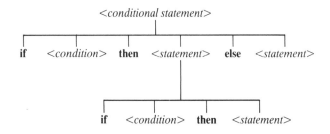

Figure 12.3
Derivaton trees for
conditional
statement.

or as:

if *<condition>* **then**
begin
   if *<condition>* **then** *<statement>*
end else *<statement>*

depending on which interpretation was required. A general discussion of this problem was given in Section 4.3.

General proofs that a given grammar is unambiguous are not possible, but a simple and useful rule is that a grammar is always ambiguous if it is any two of left-recursive, self-embedding and right-recursive with respect to the same nonterminal.

EBNF

Several variants of the BNF notation have been used in language definitions, for example replacing ::= with →, not using diamond brackets and enclosing terminals within quotes. Hence, instead of writing:

   <exp> ::= *<exp>* + *<term>*

the rule might be written as:

   exp → *exp* '+' *term*

The following extensions to BNF (called EBNF) are of a more substantive nature and were used in the definitions of Pascal and Ada:

(a)

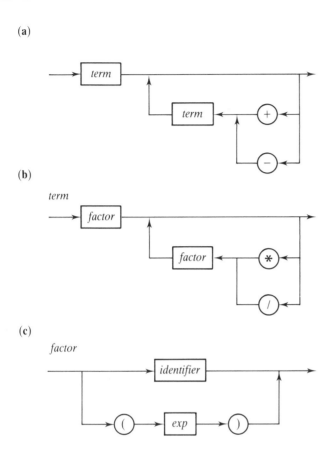

(b)

(c)

Figure 12.4
Syntax diagrams for
exp, *term* and
factor.

- Optional constructs are enclosed in square brackets, [ ].
- Zero or more repetitions of a construct are indicated by braces, { }. In some EBNF notations the ellipsis symbol ... is used instead of { }.
- Round brackets, ( ), can be used for grouping items together.

Their main effect is to replace left recursion by iteration.

The BNF definition for an algebraic expression has already been given. The equivalent EBNF production rules are:

exp ::= *term* { ('+' | '–') *term* }
term ::= *factor* { ('*' | '/') *factor* }
factor ::= '('*exp*')' | *identifier*

EBNF production rules can be presented diagrammatically by what are known as **syntax diagrams**. These diagrams are particularly useful for students at the early stages of understanding the syntax of a language as they are easier to follow than production rules.

Syntax diagrams have the following properties:

- Arrows are used to indicate the direction of flow.
- Rectangular boxes are used for nonterminals.
- Round boxes are used for terminals.
- There is a diagram for each nonterminal. A nonterminal is defined by the possible paths through its defining diagram.

The production rules for *factor*, *term* and *exp* are shown as syntax diagrams in Figure 12.4. It should be noted that the syntax diagrams are recursive; *exp* is defined in terms of *term*, which is defined in terms of *factor*, which may, in turn, be defined in terms of *exp*.

Syntax-directed compiling

The production rules used in the definition of a language are embedded in modern compilers and control the syntax analysis phase of the compiler. Such compilers are said to be **syntax directed**.

During the derivation of a sentence, there is often a choice as to which right part should be used to replace a left part and it is often far from obvious which alternative should be chosen. Programming languages are therefore usually defined using a restricted form of context-free grammar so that the choice is always obvious.

If, using the top-down approach, it is always clear which of the possible right parts should be chosen by looking one symbol ahead, then the grammar is said to be LL(1). When syntax is defined using EBNF, it is much easier to put a grammar into LL(1) form than when BNF is used. If, using the bottom-up approach, it is always clear, by looking one symbol ahead, which part of a sentential form should be reduced, then the grammar is said to be LR(1). LL(1) and LR(1) grammars are always unambiguous and lead to languages that can be efficiently compiled. Such issues are taken into account by language designers. The language Pascal, for example, was designed in such a way that its syntax could be defined by means of an LL(1) grammar.

12.2   Semantics

In contrast to the early progress made in the formal definition of syntax, the task of formulating a suitable definition for the semantics of programming languages has presented many problems. Attempts have been made by researchers to arrive at a readable, concise and unambiguous notation for the definition of semantics, and, although considerable progress has been made, an easily understandable solution to the semantics of programming languages is still not available. BNF was first used in the definition of ALGOL 60, but as the ALGOL 60 committee was unable to come up with a solution to the semantic problem to match the BNF syntactical description, they resorted to English language for the semantic explanations. Unfortunately, the use of English prose is ambiguous, so that two readers can often arrive at different interpretations of a typical sentence. However, the semantics in the ISO and ANSI definitions of recent programming languages are still defined in English.

One approach, called operational semantics, defines a simple abstract machine that has a set of data structures and operations whose semantics is assumed to be known. The semantics of a programming language can then be defined by the rules governing how programs written in that language can be executed on the abstract machine. Although the abstract machine is unlikely to be similar to any existing computer, the operational semantics of a language can be of direct benefit to the language implementor. This approach does, however, often involve too much implementation detail to be of much use to the language user.

Two more formal methods used to describe the semantics of a language are the **denotational** approach and the **axiomatic** approach. The notations used with these approaches are not easy to follow and require a higher level of mathematical sophistication than is assumed in this book. However, for completeness, a brief overview of each approach is given.

Denotational semantics

In denotational semantics, information is given about the effect of program execution and not about how the execution is to be carried out. It is, therefore, unlike the operational approach, of more use to language designers than to language implementors. The following description does not attempt to be rigorous, but only to give an idea of what is involved. Difficult points, such as the handling of errors, are ignored.

Language constructs are modelled by appropriate mathematical objects, usually numbers or functions, whose meaning is already known. Consider, for example, a language that only consists of constant declarations and expressions. A series of declarations is modelled as a function that maps identifiers to their associated values; this kind of function is known as an **environment**. A new pair is added to the environment by the function *bind*, which takes an identifier, a value and an environment and returns a new environment to which the new identifier/value binding has been added. A declaration can then be defined by the semantic function *D*:

$D(\text{const } i = e, env) = bind(i, E(e, env), env)$

which takes the declaration const i = e and an environment *env*, and returns a new environment which differs from *env* in that a binding between the identifier i and the value obtained by evaluating the expression e has been added. The semantic function *E* takes an expression and an environment and returns the value obtained by evaluating the expression in that environment. During the evaluation of the expression, the value of any identifiers encountered are determined by looking them up in the environment using a *lookup* function which takes an identifier and an environment and returns the value to which that identifier is currently bound. As purely functional languages consist of only declarations and expressions, their semantics can be fully defined without the need to introduce the concept of a computer store.

When commands, such as the assignment statement, exist in a language, the notion of a store is necessary and functions such as E must include the current store as a parameter. In the declaration of a variable, an identifier is bound to the address of a store location (a reference) and this binding is added to the environment. The store itself is modelled in a similar way to the environment, but this time as a function which maps references to their associated values. A function *set* can be defined which takes a reference, a value and a store and returns a new store to which the reference/value binding has been added.

Consider now the assignment statement. Its effect is to modify the store. The semantic function C takes a command, an environment and a store and returns a new store. The definition:

$$C(i := e, env, st) = set(lookup(i, env), E(e, env, st), st)$$

is interpreted as stating that the effect of executing the command i := e in the environment *env* and store *st*, is to create a new store which differs from *st* in that the reference bound to the identifier i (found by looking up i in the environment *env*) is bound to the value obtained by evaluating the expression e in the environment *env* and store *st*. As the definition of assignment is in terms of a new store, rather than in terms of a modification to the old store, this is obviously not intended as a model for a possible implementation. The difference between the old and the new store does, however, define the *effect* of the assignment operation.

Denotational semantics is hierarchical in nature with high-level features being defined in terms of lower level features whose meaning has already been defined. The effect of an if statement can be defined as:

$$C(\text{if } e \text{ then } s1 \text{ else } s2, env, st)$$
$$= E(e, env, st) \rightarrow C(s1, env, st);$$
$$C(s2, env, st)$$

This is interpreted as stating that the effect of executing the if statement in the environment *env* and store *st* is first to evaluate the expression e in *env* and *st* and, if the value is true, to return the store obtained by executing the command s1 in *env* and *st* and, if the value is false, to return the store obtained by executing the command s2 in *env* and *st*. It has been assumed that evaluation of the expression e does not produce any side effect, that is, modify the store.

A while statement can be defined in a similar way, with iteration being defined using recursion. The definition:

$$C(\text{while } e \text{ do } s, env, st)$$
$$= E(e, env, st) \rightarrow C(\text{while } e \text{ do } s, env, C(s, env, st));$$
$$st$$

is interpreted as stating that the effect of executing the while statement in environment *env* and store *st*, is first to evaluate the expression e in *env* and *st* and, if the value is false, then the while statement has no effect and the result is the original store *st*. If the value is true, the while statement is again executed, this time using the store obtained by executing the command s.

Axiomatic semantics

The axiomatic method, which is based on symbolic logic, uses **rules of inference** to deduce the effect of executing a construct. The meaning of a statement, or group of statements, S is described in terms of:

(1) the condition P (the **pre-condition**) that is assumed or asserted to be true before S is executed, and

(2) the condition Q (the **post-condition**) which can be deduced to be true after execution of S.

This is usually written as:

$\{P\}\ S\ \{Q\}$

The post-condition that holds after the execution of one group of statements can of course act as the pre-condition for the next.

Consider the assignment statement $x := x + 1$. If the condition $x \geq 0$ is true before execution of this statement, then $x > 0$ will be true after execution of the statement. This is written as:

$\{x >= 0\}\ x := x + 1\ \{x > 0\}$

Assertions about a structured statement can be deduced from assertions about its components. The rule of inference for the if statement is:

$$\frac{\{P\ and\ e\}\ s1\ \{Q\},\quad \{P\ and\ not\ e\}\ s2\{Q\}}{\{P\}\ \texttt{if}\ e\ \texttt{then}\ s1\ \texttt{else}\ s2\ \{Q\}}$$

which states that when P is true before the if statement is executed, Q will be true after the statement is executed if either:

• Q is true after s1 is executed, provided that P and e were both true before s1 was executed, or

• Q is true after s2 is executed, provided that P was true and e was false before s2 was executed.

Unlike the other two approaches, the meaning of a statement S is, therefore, not described directly; instead, the effect of executing S is described indirectly by the relationship between P and Q. This means that the axiomatic method is of most use in verifying and reasoning about the effect of programs. Using axiomatic semantics, program verification of:

$\{P\}\ S\ \{Q\}$

consists of proving, using rules of inference like the one shown above, that if the pre-condition P is true before S is executed, the post-condition Q is true after S has been executed.

Instead of being used to verify the correctness of an existing program, axiomatic semantics can be used in program construction by constructing the program and its proof at the same time. The starting point is the pre- and post-conditions, from which the statements which satisfy these assertions are to be constructed. In order to support this approach to program construction, assertions are included in some programming languages, an example being Eiffel.

As operational, denotational and axiomatic semantics are useful under differing circumstances, they can be seen to be complementary to one another, rather than being competitors.

Summary

(1) The syntax of a programming language is usually defined using BNF.

(2) BNF is an example of a metalanguage, that is, a language used to define other languages.

(3) A BNF definition consists of nonterminals, terminals and a series of production rules. Sentences in the language are derived from a special nonterminal known as the start symbol.

(4) A BNF grammar imposes a phrase structure on sentences.

(5) An ambiguous grammar allows different interpretations for the same sentence.

(6) The production rules used in the definition of a language are often used to control the syntax analysis phase of its compiler.

(7) In most language reference manuals, the semantics of language constructs are not described formally; rather they are given in a natural language such as English.

(8) There are three approaches to formal semantics; operational, denotational and axiomatic.

(9) In denotational semantics, language constructs are modelled by appropriate mathematical objects whose meaning is already known.

(10) In axiomatic semantics, rules of inference are used to deduce the effect of executing a language construct.

EXERCISES

12.1 Give BNF definitions for:

    (a) an unsigned integer number,

    (b) an unsigned real number, where there must be at least one digit before and after the decimal point.

12.2 Using the definition for *⟨exp⟩*, *⟨term⟩* and *⟨factor⟩* in Section 12.1, give a derivation tree for the expression $a * b + c$.

12.3 Section 12.1 gives a BNF definition for an algebraic expression. Extend this definition so that the expressions can include the relational operators >, >=, <, <=, = and <> which all have a lower precedence than the arithmetic operators.

12.4 For each of the following grammars, in which <*start*> is the start symbol, determine the language (the set of sentences) which is generated.

(a) <*start*> ::= a | a <*start*>

(b) <*start*> ::= a | a <*next*>
     <*next*> ::= a <*start*>

(c) <*start*> ::= a <*start*> | a <*next*>
     <*next*> ::= b | b <*next*>

(d) <*start*> ::= a <*start*> b | ab

12.5 List all the valid sentences with one, two or three characters that can be derived from the EBNF grammar:

    sequence → 'A' { 'B' | 'C' } ['D']

Represent the EBNF grammar as a syntax diagram and give an equivalent grammar in BNF.

12.6 How is the 'dangling else' problem dealt with in Pascal?

12.7 When there are alternative right parts, it can be far from obvious, even with very simple grammars, which one is to be chosen at each stage. As an example, derive the sentences *abag* and *aabg* using the following grammar in which <*sentence*> is the start symbol.

    <*sentence*> ::= a <*first*> | <*second*> g
    <*first*> ::= <*third*> g | b <*first*> | a <*first*>
    <*second*> ::= <*third*> b | <*third*> <*second*>
    <*third*> ::= a

12.8 Using the grammar:

    <*sentence*>   ::= p <*char*> <*continue*>
                  | r <*char*> <*continue*>
    <*char*> ::= a | b
    <*continue*>   ::= , <*char*> <*continue*> | ;

in which <*sentence*> is the start symbol, derive the sentence:

    p a, b, a;

Why was this straightforward? At each stage, how many symbols ahead must be scanned to determine which of the alternative right parts was to be used?

BIBLIOGRAPHY

Most programming language texts include a definition of the language's syntax using either BNF or syntax diagrams while an introduction to language grammars is given in most books on compiling such as that by Aho (1986).

Books on semantics are far from simple. One that is more accessible than most is by Nielson (1992).

Aho, A. V., Sethi, R. and Ullman, J. D. (1986), *Compilers: Principles, Techniques and Tools*, Addison-Wesley.

Ichbiah, J. D. *et al.* (1983), *Reference Manual for the Ada Programming Language*, ANSI MIL-STD-1815A-1983.

Naur, P. *et al.* (Eds.) (1960), 'Report on the Algorithmic Language ALGOL 60', *Comm. ACM*, **3**, pp. 299–314.

Nielson, H. R. and Nielson, F. (1992), *Semantics with Applications*, John Wiley.

Input and output

13

CONTENTS

13.1 **Introduction**   **298**
13.2 **Input and output of text**   **299**
13.3 **Binary and direct access files**   **307**
13.4 **Concluding remarks**   **309**

This chapter looks at the Cinderella of language design – input and output (I/O) – and shows how the input and output of textual information is handled in several languages, including those such as C, Modula-2 and Ada where I/O is not really part of the language at all, but is handled by a set of pre-defined routines.

I/O routines must be able to deal with a wide range of different peripheral devices, but for reasons of simplicity, languages abstract away from the physical details of particular peripheral devices and deal with both input and ouput in terms of sequences of records. When the information is in human readable form, each record usually corresponds to a line of text. The problems that arise when interactive I/O is dealt with in the same way as accessing sequential files on disk are discussed. Binary files and direct access files, where records may be written or read in any order, are then considered.

An alternative model of I/O, where the program and the user are considered as two concurrent interacting processes, is examined in the final section.

13.1 Introduction

The most effective way in which human users can interact with computers has only recently received a significant amount of attention with the advent of menu-driven systems, mouse input, multiple windows and icons. Such systems were originally aimed at non-experts using a personal or business computer where the facilities are regarded as being part of the operating system or an application package, rather than being features of a high-level language. However, they are also a feature of the powerful workstations used by more specialized users and are of course central to the Smalltalk environment, where many of the ideas originated.

The effect this is going to have on languages is not clear. One approach is that screen handling properly belongs in the realm of operating systems and that a language independent window manipulation system, such as the X Window System, should be used. In this case, the only impact on languages is the provision of a set of library routines to provide a suitable interface to the window manipulation system.

The other view is that graphical facilities should be integrated into a language. Many implementations of BASIC have extended the language to include instructions for screen manipulation and such facilities are also often included in fourth-generation languages. Object-oriented systems, where the distinction between the language and the support environment is not clear cut, are at an intermediate point between these two situations. Graphical facilities are offered as a set of library classes, but are regarded by many as forming an integral part of the language.

Despite the changes in how users interact with computers, it remains the case that in traditional languages, the commands for reading and writing human-readable information still deal in terms of lines of text, and the language facilities have not changed much from the days when the standard devices were a card reader and a line printer.

Although information is usually presented to and received from a computer as lines of text, this is not how the information is held within the computer. Part of the reading process is, therefore, to convert information from an external human readable form (usually text) to a suitable internal representation. With integer data, for example, the external representation is a series of digit characters with a possible leading + or − sign. A command to read an integer will read such a character string and convert it into the computer's internal representation for integer numbers (for example, two's complement). Similarly, when results are output the internal representation has to be converted back into the appropriate character string.

Input and output devices (I/O devices) are much slower than the central processor. To prevent I/O instructions slowing down the operation of the whole computer, they are executed concurrently with processing by the CPU, and buffers are used to hold intermediate information. This process is normally handled by the operating system and is transparent to the programmer, the exception being when the language is to be used for systems programming. Even then, programmers do not need to get involved with low-level detail, unless they wish to, because systems programming languages usually have different levels of I/O instructions.

I/O instructions have to indicate the device to be used as well as the layout and type of the data or results. To avoid the necessity of having a different instruction for each new device, language designers have made an abstraction of the input/output process. In the original definition of FORTRAN, for example, it was assumed that input came from punched cards and output went to a line printer. These devices can be considered as delivering or receiving a series of fixed-length records with each record being regarded as a line of characters divided into fields. Similarly, information held in a file on backing store can be considered as a series of such records and so can be dealt with in the same way.

The abstraction used in Pascal is that all I/O, even when it involves a terminal, is considered to be to or from a sequential file; that is, a file in which the records may only be accessed in the order in which they were originally written. A Pascal program has two standard files, called *input* and *output*, which are attached to what are called the standard input and output devices; usually the keyboard and terminal screen. These logical file names are given in the program heading:

    program *example*(*input*, *output*);

and are of the predefined type *text*. A file of type *text* is a file of lines where each line consists of a series of characters terminated by an end-of-line indicator. A text file is not the same as a file of characters since the implementation of the end-of-line indicator depends on the particular operating system used, and some systems have no way of representing the end of a line within their character set. This abstraction of text I/O is more or less the same as that used in Ada, Modula-2 and C. Unlike FORTRAN, the lines are not of a fixed length in these languages.

Files are not only used for communication between different programs on the same computer, but for the transfer of information between computers with different operating systems. For the reasons just stated, this type of transfer can cause problems. However, it is usually possible to achieve the transfer of a file of records, where each record consists of a line of printable (non-control) characters. If the end-of-line indicator used in the transmitting system is known to the network, a series of records can be sent. On receipt of each record, the receiving system can insert its own end-of-line indicator.

File transfer is not within the realms of language design, but what is important is that a language's abstract model for files of text should fit the scenario described here. The next section looks at how sequential input and output of textual information is handled in FORTRAN, Pascal, Ada, Modula-2, C, PROLOG and LISP.

13.2   Input and output of text

FORTRAN

FORTRAN uses FORMAT statements to specify the layout of data and results, and channel numbers to specify their source or destination. The channel number corresponding to the standard input device depends on the operating system. Assuming that it is channel 5, the statement:

```
READ (5, 50) ITEM, NUMBER
```

causes two values to be read into the integer variables ITEM and NUMBER with a layout as specified by the FORMAT statement labelled 50. This could have the form:

    50 FORMAT(I8, I7)

where the I8 indicates that an integer value is to be found in the first eight columns of the input record and the I7 that a second integer value is to be found in the next seven. Leading blanks are ignored, but trailing blanks are treated as zeros.

The command for writing information is similar. Hence:

       WRITE (6, 51) ITEM, NUMBER
    51 FORMAT (' ANSWERS =', I9, I7)

causes a character string and two integer values to be written out on a new line on channel 6 with the layout specified by the FORMAT statement labelled 51. This format specifies that after ANSWERS=, the next nine columns should be used to contain an integer value (with leading blanks if required) and the next seven used for a second integer value. It has been assumed that channel 6 corresponds to the standard output device.

Format specifications are available to read and write integer, real, character, complex and logical values. The FORTRAN FORMAT statements make it relatively straightforward to print out tables of information although, as many different kinds of format specification are possible, novice programmers tend to make mistakes.

Reading in data in a fixed format was sensible when cards were the main input mechanism, but it is inconvenient when input occurs at a terminal. List directed I/O was therefore introduced in FORTRAN 77. The statement:

    READ (5, *) ITEM, NUMBER

will read from channel 5 two integer values into ITEM and NUMBER, respectively. The values must be separated by a comma or by spaces. No FORMAT statement is required.

Instructions to transfer information to and from sequential files of text have the same form as ordinary input and output instructions. However, it is also necessary to have a way of associating the physical file on backing store, usually disk, with the channel number used in the program.

The statement:

    OPEN(2, FILE = 'INFO', STATUS = 'OLD')

associates an existing (OLD) disk file called INFO with channel 2. Ordinary READ statements can then be used to read information on this channel. The statement:

    OPEN(4, FILE = 'MOREINFO', STATUS = 'NEW')

creates a new file called MOREINFO which can then have information written to it on channel 4. The file associated with a channel may be closed by a command such as:

    CLOSE(2)

after which another file may be connected to that channel or the original file may be connected to another channel.

ALGOL 60

FORTRAN I/O is simple and powerful and machine dependence is limited to the channel numbers. One of the aims of the designers of ALGOL 60 was to produce a language that was machine independent, and as I/O requires interaction with the operating system, it was completely ignored in the design of the language. This had exactly the opposite effect to that intended. Since read and write instructions are essential, each implementor of ALGOL 60 devised a different mechanism with the result that ALGOL 60 programs are less portable than FORTRAN ones.

Pascal

To write a character string, followed by the values of the integer variables *item* and *number*, to the standard output device in Pascal, the following statement is used:

write(' ANSWERS =', *item, number*)

which is shorthand for:

write(*output*, ' ANSWERS =', *item, number*)

There are no FORMAT statements in Pascal and the default layout is implementation dependent, although the number of columns to be used in writing a value can be specified, as in:

write(' ANSWERS =', *item* : 9, *number* : 7)

which will give the same layout as the FORTRAN WRITE statement given earlier.

Unlike FORTRAN, where each new WRITE statement causes information to be written on a new line, values are written on the current line in Pascal. To output an end-of-line indicator, *writeln* is used. The statements:

write(*item*); *write*(*number*)

will cause two values to be written on the current line while:

writeln(*item*); *write*(*number*)

will cause the first value to be written on the current line and the other on the next line. The end-of-line indicator can only be written using *writeln*.

To read two values, the statement is:

read(*item, number*)

which is shorthand for:

read(*input, item, number*)

The statement:

readln(*item, number*)

will read two values and then skip all the remaining characters in the line up to and including the end-of-line indicator. When reading data, it is possible to find out if the current position is at the end of a line by using the predefined Boolean function *eoln*. The end-of-line indicator itself is read as the space character.

Associated with a file *x* is the file buffer variable *x* ↑. The standard file buffer variables *input* ↑ and *output* ↑ are of type *char*. The *read* and *write* statements can be defined in terms of the more fundamental I/O statements *get* and *put*. If *ch* is a character variable, the effect of *read(ch)* is defined as:

    ch := input ↑; *get(input)*

which sets *ch* equal to the current value of the file buffer variable *input* ↑ and then uses *get* to read the next character into *input* ↑. The effect of *write(ch)* is defined as:

    output ↑ := *ch*; *put(output)*

The value of *ch* is assigned to *output* ↑ and *put* is then used to add the value of *output* ↑ to the end of file *output*. After a call of *put(output)*, the value of *output* ↑ is undefined.

As, after a call of *read* or *readln*, the file buffer variable contains the next character to be read, problems can arise with interactive I/O. A statement such as *readln(item)* reads the value of *item*, skips the rest of the characters on the line, including the end-of-line indicator, and then inputs the first character on the next line into *input* ↑. In interactive input, this character may not yet have been typed in and so cannot be read. In early implementations of Pascal, this caused programs to hang up at unexpected times, waiting for input. Most recent implementations of Pascal solve this problem by using what is called **lazy I/O**, where the reading of the next character into the file buffer variable is delayed until it is required.

Interactive I/O is the only place in the semantics of a sequential language like Pascal that two parallel processors must be considered; namely, the computer and the human user. If problems are to be avoided, their synchronization must be explicitly considered in the language design. Unfortunately, this does not happen. I/O is usually the last feature to be considered and it often seems that interactive I/O is not given any special consideration at all.

Items of type *char, integer, real* and *Boolean* together with packed arrays of *char* may be written in Pascal, but *Boolean* variables may not be read and strings have to be read in as a series of individual characters.

To read or write information to disk, logical file names must be listed in the program heading along with *input* and *output* and their type given in a declaration:

    program *example(input, output, oldfile, newfile)*;
    ...
    var *oldfile, newfile* : *text*;
    ...

As has been seen, *input* and *output* are automatically associated with the standard input and output devices. The way in which other logical file names are associated with physical files on backing store is up to the operating system. This association is fixed and cannot be changed during program execution, for there is no equivalent in standard Pascal of the *open* and *close* procedures found in many other languages.

To open the file associated with *oldfile* for reading, the command is:

    reset(*oldfile*)

and to open the file associated with *newfile* for writing, the command is:

    rewrite(*newfile*)

read and *write* statements are then used in the same way as with the standard input and output files; for example:

    read(*oldfile, item*); *write*(*newfile, item*)

When reading a file, it is possible to determine if the end has been reached through the value of the Boolean function *eof*.

Although there is no instruction to close a file in Pascal, if *reset* or *rewrite* is applied to an open file, the file is first closed and then opened for reading or writing, respectively.

Ada and Modula-2

I/O in Ada is provided by a hierarchy of predefined packages called *low_level_io*, *direct_io, sequential_io* and *text_io*. All validated Ada systems must provide an implementation of these packages, as specified in the Ada Reference Manual.

Modula-2 also provides I/O through a hierarchy of modules, although it differs from Ada in that the module contents are only recommended and are not mandatory. The problem of non-standard implementations and the resulting difficulties in program portability therefore arise, and could be a major obstacle to the acceptance of Modula-2. As the current recommendations correspond to a simplified and incomplete version of Ada I/O, they will not be considered further.

High-level text I/O in Ada is provided by the package *text_io*, which provides facilities at a similar level to Pascal I/O. This package defines procedures called *get* and *put* to read and write characters or strings. The *get* and *put* routines to read and write integers, fixed point numbers, reals and enumerated types are declared in local generic packages *integer_io, fixed_io, float_io* and *enumeration_io*, which are declared within package *text_io*. However, these packages must be instantiated before such I/O can take place. (The instantiation of generic packages was looked at in Section 7.5.) For example, to be able to read and write integers, the following must be written:

```
with text_io; use text_io;
procedure example is
   ...
   package int_io is new integer_io(integer);
   use int_io;
   ...
```

Calls of *get* and *put* to read and write character, string and integer values may now be made in procedure *example*. As Ada allows procedures and functions to be overloaded, the type of the parameter determines which version of *get* or *put* is required. The drawback of this approach is that generic instantiation has to be introduced at the beginning of an Ada course.

A difference between Pascal and Ada is that the Ada I/O routines all follow the ordinary Ada rules for procedures and functions, while Pascal I/O routines only look like ordinary subprograms and can have a variable number of parameters of differing types.

As with Pascal, Ada lines are terminated by an end-of-line indicator, which can only be written by calls of procedures such as *new_line*. Corresponding to the Pascal *eoln* function is the function *end_of_line*. In addition, lines are grouped into pages. End-of-page indicators are written by calls of *new_page* and recognized by calls of the Boolean function *end_of_page*.

In Ada, logical file names are declared to be of type *file_type*; for example:

old_file, new_file : file_type;

Ada files may have the mode *in_file* or *out_file* where type *file_mode* has been declared in *text_io* as:

type file_mode **is** (in_file, out_file);

The procedure call:

open(old_file, in_file, info);

will cause the logical file called *old_file* to be associated with the backing store file whose name is held in the string variable *info* and for that file to be opened for reading. The call:

create(new_file, out_file, new_info);

will create a new file with the name which is held in the string variable *new_info*. It will then associate that file with the logical file *new_file* so that it can be written to.

As a value can be read into a string variable, the association between logical and physical files can be set up and changed during program execution. In Pascal, on the other hand, all such associations must be set up before execution begins.

Overloaded versions of *get* and *put* are used for file I/O; for example:

get(old_file, item); put(new_file, item);

To close the file associated with *new_file*, the command is *close(new_file)* and to delete it, the command is *delete(new_file)*. Files should be explicitly closed before a program is terminated. Many other procedures and functions are available in Ada to manipulate files and to control the layout of data or results. Another difference between Pascal and Ada is that in Ada it is possible to read and write the values of an enumerated type (by instantiating the generic package *enumeration_io* for a particular enumeration type) and to read strings as a single unit as well as write them.

The C language

The definition of the C language does not deal with input and output, but in implementations high-level I/O is provided by a standard library called *stdio*. To ensure that certain necessary definitions are available, programs using this library should start with:

#include <stdio.h>

To control layout a FORTRAN-like format specification is incorporated within the print statement. Hence:

printf(" ANSWERS =%9d%7d", item, number);

causes ANSWERS = to be output followed by the value of *item* in the next 9 columns and the value of *number* in the following 7. The format %d indicates that an integer number is to be printed. Other formats are possible, such as %s for string, %c for character and %f for floating point number.

Input is provided by the *scanf* routine, as in:

scanf("%d%d", &item, &number);

Instead of having a special end-of-line indicator, lines are terminated by an ordinary character, which is represented in programs as \n. Being at the end of a line is determined by testing for this character.

Logical file names are declared to be pointers to type FILE, as in:

FILE *oldfile, *newfile;

To associate the logical file called *oldfile* with the backing store file whose name is held in the string variable *info* and to open the file for reading, the call is:

oldfile = fopen(info, "r");

while to create a new file with the name held in the string variable *newinfo* so it can be written to, the call is:

newfile = fopen(newinfo, "w");

If a file cannot be opened, the null pointer is returned. Pointers to three standard files (*stdin, stdout* and *stderr*) are declared in *<stdio.h>*. These are associated with the standard input, standard output and standard error output files. To close a file such as *newfile*, the command is *fclose(newfile)*. To read and write files, *fscanf* and *fprintf* are used, as in:

fscanf(oldfile, "%d", &item); fprintf(newfile, "%d", item);

At a slightly lower level, characters can be read and written by calls of *fgetc* and *fputc*, as in:

ch = fgetc(oldfile); fputc(ch, newfile);

The function *fgetc* actually returns an integer value, but this can usually be treated as a character. The exception is that when the end of file is encountered; then, the integer constant EOF is returned. The value of EOF is defined in *<stdio.h>* and is implementation dependent.

As with the other languages discussed, I/O is buffered in C. It is often necessary to be able to 'peek' ahead at the character following the item currently being read. Pascal uses the file buffer variable for this while in C it is possible to read a character as normal and then, after examining it, to put it back by means of the *ungetc* function! The next call of *fgetc* will read the character that was put back.

Scanning strings

From a programmer's point of view, reading a line of text and converting it into some internal representation is not too different from scanning a string of characters. Hence, C and Ada have routines, analogous to their I/O routines, for converting strings of, for example, digits into the internal representation of a number. If *str* is the string "34 42 –181 853", the effect of:

> *get(str, item, pos);*

in Ada is analogous to:

> *get(old_file, item);*

when 34 is the next string of characters in the file associated with *old_file*. The variable *pos* is set equal to the position in the string *str* of the last character read so that, by using array slices, the next item from the string can be read. The effect of executing the code segment:

```
pos := 0;
for count in 1 .. 4 loop
    get(str(pos + 1 .. str'length), item, pos);
    put(item);
end loop;
```

is to write out the four numerical values which were in the string *str*. The value of *pos* will be in turn 2, 5, 10 and 14. *str'length* is an array attribute that has as its value the length of the string *str*.

It can at times be useful to read a complete line of numerical data into a string before extracting its contents. By doing this, it is possible to build in an error recovery routine if an input error is detected.

PROLOG and LISP

PROLOG and LISP are normally used interactively. A PROLOG session often consists of a series of questions to which the system is required to respond. Similarly, a LISP session consists of a series of function definitions and expressions which are to be evaluated. The LISP system responds to a request to evaluate an expression by printing the result. More conventional I/O is, however, possible in both of these languages.

In PROLOG, as in Pascal, the user's keyboard and screen are treated as sequential files. Only one input and one output file are active at any one moment and at the beginning of a PROLOG session these are the user's keyboard and screen. To change the current input file to file **oldfile**, the following clause is used:

   see(oldfile)

while to change the output file to file **newfile**, the following clause is used:

   tell(newfile)

These goals succeed when it is possible to open the relevant file, otherwise they fail. To return to the standard input file, the goal **see(user)** is attempted; to return to the standard output file, the goal **tell(user)** is tried.

The effect of **read(X)** in PROLOG is to read a value (terminated by a full stop) from the current input file and attempt to match it with the variable **X**. Similarly, **write(X)** will write out the value of **X**. There is no restriction on the complexity of the data object associated with **X**. Input and output in PROLOG is, therefore, relatively simple, the main aim being to read and write values for the data objects that are manipulated by the PROLOG program. There is automatic translation between the internal representation and some suitable external form.

LISP systems have functions READ and PRINT which achieve their effect by side effects. Like PROLOG, the values input or output are the basic data objects of the system, which in the case of LISP are S-expressions. Input from or output to a file is achieved by calls to predefined functions and these differ from one implementation to the next.

Thus, the I/O facilities of LISP and PROLOG are aimed at supporting the interactive environment in which they are usually used, rather than supporting sophisticated file handling facilities.

13.3 Binary and direct access files

Binary files

Up till now, the discussion on I/O has concentrated on text files. However, when a file is created by one program, so that it can be read by another, there is no need for conversion between some internal representation and a human readable external form.

In Pascal, instead of declaring a file to be of type *text*, it can be declared to be a file of, for example, *integer*:

   var *old* : **file of** *integer*;

The exact way in which the integers are represented in the file is implementation dependent, although the probability is that they will be in binary; that is, in the same form as their internal representation. All that can be guaranteed here is that a file written by a Pascal program on a particular system as a file of *integer* can be read as a file of *integer* by another Pascal program on the same system.

A file can be considered to consist of a series of records where each record consists of a series of fields. This structure can be represented in Pascal by declaring a record type with the appropriate field structure. Assuming a record type *recorditem*, file variables can then be declared as:

> **var** *datafile, resultfile* : **file of** *recorditem*;

If the variable *thisrecord* has been declared to be of type *recorditem*, the following loop will cause the contents of file *datafile* to be copied to file *resultfile*:

> *reset(datafile)*; *rewrite(resultfile)*;
> **while not** *eof(datafile)* **do**
> **begin**
>   *read(datafile, thisrecord)*;
>   *write(resultfile, thisrecord)*;
> **end**;

Each call of *read* reads the contents of the next complete record in file *datafile* into the record variable *thisrecord*, while each call of *write* outputs the contents of a complete record.

In FORTRAN, binary files are said to be UNFORMATTED. A binary file called BIN can be associated to channel 2 and opened for reading by:

> OPEN(2, FILE = 'BIN', STATUS = 'OLD', FORM ='UNFORMATTED')

READ and WRITE statements are declared as before except that no format number need be given, as in:

> READ (2) ITEM, NUMBER

In Ada, the generic package *sequential_io* contains the definition of I/O for sequential files. To deal with a sequential file of items of the record type *recorditem*, this package has to be instantiated as:

> **package** *seq_int_io* **is new** *sequential_io(recorditem)*;

The package contains definitions of file management procedures such as *open*, *create* and *delete* similar to those declared in *text_io*. One difference is that reading and writing is done by calls to *read* and *write* instead of *get* and *put*.

Direct access files

As well as having sequential files, many languages support direct access files where items may be read or written in any order. Thus, there must be some means of indicating which position in the file is being referred to. Such facilities are available in FORTRAN 77, C and Ada, but not in Pascal.

To illustrate how direct access is handled, consider the facilities available in the Ada generic package *direct_io*. It is very similar to *sequential_io* except that as well as having procedures *read* and *write* with the specification:

procedure *read*(*file* : **in** *file_type*; *item* : **out** *element_type*);
procedure *write*(*file* : **in** *file_type*; *item* : **in** *element_type*);

which transfer an item to or from the current position in a file, it also has:

procedure *read*(*file* : **in** *file_type*; *item* **out** *element_type*;
          from : *positive_count*);
procedure *write*(*file* : **in** *file_type*; *item* **in** *element_type*;
          to : *positive_count*);

in which the position of the item can be specified. The subtype *positive_count* is an implementation-defined integer subrange.

This package also has a file of mode *inout_file* as well as *in_file* and *out_file*, which allows the contents of a file to be updated while it is still open for reading.

13.4 Concluding remarks

This chapter has shown how several languages handle I/O and how, in general, I/O is not a central part of the language, but is implemented by means of a series of pre-defined subprograms. In languages like Pascal, these subprograms allow a variable number of parameters of varying types and so do not follow the usual language rules for subprograms. In more recent languages such as Ada and Modula-2, modules are used to encapsulate the subprograms that implement I/O, but the general approach remains the same. This leads to the question of whether there is a simple conceptual model that would allow I/O to be brought into the mainstream of language design.

One novel approach has been receiving attention. In a concurrent system, sequential processes can communicate with one another by passing messages. The output of information to, or input of information from, a peripheral device has a marked similarity with a process passing information to, or receiving information from, another process. This similarity underlies the approach taken in inter-process communication in the language CSP and implemented in occam. The command:

```
keyboard ? ch
```

means read a value from a keyboard and assign it to the variable ch. The command:

```
vduscreen ! ch
```

means send the value of the variable ch to a VDU screen. It is assumed here that keyboard and vduscreen are peripheral devices. However, they could equally well have been the names of processes, and in that case the form of the CSP command would have been the same.

The identification of I/O with inter-process communication is useful at the implementation level, since a process controlled by the CPU really is operating concurrently with a peripheral device. It is also useful when thinking about the effect of a user program. In interactive I/O, for example, the two communicating sequential processes can be considered to be the program and the activities of a human being sitting at a terminal. Furthermore, if a user is to take part in a dialogue at a terminal, then this requires that input and output are not independent of one another but are synchronized.

Although Ada adopted the CSP model as the basis for task communication and synchronization it, unlike occam, uses the conventional approach to I/O. There is, however, no reason why an alternative set of I/O packages could not be defined to make explicit use of tasking. It would in fact be interesting to see if such an approach resulted in an improved way of defining interactive I/O.

When dealing with I/O, it is often unclear where language issues end and the operating system begins. This is especially true with C due to its intimate connection with the UNIX operating system. To illustrate the situation in C, suppose that the program *first* outputs results to a terminal while the program *second* inputs data from a terminal. Program *first* can be made to output its results to a file called *intermediate* by 'redirecting' the output by means of the UNIX command line:

first > intermediate

Similarly, *second* can be made to read its input from the file *intermediate*, instead of from a terminal, by means of the command line:

second < intermediate

Neither C program would have to be changed in any way.

To make the two programs communicate with one another without having to specify an intermediate file, a UNIX pipe is used. The command line is:

first | second

The output from *first* is taken as the input to *second*. The same mechanism is, therefore, used in UNIX for I/O and for the communication between two independent processes.

Summary

(1) After information in human readable form has been input into a computer, it must be converted into a suitable internal representation. Conversion in the opposite direction is required on output.

(2) FORTRAN uses FORMAT statements to specify the layout of data and channel numbers to specify the peripheral device. Pascal has no FORMAT statements and uses symbolic names to specify the peripheral device. C uses FORTRAN-like FORMAT specifications but, unlike FORTRAN, they are incorporated into the appropriate I/O routine.

(3) In Pascal, all I/O, including interactive I/O, is considered to be to or from a sequential file. A Pascal text file is a file of lines. This approach has been followed in Ada and in Modula-2.

(4) In standard Pascal, the association between logical file names and particular physical files cannot be changed during program execution. This is in contrast to many other languages which have explicit open and close instructions.

(5) I/O in Ada is provided by a hierarchy of predefined packages called *low_level_io, direct_io, sequential_io* and *text_io*. *text_io* is for human readable text, *sequential_io* for binary files, *direct_io* for direct access files while *low_level_io* allows direct control of peripheral devices.

EXERCISES

13.1 Compare the relative ease of presenting the results of executing a program as a table in Pascal and in FORTRAN.

13.2 What I/O instructions would have to be added to Pascal so that it could be used as a systems programming language?

13.3 Languages like FORTRAN have special I/O instructions while later languages use predefined procedures and functions to handle I/O. Which approach is to be preferred and why?

13.4 Many languages treat all I/O as if it were 'to' or 'from' a sequential file. What difficulties does this cause with interactive I/O?

13.5 Should languages like Pascal and Ada have features that directly support menus, icons and the movement of turtles about a VDU screen? Pascal systems on microcomputers often have enhanced screen handling facilities. Collect as much information as you can on existing systems, compare their facilities and design a suitable set of machine-independent routines.

BIBLIOGRAPHY

Input and output in the various languages is described in the language texts listed at the end of this book. The text on C by Kernighan (1988) also describes the interface between C and UNIX. CSP was introduced by Hoare (1985).

Hoare, C. A. R. (1985), *Communicating Sequential Processes*, Prentice-Hall.

Kernighan, B. W. and Ritchie, D. M. (1988), *The C Programming Language* (Second Edition), Prentice-Hall.

The future

14

CONTENTS

14.1 **Imperative languages**   314
14.2 **Fourth-generation languages**   316
14.3 **Declarative languages**   316
14.4 **Object-oriented languages**   317
14.5 **Language design**   318
14.6 **Implementation considerations**   320
14.7 **Reasoning about programs**   321
14.8 **Efficiency versus ease of use**   322

The first part of this chapter looks at the development of programming languages through the 1990s. Speculation beyond this point is probably too unreliable to be useful to current computer users. The second part of the chapter then looks at language design in general and examines how it is likely to develop. Particular attention is paid to those features that support the production of reliable programs, such as data abstraction, the need for language structures that make it easier to reason about a program's effect and the move towards declarative languages where more of the details are handled by the system rather than by the programmer.

14.1 Imperative languages

Current imperative languages can be divided into three categories. The old languages (FORTRAN and COBOL) which were developed in the 1950s and early 1960s but which are still in use in a revised form; the middle-aged languages (Pascal, BASIC and C) which were developed in the 1960s and early 1970s and which are still going strong; and, finally, the newer languages (Modula-2, C++ and Ada) whose share of the market is likely to grow.

Old imperative languages

Given the far-reaching changes that have occurred in both hardware and software design, it is surprising to find that, 30 years on, the old warhorses FORTRAN and COBOL still hold a sizable share of the scientific and business programming markets, respectively. As was stated at the beginning of this book, there is a great deal of inertia in the computing world and so once a language has been accepted and a large body of algorithms, systems and programs developed, it is difficult (if not impossible) to replace it. Certainly, FORTRAN and COBOL will continue to be used in the foreseeable future, although the attitude of most programmers is one of acceptance of them with all their warts, rather than true love. Newer versions (for example, FORTRAN 90 replacing FORTRAN 77) will no doubt continue to emerge but few people believe that such updates will produce more than a temporary life extension for these languages since it is the basic structure that needs to be replaced.

Middle-aged imperative languages

The languages Pascal, BASIC and C are likely to extend their useful lives well into the 1990s, but for quite different reasons.

Pascal was developed as a language for teaching good programming practice and, after a somewhat slow start, it convinced a fair body of opinion of its ability to do just that. Hence, at many universities it is the first language taught to students especially those taking specialist computing degrees. As Pascal is backed up by efficient compilers for the majority of computers, its role in this area is hardly being challenged. Indeed, two major new imperative languages, Modula-2 and Ada, are Pascal based. Hence, Pascal is an excellent first language if it is intended to move on to Modula-2 or Ada. Also, as most Pascal implementations contain extensions such as a module facility and enhanced string handling, Pascal itself is now widely used in industry.

BASIC's surprising success in the 1970s was due to its simplicity and the fact that it contained sufficient operating system features for it to be self-contained. Such features enabled BASIC to take full advantage of the opportunities in the small computer market. However, its hold on the microcomputer market is not likely to be as long lasting as that of FORTRAN and COBOL in their areas. One reason for this is that the small computer market has not the same strong inertia factor for systems written in BASIC. When users move from small computers, they do not normally insist on a large body of algorithms, systems and programs moving with them. Another factor is that with the reduction in hardware costs, the power and size of microcomputers has increased substantially. In the early 1980s, micros typically had main memory sizes of 16, 32 or 64 kbytes while by 1990 main memory sizes of several megabytes had become commonplace. This change has meant that micros are now capable of handling more sophisticated languages than BASIC and so has given other languages a chance to challenge BASIC in the small computer market.

Thus, at one end, there is an erosion as more users prefer the precision and structure of Pascal, a trend that has been helped by the development of extensions, such as Turbo Pascal, which are designed specifically for use on microcomputers. At the other end, there have been several attempts to produce languages simpler than BASIC, usually at a higher level and for specific applications.

C continues to grow in importance and many of its early deficiencies in the area of typing have been dealt with in the development of ANSI C and C++. As C++ is a superset of ANSI C, this gives a straightforward development path for programmers moving from C to the richer data abstraction facilities of C++.

C is now the most widely used systems programming language. A major factor in its rise is that it is the host language for the UNIX operating system which dominates the market for high-performance scientific workstations and is making increasing inroads into the commercial and business markets.

Newer imperative languages

Apart from C++, Ada and Modula-2 seem the most likely heirs to the imperative language empire. Of these two languages, Ada is an obvious candidate since it underwent a rigorous selection procedure at birth and has the backing of the US Department of Defense (DOD). Doubts about Ada mainly stem from its large size and, while appreciating that complex problems may well need more than a simple language, it still worries many computer scientists that Ada could well encounter the size and complexity problems that beset PL/I.

It is perhaps unfair to associate Ada with the problems of PL/I, particularly as the design of Ada was dealt with in a much more effective and professional manner. Ada compilers are, however, large and expensive and require substantial computing power due to the size and complexity of the language. In addition, the widespread adoption of the language is not helped by the inflexibility of the DOD in not allowing any subsets. A sensible approach to this problem would be to have a small teaching subset of Ada – in essence, the part of Ada that is similar to Pascal with the addition of packages. Other useful subsets could also be evolved, but at present official policy is to ban all subsets of Ada.

The other new imperative language that gained popularity in the 1980s is Modula-2. As Modula-2 does not have the complexity of Ada, the compiler difficulties are much less serious. Of course, Modula-2 has no large backing organization like the DOD, and this has its drawbacks, but it also allows experimentation and an ability to take opportunities when they arise. There are, however, reservations among programmers as to whether Modula-2 has the right features to make a significant impact in the embedded systems and concurrency areas and it is likely that, in the 1990s, the competition of C++ and Ada will prove too strong and that the use of Modula-2 will decline.

14.2   Fourth-generation languages

The so-called fourth-generation languages (4GLs) have not been discussed in any depth in this book, a detail that will no doubt confirm James Martin's view that academics have not realized the true importance of these languages. It is indeed the case that universities have done little to advance the cause of 4GLs, but their reasons are not just ignorance and prejudice. Although 4GLs cover a wide range of programming activity, their most obvious area of application is in the business programming area; they are, in effect, attempts to produce a higher level COBOL. Perhaps what is required is for the business programming fraternity to sit down together and design one 4GL for their field of computing. So far, however, this has not happened and the net result is a whole mass of 4GLs, each purporting to do everything that one could possibly wish for. Alas, the reality is that while these languages have some strong high-level features, they are incomplete and never comprehensive. It seems that manufacturers, in an attempt to catch the market, produce them too quickly and before they are wholly and consistently specified. Nevertheless, the fact that the current incomplete and often ill-designed 4GLs are making a considerable impact in the market-place suggests that there is indeed a need for a high-level business-oriented language – this is hardly surprising since COBOL was a product of the late 1950s and computers have advanced considerably since then. Perhaps what is needed is a development on the business side similar to the development of Ada. However, there is no sign of such a move and so the probable outcome will be the emergence of the best of the current business-oriented 4GLs.

14.3   Declarative languages

The main declarative languages are the functional subset of LISP, together with the newer functional languages such as Miranda, ML and Haskell and the logic language PROLOG. It is clear that the supremacy of imperative languages is being seriously challenged by declarative languages, although both functional and logic languages are at a considerable disadvantage when they are used on current computer architectures. Furthermore, although they have shown their ability to specify problems, particularly in artificial intelligence, they have revealed a major weakness when attempts have been made to use them on large problems.

There are two approaches to these difficulties. The first is to use the declarative language to specify the problem and then convert the specification, perhaps automatically, to an imperative language for running on the computer. A more fundamental approach is to seek alternative architectures that support concurrent activities and thus build computers more attuned to declarative languages.

For a long time, functional languages and PROLOG were seen as competitors, and this may have been partly due to the fact that they both arose in artificial intelligence research activities. A fair amount of wasted effort and energy went into attempts to prove that the functional approach was superior to the logic method and vice versa. However, these efforts did help to identify the strengths and weaknesses of each language and have led to more constructive research aimed at finding a compromise based on the strong points of each. This is a welcome development and could perhaps be taken further by adding some of the better features of modern imperative languages to declarative languages.

14.4   Object-oriented languages

Object-oriented languages are an active area of research and will become increasingly important in the 1990s. Being able to reuse existing software components has, for long, been one of the main aims of software developers, and object-oriented languages offer the most promising way ahead.

Object-oriented programming languages are also ideally suited to application areas such as the implementation of graphical user interfaces. Components of a graphical interface, such as windows, icons and menus, have to be opened, closed, moved and re-sized. They can therefore be modelled naturally as objects that have a local state and that respond to messages. Once a library of basic graphical component definitions (classes) has been provided, the definitions can be customized, using inheritance, to provide exactly what is required. As user-friendly graphical interfaces are an increasingly important part of all new systems, this area alone guarantees the continuing practical importance of object-oriented programming languages.

Although some newer object-oriented languages, such as Eiffel, are statically typed, many object-oriented languages are dynamically typed and so would seem to be more suited to prototyping and for use in a research environment rather than used as tools in the creation of large industrial-quality systems. It is therefore likely that purely object-oriented systems will not become widely used in industry and the main impact of object-oriented concepts will be their incorporation into new versions of imperative languages, as has already happened with the development of C++ from C. The use of a hybrid language like C++ is attractive to industry as it allows a gradual move from conventional languages and approaches. Many would argue, on the other hand, that the object-oriented approach must be followed through all stages of software development if its full benefits are to be realized.

Object-oriented software development supports an integrated approach to the analysis, design and implementation phases of the software life cycle. In object-oriented analysis, a problem-oriented model is created with real-world entities being modelled as objects which provide services to, and require services of, other objects. This model acts as a specification of the required system. In object-oriented design, the problem-oriented model is transformed into a form which is oriented towards computer implementation. Ideally, there will be a simple mapping from objects in the problem-oriented model to objects in the design model. In the implementation phase, the objects in the design phase are implemented in either an object-based or an object-oriented programming language.

This approach to software development leads naturally to modular systems and, as it supports the goals of data abstraction, encapsulation and information hiding, the resulting systems can be easily maintained or enhanced. The modelling of real-world entities as objects leads to implementations that resemble the original problem. This can be a major help in the understanding of large software systems.

Object-oriented development is already widely used by the Ada community and is likely to increase in importance. Its impact on the software development process will spread the influence of object-oriented concepts and will add to the pressure for the incorporation of object-oriented constructs into existing imperative languages.

14.5 Language design

The aim of this section is to look at language design in general to see if any conclusions can be made about the features that are central to the design of a modern language. To some extent, this will of course depend on what the language is to be used for, but it should be possible to identify common goals.

A principal aim of a programming language should be to support the development of reliable programs. This means that it should be a help to the designer or programmer during the development process and should lead to programs that are straightforward to read and understand. It is, of course, possible to write obscure programs in any language, but there can be no doubt that the development of techniques such as programming by stepwise refinement, coupled with the introduction of languages such as Pascal that support the systematic development of programs, has led to an improvement in programming standards.

What, then, are the features that support the production of reliable programs? One approach is to use high-level constructs where the programmer states 'what' is to be done rather than 'how' it is to be achieved. By removing such details, the opportunity for error is reduced. Short high-level programs are generally easier to read, write and understand than long low-level programs. This factor has led to the great interest in functional and logic languages, but unless radically new computer hardware is developed, it seems likely that imperative languages will remain dominant for the foreseeable future.

Reliable programs should be straightforward to read and understand. Ideally, a language should contain a minimum number of independent concepts which can be combined according to simple rules. As there will then be few, if any, special cases to be considered, such a language should be simple.

Unfortunately, the combination of independent concepts in all possible ways usually leads to certain features that are of dubious value and which are difficult and expensive to implement, as was found with ALGOL 68. In certain cases, the introduction of restrictions on how features may be combined can actually increase the simplicity of a language. After all, a feature of high-level languages is that they do restrict usage, examples being strong typing, restrictions on the arbitrary transfers of control and on performing arithmetic on addresses.

A programming language's design must, therefore, exhibit a proper sense of balance. On the one hand, it is important to have a small set of concepts that can be combined, since this leads to a set of regular rules that can be learned and used much more easily than a set of *ad hoc* rules. On the other hand, it is important to have a small set of restrictions that outlaw those constructs which few, if any, people would ever want to use.

Another important feature of a language design is that there should be no surprises. Features that are similar should look similar; for example, procedure and function declarations should have the same structure. Conversely, features that are different should look different so that similarities are not sought where none exist; for example, the notation used in Pascal to indicate a file buffer variable (*filename*↑) is the same as that used with pointers and students are often misled into pushing the analogy further than is useful.

Reliability is greatly enhanced if most errors can be detected by a static scan of the program text rather than having to wait till program execution. This suggests the need for strong typing so that certain logical errors, which would otherwise lie dormant until run time, show up during program translation.

It is also important that a simple typing mistake should cause a syntax error rather than leading to a program which, although logically wrong, is syntactically correct. The classic example of this is the FORTRAN statement:

```
DO 20 I = 1.6
```

where a decimal point has mistakenly been typed instead of a comma. Thus, the statement, instead of describing the beginning of a loop, represents an assignment statement where 1.6 is assigned to the variable DO20I. Errors of this nature cannot occur when spaces are significant in the program text and when all identifiers are declared before being used, rather than being implicitly declared by their first use.

Security is also enhanced by the introduction of redundant reserved words so that errors can be detected as soon as they occur. For example, in the Pascal statement:

if $a > 2$ **then** $b : = 47$

the reserved word **then** is not strictly necessary. In a statement such as:

if $a > 2 \, b : = 47$

it is always possible to tell when the end of the Boolean expression has been reached. The appearance of **then** is not therefore necessary, but it does help readability.

If a language is to be used in the development of reliable large programs, it is essential that it contains some mechanism to support modular decomposition. There seems to be general agreement that this should be achieved by organizing programs as a collection of modules. Each module is then divided into two parts; a visible part that defines its interface with other modules and an implementation part that is hidden. If a user of a module cannot see, and therefore cannot use, the information in the implementation part then, provided that it has no effect on the module interface, a change in the implementation part cannot have an effect outside the module. The consequences of change are therefore localized and this is essential if reliability is to be maintained when a large system is modified.

In object-oriented languages, the module (class) is a type. This gives many advantages in the construction of abstract data types, but a case can be made for separating the notion of modules and classes. A module is primarily concerned with properties concerning program structure such as information hiding and determining which units may be separately compiled, while classes are primarily concerned with the definition of new types. This separation already occurs in C++. Classes are usually held in separate files and it is these files that provide a program's module structure.

14.6   Implementation considerations

The syntax of modern programming languages are formally and unambiguously defined by meta-languages such as Backus-Naur Form (BNF), or graphically by means of syntax diagrams. Having a language syntax defined in this way leads to a regular language structure. Modern compilers directly use a language's syntax rules to translate a source program into machine code. It is therefore important that the syntax can be defined in such a way that it can be easily handled using conventional compiler techniques. This really means that the language should be defined by either an LL(1) or an LR(1) grammar. Such languages are always unambiguous and can be parsed by efficient standard techniques.

The needs of the compiler and the human user as regards the definition of a language's syntax appear to coincide exactly, since language constructs that can be easily translated also seem to be simple for humans to understand, whereas constructs that are difficult to translate are also difficult for humans to comprehend. Indeed, Wirth suggests that the process of language design and language implementation should go together for this very reason, and he has followed this approach in the design of Pascal, Modula and Modula-2. Given the success of these languages, Wirth's views must be taken seriously, although concern with implementation issues can be taken too far.

Often, when a language is being designed, a lot of pressure is placed on the designer to include additional features because they might be useful. Such pressures can be balanced by requests to keep things simple if the language implementation team are in day-to-day contact with the design team.

The importance of size should not be underestimated. The size and complexity of a language affects the speed at which it can be translated and the size of machine required to host the translation. The relative ease with which Pascal could be implemented, coupled with the existence of a portable compiler, greatly enhanced its acceptance while the size of PL/I and the complexity of ALGOL 68 led to their relative lack of success. Similarly, the widespread adoption of Ada is being hampered by the size, cost and lack of speed of its compilers and is helping C, C++ and Modula-2 gain a niche in the market-place.

14.7 Reasoning about programs

Once a program has been produced, it is important to ensure that it satisfies its specification. The usual way of doing this is to run the program with suitably chosen data. Although testing is an important stage of the software development process, it does suffer from one major drawback; it can show the presence of errors, but it cannot prove that no errors remain. The ideal approach is therefore to verify a program; that is, to *prove* that the program conforms to its specification. A specification is often written in an informal notation although the trend is increasingly towards using a formal (mathematical) notation, which has led to the development of special specification languages. Such languages are beyond the scope of this book but the interested reader is referred to the collection of papers edited by Gehani (1986).

A lot of research has gone into proving that programs meet their specification and into how specifications can be automatically transformed into executable programs. Although progress has been made, this research is still a long way from either being able to prove the correctness of large programming systems or automatically generating them from their specification. However, it is at present possible to reason about the effect of programs and thereby to increase one's confidence that the specification is met. To reason about the effect of a large program, it is important that it has been constructed in such a way that it can be decomposed into separate components. It is then possible to reason about these components independently and so use the separate results when reasoning about the program as a whole.

Among the language features that help support this approach are modules and the structured control statements introduced in ALGOL 60 and refined in later languages. Each structured statement has only one entry and one exit point. A program constructed from such statements consists of a linear sequence of program components and the flow of control closely follows the program text. The reason for the unpopularity of the **goto** statement is that the arbitrary transfer of control that is then possible makes reasoning about programs much more difficult.

The ability to modify global variables means that one program component can have an unforeseen effect on another and is an obstacle to the decomposition of large programs into self-contained units that can be reasoned about independently. This is especially so when aliasing is involved.

Two approaches can be taken in language design. One is to offer sufficiently powerful language constructs so that programmers can produce well-structured programs; the other is to restrict languages so that the offending constructs are outlawed. These two approaches can, of course, be considered to be complementary.

One of the recently identified villains in the programmer's repertoire is the assignment statement, as without this it would not be possible to have global variables or aliases. Although pure functional languages manage without assignment, it is central to imperative languages and so curbing its abuses seems more appropriate than total abolition.

14.8   Efficiency versus ease of use

An important practical concern of a language is its efficiency at run time, both in terms of speed and the amount of store required. Associated with this, are the data types allowed and their built-in operations.

An important reason for the success of functional languages is that they treat structured data types, such as lists, as primitive types. Conventional imperative languages, on the other hand, tend to have a much richer set of operators available on scalar types than they do on structured types. In Pascal, for example, a function cannot return a structured value and, with the exception of strings, structured constants are not possible.

Having either built-in operators on structured types or the ability to create such operators easily leads to shorter programs, which should therefore be easier to understand. Detailed programming no longer has to be done by the programmer, but is handled automatically by the language system. The drawback of this approach is that in many cases heap storage allocation must be used with the attendant need for garbage collection and the reduction in execution speed.

Strong typing has been criticized for its lack of flexibility. For example, to sort an array of reals and an array of integers in Pascal, two separate sort procedures are required. In Ada, on the other hand, this can be achieved by generic subprograms and packages and it is no longer necessary to write two separate sort procedures. Instead, there are two instantiations of a generic sort procedure: one for integers and one for reals. This means, however, that two separate sort procedures still exist. In a language like ML, a single polymorphic sort procedure can be used and there is no need to create special purpose forms.

There has been a long debate about the need for types in programming languages. The balance seems to have swung decisively towards the strong typing school on the grounds that the need for reliability is more important than flexibility. The functional language ML makes an interesting contribution to this debate. It has types, but the types of objects do not have to be declared. The ML system deduces what the type of objects must be from their use and can report on inconsistent use.

Finally, the development of multiprocessor systems makes it likely that languages of the future must have a high-level way of handling concurrency. Perhaps the most interesting development (Yonezawa, 1987) is the generalization of the Smalltalk object so that systems are composed of objects that can execute independently and in parallel with all the others. The objects then interact with one another by passing and receiving messages. This concurrent object-oriented approach has a lot in common with the process model used in occam and in Ada, and so yet again there is a convergence of the developments in different areas. It is therefore important that all computer scientists have a working knowledge of the imperative, functional, logic and object-oriented programming paradigms so that they can make such connections instead of acting as a series of non-communicating sequential processes.

Summary

(1) Languages such as FORTRAN, COBOL and LISP, although developed in the 1950s and early 1960s, are still in widespread use.

(2) C is currently the most widely used systems programming language although Modula-2, Ada and C++ have better features for the support of reliable programming.

(3) Declarative languages may require the development of new architectures if they are to become dominant.

(4) The object-oriented approach is becoming increasingly important in the requirements analysis, specification and design phases of software development as well as in programming language design.

(5) The principal aim of a programming language should be to support the development of reliable programs.

(6) There is a correlation between language constructs that are simple for a human to understand and those that are easy for a compiler to translate.

(7) There is still much research to be done before it will be possible to prove the correctness of large programs or to generate them automatically from their specification. Reasoning about the effect of a program can, however, increase one's confidence that it meets its specification.

BIBLIOGRAPHY

The book by Gehani (1986) contains a large collection of papers on specification languages and methods. A good description of the formal approach to software development has been given by Partsch (1990) while the object-oriented software development life cycle has been described by Henderson-Sellers (1990).

Gehani, N. and McGettrick, A. D. (Eds) (1986), *Software Specification Techniques*, Addison-Wesley.

Henderson-Sellers, B. and Edwards, J. M. (1990), 'The Object-Oriented Systems Life Cycle', *Comm. ACM*, **33**, pp. 143–159.

Partsch, H. A. (1990), *Specification and Transformation of Programs*, Springer-Verlag.

Yonezawa, A. and Tokoro, M. (1987), *Object-Oriented Concurrent Programming*, MIT Press.

Appendix 1
Language summaries

This appendix summarizes the features of the principal languages dealt with in the text. The languages are given in alphabetical order and are Ada, ALGOL 60, ALGOL 68, C, C++, COBOL, Eiffel, FORTRAN, LISP, ML, Modula-2, Pascal, PL/I, PROLOG and Smalltalk. References to these and the other languages referred to in the text are given in Appendix 2.

Ada

Ada is a large and powerful language based on Pascal. It includes features to support data abstraction, concurrency and the production and maintenance of large systems.

Program structure and visibility

An Ada program is a collection of modules (subprograms or packages) whose inter-dependency is given by context clauses. One of the modules is the main program and it must be a procedure. A module is compiled in the context of those modules from which it imports information. A package is in two parts: a specification which gives its interface with the rest of the program, and a hidden implementation part. This allows separate compilation.

Data types

The predefined types are *integer, float, character, Boolean* and *string*. Scalar user-defined types are the derived subrange types and the enumeration types. Structured types can be defined using arrays, records and pointers. Abstract data types can be implemented using packages and parameterized abstract data types using generic packages.

Type checking

Ada is strongly typed.

Manipulation of structured objects

Arrays and records can be passed as parameters and returned as function values. Fixing the size of an array can be delayed until block entry. Dynamic data structures are created using records that have one or more fields of a pointer type. Strings are arrays of *character*.

Control structures

Structured control statements have explicit terminators. The conditional statements are **if** and **case**. The iterative statements are **while, for** and a **loop ... end loop** construct which may be left using an **exit** statement. Exception handling is also supported.

Concurrency

Parallel processing is achieved using tasks. Message passing is used both to pass information and to achieve synchronization.

Input/output

I/O is supported by a hierarchy of packages whose specifications are given in the Ada Reference Manual. At the highest level, text I/O is supported while the lowest level supports direct access to peripheral devices.

ALGOL 60

ALGOL 60 was the original block-structured language and is the direct ancestor of Pascal and most modern imperative languages. It was the first language to have its syntax defined formally using BNF.

Program structure and visibility

It is block structured with blocks inheriting declarations made in enclosing blocks. Procedures may be recursive in ALGOL 60 and all its descendants. There are no facilities for dealing with very large programs or for separate or independent compilation.

Data types

The predefined types are *real, integer* and *Boolean*. The only structured type is the array. User-defined types are not available.

Type checking

Implicit conversions are allowed between numeric types.

Manipulation of structured objects

Arrays may be passed as parameters, but may not be returned as the value of a function. The bounds of an array do not have to be fixed until block entry.

Control structures

The **if** statement has been copied in most ALGOL-like languages. Iteration is performed by the **for** statement which has several forms, one of which includes a **while** variant.

Concurrency

Not supported.

Input/output

Not defined in the language. Each implementation introduced its own statements.

ALGOL 68

ALGOL 68 was designed as the sophisticated and elegant successor to ALGOL 60, but although it proved popular with theoreticians it was far less popular with programmers. Its definition was difficult to follow and no concessions were made to ease the implementation – a compiler writer's nightmare.

Program structure and visibility

It is a block-structured language. There are no facilities for dealing with very large programs or for separate or independent compilation.

Data types

Predefined types are *int, real, char, bool* and *string*. Array, pointer and structure (record) types can be user defined.

Type checking

It is strongly typed.

Manipulation of structured objects

There are better facilities for the manipulation of structured objects in ALGOL 68 than in most other languages. The size of a (flexible) array can be changed during program execution. Strings are implemented as flexible character arrays.

Subprograms can have subprograms as parameters and functions can return subprograms as values.

Control structures

Unlike ALGOL 60, control statements in ALGOL 68 have explicit terminators. The conditional statements are **if** and **case** but, as all statements have values, they are also conditional expressions. As in ALGOL 60, loops are constructed from the many variants of the **for** statement, which include a **while** statement.

Concurrency

Parallel processing is supported with semaphores being used for synchronization.

Input/output

I/O (called transput) is by a set of predefined routines. Files may be opened and closed at run time and formatted, unformatted and binary transput are supported.

C

C is a systems programming language and is at a lower level than the other languages dealt with in this book. It has the control and data structures found in modern high-level languages and, as its wide range of operators mirror the machine code instructions found in many computers, C programs are comparable in efficiency to assembly language programs. C is closely identified with the UNIX operating system.

Program structure and visibility

The source text of a C program can be distributed among several files, each of which can be compiled independently. Full type checking is not possible, however, across these boundaries. Although it has some features of a block-structured language, subprograms may not be nested.

Data types

The predefined data types are *int, char* and *float* together with *short* and *long* (for integers) and *double* (for floating point). User-defined types are enumeration types, arrays and structs (records). Dynamic data structures can be created using pointers.

Type checking

As it is a relatively low-level systems programming language, strict type checking is not imposed although this situation has been greatly improved in ANSI C.

Manipulation of structured objects

This is largely achieved by manipulating pointers to structured objects. Strings are implemented as arrays of character.

Control structures

It has structured control statements. The conditional statements are **if** and **switch** (similar to **case** in Pascal) and the iterative statements are **while** and **for** together with a **do ... while** construct which tests at the end of a loop.

Concurrency

Not supported directly, but new processes can be created through calls to UNIX system routines.

Input/output

I/O is not directly defined in the language, but is implemented by means of a standard library.

C++

C++ was designed to add data abstraction and object-oriented features to C.

Program structure and visibility

Classes support the decomposition of large programs into self-contained units.

Data types

The types are as in C with the addition of classes. This gives information hiding and allows the definition of abstract data types. Derived classes inherit the properties of a base class which they can extend through the definition of new, or the redefinition of existing, data and function members. Dynamic binding is supported.

Type checking

The type checking of C has been tightened up significantly.

Manipulation of structured objects

As in C, this is largely done using pointers. Class variables (objects) can be allocated space dynamically.

Control structures

As in C.

Concurrency

As in C.

Input/output

A library of predefined routines is available.

COBOL

COBOL is the most extensively used programming language in data processing and is oriented to dealing with large files of data. It has been revised several times, but these revisions, like the FORTRAN revisions, have been unable to take into account in any sensible way the new programming concepts of structure and modularity.

Program structure and visibility

A COBOL program is divided into four divisions. The IDENTIFICATION DIVISION provides commentary and is essentially program documentation; the ENVIRONMENT DIVISION contains machine-dependent program specifications relating logical and physical entities; the DATA DIVISION describes the data and its structure; and, finally, the PROCEDURE DIVISION gives the algorithms. Subprograms do not exist as such although it is possible to use labelled sequences of statements. There is no recursion.

Data types

The basic types are character strings and numbers whose precision is defined by the programmer in the DATA DIVISION. Arrays exist, but the main structured variables are records, which can be combined together to make files. Dynamic data structures are not supported.

Type checking

Since implicit type conversions are an integral part of COBOL, little type checking is possible.

Manipulation of structured objects

The REDEFINES clause allows more than one data structure to be mapped to the same piece of storage. Array bounds are fixed.

Control structures

There is a restricted `IF` ... `THEN` ... `ELSE` statement, but most control is exercised by the `PERFORM` statement, which can be used as an iterative statement or as a primitive form of subprogram call. There are labels and `GOTO` statements.

Concurrency

Not supported.

Input/output

Extensive read and write facilities are provided for both sequential and random access to the records of a file.

Eiffel

Eiffel is an object-oriented language that combines dynamic binding and static type checking. The reuse of software components is the central issue.

Program structure and visibility

Programs are composed of class definitions. The equivalent of a main program is the *Create* feature of the root class.

Data types

Simple data types such as integer, real, character and Boolean are built in. All other types are defined using classes and are accessed via pointers (references). New classes normally inherit information from parent classes. Generic classes are supported.

Type checking

It is strongly typed.

Manipulation of structured objects

Excellent. Classes, defining structured objects and their operations, are central to the language. Automatic garbage collection is supported.

Control structures

The control structures of a typical imperative language are available, but iteration classes can be defined and used in addition to loops.

Concurrency

It is a sequential language.

Input/output

The Eiffel environment typically includes classes to manipulate graphics in addition to the usual text I/O.

FORTRAN

FORTRAN is still widely used for numerical applications by scientists and engineers, but although it has been revised to take account of some of the ideas of structured programming, it lacks the regular structure of languages such as Pascal.

Program structure and visibility

A FORTRAN program consists of a set of independently compiled subprograms. There is no block structure and subprograms communicate through parameter lists and COMMON lists. Recursion is not supported.

Data types

The predefined data types are INTEGER, REAL, DOUBLE PRECISION, LOGICAL, CHARACTER and COMPLEX. The only structured types are fixed-size arrays. User-defined types are not available.

Type checking

Type checking of actual and formal parameters cannot take place due to the requirements of independent compilation. There is implicit conversion between integer and real in assignment statements.

Manipulation of structured objects

Arrays can be passed as parameters, but may not be returned as the value of a function. Strings are character arrays.

Control structures

Early versions of FORTRAN did not have structured control statements. This was remedied in FORTRAN 77 with the block IF statement. Iteration is provided by the DO loop, which corresponds to the **for** loop of Pascal.

Concurrency

Not supported.

Input/output

Special read and write statements with channel numbers to indicate the device and optional FORMAT statements are provided.

LISP

LISP is primarily used in artificial intelligence applications and although it is not a purely functional language it has all the features needed for functional programming. Its syntax is simple although it is rather offputting to the beginner.

Program structure and visibility

A program consists of function definitions and expressions in which the functions are applied. There is no support for dealing with very large programs.

Data types

The objects manipulated in the language are S-expressions, which can be lists, atoms or functions. Atoms may be symbolic or numerical.

Type checking

LISP is dynamically typed.

Manipulation of structured objects

Lists are first-class objects and so they can be manipulated as easily as scalar objects in imperative languages. Functions may be higher order. Automatic garbage collection is supported by LISP systems.

Control structures

Recursion is used instead of iteration.

Concurrency

Not dealt with explicitly although, as pure functions have no side effects, they may be executed in parallel.

Input/output

A set of predefined functions are used to read and write S-expressions.

ML

ML is a modern functional language which, unlike LISP, is strongly typed. Pattern matching is used, as an alternative to conditional expressions, in function definitions.

Program structure and visibility

A program consists of a set of function definitions. Standard ML includes modules as originally defined in the language Hope.

Data types

It supports the implementation of abstract data types.

Type checking

It is strongly typed, but has a type inference system. The user does not have to specify all types as the system can work out what they must be and report on any incompatibilities. Polymorphic functions are supported.

Manipulation of structured objects

Lists, functions and instances of abstract data types are first-class objects and so they can be manipulated as easily as scalars in imperative languages. Functions may be higher order and automatic garbage collection is supported.

Control structures

Recursion is used instead of iteration.

Concurrency

It is a sequential language.

Input/output

This is done in a non-functional way.

Modula-2

Modula-2 can be regarded as Pascal extended with modules and with low-level features to support systems programming.

Program structure and visibility

A Modula-2 program consists of a series of modules which can be divided into a definition and an implementation part. Modules interact by importing information exported by other modules. Modules support the creation of large programs as they are the basis of information hiding, data abstraction and separate compilation. Procedure declarations may be nested within modules.

Data types

The predefined types are INTEGER, CARDINAL, REAL, CHAR and BOOLEAN together with LONGINT, LONGCARD and LONGREAL. Scalar user-defined types are subrange and enumeration types. Structured types are arrays, records and sets. Dynamic data structures can be constructed using pointers. Abstract data types can be implemented using modules.

Type checking

The language is strongly typed with the exception of variant records, although Modula-2 systems usually include a SYSTEM module, which includes definition of system-dependent types such as BYTE, WORD and ADDRESS and which allows all kinds of unsafe type conversions.

Manipulation of structured objects

As in Pascal, except that string comparisons are not allowed.

Control structures

Structured control statements have explicit terminators and so compound statements are not required. There are **if** and **case** conditional statements. As well as the Pascal-like iterative statements, **while, repeat** and **for** there is a LOOP ... END statement, which may be left by execution of an EXIT statement.

Concurrency

Processes communicate through shared variables with monitors being used to guarantee mutual exclusion. Signals are used to synchronize processes.

Input/output

I/O is not defined in the language, but is provided by a set of library modules.

Pascal

Pascal was designed as a vehicle for the teaching of good programming style. Its emphasis on the importance of types and data structures has been very influential and virtually all recent imperative languages can be classified as Pascal derivatives. It is relatively small and, partly as a consequence of it being designed so that it would be easy to implement, it is available on most computers.

Program structure and visibility

It is a block-structured language, but as there is a single outermost block, neither independent nor separate compilation is supported. The only inner blocks are procedures and functions. Inner blocks inherit all declarations made in enclosing blocks.

Data types

The predefined data types are *integer, real, Boolean* and *char*. Array, record, set, pointer, subrange and enumeration types can be user defined.

Type checking

It is strongly typed, apart from variant records.

Manipulation of structured objects

Arrays and records may be parameters, but may not be returned as function values. Dynamic data structures are created using records, which have one or more fields of a pointer type. The size of arrays is fixed at compile time, although arrays of different sizes may be passed as parameters. Strings are packed arrays of *char*.

Control structures

It has structured control statements. The conditional statements are **if** and **case**; the iterative statements are **while, repeat ... until** and **for**. The compound statement is used to group statements together.

Concurrency

Not dealt with.

Input/output

Handled by a set of predefined procedures and functions that do not follow the usual language rules. The association of internal file names with physical external files is not handled in the language. Interactive I/O is dealt with in the same way as I/O to a sequential file.

PL/I

PL/I is a large general-purpose language that was designed to be suitable for both scientific and data processing work. It brought together ideas from FORTRAN, ALGOL and COBOL, but turned out to be large and unwieldy.

Program structure and visibility

A program consists of a set of external procedures, which may be compiled independently. External procedures may communicate with one another by passing parameters or through EXTERNAL variables. Within an external procedure, the declarations of internal procedures may be nested. Internal procedures inherit declarations from their enclosing blocks.

Data types

Types may be defined in great detail. For example, numeric types can have a mode (REAL or COMPLEX), a scale (FIXED or FLOAT), a base (DECIMAL or BINARY) and a precision. However, the default options are heavily used in defining types. Structured types are arrays and structures (records). Dynamic data structures can be created using pointers. Character strings can be defined to have either a fixed size or to be variable up to a fixed maximum size.

Type checking

When types do not match, implicit conversion rules are applied.

Manipulation of structured objects

Structured objects can be parameters of procedures, but they may not be returned as values of user-defined functions. There is an extensive set of operators and built-in functions for string handling.

Control structures

A structured **if** statement is available and the DO (**for** loop) can include a WHILE variant. Exception handling is also available.

Concurrency

Primitive tasking facilities are defined, but seldom used.

Input/output

Extensive facilities are available to support data processing work as well as the simpler requirements of scientific programmers.

PROLOG

PROLOG is a logic programming language in which the programmer states what is to be done rather than how it is to be carried out. The PROLOG approach is goal oriented and along with LISP dominates the artificial intelligence scene.

Program structure and visibility

A PROLOG program consists of a database of facts and a series of rules. Although programs can easily be extended by adding new facts and rules, there is no support for the creation of very large programs.

Data types

PROLOG has (symbolic) atoms, numbers and structures.

Type checking

It is dynamically typed.

Manipulation of structured objects

Structures (which are similar to records in Pascal) can be manipulated as easily in PROLOG as can lists in LISP. Structures are mainly used to represent lists, trees and graphs.

Control structures

To achieve a goal, subgoals are generated and achieved. Tree searching and associated backtracking are built into the interpreter and are not explicitly programmed.

Concurrency

Not dealt with.

Input/output

All data objects in PROLOG programs can be directly read or written. The standard input and output streams can be redirected to give access to disk files.

Smalltalk 80

Smalltalk is the archetypal object-oriented language. It is not just a language, but is a complete programming environment. Everything in a Smalltalk system is an object, which means that the number of separate concepts is kept to a minimum.

Program structure and visibility

Objects support information hiding. Data local to an object may only be accessed by sending a message to the object. An object responds to a message by selecting a procedure (called a method) to carry out the requested task. Objects give a hierarchical structure to large programs.

Data types

The only type is the object. Objects belong to a class, which is itself an object. New classes (subclasses) can be defined which inherit the properties of an existing class (their superclass) which they extend through the definition of new methods. There is automatic garbage collection of inaccessible objects.

Type checking

When messages are sent to an object, the required method is selected dynamically at run time. The nearest thing to a type error is when an object is unable to respond to a message.

Manipulation of structured objects

As the Smalltalk approach is centred on the manipulation of objects, its facilities are excellent in this area.

Control structures

Control structures are implemented as messages involving objects of class *block*. A *block* object represents a sequence of instructions which are to be executed when a suitable message is received.

Concurrency

A concurrent system can be built as a collection of concurrent objects that communicate with one another by sending messages.

Input/output

The Smalltalk environment introduced windows, icons and the mouse.

Appendix 2
Language texts

Ada

The Ada reference manual was published in 1983. There are a large number of Ada texts, three of which are given below.

Barnes, J. G. P. (1989), *Programming in Ada* (Third Edition), Addison-Wesley.

Booch, G. and Bryan, D. (1992), *Software Engineering with Ada* (Third Edition), Benjamin/Cummings.

Clark, R. G. (1985), *Programming in Ada: A First Course*, Cambridge University Press.

Ichbiah, J. D. *et al.* (1983), *Reference Manual for the Ada Programming Language*, ANSI MIL-STD-1815A-1983.

ALGOL 60

There are many books on ALGOL 60. Three of the early ones are given below as well as the classic paper edited by Peter Naur which gives the language definition.

Dijkstra, E. W. (1962), *A Primer of ALGOL 60 Programming*, Academic Press.

Ekman, T. and Froberg, C.-E. (1967), *Introduction to ALGOL Programming*, Oxford University Press.

Naur, P. (1963), 'Revised Report on the Algorithmic Language ALGOL 60', *Comm. ACM*, 6, pp. 1–17.

Reeves, C. M. and Wells, M. (1964), *A Course on Programming in ALGOL 60*, Chapman and Hall.

ALGOL 68

The defining document is not easy to read. The description by Lindsey and van der Meulen is more accessible.

Van Wijngaarden, A., Mailloux, B. J., Peck, J. E. L., Koster, C. H. A., Sintzoff, M., Lindsey, C. H., Meertens, L. G. L. T. and Fisker, R. G. (1975), 'Revised Report on the Algorithmic Language ALGOL 68', *Acta Informatica*, **5**, pp. 1–236.

Lindsey, C. H. and van der Meulen, S. G. (1977), *Informal Introduction to ALGOL 68* (Revised Edition), North-Holland.

ALGOL W

This language is described in the following paper.

Wirth, N. and Hoare, C. A. R. (1966), 'A Contribution to the Development of ALGOL', *Comm. ACM*, **9**, pp. 413–431.

Alphard

There is only one text.
Shaw, M. (1981), *Alphard: Form and Content*, Springer-Verlag.

APL

The designer Kenneth Iverson wrote the original book on the language before a computer implementation was considered. The implemented version is somewhat different.

Falkoff, A. and Iverson, K. E. (1973), 'The Design of APL', *IBM Journal of Research and Development,* **17**, pp. 324–334.

Iverson, K. E. (1962), *A Programming Language*, John Wiley.

Polivka, R. P. and Pakin, S. (1975), *APL: The Language and its Usage*, Prentice-Hall.

BASIC

The designers John Kemeny and Thomas Kurtz wrote the first book about the language. Since then the market has been flooded.

Kemeny, J. G. and Kurtz, T. E. (1967), *BASIC Programming*, John Wiley.

C

Recently a large number of C books have been published, but for a long time the only text was by Kernighan and Ritchie. Their second edition deals with ANSI C, but as traditional C is still widely used, the first edition is still relevant. A simpler introduction is given in the book by Kelley and Pohl.

Kelley, A. and Pohl, I. (1990), *A Book on C* (Second Edition), Addison-Wesley.

Kernighan, B. W. and Ritchie, D. M. (1978), *The C Programming Language*, Prentice-Hall.

Kernighan, B. W. and Ritchie, D. M. (1988), *The C Programming Language* (Second Edition), Prentice-Hall.

C++

This is an object-oriented extension to C and the latest version is a superset of ANSI C. Stroustrup is the designer of C++. The book by Pohl gives a good introduction to programmers experienced in Pascal.

Ellis, M. A. and Stroustrup, B. (1990), *The Annotated C++ Reference Manual*, Addison-Wesley.

Pohl, I. (1990), *C++ for Pascal Programmers*, Addison-Wesley.

Stroustrup, B. (1991), *The C++ Programming Language* (Second Edition), Addison-Wesley.

CLU

The most accessible reference is given below.

Liskov, B., Snyder, A., Atkinson, R. and Schaffert, C. (1977), 'Abstraction Mechanism in CLU', *Comm. ACM*, **20**, pp. 564–576.

COBOL

There are many textbooks to choose from, two of which are listed below.

McCracken, D. D. and Golden, D. G. (1988), *A Simplified Guide to Structured COBOL Programming* (Second Edition), John Wiley.

Parkin, A., Yorke, R. and Barnes, R. (1990), *COBOL for Students* (Third Edition), Edward Arnold.

Eiffel

The two books by Meyer describe, respectively, the use of the language and the latest version.

Meyer, B. (1988), *Object-oriented Software Construction*, Prentice-Hall.

Meyer, B. (1992), *Eiffel: The Language*, Prentice-Hall.

Euclid

A complete issue of SIGPLAN Notices was devoted to the language.

Lampson, B. W., Horning, J. J., London, R. L., Mitchell, J. G. and Popek, G. J. (1977), 'Report on the Programming Language Euclid', *ACM SIGPLAN Notices*, **12**(2).

FORTRAN

There are textbooks on FORTRAN to suit all tastes. The following text adopts a structured approach.

Ellis, T. M. R. (1990), *FORTRAN 77 Programming: With an Introduction to the Fortran 90 Standard*, Addison-Wesley.

GPSS

O'Donovan, T. M. (1979), *GPSS Simulation Made Simple*, John Wiley.

LISP

The classic text is written by John McCarthy *et al*. Since then, many texts have been written. The book by Winston and Horn is oriented towards COMMON LISP and the book by Steele gives a full definition of COMMON LISP.

McCarthy, J., Abrahams, P. W., Edwards, D. J., Hart, T. P. and Levin, M. I. (1965), *LISP 1.5 Programmer's Manual*, MIT Press.

Winston, P. H. and Horn, B. K. P. (1988), *LISP* (Third Edition), Addison-Wesley.

Steele, G. L. (1984), *COMMON LISP: The Language*, Digital Press.

LOGO

Early publicity on LOGO was centred on the book by Papert. Since then, many texts have been published, most of which concentrate on turtle graphics.

Papert, S. (1980), *Mindstorms: Children, Computers and Powerful Ideas*, Harvester Press.

ML

The first book devoted to ML is by Wikstrom. The book by Reade uses ML as the main language.

Reade, C. (1989), *Elements of Functional Programming*, Addison-Wesley.

Wikstrom, A. (1987), *Functional Programming using Standard ML*, Prentice-Hall.

Modula-2

Books on Modula-2 are now appearing in quantity. The original text is by Wirth and like most books on Modula-2 assumes prior knowledge of a language like Pascal. The book by Terry is suitable for a first course on programming.

Wirth, N. (1985), *Programming in Modula-2* (Third Edition), Springer-Verlag.

Terry, P. D. (1987), *An Introduction to Programming with Modula-2*, Addison-Wesley.

occam

The first version of the occam programming manual is now rather out of date as the language has continued to be developed. The text by Burns describes occam 2.

Burns, A. (1988), *Programming in occam 2*, Addison-Wesley.

INMOS Ltd (1984), *occam Programming Manual*, Prentice-Hall.

Pascal

The original book is by Jensen and Wirth, but many more readable books are available, such as the ones by Findlay and Watt and by Dale and Weems. The third edition of Jensen and Wirth describes the language defined in the ISO Pascal Standard.

Dale, N. and Weems, C. (1987), *Pascal* (Second Edition), D. C. Heath.

Findlay, W. and Watt, D. A. (1984), *Pascal* (Third Edition), Pitman.

Jensen, K. and Wirth, N. (1974), *Pascal User Manual and Report*, Springer-Verlag.

Jensen, K. and Wirth, N. (1985), *Pascal User Manual and Report* (Third Edition), Springer-Verlag.

PL/I

There are many textbooks available. Conway and Gries is worth noting as it contains a well-known and useful subset called PL/C.

Conway, R. and Gries, D. (1979), *An Introduction to Programming – A Structured Approach Using PL/I and PL/C* (Third Edition), Winthrop.

PROLOG

The first book available was by Clocksin and Mellish although other texts are now being published, such as the texts by Bratko and Hamilton.

Bratko, I. (1990), *Prolog Programming for Artificial Intelligence* (Second Edition), Addison-Wesley.

Clocksin, W. F. and Mellish, C. S. (1984), *Programming in Prolog* (Second Edition), Springer-Verlag.

Hamilton, A. G. (1989), *The Professional Programmers Guide to Prolog*, Pitman.

RPG

Essick, E. L. (1981), *RPG II Programming*, SRA.

Scheme

The revised report on Scheme was published in 1986. The book by Abelson on the teaching of programming using Scheme was very influential.

Abelson, H. and Sussman, G. J. (1985), *Structure and Interpretation of Computer Programs*, MIT Press.

Rees, J. and Clinger, W. (1986), 'Revised Report on the Algorithmic Language Scheme', *ACM SIGPLAN Notices*, **21**(12), pp. 37–79.

SIMULA 67

The main text is as follows.

Birtwistle, G. M., Dahl, O.-J., Myhrhaug, B. and Nygaard, K. (1975), *Simula Begin*, Auerbach.

Smalltalk

Smalltalk is not just a language, but is a complete programming environment. The main text is given below.

Goldberg, A. (1989), *Smalltalk-80: The Language*, Addison-Wesley.

SNOBOL

The original designers have written the standard textbook.

Griswold, R. E., Poage, J. F. and Polonsky, I. P. (1971), *The SNOBOL4 Programming Language*, Prentice-Hall.

Solutions to selected exercises

Chapter 3

3.2 For consistency, user-defined type identifiers and built-in type identifiers should be represented in the same way. Hence, in Pascal, *integer* and *real* should be predefined identifiers. As ALGOL 60 does not have user-defined types, it is reasonable for *integer* and *real* to be reserved words. A similar argument applies to *false* and *true* which, in Pascal, are examples of pre-defined enumeration values.

3.11 **type** *month* **is** (*January,   February,   March,   April,   May,   June,   July,   August, September, October, November, December*);
Operations: *next_month, last_month, month_number, month_name*

3.12 Array index, case label, in a subrange, element of a set, value of a loop control variable.

Chapter 4

4.2 In either of the expressions:

> *A* **or** *B*   where   *A* is true
> *A* **and** *B*   where   *A* is false

and *B* contains an expression that cannot be correctly evaluated or whose evaluation has a side effect.

4.5 Ada leads to the more reliable programs as the programmer has to make a positive decision when writing a program about all possible cases. This allows some errors to be picked up at compile time, which in Pascal would lead to run-time errors.

4.7 The Pascal solution requires *n* and a half loops because, as Pascal does not have an **exit** statement, the statement to read a number has to appear twice.

```
sum := 0;
read(number);
while number >= 0 do
begin
    sum := sum + number;
    read(number)
end
```

Chapter 5

5.6   The result $j = 2$, $a[1] = 1$, $a[2] = 3$ is obtained except with call by name which gives $j = 2$, $a[1] = 2$, $a[2] = 1$ when the call is *swap(j, a[j])* and the same result as the others when the call is *swap(a[j], j)*. As long as the addresses of all the actual parameters are computed on subprogram exit before any of the actual parameters are updated, call by value-result (ALGOL W) gives the same answer as call by value-result. If this is not the case, it gives the same result as call by name.

5.9
```
function next_month(mo : month) return month is
begin
    if mo = December then
        return January;
    else
        return month'succ(mo);
    end if;
end next_month;

function last_month(mo : month) return month is
begin
    if mo = January then
        return December;
    else
        return month'pred(mo);
    end if;
end last_month;

function month_number(mo : month) return integer is
begin
    return month'pos(mo) + 1;
end month_number;

function month_name(num : integer) return month is
begin
    return month'val(num – 1);
end month_name;
```

The Pascal implementations are essentially the same with the exception of *month_name* where a **case** statement has to be used as there is no equivalent of the *val* operation.

Chapter 6

6.2 Assume *BA*, the base address, is where the first element of the array is stored and each element occupies *s* locations.

Mapping function for $x[i] = BA + s * (i - 2)$
Mapping function for $a[i, j] = BA + s * (6 * (i - 1) + j)$

Hence:

$x[7]$ is in $BA + 5 * s$
$a[3, 2]$ is in $BA + 14 * s$

6.9 **subtype** *size* **is** *integer* **range** 1 .. *max*;
type *values* **is array**(*size*) **of** *real*;
type *queue* **is**
  record
    data : *values*;
    front, rear : *size* := 1;
    -- front points to the front of the queue
    -- rear points to where the next element will be inserted
  end record;

procedure *add*(*x* : *real*; *q* **in out** *queue*) **is**
begin
  if (*q.rear* = *max* **and** *q.front* = 1) **or else**
     (*q.rear* + 1 = *q.front*) **then**
    full_error_message;
  else
    q.data(*q.rear*) := *x*;
    if *q.rear* = *max* **then**
      q.rear := 1;
    else
      q.rear := *q.rear* + 1;
    end if;
  end if;
end *add*;

procedure *delete*(*q* **in out** *queue*) **is**
begin
  if *q.front* = *q.rear* **then**
    empty_error_message;
  elsif *q.front* = *max* **then**
    q.front := 1;
  else
    q.front := *q.front* + 1;
  end if;
end *delete*;

It is assumed that the queue is represented by a circular list and that the element following *q.data(max)* is in *q.data(1)*. To be able to differentiate between a full and an empty queue, the maximum number of elements that can be held is max − 1.

6.11   **procedure** *Polish(p : ptr)*;
  begin
    if *p* <> **nil then**
    begin
      write(p↑.data);
      Polish(p↑.left);
      Polish(p↑.right);
    end;
  end {Polish};

6.13   CORRECT

Chapter 7

7.7   **generic**
    type *item* **is private**;
    max : integer;
  package *queues* **is**
    type *queue* **is limited private**;
    procedure *add(x : item; q* **in out** *queue)*;
    procedure *delete(q :* **in out** *queue)*;
    function *first(q : queue)* **return** *item*;
    function *is_empty(q : queue)* **return** *Boolean*;
  private
    --implementation of type queue as in 6.9
  end *queues*;

7.9   **package** *months* **is**
    type *month* **is** (*January, February, March, April, May, June, July,*
                August, September, October, November, December);
    function *next_month(mo : month)* **return** *month*;
    function *last_month(mo : month)* **return** *month*;
    function *month_number(mo : month)* **return** *integer*;
    function *month_name(num : integer)* **return** *month*;
  end *months*;

  package body *months* **is**
    --function definitions as in 5.9
  end *months*;

7.13   **generic**
    type *item* **is private**;
  package *retrieve* **is**

```
    type table is private;
    procedure initialize(info : in out table);
    procedure insert(x : item; info : in out table);
    function lookup(x : item; info : table) return integer;
private
    type table is array(1 .. 100) of item;
end retrieve;
```

Chapter 8

8.5 **class** *publication* {
protected:
    char the_title[255], *the_cat_no*[20], *the_pub*[40];
    int the_year;
public:
    *publication(char * ti, char * cat_no, char * pub, int year)*
    { *strcpy(the_title, ti)*;
      strcpy(the_cat_no, cat_no);
      strcpy(the_pub, pub);
      the_year = year;
    }
    virtual void *date() {cout << the_year << '\n';}*
    // other member functions as before
};

class *journal* : **public** *publication* {
    int the_vol, the_part, the_month;
public:
    *journal(char * t, char * c, char * p, int y, int vol, int part, int month)*
      : *publication(t, c, p, y)*
    { *the_vol = vol*;
      the_part = part;
      the_month = month;
    }
    void date() {cout << the_month << ", " << the_year << '\n';}
    // other member functions as before
};

The only change required in class *book* is to its constructor. This is because the constructor of *publication* has been modified.

8.10 **class** *SESSION*
inherit
    CHAIN_ITER[INTEGER]
      rename *item_action* **as** *pr_item*,
            item_test **as** *pr_test*,
            do_all **as** *pr_do_all*,
            do_while **as** *pr_do_while*
      redefine *pr_item, pr_test*;

CHAIN_ITER[INTEGER]
    rename *action* **as** *zero_action,*
            test **as** *neg_test,*
            do_if **as** *neg_do_if*
    redefine *zero_action, neg_test*
feature
   list: *LINKED_LIST[INTEGER]*;

   zero_action(li : TRAVERSABLE[INTEGER]) **is**
   do
     list.put(0)
   end; – – zero_action

   neg_test(li : TRAVERSABLE[INTEGER]) : BOOLEAN **is**
   do
     Result := li.item < 0
   end; – – neg_test

   pr_item(i : INTEGER) **is**
   do
     io.putint(i);
     io.putstring ("\n")
   end; – – pr_item

   pr_test(i : INTEGER) : BOOLEAN **is**
   do
     Result := i /= 0
   end; – – pr_test

   ...

end; – – SESSION

Chapter 9

9.4   (ISMEMBER 24 '(17 24 59))
  => (COND ((NULL '(17 24 59)) NIL)
        ((EQ 24 (CAR '(17 24 59))) T)
        (T (ISMEMBER 24 (CDR '(17 24 59)))))
  => (COND (NIL NIL)
        ((EQ 24 (CAR '(17 24 59))) T)
        (T (ISMEMBER 24 (CDR '(17 24 59)))))
  => (COND ((EQ 24 (CAR '(17 24 59))) T)
        (T (ISMEMBER 24 (CDR '(17 24 59)))))
  => (COND ((EQ 24 17) T)
        (T (ISMEMBER 24 (CDR '(17 24 59)))))
  => (COND (NIL T)
        (T (ISMEMBER 24 (CDR '(17 24 59)))))
  => (COND (T (ISMEMBER 24 (CDR '(17 24 59)))))
  => (ISMEMBER 24 (CDR '(17 24 59)))

```
=> (ISMEMBER 24 '(24 59))
=> (COND ((NULL '(24 59)) NIL)
            ((EQ 24 (CAR '(24 59))) T)
            (T (ISMEMBER 24 (CDR '(24 59))))))
=> (COND ((EQ 24 (CAR '(24 59))) T)
            (T (ISMEMBER 24 (CDR '(24 59))))))
=> (COND (T T)
            (T (ISMEMBER 24 (CDR '(24 59))))))
=> T
```

IsMember(24, [17, 24, 59])
=> **if** 24 = 17 **then** *true*
 else *IsMember*(24, [24, 59])
=> **if** *false* **then** *true*
 else *IsMember*(24, [24, 59])
=> *IsMember*(24, [24, 59])
=> **if** 24 = 24 **then** *true*
 else *IsMember*(24, [59])
=> **if** *true* **then** *true*
 else *IsMember*(24, [59])
=> true

9.10 **(a)** **fun** *Sum*(*nil*) = 0
    | *Sum*(*first* :: *rest*) = *first* + *Sum*(*rest*);

Its functionality is :

val Sum = fn : (*int list*) → *int*

(b) **fun** *Length*(*nil*) = 0
    | *Length*(*first* :: *rest*) = 1 + *Length*(*rest*);

Its functionality is :

val Length = fn : ('*a list*) → *int*

(c) **fun** *RemoveNeg*(*nil*) = *nil*
    | *RemoveNeg*(*first* :: *rest*) =
     if *first* < 0 **then** *RemoveNeg*(*rest*)
     else *first* :: *RemoveNeg*(*rest*);

Its functionality is :

val RemoveNeg = fn : (*int list*) → (*int list*)

9.11 **fun** *filter f nil* = *nil*
  | *filter f* (*first* :: *rest*) =
   if *f first* **then** *first* :: *filter f rest*
   else *filter f rest*;

Its functionality is :

val filter = fn : ('*a* → *bool*) → (('*a list*) → ('*a list*))

9.14 **fun** *generate*10(*m*) =
  if *m* <= 10 **then** *m* :: *generate*10(*m* + 1)
  else *nil*;

Reduction without lazy evaluation:

lowsquares(*generate*10 1)
=> *lowsquares*(1 :: *generate*10(2))
=> *lowsquares*(1 :: 2 :: *generate*10(3))

...

=> *lowsquares*(1 :: 2 :: 3 :: 4 :: 5 :: 6 :: 7 :: 8 :: 9 :: 10 :: *nil*)
=> 1 * 1 :: *lowsquares*(2 :: 3 :: 4 :: 5 :: 6 :: 7 :: 8 :: 9 :: 10 :: *nil*)
=> 1 :: 2 * 2 :: *lowsquares*(3 :: 4 :: 5 :: 6 :: 7 :: 8 :: 9 :: 10 :: *nil*)

...

=> 1 :: 4 :: 9 :: 16 :: 25 :: *lowsquares*(6 :: 7 :: 8 :: 9 :: 10 :: *nil*)
=> 1 :: 4 :: 9 :: 16 :: 25 :: *nil*

Reduction with lazy evaluation :

lowsquares(*generate*10 1)
=> *lowsquares*(1 :: *generate*10(2))
=> 1 * 1 :: *lowsquares*(*generate*10(2))
=> 1 :: *lowsquares*(2 :: *generate*10(3))
=> 1 :: 2 * 2 :: *lowsquares*(*generate*10(3))
=> 1 :: 4 :: *lowsquares*(3 :: *generate*10(4))
=> 1 :: 4 :: 3 * 3 :: *lowsquares*(*generate*10(4))
=> 1 :: 4 :: 9 :: *lowsquares*(4 :: *generate*10(5))
=> 1 :: 4 :: 9 :: 4 * 4 :: *lowsquares*(*generate*10(5))
=> 1 :: 4 :: 9 :: 16 :: *lowsquares*(5 :: *generate*10(6))
=> 1 :: 4 :: 9 :: 16 :: 5 * 5 :: *lowsquares*(*generate*10(6))
=> 1 :: 4 :: 9 :: 16 :: 25 :: *lowsquares*(6 :: *generate*10(7))
=> 1 :: 4 :: 9 :: 16 :: 25 :: *nil*

Chapter 10

10.2 The question:

   ?– goodmatch(A, B).

requires the subgoals:

   loves(A, B), loves (B, A)

to be satisfied. The substitutions **A ← john** and **B ← jane** allow the first subgoal to be matched with the first fact, but the second subgoal then fails. The system backtracks to the first subgoal and tries **A ← bill** and **B ← jane** so that the second fact is matched. The second subgoal again fails. The system again backtracks and tries **A ← james** and **B ← jane** which satisfies both subgoals.

10.3 within(X, Y) :- district(X, Y).
within(X, Y) :- region(X, Y).

...

within(X, Y) :- district(Z, Y), region(X, Z).
within(X, Y) :- region(Z, Y), country(X, Z).

...

within(X, Y) :- district(A, Y), region(B, A), country(C, B),
                continent(X, C).

Better to define:

inside(X, Y) :- district(X, Y).
inside(X, Y) :- region(X, Y).
inside(X, Y) :- country(X, Y).
inside(X, Y) :- continent(X, Y).

and then to define:

within(X, Y) :- inside(X, Y).
within(X, Y) :- inside(X, Z), within(Z, Y).

Chapter 11

11.7 Assuming the type declaration:

type *ready_state* **is** (*off, snooze*);

the two task bodies are:

```
task body person is
   state : ready_state;
begin
   loop
      accept alarm_call(response : out ready_state) do
         -- determine value for state
         response := state;
      end alarm_call;
      exit when state = off;
      -- go back to sleep
   end loop;
   -- get up
end person;

task body alarm is
   continue : ready_state;
begin
   loop
      person.alarm_call(continue);
      exit when continue = off;
```

            delay 2.0;
           end loop;
         end *alarm*;

11.8 Two, as a channel will be required for the person's response.

Chapter 12

12.1a *<digit>* ::= 0 | 1 | 2 | 3 | 4 | 5 | 6 | 7 | 8 | 9
     <digitsequence> ::= *<digit>*
                 | *<digit> <digitsequence>*

12.1b *<realnumber>* ::= *<digitsequence>.<digitsequence>*

12.2 *<exp>*
     <exp> + *<term>*
     <term> + *<term>*
     <term> * *<factor>* + *<term>*
     <factor> * *<factor>* + *<term>*
     <identifier> * *<factor>* + *<term>*
     a * *<factor>* + *<term>*
     a * *<identifier>* + *<term>*
     a * *b* + *<term>*
     a * *b* + *<factor>*
     a * *b* + *<identifier>*
     a * *b* + *c*

12.5 The sentences are A AB AC AD ABB ABC ABD ACB ACC ACD.
     The equivalent BNF grammar is:

     <sequence> ::= A | A *<bcdpart>*
     <bcdpart> ::= *<borc>* | *<borc> <bcdpart>* | D
     <borc> ::= B | C

12.7 *<sentence>*
     a <first>
     a b <first>
     a b <third> g
     a b a g

     <sentence>
     <second> g
     <third> <second> g
     a <second> g
     a <third> b g
     a a b g

12.8 *<sentence>*
p <char> <continue>
p a <continue>
p a , <char> <continue>
p a , b <continue>
p a , b , <char> <continue>
p a , b , a <continue>
p a , b , a ;

The derivation was straightforward because, at each stage, the right part to be used could be determined by scanning one symbol ahead.

Chapter 13

13.2 Instructions are needed to associate named physical files with logical files at run time and to create, open, close and delete such files. Operations on direct access files should also be included.

Index

absolute time 278
abstract data type 36, 172–9, 184, 192, 207, 320
   Ada 173, 174, 177–9, 184–6
   C++ 174–7
   ML 236, 237
   Modula–2 174, 265
   SIMULA 36
abstraction 99, 173, 192, 206, 238, 318
accept statement 268–73, 277, 279
access type 149, 170
accuracy 64
ACM 19, 42
activation record 119
Ada, Countess of Lovelace 14, 42
Ada 4, 38, 41, 42, 325, 326
   abstract data type 173, 174, 177–9, 184–6
   accept statement 268–73, 277, 279
   aggregates 141, 142, 145
   arrays 140–3, 157, 158
   bit string 158
   default parameters 115, 116
   definition 41, 207, 284, 315
   delay statement 277–9
   derived types 60, 63
   entry call 268, 270–3, 277
   enumeration type 67, 68, 90
   exception handling 42, 92–4
   file 304, 309
   function 116–19, 126, 128, 129, 142
   generics 128, 129, 182–6, 234, 303, 322
   guarded command 273, 274
   information hiding 169–72
   I/O 114, 303, 304, 309
   named association 115, 116

   overloading 61, 68, 114, 119, 178, 183, 304
   package 42, 164–74
   parameters 106–19, 128, 129, 182, 183, 272
   private 169, 170, 173, 174
   program structure 166, 179–81
   real–time 42, 276–9
   redefining operators 118, 119, 178
   rendezvous 263, 268–72, 277
   select statement 273, 274, 279
   separate compilation 179–81
   short–circuit evaluation 78
   strong typing 42, 54, 182
   synchronization 268, 270
   tasks 42, 268–73
address 52, 136, 137, 212, 277
aggregate 141, 145
AIMACO 23
ALGOL 58 19, 28
ALGOL 60 18–22, 326, 327
   arrays 138
   block structure 19, 104
   character set 8
   declarations 19, 60
   definition 19, 284, 287, 290
   for statement 19, 87, 89
   function 116, 117
   if statement 19, 82, 83, 287
   I/O 20, 301
   own variables 57
   parameters 21, 113, 237
   Report 19
   structured control statements 19
ALGOL 68 21, 22, 327, 328
   arrays 138, 139
   collateral statement 260

exception handling 92
flexible arrays 138, 139, 154
higher–order function 128, 217
orthogonality 5, 22
parameters 6, 107
Report 21
side–effects 79
strings 154
ALGOL W 21, 38
case statement 21, 84
for loop 21, 90
parameters 21, 42, 110, 113
records 21
algorithm 5, 98
alias 69, 71, 111–14, 213, 260, 322
Alphard 90, 105, 107
ambiguity 82, 83, 287, 288, 291
Analytical Engine 14, 42
ANSI 17, 23, 40, 126, 127
Apple Macintosh 45
APL 31–3, 55
array 138, 141, 142, 261
character set 8
expression evaluation 76
application generator 27
application package 37, 38, 298
applicative language 212
array 134–43, 152–4
address calculation 136
aggregate 141
assignment 141, 142, 153, 261
associative 33
conformant 139, 140
dynamic 138, 139, 154
parameter passing 39, 108, 137, 139,
140
processor 261
slice 141, 142, 306
static 39, 137, 138
type equality 140, 141
unconstrained 140
variable bounds 19, 138–40, 154
artificial intelligence 35, 44, 244, 256
ASCII 9, 66, 68
assembly language 14, 28, 37, 40, 276
assertion 21, 203, 293, 294
assignment 57, 79–81, 213, 291, 322
array 141, 142, 153, 261
compatibility 79, 80
multiple 81

operator 80, 81
problems 57, 213, 322
record 145
string 153, 154
asynchronous communication 262, 263
attributes 52, 59, 136, 140, 184, 199,
200, 306
autocode 14, 15, 31
axiomatic semantics 291, 293, 294

Babbage, Charles 14, 42
backtracking 244, 247–9, 252, 253
Backus, J. 15, 43
Backus–Naur Form 284
Barron, D. 52
base
address 121, 122, 136
class 194–6, 201
BASIC 31, 32, 298, 314, 315
batch processing 28, 31
BCPL 37, 40
Bell Laboratories 33, 40
binary
file 307, 308
operator 77
tree 150, 151
binding 291
block entry 53, 56–8, 70, 120, 138
compile–time 53–6, 58, 137, 138, 196
declaration–reference 56, 57, 70, 119,
120
dynamic 55, 192, 196–8, 201, 206,
223
load–time 53, 57, 119
name–declaration 53–7, 60
name–size 137–9
name–type 54, 55
name–value 58
reference–value 57, 79
run–time 53, 55, 56, 198
statement execution 53, 57, 58, 70,
138
static 54, 196
time 53
bit strings 158
BLISS 37
block structure 19, 53, 104, 105
BNF 19, 25, 284–90, 320
Boole, G. 65
Boolean 59, 65

operators   77, 78, 157, 158
bottom up   285, 290
buffer   264, 266, 267, 298
   variable   302, 319
buffered I/O   298
built-in type   42, 59, 172
business data processing   22–7

C   37, 38, 40, 41, 264, 328, 329
   ANSI standard   40, 126
   array   137, 141, 142
   assignment operators   41, 80, 81
   cast   70
   constants   58
   external identifier   106
   file   106, 305
   for statement   88, 137
   function   100, 102, 116–18, 142
   function prototype   126
   independent compilation   181
   integer types   62
   I/O   264, 265, 305, 306, 310
   logical   65, 78
   mixed–mode   78
   parameters   112, 137
   pointers   68–70, 137, 149, 150
   preprocessor   58
   static variable   56
   strings   152, 153
   structs   149, 150, 176
   type checking   40, 126
C++   38, 40, 45, 329, 330
   base class   194–6, 201
   class   40, 42, 174–7, 186, 193–8, 320
   constructor   175
   data members   175
   derived class   194–6
   destructor   176
   dynamic binding   196–8
   function prototype   175
   header file   181
   inheritance   147, 193
   member function   175
   overloading   114, 119, 195–8
   parameters   112
   pointers   149, 150, 195–8
   private member   175, 194, 195, 201
   protected member   193, 194, 201
   public member   175, 194, 195, 201
   pure virtual function   203

   redefining operators   118, 119
   scope resolution   175, 204
   type checking   126, 181
   virtual functions   196
call
   by constant–value   107–9
   by name   21, 107, 113, 220, 237
   by reference   107, 108, 110–14, 137
   by reference–constant   107–9
   by result   21, 107, 108
   by value   107, 108, 112–14, 137, 220
   by value–result   21, 107, 110–14
case statement   21, 84, 85, 147
cast   70
channel   268, 270, 271, 274, 278, 299,
      300
character
   constant   66, 153
   control   9, 299
   set   8, 68, 299
   string   33, 66, 67, 152–6, 306
   type   66
class   36, 42, 45, 192–207, 320
   base   194–6, 201
   C++   40, 42, 174–7, 186, 193–8, 320
   deferred   203, 204
   derived   194–6, 200
   Eiffel   36, 198
   generic   204–6
   inheritance   147, 186, 192–5, 204
   instance   192
   root   202
   SIMULA   36, 40, 42, 45
   Smalltalk   36, 45, 198
client   176, 194, 199–201
clock   42, 277
closed–world assumption   249, 250, 256
closed scope   105
CLU   90, 92
COBOL   22–6, 314, 330, 331
   data division   23, 24
   environment division   23, 24
   identification division   23, 24
   procedure division   23, 25
   records   143
   strings   154
CODASYL   26
COMIT   33
COMMON   102, 103
COMMON LISP   35, 225

Communicating Sequential Processes
263, 264, 309
communication 263, 268, 270
communication network 261
compilation unit 180
compile time 121, 123
    binding 53–6, 58, 137, 138, 196
    error 7, 60, 63, 80, 119, 197, 217, 238
    instantiation 129, 182
    type checking 4, 42, 45, 54, 55, 149,
        197
compiler 6, 78, 170, 320, 321
    one–pass 125
    optimization 30, 260, 272
    syntax–directed 19, 290
complex type 65, 177–9
composite symbol 9
composition 230
compound statement 81
computable index 134, 136, 145
concatenation 152, 154
concurrency 41, 213, 214, 260–79, 309
conditional statement 82–4
conformant array parameters 139, 140
constant–value parameters 107–9
constants 57, 58
constraint 60, 66, 92
constructors 35, 175, 200–2, 216, 236
context clause 166, 168, 180
context free 285
control
    character 9, 299
    variable 87–90, 136
Coral 66 37, 276
coroutines 43, 265
correctness 7, 213, 293
critical region 262, 270, 271
CSP 263, 264, 309, 310

Dahl, O–J. 36
dangling else 82, 287, 288
dangling reference 71
data abstraction 172–9, 192, 206, 238,
    251, 318
data area 119–23, 125, 138, 140
database 27, 44, 251
data processing 22, 143
data structures
    arrays 134–43, 152–54
    dynamic 72, 148–52

files 158, 159, 299, 300, 302–9
Prolog 250–2
records 21, 134, 135, 143–50
recursive 125, 151, 215
sets 156–8
stepwise refinement 98
deadlock 262, 263
decision–support language 27
declaration 53–8
    default 28, 59, 115, 116
    implicit 7, 17, 30, 59, 90
    local 102, 104
declaration–reference binding 56, 57, 70,
    119, 120
declarative language 316, 317
declarative meaning 244, 253
default
    case statement 84
    declarations 28, 59
    parameters 115, 116
    value 115, 146
    visibility 167
deferred class 203, 204
definition module 164, 167, 170, 174,
    181
delay
    guard 279
    statement 277–9
denotational semantics 291, 292
depth first tree search 252
dereferencing 57, 68, 69
derivation 285–7
derived
    class 194–6, 200
    type 60, 63
descriptor 156
design
    language 3–8, 318–20
    software 2–4, 164, 183–6, 192, 239,
        263, 318
destructor 176
development environment 6, 45, 192,
    225, 264, 298, 317
dialogue 310
differentiation 221, 222, 228, 229, 253–5
Dijkstra, E. 91, 275
direct access file 308, 309
discrete
    simulation 35
    type 59, 84, 89, 90

distributed system   261, 270
DOD   23, 41, 315
domain   212
double precision   64
dyadic operator   77
dynamic
    arrays   138, 139, 154
    binding   55, 192, 196–8, 201, 206, 223
    chain   122, 123
    data structures   72, 148–52
    scope   54, 222, 226
    storage allocation   70, 156, 198, 216
    strings   152–6
    typing   55, 193, 217, 232, 234, 317
    variable   69, 72, 149

EBCDIC   68
EBNF   288, 289
editor   226, 264
EDSAC I   14
Eiffel   4, 38, 45, 331, 332
    assertion   203, 294
    attributes   199, 200
    class   36, 198
    deferred class   203
    descendant   201
    exceptions   94, 203
    features   199
    garbage collection   198
    generics   204–6
    multiple inheritance   204–6
    object   198
    parent class   201
    reference variable   198, 202
    root class   202
    typing   198, 317
embedded system   41, 94, 277, 316
Emerald   263
encapsulated data type   173, 201
end–of–file   91, 303, 306
end–of–line   299, 302, 304, 305
end–of–page   304
entry call   268, 270–3, 277
enumeration type   39, 66–8, 118
    I/O   67, 303
environment   6, 45, 105, 192, 225, 264,
        291, 298, 317
error
    compile time   7, 60, 63, 80, 119, 197,
        217, 238

    input   93
    logical   6, 60, 63, 238, 319
    recovery   41, 91–4
    run time   7, 92, 197, 217
    syntax   114
Euclid   105, 112, 118, 164
exception handling   29, 42, 91–4, 236,
        237
expert system   44, 252
exponent   63
exponentiation   62
export list   164, 167, 168
exported operation   167, 184, 186, 192,
        201, 265
expression evaluation   76–8
    short–circuit   78
expressive power   5
extent   56, 165, 172

fair scheduling   262
fault–tolerant   92, 261
Ferranti Pegasus   14, 15
fifth generation   44
file   158, 159, 299, 300, 302–9
    binary   307, 308
    buffer variable   302, 319
    direct access   308, 309
    local   158
    logical   299, 302, 304, 305
    of records   143, 308
    sequential   158, 299–308
fixed point   64, 65
flexible arrays   138, 139, 154
floating point   63, 64
FLOW–MATIC   22
for statement   19, 87–90
FOCUS   27
formal
    functions   127, 128, 217
    parameters   99, 109, 179
    procedures   127, 128
    reasoning   8, 213, 238, 293, 321
format   16, 299, 300
FORTRAN   15–18, 332, 333
    array   17, 137, 261
    assignment   16, 80
    character set   9
    COMMON   102, 103
    complex   65, 177
    DO statement   16, 88, 319

format 16, 299, 300
FORTRAN 66 17, 82
FORTRAN 77 17, 18, 83, 300, 308, 314
FORTRAN 90 17, 18, 314
function 16, 116, 117
if statement 82
implicit declarations 7, 59
independent compilation 103, 119, 179
I/O 299, 300, 308
parameters 102, 112
program structure 102–4
storage allocation 119, 120
subroutine 16, 100
forward declarations 125–7
fourth generation languages 5, 26, 27, 316
FP 43, 229–31
composition 230
condition 230
construction 230
functional form 229, 230
higher order 229
primitive functions 230
sequences 229–31
frame 92, 93
free space list 34, 72
free variable 223
function 98, 116–19, 212
domain 212
expression 232, 233, 235
formal 127, 128, 217
generic 128, 234
higher order 217, 222–4, 229, 234–6
polymorphic 55, 234–8, 322
primitive 213
prototype 126, 175
range 212
virtual 196, 201, 203
functional form 229–31
functional language 4, 35, 38, 43, 212–39, 316, 317
purely 7, 43, 57, 213, 229, 261, 291
functionality 232–6
functor 250

garbage 71
garbage collection 35, 72, 198, 216, 322
generic

class 204–6
instantiation 129, 182, 185, 303
package 182, 183, 185, 186, 303
parameter 128, 129, 182, 183, 185, 204
subprogram 128, 129, 234, 322
global variable 54, 106, 322
goal 244–50, 252–5, 307
goto statement 8, 91, 224
GPSS 36
grammars 284–6
graphical user interface 298, 317
guarded command 273–6

Haskell 38, 43, 316
heap storage 72, 138, 156, 322
heuristic 249
hidden detail 98, 164–79, 201, 320
hierarchical 143, 215, 219
higher–order
function 217, 222–4, 229, 234–6
language 217
Hoare, C.A.R. 42, 263
Hopper, Grace 23
hole in scope 54
Hope 43

IAL 18, 28
IBM 14, 15, 26, 28, 30
Ichbiah, J. 42
icon 45, 298, 317
identifiers 9, 52
if statement 82–4
IFIP 21
imperative language 4, 35, 56, 212, 250, 314–17
implementation
dependent 78, 307
hidden 164, 172–9, 201
language 3, 6, 212, 320, 321
module 165, 167, 170, 181, 320
implicit
declaration 7, 17, 30, 59, 90
increment 87
import list 105, 112, 168
incarnations 125
independent compilation 29, 103, 106, 119, 179
index 134, 136, 145
indirect reference 111

inference
    rules 293
    type 43, 55, 232
infix 118, 219, 227
information hiding 42, 98, 164–79, 192, 194, 201, 206, 318, 320
INGRES 27
inheritance 147, 186, 192–5
    multiple 204
initial value 115, 116, 141, 149, 172, 215
in parameters 106–8, 115
in out parameters 106, 110, 118
input/output 20, 298–310
    buffered 298, 306
    error handling 93
    interactive 238, 302
    lazy 43, 238
    library 114, 303, 305
    redirecting 310
instance variable 199
instantiation 128, 182, 185, 234, 246, 303
integers 59, 61–3
interactive
    environment 6, 31, 219, 307
    I/O 31, 238, 302, 306
    language 6, 30–3, 138, 219
interface 45, 164
    module 164, 320
internal representation 298, 307
interpreter 6, 36, 40, 55, 227
interrupt 37, 42, 276, 277, 279
IPL–V 34
ISML 38
ISO Pascal Standard 39, 139, 169
iterative statement 85–91
iterator 90, 91, 204–6
Iverson, K. 32

JOSS 31
JOVIAL 27, 28, 37
jump instruction 82, 91, 92

keywords 9

L–value 57
L6 35
label 82, 91, 224, 300
    case 84
lambda

calculus 35
    expression 219–24, 232, 233
language
    assembly 14, 37, 40, 276
    declarative 316, 317
    design 3–8, 318–20
    fifth generation 44
    fourth generation 5, 26, 27, 316
    functional 4, 35, 38, 43, 212–39, 316–18
    higher order 217
    imperative 4, 35, 56, 212, 314–18
    implementation 3, 6, 212, 320, 321
    interactive 6, 30–3, 138, 219
    logic 4, 44, 244–56, 316, 318
    object oriented 4, 36, 38, 40, 174, 192–207, 317, 318
    procedural 212
    pure logic 255
    purely functional 7, 43, 57, 213, 229, 261, 291
    specification 3, 321
    systems programming 37, 40, 43, 157, 298, 315
    third generation 26
lazy evaluation 43, 237, 238
lazy I/O 43, 238
lexical elements 8–11
library 42, 103, 164, 204, 265, 317
    file 180
lifetime 56, 121, 158
limited private 174
linked list 21, 34, 39, 148–50, 174, 204–6, 215, 250
LISP 6, 34, 35, 72, 214–25, 256, 333, 334
    assignment 224
    COMMON 35, 225
    development environment 6, 219, 225
    dialects 223, 225, 226
    dynamic scope 55, 222
    free variable 223
    higher–order function 217, 221–4
    imperative features 224, 225
    I/O 306, 307
    lambda expression 219–24
    parameters 219, 220, 223
    predicate 220
    prefix notation 219
    S–expression 219, 220

scope rules   222, 223
    special form   219, 224
list processing   34, 35, 172, 204–6, 215,
    228, 233, 234
literals   63, 67
LL(1) grammar   290, 320
load time   53, 57, 119, 120, 165
local declarations   102, 104
local variable   54, 56, 107, 110, 111,
    120–3, 271
    static   56, 57, 172
locations   56, 57, 102, 119, 120, 136,
    212, 213, 216, 276
logic
    language   4, 44, 244–56, 316, 318
    programming   44, 244–56
logical
    error   6, 60, 63, 238, 319
    file name   299, 302, 304, 305
    operators   65, 77, 78
    type   59, 65
LOGO   226–9
    built–in editor   226
    dynamic scope   226
    parameters   227
    recursion   226
    scope rules   226
    side effect   226
    turtle graphics   226
loop
    control variable   87–90, 136
    parallel execution   261
loosely coupled   261
LOTUS 1–2–3   27
LR(1) grammar   290, 320

machine
    code   6, 14, 26, 212, 320
    independence   16, 26, 28, 301
maintenance   3, 4, 181
mantissa   63
mapping function   136, 143
mathematical function   212, 213
McCarthy, J.   34
menu   45, 193, 298, 317
message passing   37, 45, 197, 198, 262,
    263, 270, 309, 317, 323
metalanguage   284
method   197, 200
Meyer, B.   45

microcomputer   31, 40, 226, 315
Miranda   38, 316
MIT   33, 34
mixed–mode   78
ML   4, 38, 43, 232–9, 334
    abstract data type   236, 237
    constructors   236
    exceptions   236, 237
    function expresion   232, 235
    higher order functions   234
    lazy evaluation   237, 238
    pattern matching   233–8
    polymorphic functions   55, 234–8, 322
    scope rules   234
    strong typing   55, 232
    type inference   55, 232, 323
mnemonic   14
mode   106–9, 154
model building   36, 45, 183, 318
Modula   42, 320
Modula–2   4, 38, 42, 43, 316, 320, 335,
    336
    abstract data type   174, 265
    array   137, 171
    coroutines   43, 265
    export list   167, 168
    for statement   88, 90
    formal subprogram   128
    function   117, 128, 142
    import list   168, 171
    information hiding   164, 167
    I/O   115, 303
    low–level facilities   43, 267
    modules   43, 101, 164, 167–72, 181,
        265–7
    monitor   265–7
    parameters   107, 110, 128
    pointers   70, 170, 174
    procedure   101, 128
    procedure types   43, 128
    program structure   101, 102, 170, 171
    separate compilation   181
    sets   156, 157
    shared variables   265–8
    short–circuit evaluation   78
    signal   265
    strings   152, 153
    synchronization   265, 267
modular decomposition   165, 320
module   4, 42, 43, 101, 164–86, 320, 321

definition   164, 167, 170, 174
implementation   165, 167, 320
interface   164, 165, 320
monitor   262, 265–7
type   174, 192, 320
monadic operator   77
monitor   262, 265–7, 272
mouse   45, 298
multiple
   assignment   81
   inheritance   204
multiprocessor   212, 261, 276, 323
multiprocessing   262
multiprogramming   42, 262, 277
mutual
   exclusion   262, 265, 267
   recursion   125

NAG   38
name equivalence   141
name parameters   21, 107, 113, 220,
   237
name–declaration binding   53–7, 60
name–size binding   137–9
name–type binding   54, 55
name–value binding   58
Naur, P.   19
nested
   block   53, 104, 105, 123
   scope   54
   subprograms   40, 104
network   261, 299
non–determinism   264, 273, 275, 276
non–local identifiers   54, 105, 118, 123,
   172, 213, 268
nonterminal   284–90
numeric types   61–5
numerical analysis   64, 127
Nygaard, K.   36

Oberon   42, 43
objects   173, 185, 192–207
   attributes   59, 140, 199, 200, 306
   scalar   214
   structured   134, 214–16
   type   59, 174, 192, 198
object based language   192
object oriented
   concurrent   263, 323
   development   183–6, 263, 318

languages   4, 36, 38, 40, 174,
   192–207, 317, 318
   programming   36, 38, 45, 192, 317
occam   37
   ALT construct   274
   channel   37, 268, 270, 271, 274, 278
   clock   278
   communication   37, 263
   concurrency   260, 268, 271
   delay   279
   guard   274, 279
   I/O   309
   process   260, 268, 271, 272, 274
   TIMER channel   278
offset   121, 122
ON–condition   29, 42, 92
open scope   105
operand   76, 78, 261
operating system   32, 261, 265, 298, 299,
   310
operational semantics   291
operators   76, 118, 119
   arithmetic   61, 62
   binary   77
   Boolean   65, 77, 78
   division   61
   precedence   76–8, 80, 286
   redefining   118, 119, 178
   relational   62, 77, 78
   time   277–9
   unary   77
ORACLE   27
ordinal type   59
orthogonality   4, 5, 22
out parameters   106, 109, 110, 114, 118,
   272
overlaying   30, 102
overloading   61, 68, 78, 114, 119, 178,
   183, 185, 195–8, 304
own variables   57

package   37, 38, 42
   body   164–6, 169–74, 180–3, 268
   specification   164–6, 169–74, 180–6,
   268
Palo Alto   45
parallel execution   42, 260, 267
parameters   99–119
   array   39, 108, 137, 139, 140
   constant–value   107–9

default   115, 116
entry call   270
formal   99, 109, 179
formal subprogram   127, 128, 217
generic   128, 129, 182, 183, 185, 204
mode   106–9
name   21, 107, 113, 220, 237
named association   115, 116
positional association   99, 115
record   108
reference   107, 108, 110–14, 123, 137, 213
reference–constant   107–9
result   21, 107, 109, 110
type   234
value   21, 107, 108, 112–14, 123, 220, 226, 237
value–result   21, 107, 110–14
Parnas principles   188
Pascal   4, 38–40, 336, 337
arrays   39, 137–42
block   53, 104
Boolean operators   77, 78
case statement   84, 147
conformant array parameters   139, 140
constants   58
enumeration type   39, 66, 67, 90
file type   158, 299
for statement   87–90
formal subprogram   127
forward declarations   125, 126
function   116–18, 142
I/O   114, 301–3, 307, 308
ISO Standard   39, 139, 169
parameters   6, 107–12, 127
pointers   39, 69, 71, 148
precedence rules   76–8
program structure   104
records   143–7, 155, 308
scope rules   53–5, 104
sets   156, 157
static array   39, 137, 138
strings   152, 153
subrange   39, 60, 62
Turbo   315
type declarations   39, 60, 173
type insecurity   147
pattern matching   28, 34, 233–8, 251, 252
pervasive   105
phrase   286

pipe   264, 265, 310
PL360   38
PL/I   28–30, 337, 338
array operations   141, 142
block structure   29
default   28
fixed–point   64
list processing   29
mixed–mode   78
ON–conditions   29, 42, 92
pointers   68, 149
size   30
strings   155
structures   143–5
pointers   68–72, 148–52, 195–8, 202, 215
polymorphic operations   55, 234–8, 322
portability   8, 301, 303, 321
post–condition   203, 293
precedence rules   76–8, 286
precision   75
pre–compiled   103
pre–condition   203, 293
predefined identifiers   10
predicate   220, 224, 230
prefix   118, 219, 227
primitive type   59, 66, 172, 179, 322
priority   265, 270, 277
private
instance variable   199
limited   174
member   194
part   169, 170, 173
type   169, 170, 174
procedural language   212
procedural meaning   244, 253
procedures   98–116
formal   127, 128
process   37, 260–79
communication   37, 262–71, 309
interaction   263, 264, 271
model   323
priority   265, 270, 277
scheduling   261, 262, 270
suspended   262, 267, 270, 273, 277
synchronization   37, 214, 262, 264, 265, 267, 268, 270, 302
process control   277
production rule   284–90
program
correctness   7, 213, 293

design language   3
library   180
maintenance   3, 181
portability   8, 301, 303
proving   2, 8, 293
testing   2, 4, 91
unit   165
verification   2, 293
programming
   environment   6, 45, 192, 225, 298, 317
   functional   35, 43, 212–39, 316
   goal oriented   244
   in the large   164
   logic   44, 244–56
   object oriented   36, 38, 45, 174, 183–6,
      192, 317
   pure logic   244, 256
   real–time   276–9
   structured   4, 39, 82
PROLOG   44, 244–56, 316, 317, 338
   arithmetic   254
   backtracking   244, 247–9, 252, 253
   clause   246, 251, 253
   closed–world assumption   249, 250,
      256
   cuts   252, 253, 256
   declarative meaning   244, 253
   efficiency   252, 253, 256
   facts   44, 244–8, 250
   functor   250
   goals   244–50, 252–5
   I/O   306, 307
   negation   249, 250
   procedural meaning   244, 253
   questions   245
   recursion   249
   rules   44, 244–50, 252–4
   selector relation   251
   subgoals   244, 246–9, 254, 255
   unification   247
protected member   193, 194, 201
prototyping   3, 4, 239, 317
public member   175, 194, 195, 201
purely functional language   7, 43, 57,
   213, 229, 261, 291, 322
pure logic
   language   255
   programming   244, 256

qualified name   167, 170

query language   27
QUICKTRAN   31

R–value   57
raising exceptions   92–4, 236
RAMIS   27
RAND   31
range
   constraint   60, 66, 92
   function   212
rapid prototyping   3, 4, 239, 317
Rapidwrite   23
real time   28, 37, 42, 276–9
real type   61, 63, 64
reasoning   8, 213, 238, 293, 321
recompilation   103, 179–81
records   21, 134, 135, 143–50
   aggregates   145
   assignment   145
   parameters   108
   tree structure   143, 145
   variant   146, 147
   with statement   145, 147
recursive data structures   125, 151, 215
recursion   19, 35, 119, 123–5, 215, 217,
   226, 249
   mutual   125
reduction   218
reference   52, 57, 79
   parameters   107, 108, 110–14, 123,
      137, 213
reference–value binding   57, 79
referential transparency   213, 261
refinement   98, 164, 318
relational
   expression   77, 78, 153
   operator   62, 76, 155
relative time   278
reliability   4, 45, 103, 104, 206, 318
rendezvous   263, 268–72, 277
requirements   164
   analysis   2
reserved words   9, 225, 319
result parameters   21, 107, 109, 110
return statement   116, 117, 142
reverse Polish   151, 152
rewrite rule   218, 284
root class   202
rounding   80
   error   89

RPG   26
rules
  inference   44, 293
  precedence   76–8, 286
  production   284–90
  rewrite   218, 284
  scope   54–6, 104, 105, 123, 165, 224,
    232
run–time
  binding   53, 55, 56, 198
  check   54, 217, 220
  efficiency   15, 16, 36, 54, 55, 137–9,
    156, 212, 217, 238, 244, 322
  error   7, 92, 197, 217
  stack   121–3
  system   72

S–expression   219, 220
S–ALGOL   85
SAGE   28
scalar type   59, 109, 112, 214, 322
scheduling   261, 262, 270
scope rules   54–6, 104, 105, 123, 165,
    224, 232
  closed   105
  dynamic   54, 222, 226
  hole   54
  open   105
  resolution operator   175, 204
  static   54, 123, 222, 224, 232, 234
select statement   273, 274, 279
selection   82–5
selector   35, 84, 236, 251
self–referential   149
self–contained unit   4, 165, 321
semantics   8, 284, 290–4
  axiomatic   291, 293, 294
  denotational   291, 292
  operational   291
semaphore   281
sentential form   285
separate compilation   104, 170, 179–81,
    320
sequence   229–31
sequential file   158, 299–308
set   90, 156–8
shared
  behaviour   186
  memory   261, 262, 268, 270
  resources   263

store   213, 262
  variable   262, 265–8, 270
short–circuit evaluation   78
SHORTCODE   14
side effect   43, 76, 79, 105, 118, 172,
    213, 218, 226, 238, 307
signal   265–7, 274
SIMULA   36, 40, 192
  abstract data type   36
  class   36, 40, 42, 45
  simulation   36, 263
simulation languages   35, 36, 263
slice   141, 142, 306
SLIP   35
Smalltalk   4, 38, 45, 192, 198, 339
  class   192, 198
  environment   192, 193, 298
  messages   45
  methods   200
  object   45, 192, 198
  private instance variable   199
SNOBOL4   33, 34, 55, 66, 152, 156
  dynamic arrays   138
  pattern matching   34, 154
software
  components   164, 192, 317
  design   2–4, 164, 183–6, 192, 239,
    263, 318
  development   2, 3, 192, 263, 318
  engineering   225, 251
  life cycle   2–4, 318
  reliable   4, 45, 103, 104, 206, 318, 320
  reuse   45, 164, 192, 194, 201, 206
  specification   2, 3, 7, 98, 164, 237,
    263, 317, 318, 321
special form   219, 224
specialization   192, 186, 194
specification   2, 3, 7, 98, 164, 237, 263,
    317, 318, 321
  languages   3, 321
  package   164–6, 169–74, 180–6, 268
Speedcode   14
SPSS   38
SQL   27
SSP   38
stack storage allocation   119–23
Standard ML   43
standard
  file   302, 305, 307
  function   77, 80

I/O device   299, 301, 302
start symbol   285
statement   79–81
   assignment   57, 79–81, 141, 142, 145,
      153, 154, 213, 261, 291, 322
   case   21, 84, 85, 147
   compound   81
   conditional   82–4
   exit   86
   for   19, 87–90
   goto   8, 91, 224
   if   82–4
   iterative   85–91
   label   82, 91
   loop   86, 87
   repeat   39, 86, 87
   return   116, 117, 142
   separation   10, 11, 82
   structured   19, 39, 82, 98, 321
   termination   11, 82
   while   85, 87
static
   array   39, 137, 138
   binding   54, 196
   chain   123
   scope   54, 123, 222, 224, 232, 234
   storage allocation   119–21, 165
   typing   54, 198, 217, 317
   variable   56, 57, 172
stepwise refinement   98, 164, 318
storage allocation
   dynamic   70, 156, 198, 216
   stack   119–23
   static   119–21, 165
Stroustrup, B.   40
string processing   33, 152–6, 306
strings   33, 39, 66, 67, 152–6, 306
   implementation   155, 156
   I/O   302, 304
strong typing   42, 43, 45, 54, 182, 319,
     322
structural equivalence   141
structured control statements   19, 39, 82,
     98, 321
structured objects   134, 214–16
structured programming   4, 39, 82
subclass   192, 195
subgoal   244, 246–9, 254, 255
subprograms   98–129
   nesting   40, 104

overloading   114, 119, 178, 183, 185,
     195–8, 304
subrange type   60, 66
subscript   92, 136
subtype   60
superclass   192, 194
suspended process   262, 267, 270, 273,
     277
symbolic differentiation   221, 222, 228,
     229, 253–5
symbolic information   215
synchronization   37, 214, 262, 264, 265,
     267, 268, 270, 302
synchronous communication   262, 263
syntax   8, 284–90
   analysis   285
   diagrams   289, 290, 320
   directed compilers   19, 290
   error   114
systems programming language   37, 40,
     43, 157, 298, 315

tag field   147, 150
task   42, 260, 268–273
   overhead   272
template   128, 182, 185
terminal   30, 284–90
text I/O   299–306
third generation language   26
time   276–9
   absolute   278
   relative   278
   sharing   30
   slice   262
top–down   98, 255, 285, 290
top–level algorithm   98
transputer   37, 272
tree search   252
tree structure   34, 143, 145, 150, 151,
     250, 251
   derivation   285
truncation   80
turtle graphics   226
two's complement   62, 172, 298
type   52, 59–67
   abstract   36, 172–9, 184–6, 192, 207,
     236, 237, 265, 320
   array   134–43
   built–in   42, 59, 172
   character   66

checking 4, 40, 45, 54, 55, 103, 127, 149, 179, 193, 197, 198, 217, 234
complex 65, 177–9
conversion 61, 70, 78, 80, 178
definitions 39, 59–61
derived 60, 63
discrete 59, 84, 89, 90
enumeration 39, 66–8, 118
file 158, 302, 304, 305, 307, 309
inference 43, 55, 232
logical 59, 65
mark 61
module 174, 192, 320
numeric 61–5
ordinal 59
parameter 234
primitive 59, 66, 172, 179, 322
private 169, 170, 174
real 61, 63, 64
record 143–50
scalar 59, 109, 112, 214, 322
structured 59, 134–59, 322

unary operator 77
unconstrained arrays 140
unification 247
UNIVAC 14, 22
UNIX 38, 40, 310
  pipe 264, 265, 310
use clause 166, 168, 201
user–friendly 45

validation 8
value parameters 21, 107, 108, 112–14, 123, 220, 226, 237

value–result parameters 21, 107, 110–14
variable 52
  control 87–90, 136
  dynamic 69, 72, 149
  global 54, 106, 322
  lifetime 56, 121
  local 54, 56, 107, 110, 111, 120–3, 271
  non–local 54, 105, 118, 123, 172, 213, 268
  shared 262, 265–8, 270
  static 56, 57, 172
variant records 146, 147
verification 2, 293
virtual functions 196, 201
  pure 203
visibility 164–73, 194
von Neumann computer 56, 212, 256

wait instruction 262, 265–7
while statement 85, 87
widening 80
windows 45, 193, 298, 317
Wirth, N. 6, 21, 39, 42, 265, 320
WISP 35
with clause 166, 180
with statement 145, 147
workspace 267
workstation 261, 298

X–window system 298
Xerox 45
XPL 37